Michael B. Hundley

Keeping Heaven on Earth

Safeguarding the Divine Presence
in the Priestly Tabernacle

Mohr Siebeck

MICHAEL B. HUNDLEY, born 1978; 2000 BA from Amherst College; 2010 Ph.D., University of Cambridge; currently Humboldt Postdoctoral Research Fellow at Ludwig-Maximilians-Universität Munich.

ISBN 978-3-16-150697-0
ISSN 1611-4914 (Forschungen zum Alten Testament, 2. Reihe)

The Deutsche Nationalbibliothek lists this publication in the Deutsche Nationalbibliographie; detailed bibliographic data is available in the Internet at *http://dnb.d-nb.de*.

© 2011 by Mohr Siebeck, Tübingen, Germany.

This book may not be reproduced, in whole or in part, in any form (beyond that permitted by copyright law) without the publisher's written permission. This applies particularly to reproductions, translations, microfilms and storage and processing in electronic systems.

The book was printed by Laupp & Göbel in Nehren on non-aging paper and bound by Buchbinderei Nädele in Nehren.

Printed in Germany.

For Susan

אעלה אתך מארץ מצרים
לתת לך ארץ זבת חלב ודבש

Preface

The present monograph represents, with light revisions, my Ph.D. Dissertation at the University of Cambridge submitted in September 2009. Most prominently, I have inserted many of the footnotes into the main text, provided further rationale for my focus on ANE comparisons instead of the internal Israelite development, and reinserted a chapter on Leviticus 4–5 and 12–15 that previously was cut for space. Chapters 2 and 4 were presented in modified form at the SBL International Conference in Rome 2009 as "God's Technicolor Coat: An Examination of Divine Glory in the Priestly Texts" and at the University of Cambridge Faculty of Divinity and Faculty of Asian and Middle Eastern Studies Old Testament Seminar in 2009 as "Keeping God's House: Regular Divine Service in the Priestly Tabernacle" respectively and have since been slightly revised in response to the helpful comments I received.

As with any such endeavor, many thanks are due. I am indebted first of all to Professor Richard Averbeck from Trinity International University, who introduced me to Israelite cultic texts and inspired me to plumb their depths. I had the great fortune of studying under Baruch J. Schwartz of the Hebrew University of Jerusalem, who challenged and refined my thinking and who, more than anyone else, informed my perspective on the Priestly texts. I am grateful for his support and encouragement, which have endured well after I left his care. Christophe Nihan of the University of Lausanne, whose monograph was a source of much inspiration, also provided helpful and encouraging comments during the final stages of the manuscript. My doctoral supervisor, Graham I. Davies, deserves a lion's share of the credit, since without his warm and judicious support this work never would have been written. Professor Davies was the ideal supervisor for me and my research project. He gave me far more leeway than most would dare and far more than I deserved, while preventing me from many a misstep along the way. When the scope of my project threatened to grow to unmanageable proportions and when tangents captured too much of my attention, he reined me in, helped me to focus, and guided me to complete my study in the allotted time. My only regret is that, with his impending retirement, more students will not be able to benefit from his excellent guidance.

My internal examiner Professor Robert Gordon and my external examiner Professor Walter Houston of the University of Oxford each offered valuable comments on my research and generated a challenging and helpful discussion that helped me to refine my thinking and writing. Thanks are also due to Mohr Siebeck and in particular to the theology editor, Henning Ziebritzki, and to the editors of the series *Forschungen zum Alten Testament*, Professors Bernd Janowski, Mark S. Smith, and Hermann Spieckermann, for accepting this work for publication. Tanja Mix also deserves credit for her technical supervision.

Finally, I owe the greatest debt to my family, without whom none of this would have been possible. My parents and parents-in-law, Timothy and Virginia Hundley, Charles David and Virginia Susann Jones, have provided invaluable financial and practical support throughout the course of my research. My daughters, Kaya and Evangeline, have been a source of great inspiration, joy, and at times great distraction. Above all, I would like to thank my wife, Susan. She has read and edited the manuscript several times in its various incarnations, immeasurably improving its style and content. More importantly, she has patiently and unflaggingly supported me throughout the highs and the lows of this arduous process, often to her own detriment. For all these reasons and many more, I dedicate this book to her with my love and gratitude.

Princeton NJ, September 2010　　　　　　　　　　　　　　Michael B. Hundley

Table of Contents

Preface VII
Contents IX
Abbreviations XIII

Introduction 1

Chapter One: Ritual Theory 17

    1.1. Problems with Ritual 17
    1.2. What is Ritual? 20
        Why is it Both Useful and Undefinable? 20
        Features of Ritual Signs 22
        The Effects of Performing Ritual 24
    1.3. Analyzing Ritual 26
        Catherine Bell and Ritualization 26
        Klawans and the Symbolic Approach 26
        Gilders and the Indexical Approach 29
        Modéus and Causa 32
        Gane and Systems Theory 33
    1.4. The Cumulative Approach 34
        How the Theories Address Multiple Levels of Meaning 35

Chapter Two: The Divine Presence 39

    2.1. The Difficulty of Describing the Divine Presence 39
    2.2. Linguistic Context 40
    2.3. The Varying Intensity of Glory 43
    2.4. The Divine Form Beyond the Glory 44
    2.5. The Glory and the Fire 45
    2.6. The Glory and the Cloud 46
    2.7. Priestly Assimilation of Theophanic Elements 47
    2.8. Synthesis 49

Chapter Three: The Dedication and Inauguration of the Tabernacle and its Cult 53

3.1. Temple Dedication in 1 Kings 8 and the Ancient Near East 54
3.2. The Dedication of the Tabernacle in P 57
3.3. Tabernacle Dedication and Priestly Installation 59
    Structure 60
    Use 63
    Ideology 65
        Ideology of the Individual Elements 70
        a) Washing 70
        b) Consecration 71
            Consecration in Exodus 29 and Leviticus 8 73
        c) Clearing 81
            Clearing in Exodus 29 and Leviticus 8 82
        d) Pleasing Gift 86
        e) Important Uninterpreted Acts 87
        The Cumulative Effect 89
        The Ideology of the Tabernacle Inauguration 90
3.4. Ritual Sequence and Function in Exodus 29, 40, and Lev 8–9 91

Chapter Four: Regular Divine Service 95

4.1. Ancient Near Eastern Background 95
4.2. How Do the Israelites Maintain the Precarious Presence of YHWH in their Midst? 96
4.3. The Individual Elements 99
    The Bread of Presence 99
    Light 103
    Incense 105
        a) Incense in the ANE 105
        b) Incense in the Tabernacle 107
    Burnt, Grain, and Drink Offerings 109
4.4. What is YHWH's Relationship to His Food? 113
4.5. Access for Divine Service 115
4.6. Synthesis 116

Chapter Five: Damage Control in the Ancient Near East 119

5.1. The State of Scholarship on ANE Damage Control 120
5.2. The Gods' Relationship to Creation and its Inhabitants 120

5.3. Damage Control in the ANE 123
   Nature and Source of Evils.. 124
   Removal Rites.. 125
      Temple Removal Rites 126
      Individual and Community Removal Rites 130
   Synthesis.. 133

Chapter Six: Damage Control in the Priestly Texts 135

6.1. YHWH's Relationship to the World and His People in P........... 136
6.2. Individual and Communal Removal Rites
   (Leviticus 4–5 and 12–15) 136
      Structure 138
         Offerings for Sin (Leviticus 4–5) 138
         Remedies for Impurity (Leviticus 12–15)............................. 140
      Use 142
         Offerings for Sin... 142
         Remedies for Impurity 143
      Ideology 144
         Offerings for Sins 144
            The Nature and Function of חטאת and אשם
            Offerings for Sin in Leviticus 4–5................................... 147
         Remedies for Impurity 149
            The Nature and Function of the Rituals for Removing Impurity 155
      Synthesis of Leviticus 4–5 and 12–15 158
6.3. Clearing Day.. 159
      Structure 159
      Use 162
      Ideology... 163
         Pollutants Removed 164
         The Clearing Process 168
         The Loose Ends 171

Chapter Seven: Damage Control: Evaluation 173

7.1. The Rhetorical Trajectory of Leviticus 1–16 173
7.2. The Implications of Priestly Damage Control............................ 175
   Excursus: The Possibility of System Failure in H and Ezekiel.... 178
7.3. Key Priestly Concepts.. 179
   Sins and Impurities 179
      How Do Contaminants Pollute the Sanctuary? 182

חטאת and אשם	182
כפר	186
Why Choose a Multivalent Term?	189
The Consequences of Priestly Language	192
7.4. A Comparison of Priestly and ANE Damage Control Systems	192
Sanctuary Rites	194
Individual and Communal Rites	197
Why Does the Priestly System Allow Pollution in the Divine Sphere?	199

Conclusion 201

Works Cited 209

Source Index 233
Author Index 242
Subject Index 246

Abbreviations

AA	*American Anthropologist*
AB	The Anchor Bible
ABD	*The Anchor Bible Dictionary*, ed. D. N. Freedman
AfO	Archiv für Orientforschung
AHw	*Akkadisches Handwörterbuch*, W. von Soden.
ALASPM	Abhandlungen zur Literatur Alt-Syrien-Palästinas und Mesopotamiens
ANE	Ancient Near East/ Ancient Near Eastern
ANET	*Ancient Near Eastern Texts Relating to the Old Testament*, ed. J. Pritchard, 3rd ed.
AO	collection of the Department des antiquités orientales, Musée du Louvre
AOAT	Alter Orient und Altes Testament
apud	cited at secondhand from
ASOR	American Schools of Oriental Research
ATD	Das Alte Testament Deutsch
ATSAT	Arbeiten zu Text und Sprache im Alten Testament
BA	*Biblical Archaeologist*
BASOR	*Bulletin of the American Schools of Oriental Research*
BBB	Bonner Biblische Beiträge
BDB	*A Hebrew and English Lexicon of the Old Testament*, ed. F. Brown, S. R. Driver, C. A. Briggs
BETL	Bibliotheca ephemeridum theologicarum lovaniensium
BEvT	Beiträge zur evangelischen Theologie
Bib	*Biblica*
BibInt	*Biblical Interpretation*
BiOr	*Bibliotheca Orientalis*
BIS	Biblical Interpretation Series
BJS	Brown Judaic Studies
BKAT	Biblischer Kommentar Altes Testament
BN	*Biblische Notizen*
BOREAS	Boreas: Uppsala Studies in Ancient Mediterranean and Near Eastern Civilizations
BS	The Biblical Seminar
BZAR	Beihefte zur Zeitschrift für Altorientalische und Biblische Rechtsgeschichte
BZAW	Beihefte zur Zeitschrift für die alttestamentliche Wissenschaft
CAD	*The Assyrian Dictionary of the Oriental Institute of the University of Chicago*, ed. J. Brinkman, et al.
CANE	*Civilisations of the Ancient World*, ed. J.M. Sasson
CAT	Commentaire de l'Ancien Testament

CBET	Contributions to Biblical Exegesis and Theology
ConBOT	Coniectanea biblica. Old Testament series
cf.	*confer*, compare
CHD	*The Hittite Dictionary of the Oriental Institute of the University of Chicago*, ed. H. G. Güterbock and H. A. Hoffner
COS	*The Context of Scripture*, ed. W. W. Hallo and K. L. Younger
CTH	*Catologue des textes hittites*, E. Laroche
D	Deuteronomy/ Deuteronomic Source
DCH	*The Dictionary of Classical Hebrew*, ed. D. J. A. Clines
ed(s).	editor(s), edited by
e.g.	*exempli gratia*, for example
esp.	especially
ET	English Translation
et al.	*et alia*, and others
FAT	Forschungen zum Alten Testament
f(f)	and the following one(s)
fig.	figure
FRLANT	Forschungen zur Religion und Literatur des Alten und Neuen Testaments
FS	Festschrift
GKC	*Gesenius' Hebrew Grammar*, ed. E. Kautsch, ET A. E. Cowley, 2nd ed.
H	Holiness Legislation
HALOT	*The Hebrew and Aramaic Lexicon of the Old Testament*, ed. L. Koehler, W. Baumgartner and J. Stamm
HAT	Handbuch zum Alten Testament
HB	Hebrew Bible
HBSt	Herders biblische Studien
HCOT	Historical Commentary on the Old Testament
HK	Handkommentar zum Alten Testament
HSAT	Die Heilige Schrift des Alten Testamentes
HSM	Harvard Semitic Monographs
HSS	Harvard Semitic Studies
HUCA	*Hebrew Union College Annual*
HUCASup	Hebrew Union College Annual Supplements
ibid	*ibidem*, the same place
id.	*idem*, the same (person)
i.e.	*id est*, that is
Int	*Interpretation*
IRT	Issues in Religion and Theology
IT	Incantation Tablet(s) in Walker and Dick 2001
JANES	*Journal of the Ancient Near Eastern Society of Columbia University*
JAOS	*Journal of the American Oriental Society*
JBL	*Journal of Biblical Literature*
JBTh	*Jahrbuch für biblische Theologie*

JCS	*Journal of Cuneiform Studies*
JEA	*Journal of Egyptian Archaeology*
JNES	*Journal of Near Eastern Studies*
JNSL	*Journal of Northwest Semitic Languages*
JPS	Jewish Publication Society
JPSTC	The JPS Torah Commentary
JQR	*Jewish Quarterly Review*
JR	*Journal of Religion*
JSOT	*Journal for the Study of the Old Testament*
JSOTSup	Journal for the Study of the Old Testament Supplement Series
JSS	*Journal of Semitic Studies*
KHC	Kurzer Hand-Commentar zum Alten Testament
KUB	*Keilschrifturkunden aus Boghazköi*
KTU	*KTU: The Cuneiform Alphabetic Texts from Ugarit, Ras Ibn Hani, and Other Places*, ed. M. Dietrich, O. Loretz, J. Samartin, 2nd ed.
LAPO	Littératures anciennes du Proche-Orient
LHBOTS	The Library of Hebrew Bible/Old Testament Studies
lit.	literally
l(l)	line(s)
MTZ	*Münchener theologische Zeitschrift*
n(n).	note(s)
NCB	New Century Bible
NEB	Neue Echter Bibel
NIDOTTE	*The New International Dictionary of Old Testament Theology and Exegesis*, ed. W. VanGemeren
NJPSV	New Jewish Publication Society Version
NK	New Kingdom Egypt
Numen	*Numen: International Review for the History of Religions*
Num. R.	*Numbers Rabbah*
OBO	Orbis Biblicus et Orientalis
OLA	Orientalia Lovaniensia analecta
OTG	Old Testament Guides
OTL	Old Testament Library
P	the Priestly texts, writers
pace	in respectful dissent with
passim	here and there
Pg	Priestly Grundschrift
p(p)	page(s)
Proof	*Prooftexts: A Journal of Jewish Literary History*
Ps	secondary additions to the Priestly texts
RB	*Revue Biblique*
RBL	*Review of Biblical Literature*

RGG	*Die Religion in Geschichte und Gegenwart: Handwörterbuch für Theologie und Religionswissenschaft*, ed. K. Galling, 3rd ed.
RHR	*Revue de l'histoire des religions*
RlA	*Reallexikon der Assyriologie und Vorderasiatischen Archäologie*, ed. E. Ebeling and B. Meissner
SAALT	State Archives of Assyria Literary Texts
SBL	Society of Biblical Literature
SBLDS	Society of Biblical Literature Dissertation Series
SBLWAW	Society of Biblical Literature Writings from the Ancient World
SBS	Stuttgarter Bibelstudien
ScrHier	Scripta Hierosolymitana
SDB	*Supplément au Dictionnaire de la Bible*, ed. H. Cazelles and A. Feuillet
SHR	Studies in the History of Religions
SJLA	Studies in Judaism in Late Antiquity
SJOT	*Scandinavian Journal of the Old Testament*
SSN	Studia semitica neerlandica
STDJ	Studies on the Texts of the Desert of Judah
STT	The Sultantepe Tablets
SubBi	Subsidia biblica
TDOT	*Theological Dictionary of the Old Testament*, ed. G. J. Botterweck and H. Ringgren
TLOT	*Theological Lexicon of the Old Testament*, ed. E Jenni and C. Westermann
TRE	*Theologisches Realenzyklopädie*, ed. G. Krause and G. Müller
TRu	*Theologische Rundschau*
TUAT	*Texte aus der Umwelt des Alten Testaments*, ed. B. Janowski and G. Wilhelm
UBL	Ugaritisch-biblische Literatur
Ug	*Ugaritica*
Urk. IV	K. Sethe. *Urkunden der 18. Dynastie*
Utt.	Utterance from the Egyptian Pyramid Texts
VAB	Vorderasiatische Bibliothek
vs.	versus
VT	*Vetus Testamentum*
VTSup	Supplements to Vetus Testamentum
v(v)	verse(s)
WbÄS	*Wörterbuch der ägyptischen Sprache*, ed. A. Erman and H. Grapow
WBC	Word Biblical Commentary
WMANT	Wissenschaftliche Monographien zum Alten und Neuen Testament
ZAW	*Zeitschrift für die Alttestamentliche Wissenschaft*
ZTK	Zeitschrift für Theologie und Kirche

Introduction

The intersection of human and divine is as central to religious studies and practice today as it was in ancient times. In the Priestly texts of the Hebrew Bible, this unnatural and precarious intersection is governed by strict cultic legislation to ensure its mutually beneficial efficacy. As its title indicates, my study examines this Priestly system designed to keep heaven on earth, more specifically, to secure and safeguard the divine presence at the heart of the Israelite community.

The Texts Examined

Since before Wellhausen, scholars have distinguished the Priestly writing (*Priesterschrift*) from the rest of the pentateuchal literature.[1] In order to examine the Priestly tabernacle system, we will focus on the portions that prescribe and describe the tabernacle construction and legislation, namely the Priestly portions of Exodus 25–Leviticus 16.[2] Other Priestly texts in Genesis and Exodus will be included where necessary to fill out the Priestly portrait. Leviticus 17–26 (27), identified as the Holiness Legislation (H),[3] and the so-called Priestly texts in Numbers will also occasionally feature. However, they will be treated as secondary to P, and will be used selectively to help fill in the gaps left by the Priestly corpus, especially in chapter 4. In chapters 3 and 7, H will also be used as a point of comparison with P.

Although convenient, my textual selection is not arbitrary. Although classically understood to pre-date P, the scholarly consensus about H seems

---

[1] On the early debate about the Priestly texts, see Rogerson 1985; Graham 1990:117–151; Nicholson 1998:3–28. For a classic defense and delineation of the Priestly source (P), see Noth 1987:107–147.

[2] I.e., everything but the majority of Ex 32–34.

[3] Following the more neutral rendering of Schwartz 1999:17–24. Rather than enter into the debate on the extent of the Holiness Legislation outside of Leviticus 17–26 (compare Knohl 1995 with Milgrom 2001:1337–1344; id. 2003; see also Nihan 2007: 559–575), I will limit H to Lev 17–26, an ascription which most commentators agree upon. While I acknowledge that Lev 16:29–34 may very well stem from H, I will instead endeavor to read Lev 16 as a cohesive ritual text.

to be shifting in the opposite direction.⁴ While H is in many ways distinct from P, hence its identification as a separate body of texts,⁵ it nonetheless can be understood as a sequel to P and, in certain instances, as P's complement.⁶ Thus, we may profitably use some H legislation to illumine the larger Priestly portrait that includes both P and H (e.g., when discussing the regular offerings [תמיד]). In other places, however, it is profitable to see how H responds differently to similar issues, expanding on the Priestly precedent (e.g., with regard to holiness and the pollution of the land).

The P-like texts in Numbers are the subject of some controversy. Traditionally attributed to P, they have nevertheless been the most difficult to isolate from the surrounding text and to situate in the Priestly narrative. Recently, there has been a tendency to date these texts after P proper. Knohl attributes to H many of the texts previously assigned to P in Numbers.⁷ Achenbach goes even further, considering these texts to be part of a later theocratic revision (*theokratische Bearbeitung*), distinct from both P and H.⁸

Furthermore, the Priestly texts in Exodus 25–Leviticus 16 form the heart of the Sinai pericope.⁹ Exodus prescribes and describes the construction of the tabernacle at Sinai (25–31, 35–40), prescribes its inauguration along with the priests and the cult (29) and describes YHWH's arrival (40). Leviticus 1–16 then provides the primary legislation for keeping YHWH in the tabernacle. After the H texts in Leviticus 17–27, Numbers 1–10 is composed with a view toward the wilderness wanderings.

In addition, since YHWH's abiding among Israel rests at the heart of the Priestly system, one could argue that the Priestly corpus climaxes at Leviticus 16 with the legislation necessary to safeguard the divine presence in

---

⁴ Elliger was the first to argue that H was conceived from the beginning as a sequel to the Priestly narrative (Pg) (id. 1959; id. 1966:14–20 and passim; followed by Cholewiński 1976:338; Kornfeld 1983:6; Preuss 1985; Kratz 2000:114). Wagner later contended that Leviticus 17–26 was composed as a sequel to 1–16 (1974: 307–316; see similarly Blum 1990:318ff; Crüsemann 1992:323–326; Albertz 1994:2.480ff; Ruwe 1999). Knohl and Milgrom take the argument one step further, contending that H both presupposes and is later than P (Knohl 1987; id. 1995; Milgrom 1991:13–42; see similarly Stackert 2007:15–16. See also Otto [1994; id. 1999], who regards H as post-P and post-D; so now Nihan 2007:545–559).

⁵ See, e.g., Joosten 1996:6–7.

⁶ Nihan 2007:546.

⁷ Id. 1995 (see 104–106 for his delineation), followed, e.g., by Stackert 2007:57–68 in his attribution of Num 35:9–34 to H instead of P.

⁸ Id. 2003:443–628; followed largely by Nihan 2007:554–555, 570–572.

⁹ The Priestly Sinai pericope includes the beginning of Ex 19 and the end of Ex 24 (see, e.g., Noth 1948:17–19; Elliger 1952:121–122; Lohfink 1978:198 n. 29; Weimar 1984:85 n. 18).

the tabernacle.¹⁰ If the P-like texts in Numbers are part of P, they may be understood as an appendix of sorts, filling out the details after the narrative high-point in Leviticus 16, providing narrative and legislation on safeguarding the divine presence during the wilderness wanderings. Whether understood as from P, H, or the theocratic revision, we may safely conclude that they are secondary, and that in places they may be used to fill out the larger Priestly portrait (encompassing P, H and the P-like texts in Numbers).

*A Synopsis of Scholarship on P*¹¹

In recent years, there has been a major shift in P scholarship, especially regarding the cultic legislation.¹² In the past, it was especially common to isolate the Priestly narrative (Pg [*Grundschrift*]) from the legal supplements (Ps [*sekundär*]).¹³ Pg received the lion's share of the attention.¹⁴ When studied, Ps was often dissected into various disparate parts,¹⁵ many of which did not seem to cohere.¹⁶

Recent treatments of P have been far more numerous,¹⁷ systematic, and synchronic, pursuing the inner logic of the Priestly corpus and particularly its ritual legislation.¹⁸ Beginning with Mary Douglas in 1966 (especially in

---

¹⁰ Nihan even concludes that Lev 16 is the original conclusion to the Priestly account (2007:382; see before him, Köckert 1989:56–61).

¹¹ Because of its recent renaissance, many important works on P will be necessarily omitted from discussion; see esp. the helpful recent survey of Nihan 2007:1–19.

¹² Nihan (2007:15–16) claims that "it is not excessive to state that these studies have revolutionized the understanding of P's legislation in many ways, either by making a case for an integrative reading of these laws or by evincing the complex theological assumptions underlying certain laws which otherwise made little sense or even appeared arbitrary."

¹³ This trend is especially pronounced in the works of Noth 1981:8ff (German original 1948) and Elliger 1952, who radicalized the distinction within P between the primary narrative and secondary ritual elements.

¹⁴ Studies were concerned with isolating Pg as a discrete document and examining its primary characteristics (e.g., Lohfink 1978 [ET 1994]; Zenger 1983; Weimar 1984).

¹⁵ The commentaries of Bertholet 1901; Baentsch 1903; Noth 1962 (ET 1965) and Elliger 1966 focused on the genesis of Ps in Lev 1–16. Elliger, in particular, posited a complex process of ritual additions to Pg that at times included more than ten layers (see, e.g., his analysis of Lev 13–14 on pp. 159–173). Following in his footsteps, Seidl (1982) posited an even more complex genesis to Lev 13–14.

¹⁶ "Earlier scholarship [on P legislation] usually posited an erratic conflation of various pieces of distinct origin" (Nihan 2007:15); see esp. previous scholarship on Lev 5.

¹⁷ See, e.g., Fabry and Jüngling 1999; Rendtorff and Kugler 2003; and Römer 2008 for various essays in various languages related to the books of Leviticus and Numbers.

¹⁸ Priestly texts have indirectly been brought to the fore through another recent development. Since the existence of a pre-Priestly composition (J) that unites the patriarchal and Moses traditions has been called into question, many European scholars now identify

her analysis of the animal classification system of Lev 11), attempts have been made to understand the Priestly concepts of impurity, particularly as a symbolic system.[19] Jewish scholars (particularly Milgrom 1963, 1970, 1976, 1983, 1986, 1989, 1990, 1991, 2000, 2001 and Haran 1978; cf. from a different perspective de Vaux 1964; Levine 1965, 1974) have interpreted the "P legislation as a comprehensive cultic system, with a coherence and rationales of its own."[20] Milgrom's students have since followed in his footsteps (see especially Wright 1987, 1991, 1992 and Gane 2005). Gorman (1990), Jenson (1992), Gilders (2004), Janzen (2004), Bergen (2005), and Modéus (2005) have drawn from anthropology to analyze the Priestly cosmology, the theory of graded holiness, blood ritual, the social meaning of sacrifice, reading ritual in a postmodern context, and the Šĕlāmîm respectively. The systematic approach has migrated from America, Israel, and the UK to the European mainland (Marx 2005 in France; Rendtorff 1985 and Eberhart 2002 [cf. Jürgens 2001; Dahm 2003 on Lev 1–7] in Germany, and Schenker 2000 in Switzerland). There has also been a renewed interest in the structure of Leviticus as a book (Douglas 1995; Smith 1996; Warning 1999; Zenger 1999; Ruwe 2003; Luciani 2005; Nihan 2007; Bibb 2009). At the same time, scholars have become more interested in the latest redactions of the Torah and their contribution to its canonical form (Otto 2002; Römer and Schmid 2007). Nihan (2007) melds the two approaches, focusing on redaction criticism while giving the internal coherence of Leviticus significant attention. Such responses to the extremes of source- and form-critical analyses are a major step forward in analyzing the Priestly rituals.[21]

My work builds upon its systematic forbears but with significant differences. While others either have sought a unifying principle for the system or merely analyzed an aspect of it,[22] my study examines the system designed to keep YHWH on earth with a wider focus and through a broader interpretive lens.

---

the Priestly writers as the first to combine the Genesis and Exodus narratives (see, e.g., Gertz, Schmid and Witte 2002; Dozeman and Schmid 2007).

[19] See Eilberg-Schwartz 1990, Houston 1993, Whitekettle (in a series of articles), Malul 2002, and Nihan 2007:301–339. Klawans 2006 has attempted to apply Douglas' symbolic approach to sacrifice.

[20] Nihan 2007:15.

[21] Cf. Nihan 2007:15.

[22] For examples of the former, see, e.g., Gorman 1990 and Jenson 1992; for the latter, see, e.g., Kiuchi 1987; id. 2003; Gane 2005 on the חטאת and Wright 1987 on the disposal of impurity.

Interpreting Ritual Texts

Although ritual theory has been profitably applied to biblical studies, the best theories are limited in scope (covering only certain aspects of rituals such as symbolism and purpose statements). To ensure fuller and more balanced results, I develop my own cumulative approach to ritual, combining several methods into three categories – structure, use, and ideology.[23]

In addition, many scholars have failed to distinguish between ritual texts and ritual practice.[24] As Watts has recently insisted, ritual texts do much more than simply describe (and explain) ritual action; they were also written for rhetorical purposes.[25] Building on this insight, my work argues that the Priestly Sinai account seeks to exalt YHWH and his system as preeminent, while ensuring participation and securing the privileged position of the priests as ritual authorities.

The Sinai narrative is set in the idealized past,[26] at the inception of the nation of Israel at a sacred location and with its most revered characters at the heart of the narrative. The legislation comes directly from the mouth of God, given to Moses, who then transfers ritual authority to Aaron, as the embodiment of the priesthood.[27] Since YHWH has designed the system as his ultimate solution for dwelling among Israel, and both he and Moses put it in the hands of the priests, none may question its or their legitimacy.

The authors of the text speak of Israel's founding moment to ensure that the legislation is understood to be eternally important.[28] Whatever the compositional present, the tabernacle is likely a thing of the distant past.[29] To communicate the authority of the system, the authors purposely distance their system from the compositional and redactional present.[30] They set their story in the timeless past to establish the timeless preeminence of YHWH and his system,[31] and the prominence of priestly authority.[32] Thus,

---

[23] See chapter one for a much fuller treatment.

[24] See, e.g., Rendtorff 1985, Milgrom 1991, and Eberhart 2002. See Watts 2007:27–32 for a differentiation between texts and rituals; see also Gilders 2004:3–6; Bergen 2005:1–3.

[25] Id. 2007 with special reference to Leviticus; cf. id. 1999; Bergen 2005; Bibb 2009. Instead of simply trying to reconstruct the system, rhetorical analysis asks why does the text include what it does, how does it express what it includes, and what is it trying to communicate.

[26] Cf. Bibb 2009:18.

[27] Ibid. 82–85.

[28] Its esteem in Jewish and Christian circles testifies to its continued success.

[29] Watts 2007:28; cf. the odd theory of Friedman where the tabernacle rests inside the temple (1981; id. 1992).

[30] Bell 1997:145–150; Bibb 2009:57, 59.

[31] For the Priestly writers, his system is the same as their system.

the Sinai narrative sets an eternal precedent for the importance of the system and the ritual authority of its priests.[33]

Clarifications

Situating the Priestly texts more concretely in their literary context is a difficult task. Of course, historical signposts help the reader to understand the text. However, the date(s) of the Priestly composition and redaction(s), as well the date(s) of the Priestly source texts remain disputed.[34] In addition, although it is becoming increasingly clear that the Priestly system is more or less coherent, it remains unclear whether it describes actual practice, presumed past practice, innovations for future practice, the ideal presumed-lost but recently recovered (like the law book in 2 Kings), a vision for the ideal future grounded in the ideal past (cf. Ezekiel's temple vision and the Temple Scroll), or none of the above. The nature of the Priestly texts is also debated (source, redactional layer(s), or something else entirely).[35]

Since its compositional history is somewhat murky, we will examine the Priestly texts in their redacted form. Rather than simply skirting the issue, such an approach has positive purposes. The Priestly writers' deliberate choice to situate their account in the ancient past invites the reader to understand and interpret the text timelessly, i.e., without concern for the historical context of the composition.

---

[32] It is also possible that Levinson's theory that the editors of Deuteronomy intentionally conceal the history behind the texts (1997) is at work here; namely, the Priestly innovations are more palatable when they are cast as ancient tradition.

[33] A similar rhetorical purpose may be applied to the tabernacle account. The Priestly authors/redactors responsible for the account were likely aware of the various inventories and construction reports of ANE temples. They seem to make use of and expand this precedent to produce the most comprehensive prescriptive and descriptive report in order to establish the authenticity of the tabernacle account. They include such painstaking detail to establish that the tabernacle was a real, historical structure, built during the foundational period under divine and Mosaic supervision. In establishing the authenticity of the structure, the Priestly writers establish the authenticity and (transferable) authority of its legislation. This theory holds whether the tabernacle is pure invention or whether it has some historical precedent. Instead of arguing with rival traditions, P casts its legislation as the historical foundational account to establish its supreme and supremely binding authority (The Temple Scroll seems to function similarly in contradistinction to the other DSS; see, e.g., Schiffmann 2008).

[34] For example, different scholars argue that P was composed in pre-exilic (Haran 1978:132–148; Hurvitz 1982), exilic (Cross 1973:323–324; Otto 1997:24ff), and post-exilic times (Fohrer 1970:185; Blum 1990:319–360).

[35] For P as source, see, e.g., Schmidt 1993:1–34; Gertz 2000; as redaction, e.g., Cross 1973:294–322; Blum 1984:420–458; id. 1990:229–285.

More importantly, interpreting the composite text is more in line with biblical and ANE perspectives than is reconstructing the text's multiple layers. Rituals practiced in the biblical and ANE worlds are often composite in nature,[36] especially given the ANE bent for accepting amalgamated approaches as more thorough, more important, and more effective. Even if the individual parts did not completely cohere, ancients had little interest in the history behind the text, only in correctly performing the composite ritual.[37] By interpreting the Priestly rituals synchronically (with a secondary interest in the text's genesis), we are in line with the intentions of the final redactors and the interpretations of those with the finally redacted text before them.[38] Finally, a timeless account does not altogether impede rhetorical analysis. Regardless of when it was composed, the text clearly communicates the preeminence of YHWH and his system and the priestly authority as its caretakers.

Comparison with Ancient Near Eastern Texts

Claims for preeminence are most persuasive when the system and its god resemble yet transcend those around them. Thus, a comparison with ANE deities and systems is especially profitable. However, although most scholars recognize the importance of such an endeavor and numerous works on ANE religion are available,[39] analyses of the Priestly texts often avoid such comparisons. For example, of all the works on P mentioned above on pages 3–4, only Milgrom and his students, Wright and Gane, pay adequate attention to the ANE parallels.[40]

When scholars do undertake ANE comparisons, they often do so in several limited ways: a) simple borrowing, establishing provenance and dependence, the classic expression of which is found in Friedrich Delitzsch's

---

[36] See, e.g., Abusch's analysis of the Mesopotamian *Maqlû* series (1991; id. 1992; id. 2002).

[37] However, there is likely more flexibility among ANE ritualists than their Priestly counterparts. Since ritual procedure is often a secret in an ANE context, the ritualists could theoretically adapt it to serve their purposes with less notice from the people. By contrast, making ritual procedure public knowledge puts it under public scrutiny.

[38] Advocating a holistic reading of P is not the same as advocating a holistic reading of the Pentateuch. Clear boundaries exist between P and the rest of the Pentateuch such that its narrative and ritual texts should be read independently (esp. Ex 25–31, 35–40 and Lev 1–16).

[39] See esp. the helpful essays in Sasson's *CANE* and Johnston 2004; see also, e.g., Kratz and Spieckermann 2006.

[40] See also, e.g., Weinfeld 1983 and id. 2004; Janowski, Koch and Wilhelm 1993. In addition, there have been various studies on the Day of Atonement in light of ANE parallels (e.g., Tawil 1980) and other comparative studies such as Geller (1980) on the *Šurpu* incantations and Lev 5, and Watts on the עלה (2006).

Babel und Bibel lectures; b) identification of similar rites to establish antiquity and differentiation from those rites to establish superiority (see especially Milgrom); c) a comparison of selected ANE rites with selected Priestly rites in order to illumine the various Priestly rites or systems (see especially Wright 1987).

The first method has been largely abandoned as too simplistic. Milgrom's analysis and his model, however, are still often referenced uncritically and thus require a fuller critique.[41] Milgrom's examination is apologetic in nature and tone. Thus, in defending the Priestly position, he adapts the ANE material selectively to serve his purposes.[42] He uses ANE parallels positively and negatively, neither of which is entirely convincing. Positively, he argues that similar ancient practices establish the antiquity of the Priestly account. However, this need not be the case. The existence of similar ancient practices does not mean that those in P are old, only that they would not be out of place in the ANE if they were old (the Priestly rituals could be a later derivation of earlier practices).[43] For example, the long-standing importance of expiation and purification in the ANE does not mean that the חטאת and the אשם are especially ancient. At most, it indicates that they could be old. It is equally possible that they could be more recent innovations, since the עלה could have previously served these ends. In addition, such a conclusion does not adequately account for the (near) absence of such terms before P. Negatively, for Milgrom, ANE rites represent the primitive beliefs and practices from which Israel differentiates itself. Since he does not seem entirely convinced that the Priestly rites have intrinsic value (or he is responding to those with such a conviction), he finds value in their difference, in their being decidedly less primitive. Where embarrassingly primitive elements remain in P, such as mention of YHWH's food, Milgrom often dismisses them by calling them fossilized vestiges.[44]

---

[41] As will be clear on nearly every page, I owe a great debt to the excellent work of Jacob Milgrom. The following correction in no way undermines the immense value of his work.

[42] His analysis of ANE practice is at times only a caricature, designed to defend the Priestly position often at the expense of the other ANE cultures. It often does not account for the sophisticated complexities of ANE religions. Of course, an exhaustive account of ANE practices and systems is not his aim. He uses ANE material for the express purpose of illustrating the Priestly system. Nonetheless, his selectivity and at times polemical tone can be misleading.

[43] See also Weinfeld 2004:42–47; Gane 2005:355–378.

[44] Regarding divine food, see Milgrom 1991:213. Although his argument against divine consumption of the bread of presence is more sophisticated, as we will see in chapter 4, it is likewise insufficient.

Wright's comparative approach and analysis are more productive. According to his method of contrastive comparison, "essentially similar phenomena in discrete cultures are studied in detail separately and then compared."[45] Such an approach is rightly careful not to import meaning from ANE cultures, while placing the Priestly rituals more firmly in their ANE context. However, while a comparison of similar rituals in different cultures is fruitful, it yields a superficial and selective portrait when isolated from the systems in which the rites are embedded.[46] If the Priestly writers construct their system in response to the various ANE systems, then the interpreter cannot fully understand the Priestly system without first understanding the ANE systems from which they emerge and to which they respond. More than simply responding to a selection of individual rites, the Priestly writers respond to the larger systems and their respective thought-worlds.

Without appropriate contextualization, it is unclear what roles the individual rites play in the larger system, whether they are primary or peripheral, in response to extreme circumstances or regular protocol. Rioting and looting after winning a football game provides a modern example. Without contextualizing the event, it would be unclear if this behavior is normal or an extreme version of the celebratory mob mentality. The ideology of the system itself is likewise unclear from a selective analysis (e.g., what is the nature of the gods and of their relationship to humanity and creation? How does each culture envision, elicit, and ensure divine presence? How do they envision and actualize divine service and damage control?). In addition, examining only the closest parallels to Priestly rituals provides merely a sliver of the larger picture, overlooking important areas where the two systems are unlike, and, thus, inhibiting a fuller understanding of the systems themselves.

Rather than comparing individual rites in isolation from their surrounding contexts, my research compares the systems (Egyptian, Mesopotamian, Hittite, Syro-Palestinian, and Priestly Israelite) in which the individual rites are embedded.[47] My study addresses how the various systems, reconstructed on the basis of archaeological and textual evidence from the ANE and the Priestly texts, are designed to work. I examine how they describe the nature of the divine presence (chapter 2), elicit that presence, prepare accommodation and servants for its arrival (chapter 3), and perform regular service (chapter 4) and damage control (chapters 5–7) – all to ensure max-

---

[45] Id. 1987:8.
[46] Although Wright's analysis of Hittite purification motifs is rather systematic (1987: 31–45), it is not integrated with the rest of his argument.
[47] Cf. Hallo (1990; id. 1997), who focuses on judicious comparisons of individual texts and textual corpora rather than on comparisons of systems.

imum efficacy. This approach is beneficial on a general comparative level and, more particularly, to elucidate the primary contribution of the Priestly writers. The latter is especially germane, since the genius of the Priestly writers is not in their total originality, but in their ability to co-opt elements already present in the surrounding cultures and adapt them to serve their own purposes. In each context, the Priestly writers minimize the perceived weaknesses of other biblical and ANE approaches. They aim to construct a system that resembles its ANE counterparts enough to be recognizable, yet differs in certain key aspects to establish its preeminence.

Unlike Wright, I compare systems and the worldviews that inform and infuse them. I am especially interested in situating each rite in the context of its larger system, whether that rite is normal or anomalous. Unlike Milgrom, I am not interested in positing a specific (early) historical context for the Priestly writings, nor do I attempt to distance Israelite practice from the more 'primitive' surrounding cultures. Instead, I strive to situate the Priestly writings within their ANE context and to recover the underlying rationale of the Priestly differentiation from it, undertaken to distance Israel from and establish Israelite superiority over those cultures closest to them.[48] In other words, instead of making value judgments myself, I attempt to uncover the Priestly rhetorical message.

However, the presentation of an extensive analysis of each system in its own right and context goes beyond the bounds of the present work on the Priestly tabernacle system (That analysis is currently in preparation for publication). Instead, my presentation of ANE material in this study must be selective. Although merely a sampling, my work necessarily builds on and is informed by my fuller treatment, providing my analysis with a depth and breadth that it would not otherwise possess.[49]

In particular, brevity forces me to minimize the various geographical and chronological differences. However, since there is a striking overlap and conservatism among ANE religious systems,[50] the necessarily artificial amalgam presented here is nonetheless profitable.

In addition, I do not limit the Priestly texts to any one period or posit borrowing from any one culture. Instead, the consistency of ideas across

---

[48] Priestly differentiation from their own Israelite context is equally important, as they seek to establish the supremacy of their system within in Israelite context over all rival claimants.

[49] Often, I can (ironically) only discuss individual elements, which, nonetheless, are analyzed and understood as part and in light of the larger system.

[50] For the commonality, see esp. my forthcoming analysis of temples and divine presence; regarding the religious conservatism, see, e.g., Lambert 1990:123 on Mesopotamia: "No major changes took place over history except in the organization of the gods into a pantheon, and except where cities completely died out and ceased to be inhabited." Regarding Egypt, see, e.g., Assmann 2001:129.

time and culture indicates that the Priestly system could be comfortably situated in multiple contexts. Regardless of its actual context, the Priestly system is both similar and a radical response to its surrounding cultures.

An explanation of the relative lack of emphasis on internal Israelite development is also necessary at this stage. The Priests undoubtedly build on present and previous Israelite ritual systems.[51] Indeed in some cases, especially for the עלה and מנחה, examining the evolution of cultic terminology and practice is possible and profitable.[52] However, in most cases, the pre-Priestly evidence is insufficient to make meaningful comparisons.[53] In order to manufacture enough data to make such connections, scholars have been forced to reconstruct the non-Priestly cult from limited material and often on the basis of hypothetical ANE parallels, which is a more perilous exegetical exercise than simply comparing the Priestly texts with their ANE counterparts. Thus, my analysis focuses on the more expansive, and perhaps no less intentional, interaction with the ANE evidence.[54]

A further point of clarification is in order, as my analysis presumes a Priestly awareness of and response to the various ANE systems. In making such a claim, I do not assume that the Priestly writers know the intricacies of ANE cult practices, much less that they perform an exhaustive study of them akin to a Ph.D. dissertation. I do contend, however, that they are fundamentally aware of and respond to the prevalent religious ideas circulating in the surrounding cultures (a contention that arises from an empirical analysis of ANE and Priestly materials). Analyzing the various ANE systems, particularly their fundamental components, provides access to the ancients' worldviews that would otherwise be out of reach. Although ritual procedure remains esoteric, most common people would know that 1) the temple is the divine abode; 2) the statue represents the god's immediate presence; 3) installing a god in its temple is a complex and important process; 4) the god is served anthropomorphically (e.g., fed, bathed, and adorned) so that he remains content, and thus, continues to bless and protect the community; and 5) rituals are necessary to remove the stains caused by evil influences from the sanctuary and from afflicted individuals. In the ANE as in P, religious personnel must communicate enough of the system to convince people that it is important, even if precise protocol is carefully guarded. Indeed, to claim that the commoner is unaware of these religious staples would be to claim that official religion is impotent, having little impact on the culture and lives of its people. Thus, studying

---

[51] Their rhetoric likely has at least as much of an internal Israelite target as it does an ANE one.

[52] See chapter 3.

[53] See, e.g., the analysis of Marx 2005.

[54] Which likely overlaps significantly with a least some (rival) Israelite perspectives.

the basic components of ANE religious systems in greater detail (than would be accessible to the commoner or ancient Israelite) provides the modern reader with access to worldviews that infuse the systems and, if successful, underlie and pervade the ANE cultures as well (i.e., as we cannot experience secondhand the living effects of these religions in practice, examination of the preserved texts and rites is the best way to understand the ANE religious worldviews). Given the ubiquity of such elements, it is likely that the Priestly system emerges from such a context and that its present form is a response to that context.

Interpreting and Comparing Religious Language

In a written composition, language is naturally one of the primary means of differentiating YHWH and his system from those in the ANE. Most scholars emphasize the precision of the Priestly writings. For example, Milgrom and Knohl use the precision of P's vocabulary as a criterion for distinguishing P from H.[55] Although at times characterized by great precision, Priestly language could be more precisely described as accurate, since it is by turns more precise and more elusive[56] than its biblical and ANE counterparts.

In the ANE, as today, religious language is problematic, as it must describe concepts in human terms which by definition transcend them. Religious language – broadly understood to encompass metaphor, model, analogy, and simile – must speak analogically.[57] Namely, religious language must use language at home in one context, the human realm, and stretch it to describe something in another, the divine realm.[58] Rather than simply substituting a different word or employing emotionally evocative language, religious interpreters use analogical language as a means of expressing something that can be expressed in no other way.[59] However, instead of capturing the divine in all its plenitude, analogical language is merely an approximation,[60] a way of giving communicable form to more

---

[55] Milgrom 1991:15; id. 2000:1327–1330; Knohl 1995:106–107.

[56] I adopt this term from Terrien 1978.

[57] I use the term 'analogically' since it is sufficiently flexible, approximates my intended meaning and does not carry the same negative freight as metaphor. For a more precise differentiation between these terms see Soskice 1985:54–66; when referring to simile and model, I mean what Soskice calls a modelling simile and a paramorphic model (60, 102).

[58] This definition purposely approximates Soskice's definition of metaphor: "metaphor is a figure of speech whereby we speak about one thing in terms which are seen to be suggestive of another" (15).

[59] Cf. Soskice 1985:44.

[60] Cf. ibid. 140: "In our stammering after a transcendent God we must speak, for the most part, metaphorically or not at all."

amorphous concepts.⁶¹ Thus, in using approximate terms, the interpreter must be careful to differentiate the subject from its referent lest the reader assume that an approximation is an encapsulation (i.e., lest the divine aspect being described is conflated with its imperfect analogue).⁶²

To represent the divine, interpreters must stretch human means of expression in an attempt to grasp or, more accurately, to approximate the ineffable. Such an endeavor is by nature anthropomorphic.⁶³ To differentiate the divine from human referents, ANE interpreters make their gods transcendently anthropomorphic.⁶⁴ In other words, while descriptions remain anthropomorphic, they stretch the boundaries of anthropomorphic expression to render the gods more transcendent. To distinguish one deity from the next, interpreters make the superior god more transcendently anthropomorphic than the inferior. While the descriptions of the gods remain anthropomorphic, their depictions become increasingly transcendent and otherworldly. For example, in the *Enūma eliš*, Marduk's body is described as impossible to understand with four eyes and ears (I 94–95). Thus, Marduk is set apart as distinct from and superior to both humans and his divine contemporaries.⁶⁵

Rather than conforming to this pattern, the Priests⁶⁶ establish the distinctiveness of YHWH and his system in order to establish their superiority. First, where possible, the Priestly texts distinguish themselves by adding precision to the non-Priestly accounts (e.g., in their distinction between purity and holiness). Second, since natural language cannot encapsulate the supernatural, precision becomes increasingly elusive the closer one gets to YHWH himself (e.g., in representing his true form). Lest they misrepresent him, the Priests then leave their language increasingly undefined. Third, instead of making YHWH more transcendently anthropomorphic than the ANE gods, the Priestly writers often minimize or eschew anthropomorphisms altogether so that YHWH is simply (more) transcendent, more other, and thus superior. For example, they never describe YHWH's form,⁶⁷

---

⁶¹ Whether language, images, ideas, or objects.

⁶² To this end, the text at times opts for similes instead of metaphors (e.g., the glory is like a consuming fire [Ex 24:17], so as to differentiate the divine entourage from its earthly analogues [fire and cloud]). Simile is more appropriate than metaphor since it is more conceptually distant (e.g., since it establishes that the glory is like but not identical to fire). Cf. Ramsey's theory of models and qualifiers (1957:49–89).

⁶³ Here understood more broadly to denote all aspects of human expression rather than simply human form.

⁶⁴ For this expression, see Hendel 1997:207.

⁶⁵ Ibid. 207.

⁶⁶ By Priests, I mean the Priestly writers, the authors of the Priestly texts.

⁶⁷ Nor do they describe YHWH's character at all, in contrast to the intervening non-Priestly material in Exodus 34.

only his attendant features, the glory, cloud, and fire. Unlike the ANE statue or the ark, these features are not made or controlled by human hands. Thus, by being less human and less humanly accessible, YHWH is more transcendent than and thus preeminent over the ANE gods. Fourth, where anthropomorphisms are inevitable, the Priestly writers employ them in a way that distinguishes them from the referent and from other ANE analogues. For example, the Priestly texts never explicitly deny that regular service includes a meal, as in the ANE. However, they include enough details to establish that, if it includes a meal, it is not like human or ANE divine meals, thus rendering YHWH more transcendent. In other words, Priestly language is both elusive enough to preserve mystery and concrete enough to differentiate it from its human and ANE analogues. Just as priests form a bridge between heaven and earth, so too must their language, to the end that YHWH is known enough to be properly served but not so much that he loses his transcendent mystery.

The Priestly writers' calculated imprecision also accords well with ritual description. Since it mixes human with divine, too much precision in a ritual context is both impossible and problematic. As with a magician and his magic show, mystery keeps the priests and the ritual system in business.

Content and Contribution

My work aims to elucidate the Priestly cultic system, the system regulating the intersection of human and divine, through a comprehensive analysis of its constituent parts. It examines the nature of the primary actor's presence, YHWH, and the human and divine actions necessary to safeguard that presence in the locus of the tabernacle, the embodiment of heaven on earth.

As explained above, my study makes five primary contributions: 1) while most studies have analyzed part of the Priestly system or examined the whole through a narrow lens, I examine the Priestly legislation as a cohesive system designed to safeguard the divine presence in the tabernacle; 2) because none of the present models are sufficient, I develop and apply a comprehensive theory for interpreting Priestly rituals; 3) because scholars often fail to differentiate between rituals and texts about rituals, I develop and apply a theory for interpreting the Priestly ritual texts, examining the persuasive purposes of the Priestly document; 4) instead of comparing isolated rites, I compare the ANE systems and their constituent parts with the Priestly system; and 5) because scholars have either overemphasized Priestly precision or ignored Priestly language altogether, I highlight the Priestly use of language, which is by turns precise and elusive, as a means of differentiating the Priestly texts from their biblical and ANE counterparts.

Rather than making each contribution in turn, my study will examine the individual elements of the Priestly system, from which these contributions will continually emerge. In order to establish my methodological framework, I begin with ritual theory (chapter 1). I will then examine the key components of the Priestly system designed to keep heaven on earth: divine presence (chapter 2), the dedication of the tabernacle and cult (chapter 3), regular service (chapter 4), and damage control (chapters 5–7).

Chapter One

Ritual Theory

1.1. Problems with Ritual

Anthropological analysis has much to give to the field of biblical studies, particularly in its ritual analysis. However, various methodological issues prevent an easy transfer of ideas. First, we encounter problems with the anthropological terms. The meaning of 'ritual' is difficult to define,[1] as is the attempt to identify its constituent parts.[2] 'Ritual' itself is an artificial term, an analytical concept, and there remains no consensus on its definition. Various analogies have been put forward, which fall into three general categories: language, text, and performance. However, none captures the essence of ritual, an essence that, if existent, transcends temporal and cultural bounds.[3] All are posited on an evolutionary model, which searches for an individual kernel of ritual that has evolved to become the multifarious forms we have expressed today. On one level, these theories are too simplistic, making unwarranted generalizations that attempt to be inclusive. On another level, these theories ignore the present state of the ritual; how it functions, finds meaning, and effects transformation in the here and now.[4] Instead, ritual defies both definition and a suitable analogue. Nonetheless, although various problems remain with the term 'ritual,' I agree with Bell that 'ritual' remains a useful term that continues to be used widely by the public and various disciplines and is due for revision, not replacement.[5] If the definition of ritual is the elusive needle in the haystack, we should at-

---

[1] Bell 1992:13–66, 69–74; Grimes 1990:7–27. Hardin calls it "a wonderfully unstable and intriguing word (1996:308)," while Grimes laments, "Of the many varieties of human behavior, ritual is probably the most difficult to evaluate" (1996:283).

[2] There remains no consensus on the intrinsic features of ritual, if they even exist. Although formality, fixity, and repetition consistently emerge, they are likely not intrinsic to ritual. Rather, they serve as a frequent but not universal strategy for producing ritualized acts (Bell 1992:91–92; see further 1997:138–169 for characteristics of ritualized activities).

[3] For a critique of the various positions, see Bell 1992.

[4] See Klawans (2006), who specifically addresses the evolutionary approaches in chapters 1–2, while building his case for a symbolic, systematic understanding of sacrificial ritual throughout the rest of the work.

[5] Id. 1992:3–7.

tempt to sort through and revise the existing stack, rather than adding more terminology to the pile.

The term 'sacrifice' is likewise problematic. 'Sacrifice' is not a homogeneous notion, and, as with theories of ritual, there is no consensus on its essence.[6] Various theories have their proponents, most prominent among them being the food, gift, communion, and substitution theories.[7] However, none can be said to capture the essence of sacrifice, instead relegating other theories to derivative and secondary roles, both in Ancient Israel and the history of the world.[8] Indeed, if homogeneous, we would almost have to argue that every sacrifice was a derivative of "a fundamental and original sacrifice." Instead, we must focus on the variety present in ethnographic literature on sacrifice.[9]

Second, ritual theories are largely incongruent with textually represented rituals. Anthropological studies identify various field models for understanding ritual. Unfortunately, these field models do not easily apply to texts. For example, ritual theorists have recently stressed the importance of participation for gaining ritual insight and understanding,[10] an option which remains out of the reach of a textual representation. The ritual text is merely one aspect of a living system that cannot be easily abstracted, for ritual texts do not encapsulate the ritual experience.

Sadly, we do not have unmediated access to the ritual performance. Instead, we are left with what the text gives us,[11] and we must carefully distinguish the textual world from the real, historically-situated world. A textually represented ritual requires an interpretation of the text in which it is embedded before moving on to the ritual itself.[12] We must uncover the ritual world of the text before we can begin to reconstruct the ritual in real space, time, and practice. We indeed may conclude that the two worlds are similar, but first must distinguish clearly between them and make conclusions accordingly. For example, in the textual world of Leviticus 4:13–20, when the whole congregation brings a חטאת offering for their sin and the ritual is performed properly, the priest makes atonement for the people and they are forgiven (20). However, simply because the ritual text attaches

---

[6] Modéus 2005:31.

[7] The gift theory was first articulated by E.B. Tylor (1871); see also Mauss (1990). The communion theory finds expression in Robertson Smith (1894:269–387). The substitution theory finds voice in Evans-Pritchard (1956:261, 279–282).

[8] Cf. Hubert and Mauss 1964.

[9] Bloch 1992:24–25; cf. Modéus 2005:31–32.

[10] See, e.g., Grimes 1990:109–144, 210–233; Jennings 1996:325, 327. "To understand ritual apart from participation is to misunderstand ritual," at least according to the participants (Bergen 2005:6).

[11] Gilders 2004:9; Gane 2005:4, 9.

[12] Gilders 2004:9–11; Watts 2007:27–32; cf. Gorman 1999:535.

this meaning to the ritual does not mean that this is what actually happened, that the participants conceived of the ritual in this way, or even practiced it at all. Furthermore, a majority of the biblical ritual texts are prescriptive; that is, they tell the audience what ought to be done if a given situation arises, rather than being descriptive, describing what was done.[13] This prescription creates distinct interpretative problems, wherein prescriptive texts appear idealized and may differ significantly from actual practice.[14]

Third, there are additional problems involved in transferring ritual theory specifically to the biblical text. The term 'ritual' is alien to the Hebrew Bible. No single Hebrew word can be appropriately translated 'ritual.'[15] In P proper, we do not even possess a ritual,[16] merely a textual representation of rituals. The observer can neither participate, observe, nor consult the native participants.

Such a situation can be likened[17] to having instructions for a board game without the pieces (the sacrifices and sacrificial equipment), the board (the tabernacle/temple), or the experience of anyone who has ever played the game (e.g., the priests).[18] Over the years, scholars have become good at reading the directions yet unfortunately have been unable to play the game. We are left with instructions that are both priceless and limited in conveying an accurate picture. Our instructions assume a working knowledge of the system. When the game is not included, we are at a loss. Left with only the instructions, scholars strive to infer from the rules and regulations what the game looked like and how it worked. They read the instructions trying to visualize the board, but naturally, the rules were written assuming participants had the board in front of them. The rules were never intended to describe what the board looked like to someone with no firsthand knowledge, and they were not intended to be separated from their context. They

---

[13] For the distinction between prescriptive and descriptive texts in relation to the Bible and ANE literature, see especially Levine 1963; id. 1965.

[14] Cf. Smith 1982:53–65, 143–145, who illustrates this discrepancy in the circumpolar bear hunting and its associated rites.

[15] Gilders 2004:2.

[16] "Unless there is a performance, there is no ritual" (Rappaport 1999:37).

[17] As with any analogy, this one is imperfect on various levels and should not be stretched too far. It merely serves to give us an approximate image of the situation we face.

[18] One could argue that the practitioners of modern Judaism continue to play the game. However, over thousands of years, the game has certainly changed. Even if we grant that the instructions (i.e., Lev 16) remain the same, various factors have converged to transform the game. Thousands of years later, we must try to play with different players (no priests), with different pieces (no sacrifices or sacrificial implements), and without a board (no temple).

were intended only to show how to operate with the board, pieces, and participants fully available.

Hopeless as our picture seems, the reality is in fact worse. Instead of providing exhaustive information, here as elsewhere the Bible is frustratingly laconic.[19] Although the text provides instructions for the performance of activities and the goals of these activities,[20] these instructions and goals are often incomplete. The text is instead selective, highlighting certain details while glossing over or ignoring others, all in pursuit of the purpose of the text and the assumption that the reader is familiar with the material. For example, in Leviticus 4, there is no mention of how to slaughter the חטאת animal and divide its parts, nor is there any mention of its purpose beyond extracting its blood and suet. Instead, the overall purposes, כפר and forgiveness, are central. This inexactitude extends to the Day of Atonement, which details how the priest is to sprinkle the altar (16:14), yet does not specify how to cast lots for the two goats and says nothing about collecting the blood of the sacrifice.[21] Thus, we neither have an exhaustive instruction booklet nor the appropriate forum to follow our incomplete instructions.

1.2. What is Ritual?[22]

1.2.1. Why is it Both Useful and Undefinable?

Ritual serves as a way of meaningfully interacting with God, to bring about a transformation or change the state of the world in some way, generally concerning the immaterial (e.g., sin and impurity).[23] Like analogical language, "ritual is not simply an alternative way to express any manner of thing, but that certain meanings and effects can best, or even only, be expressed or achieved in ritual."[24] Ritual enacts various activities that elicit[25] the response of God, thereby bringing to bear his power on the mundane

---

[19] Grabbe 1993:38; Marx 2003:103–120, esp. 103.

[20] Anderson *ABD* 5 (1992):883. Knierim contends that the biblical ritual prescriptions serve to standardize the primary steps of performance so that the rituals accomplish the goals for which they were intended (1992:89).

[21] Gane 2005:22–23, 225.

[22] By ritual, I am here referring to Priestly cultic ritual performed in the tabernacle complex, understood to involve an interchange between human and divine parties. I am not ambitious enough to construct an overarching description of ritual nor am I convinced that such a description is possible.

[23] Cf. Driver 1996:176.

[24] Rappaport 1999:30, italics his. cf. Tambiah 1968:185, 188.

[25] The ritual participants invite, rather than coerce, the response of the deity (Jennings 1996:331).

world.²⁶ In other words, ritual serves as a bridge between two worlds, the human and divine.²⁷ When these two worlds intersect, transformation inevitably occurs, as God, the wholly other, becomes accessible in the here and now. In such an interaction, simple words and actions are insufficient. Instead, we can only use whatever is at our disposal to grasp at a means of expressing this reality being ritually enacted.²⁸

To bridge the gap, we must use analogy and actions where the relationship between means and ends is not intrinsic.²⁹ Ritual systems function similarly to analogical language. Our language has no words to literally and accurately describe God. In turn, we use analogical language to communicate approximately what would otherwise be inaccessible. Along the same lines, the biblical text combines images that appear freakish to the modern reader yet functionally communicate the abstract (e.g., the cherubim with many faces). In turn, the reader should expect some flexibility in expression. In many instances mathematical precision is secondary to the conveyance of perceived reality, especially when that reality is so difficult to represent.

Ritual serves as the point of intersection between the abstract and the mundane, the human and the divine. It simultaneously enacts transformations in two different realms, drawing from each to make something unnatural to both. It at once makes practical actions transcendent and the transcendent realm concrete. In the course of ritual, mundane actions are transformed so that they are more than mere actions; they become actions that surpass what can be achieved by ordinary physical means alone. A ritual's combination of actions can simultaneously affect the interrelated states of an individual, society, the world, and God.³⁰ For example, in the case of the חטאת ritual, the ritual actions may effect כפר, bring forgiveness to the individual, reconciliation with God, and a restoration of order to the world.³¹

At the same time, these ritual actions concretize the abstract. They make complex ideas, the divine and the immaterial, practical and accessible. Ritual can condense a complex theory that functions on multiple levels into mundane ritual action. Through ritual, humans can communicate with God,

---

[26] Cf. Leach 1985:137: "The purpose of religious performance is to provide a bridge, or channel of communication, through which the power of the gods may be made available to otherwise impotent men."

[27] Cf. Smith 2005:3–4.

[28] In speaking of reality and a real encounter with the deity, I refer to the perceptions of the participants rather than to an actual (that is, empirically verifiable) interaction between human and divine.

[29] Rappaport 1999:429.

[30] Gorman 1990:37–38.

[31] The latter two interpretations are not explicit in the text.

bringing him and his power to bear in their world. Through ritual, a group of actions can make tangible the immaterial world, which is believed to be real but transcends mundane representation. In the חטאת ritual, sin and impurity become quasi-physical. The ritual transforms a bloody mess into an effective response to sin and impurity.

Rather than using an abstract philosophy to approximate (perceived) reality, ritual concretizes the abstract through real, if eccentric, actions. As we will see, much is communicated both consciously and unconsciously in the doing of ritual action. The complex and ineffable can be represented and maintained via set, practical rules. People may not comprehend or remember *why*, but they will digest and retain *how*.[32]

Furthermore, ritual action can accomplish what no mere philosophy can. While theories may propel people to perform a ritual or explain why it is necessary, no theory can practically ward off unseen dangers. To be effective, to transform reality, the theory requires ritual action.[33]

Because ritual actions enact this cosmic interchange, none of our various theories and analogies are sufficient to encapsulate 'ritual' in its ineffable glory. Rather, various approaches struggle to approximate certain aspects of the ritual process, aspects which are indeed indescribable. Performance theory, for example, highlights the fact that ritual is in some ways a performance. The participants must step into relatively fixed roles that allow for little or no deviation. However, whereas a performance is meant to have an impact on the audience, ritual action also aims to effect change in the world. Rather than merely being evocative, the very actions themselves are believed to actually do something that affects reality (beyond the disposition of the actors and participants).[34]

1.2.2. Features of Ritual Signs[35]

To address such complex situations, ritual signs must function on multiple levels. Ritual signs are characterized by condensation of meaning, multivocality, and ambiguity.[36] Ritual condenses a rich diversity of meanings

---

[32] Cf. Converse 1964:206–261.

[33] Gruenwald 2002 argues this position throughout his work, making the argument explicit in various places including VIII, 14, 29, 219.

[34] Bell 1992:43.

[35] By sign, I mean words, actions, or objects that communicate a meaning (keeping the definition as general as possible). Among other things, signs can be symbols, indexes, or icons.

[36] Kertzer 1988:11.

into a single sign,³⁷ a condensation made necessary by the diversity and abstraction of ritual expression. For example, in the single sign of the temple, we find multiple explanations, most of which can be operable at once. Among other things, the temple may symbolize the cosmos, God's dwelling, safety, danger, creation, order, the numinous.

Multivocality suggests that the same sign "may be understood by different people in different ways"³⁸ and in different ways in different contexts.³⁹ For example, fire may be understood in one context as destructive (e.g., when it burns down a home) and life-giving in another (e.g., when it heats a freezing camper). Indeed, fire can be interpreted differently in both instances depending on one's perspective. In the case of the burning house, a neighbor may interpret the event as the long-overdue judgment of God.

Ambiguity implies that an individual sign has no precise meaning. All of the examples above have no precise meaning when contextless.⁴⁰ Various meanings can be attached to them, usually culling from their natural qualities (e.g., fire heats, burns, lights). These meanings only find specificity in context. In addition, different activities can have the same meaning, even within the same ritual.⁴¹

These various possibilities all can be found in biblical ritual. For example, the suet functions differently in two different contexts. The priest presents the suet of a זבח שלמים to God as an אשה (Lev 3:3–5, 9–11, 14–16), yet the suet of the חטאת is not (e.g., 4:8–10, 19, 26, 31, 35).⁴² "Whereas a sevenfold sprinkling [of blood] in the inner sanctum on the Day of Atonement purges an area of the Sacred Tent (Lev 16:14–16a), the same activity performed on the outer altar *in the course of the same ritual* reconsecrates it (19)."⁴³ Both grain and an animal can serve as a חטאת (5:6–13).⁴⁴ Within the same ritual, a חטאת and an עלה can both make atonement in some way (16:6 and 24 respectively).

In turn, the interpreter must be careful in his interpretation. Ritual signs are not univalent.⁴⁵ We cannot simply import meaning from one context to

---

³⁷ See esp. Turner 1967. Such a sign can become cumbersome as in the case of the four-faced cherubim of Ezekiel. In this one symbol, the attributes of all four faces are brought to bear.
³⁸ Kertzer 1988:11, drawing on the works of Turner 1967:50 and Munn 1973:580.
³⁹ Gane 2005:8.
⁴⁰ Cf. Staal 1979; 1989:127–129, 131, 134, 330; Gane 2005:4–6.
⁴¹ See the example in the following paragraph.
⁴² Gane 2005:8.
⁴³ Ibid. 191, italics his.
⁴⁴ Ibid.
⁴⁵ Although the multivocality of ritual signs is practically unanimously accepted in social anthropology, biblical scholars have been slow to follow suit (Gilders 2004:5–6, e.g., on Milgrom).

another, assuming that every sign functions the same regardless of context. We cannot assume that the referent for a given sign exhausts all possibilities. Other referents may be inherent in the text or tentatively extrapolated from it.

1.2.3. The Effects of Performing Ritual

In the modern empirical sense, ritual results do not necessarily proceed from ritual actions in a cause-effect sequence. The native, however, would perceive the result as a natural outflow of the action. Cause and effect of a different sort are at work in biblical ritual. From an empirical perspective, a חטאת offering that is said to cleanse clearly fails to do so because a bloody mess does not empirically clean anything.[46] To the native participant, the same 'bloody mess,' if performed correctly, leads naturally and reliably to the sought-after result (in the above case, cleansing). As bathing makes one clean, a חטאת ritual brings about atonement and cleansing or forgiveness from sin.

Nonetheless, "although they may not make a clear distinction between what is natural and what is not, [the native actors would] know the efficacy of spells to be different than that of spears."[47] In our case, we would put ritual actions in place of spells, actions that achieve a result by interacting with the divine via actions done in a specific way at a specific place and a specific time. Although different, these actions would indeed be as efficacious as actions that instigate a cause-effect relationship. In some sense, they are more effective as they address what traditional cause-effect relations cannot. They address the immaterial relationship between God and humanity and the issues that concern it (e.g., sin that threatens it).

Ritual actions are likewise more dangerous, precarious, and ineffable than their mundane counterparts. The results of these actions are non-verifiable.[48] One cannot verify if one is actually cleansed or forgiven.[49] Instead, the system requires a measure of faith in its efficacy. One has to believe that one has been cleansed or forgiven. Although ritual is unverifiable, ritual failure emerges as a distinct possibility (see, e.g., Nadab and Abihu in Leviticus 10). At a basic level, one can assume that a ritual

---

[46] Gane 2005:17.

[47] Rappaport 1999:48.

[48] See Bell 1992:212. The biblical system differs from other ritual systems because, in the Priestly cult, there are no fertility or healing rituals, which may be more easily judged. Transactions occur on an immaterial level, addressing sin and impurity, atonement and forgiveness. Even in the case of the so-called 'leper,' the ritual occurs after he has been physically 'healed.'

[49] Perhaps further suffering or newfound blessing might indicate the ritual's failure or success to the supplicant.

failed either because it was insufficient itself or that an external force made it insufficient (e.g., the priest did not perform the appropriate ritual). Within a given system, especially when that system is relatively isolated, the ritual performer will blame himself or someone else before impugning the ritual itself.[50]

The unverifiable nature of ritual, the complexity of its performance and requirements, and high-risk repercussions make ritual action dangerous. The smallest detail could go wrong in a complex ritual performance without anyone's awareness, thereby invalidating the whole. Even afterward, such an infelicity would likely remain hidden because there is no way to rewind and check where the ritual went wrong or to verify that it went wrong at all. The cost of ritual failure, which is often death[51] and always negative, is likewise serious.

In the end, the ritual system is remarkably resilient. In it, the ritual authority decides what one is to do in response to a given situation, claiming divine initiation. The people agree and the ritual is performed. Through repetition, the ritual becomes ingrained;[52] there becomes no other way to respond. The prescribed ritual response becomes the only natural, logical, and necessary way to address a particular situation. This habituation is not something conscious or systematized. It simply becomes habitualized through consistent ritual participation. There is no reason to question the ritual as long as it works, especially when the culture is relatively isolated from outside influence.

The beauty of ritual is that it works. The ritual is unverifiable, requiring faith. Even if a degree of verifiability emerges (e.g., someone dying indicates a ritual failure), such an occurrence is rare. It is one among many rituals in a ritual system that rarely fails. It is also likely to be blamed on the human participants, a viable option given the complexity of ritual. Likewise, when the stakes are so high, there must be a great impetus to change. In turn, the ritual system remains in place.

---

[50] Grimes 1996:291; for an examination of ritual failure, see Grimes 1996:279–293, who expands upon Austin 1962; see further Hüsken 2007.

[51] The immediate death of Nadab and Abihu gave them no chance to repair their infraction (Lev 10); cf. the outburst of divine wrath against Uzzah for touching the ark (2Sa 6:6–7).

[52] Bell speaks of a 'ritual body' (1992:94–117). Among ritual bodies, the "ritualized body is a body invested with the 'sense' of ritual" (98). In other words, the ritual becomes ingrained in the person. People are changed in the very doing of ritual. "Required kneeling does not merely *communicate* subordination to the kneeler ... Kneeling produces a subordinated kneeler in and through the act itself" (100).

1.3. Analyzing Ritual

How then do we approach the system? We must tread humbly, recognizing that the system defies explanation. Its complexity stretches the mind and its ability to categorize. The texts that report biblical ritual are likewise incomplete and selective. Thus, as we try to fill in the gaps, we must be willing to say, "I don't know, but I think x based on y," and we must be willing to constantly reshape our theories. Beyond that, to understand the system, we will survey and critique several important theories. In the end, I will present my theory as an amalgamation of those analyzed.

1.3.1. Catherine Bell and Ritualization

Although Catherine Bell's work does not directly refer to the biblical text, her theories establish an important foundation, which other theorists rightly build upon. After reviewing the various treatments of ritual and finding them lacking, Bell offers the concept of ritualization as the way forward in ritual studies.[53] By ritualization, she means a "way of acting that is designed and orchestrated to distinguish and privilege what is being done in relation to other, more quotidian, activities."[54] This differentiation is enacted through various devices, among them space, time, action, specialized personnel, and order. These spheres and the ritualized action that co-opts them set apart these actions as important, creating the sacred through differentiation from the profane.[55]

Ritualization is a process employed across cultures, yet the various constitutive elements may and often do vary. When ritualized actions are abstracted from their immediate context, they are no longer the same action.[56]

1.3.2. Klawans and the Symbolic Approach

Jonathan Klawans examines the divide between the study of purity rites and sacrifice. On one hand, the symbolic approach to purity rites has become popular in biblical studies with the works of Mary Douglas, particularly *Purity and Danger*. On the other hand, biblical studies of sacrifice

---

[53] Bell's treatment of ritual is indeed complicated (1992; id. 1997). Instead of summarizing and critiquing all aspects of her theory, I will focus on the aspect of ritualization, which finds its origin in Gluckman 1962:20, 25–6.
[54] Bell 1992:74.
[55] Ibid. 91.
[56] Ibid. 81.

often have focused exclusively on tracing the evolution of the sacrificial process.[57]

In response to such methodology, Klawans accepts the position of Mary Douglas that the ritual purity system should be understood symbolically[58] and seeks to extend her symbolic approach to the entire sacrificial system.[59] Klawans' symbolic system finds its interpretive key in two concepts: "the desire to imitate God and the concern to attract and maintain the presence of God."[60]

Undoubtedly, much symbolism goes into the formation of such a complex system and grows out of its use. Indeed, few would deny the presence of symbolism in sacrificial practice. Klawans' approach rightly highlights its presence and recuperates the possibility that ancients thought abstractly.[61] Indeed understanding a sacrifice as a gift to the gods, communion with the gods, or food for the gods requires "metaphorical associations that people who offered sacrifices made themselves."[62] The evolutionary procession from literal to symbolic is too simplistic to adequately explain the sacrificial process from either a synchronic or diachronic perspective, and the search for origins often obfuscates a contextual understanding of the sacrificial system.[63]

Before embracing this approach as the way forward, we must examine its limits. In most ritual contexts, opinions differ as to the appropriate symbolic interpretation. The majority of symbolic actions can be unclear to the participants or interpreted by them in dissimilar ways,[64] and unfortunately scholars have done little better at reaching a consensus.

Unfortunately for structuralists, who have often been proponents of the symbolic approach to ritual interpretation,[65] meaning does not necessarily inhere in the structure of ritual. Actions alone do not intrinsically convey meaning.[66] Meaning may be extrapolated from the structure of the ritual, using gap-filling techniques, but it does not necessarily follow from it. Its

---

[57] Klawans 2006:6–10, 17–48. This is a pursuit that he believes "should remain largely irrelevant to the work of biblical commentators" (6). Although he overstates his case, he is right to stress the need to understand "the developed sacrificial system of ancient Israel in its context" (ibid.). Jacob Milgrom serves as Klawans' parade example of the inconsistent treatment of purity and sacrifice (ibid. 27–32).

[58] See esp. Douglas 1966.

[59] Klawans 2006:48.

[60] Ibid. 72.

[61] Ibid. 20, citing Lévi-Strauss 1978:16.

[62] Ibid. 41–42; cf. Leach 1976:83.

[63] Nihan 2007 is the most prominent exception to this trend.

[64] Bell 1992:182; Modéus 2005:42; cf. Fernandez 1965:902–929, esp. 907–912; Stromberg 1981:556–557; Kertzer 1988:67–72; Grimes 1995:106.

[65] E.g., Douglas (1966), Leach (1976), Davies (1977), and Klawans (2006).

[66] Gane 2005:10.

success as a viable interpretation depends on the skill of the one doing the gap-filling in persuading his audience that his theory best explains the data.

Klawans argues from the analogy of *imitatio dei* that "ritual purification involves a process of separating from those aspects of humanity that make one least God-like, as a preparation for a number of sacrificial performances (selecting, killing, looking into, and consuming) that are much more God-like."[67] He holds that various aspects of the sacrificial process should be understood as expressions of imitating God. As God exercises pastoral care over his people, controlling both their lives and deaths, so too do they exercise such care over their domesticated animals.[68] As God the warrior wears a blood-stained garment (Isa 61:1–3), so do the priestly officiants.[69] As God the consuming fire consumes so do the offerers burn and consume various aspects of their offerings.[70]

Klawans clearly has a lot of skill at gap-filling. He offers a fascinating perspective that can and will be criticized on a number of grounds. Rather than doing so here, we will simply note that his theory is non-verifiable. He takes various elements and skillfully weaves them into a whole, yet the whole does not automatically emerge from the sum of its parts. He draws on specific ideas attributed to God from diverse sections of Scripture (e.g., the Psalms and Isaiah) and analogically applies them to Israel in Leviticus. None of his analogical interpretations are expressed explicitly in the ritual texts (i.e., they remain uninterpreted ritualized actions). Rather he finds them implicitly in various spots, which are often uninterpreted and non-ritual themselves and have no direct bearing on the text under scrutiny, and combines them to form a unified whole. After carefully selecting his pieces from a plethora of options and putting them together, an interesting picture emerges, one that is in no way verifiable and may indeed reflect the interpreter more than the text he is interpreting.

Many other symbolic approaches[71] fall prey to the same weakness. They extrapolate aspects of what the texts supply (often from other contexts within Scripture), knit them together with various gap-filling techniques, and apply them to explain the text at hand. Like Klawans', few of the symbolic interpretations necessarily follow from the text itself.[72] Thus, it comes

---

[67] Klawans 2006:72.
[68] Ibid. 59–61.
[69] Ibid. 64.
[70] Ibid. 65.
[71] See, e.g., the various approaches to understanding the symbolism of blood noted in Gilders; see more plausibly Gorman's cosmological approach to ritual (1990).
[72] Thus, "when the texts do not provide symbolic explanations of the rituals they describe, interpreters find themselves open to the charge of imposing symbolic systems not intrinsic or necessary to the rituals" (Watts 2007: 9–10).

as no surprise that few of the symbolic interpreters agree on an appropriate symbolic interpretation.

As scholars, we often focus on the mental activity of the ritual participants at the expense of action, of ritual participation.[73] In doing so, we ignore the reality that Leviticus records no mental activity as necessary for ritual[74] and few if any symbolic interpretations.[75] Instead, if interpretations appear within the text, they are often declarations of the instrumental effects of ritual activity (e.g., sprinkling blood onto priests makes them holy [Ex 29:21]).[76]

However, the dearth of explicit symbolic interpretations should not lead us to jettison them from the realm of possibility.[77] Instead this paucity merely points to the conclusion that symbolism is not the driving force of ritual.[78] Instead of being the *raison d'être* of the ritual system, symbolism merely "grows in and around"[79] sacrificial ritual. As we will see, "in and around" the sacrificial remains a privileged spot.

1.3.3. Gilders and the Indexical Approach

From within the structuralist camp, we find an approach that offers the interpreter surer footing. Some scholars have distinguished between indexing and symbolism.[80] A symbol serves as a sign in conventional relationship with its referent.[81] For example, a dove functions as a symbol for peace. The association between a dove and peace likely derives from the passage in Genesis where a dove returns to the ark with an olive branch (also a symbol for peace) in its mouth, signifying dry land and the newfound peace between God and humanity. Within the same Christian tradition, a dove also symbolizes the Holy Spirit, for the Spirit descends like a dove on Jesus during his baptism. Nothing in the image of a dove itself necessitates

---

[73] Bergen 2005:25.

[74] Ibid.

[75] Gilders 2004:5.

[76] Ibid.

[77] We must be careful not to denigrate the symbolic approach. The lack of symbolic interpretation in ritual texts may derive simply from the nature of the text itself and its concern with the nuts and bolts of ritual. Other genres, especially poetry, are much freer with their symbolic expression. Likewise, the tabernacle and temple abound with symbolic elements (e.g., the cherubim), putting them firmly within a ritual context. Although unverifiable, the nature of ritual and the stage upon which is enacted, the temple, invite symbolic speculation.

[78] Or, at least of ritual texts.

[79] Modéus 2005:69.

[80] Charles Sanders Peirce in Buchler 1955; Jay 1992:6–7; Rappaport 1999:54–68; Gilders 2004:8.

[81] Gilders 2004:8.

30   Chapter 1: Ritual Theory

either interpretation. Instead a specific situation arose that fused the images.

In contrast, an index is a sign that is existentially related to its signifier. An index indicates rather than represents an object.[82] For example, a thermometer indicates temperature and the star Polaris indicates north. These indexes transcend temporal and cultural bounds. They are connected by a matter of fact. Likewise, in a sacrificial context, when a participant eats the flesh of a sacrificial victim, he is existentially connected with the victim.[83]

William Gilders applies this theory to the use of blood in the Hebrew Bible, specifically in the Priestly texts. In the case of the חטאת offering, because "P reserves blood manipulation activity to members of the Aaronid priesthood," blood manipulation "serves to index the distinction between priests and laity as ritual actors and also to define the spatial dimensions of the priests' activity."[84] By handling the blood, the priest is necessarily in some way related to the blood; the contact between the two indexes their relationship. The priests' exclusive access to the blood indicates a distinction between the priest and lay person, a distinction that finds further meaning in where the blood goes. While the offerer brings the offering to the entrance of the tent of meeting, the priest brings its blood to the altar. In fact, all of the actions described index the offerer's domain of meaningful activity to the entrance of the tent of meeting and the priest's to the altar.[85] Thus, the blood manipulation serves as an index that marks the distinction between priest and non-priest, the altar and tent of meeting.

A relationship between God and the offerer can also be indexed by various activities. "The offerer indexes a relationship with the animal in hand-pressing; the priest takes the blood of this animal and brings it into relationship with sancta, in Yahweh's presence ... and, thus, establishes the relationship between the offerer and Yahweh."[86] Hand leaning indexes a relationship between the offerer and his offering. As the animal is related to the offerer, the slaughter of the animal is likewise somehow related. The slaughtered animal produces the blood, which the priest brings to the altar to carry out blood manipulation, thereby indexing a relationship between the blood and the altar. Thus, "the application of the blood to the altar indexes a relationship between the offerer and the altar, a relationship mediated by the animal and its blood."[87] As the tabernacle is God's home and the altar is in the tabernacle complex, it follows that there is a relationship

---

[82] Jay 1992:7.
[83] Ibid. 6–7.
[84] Gilders 2004:139.
[85] Ibid. 80.
[86] Ibid. 140.
[87] Ibid. 81.

between God and the altar. In the end, the application of blood to the altar mediates the relationship between the offerer and God, via the animal, its blood, and the altar.[88] This remains true regardless of how we interpret the symbol of blood, "whether the blood conveys the worshiper's life, or whether it is simply the animal's life being restored to Yahweh before the animal's flesh is offered as the worshiper's gift."[89] Unlike symbolic interpretations, indexical relations are often verifiable.

However, Gane rightly criticizes the structuralist approach, arguing that when we have only physical activities, meaning will not simply appear as a sum of the parts.[90] To make his point, Gane uses the example of a man washing his feet outside of a religious shrine. His actions could be interpreted as: a) "cooling himself"; b) "making sure that he will not soil the carpet in the shrine when he enters"; c) "ritually purifying himself preparatory to worship"; or d) "engaging in a core act of worship."[91] If we continue to observe the man's behavior,

without knowing how his actions fit into his world view, we will remain unsure whether his actions constitute a complete activity system, let alone whether they are ritual in nature and, if so, what they might mean. How can we even begin to employ a structural approach, unless we import one or more *a priori* assumptions that invalidate our analysis from the outset, when we do not know whether we are looking at the top or the bottom of a ritual or nonritual activity hierarchy?[92]

Nor will a diachronic approach offer any help[93] "because a change from one unknown to another unknown does not yield something known."[94]

Gane's criticism applies to the indexical approach as it does to the symbolic approach yet with less devastating effect. If we have only ritual actions, even an indexical system will not tell us much. If the blood manipulation of the חטאת offering was ripped from context, so that we only saw the actions, we could still discern that there is some sort of indexical relationship between the one who brings the blood to the bronze object, the object itself, and the blood he brings. The blood would thus differentiate between the one who could handle it and the one who could not. Unfortunately, without a contextual framework, we would remain unaware of the implications of such an act. We would have no way of discovering if the actions and the distinctions they create are incidental or meaningful. Returning to the man washing his feet outside the shrine, we could discover

---

[88] Ibid. 81–82.
[89] Ibid. 82.
[90] Id. 2005:10.
[91] Ibid.
[92] Ibid. 10–11.
[93] Contra Jenson 1992:152.
[94] Gane 2005:11.

indexically that there is a relationship between the man, his feet, the water, and foot washing basin. Nonetheless, we could not determine if his action is ritual in nature or connected to the shrine in any way. In other words, we would have no way of interpreting the reason for the footwashing, nor could we pinpoint if there is a result beyond the instrumental, clean feet.[95]

Fortunately, biblical ritual actions do not exist in a vacuum. We do know something of the system in which they are embedded, and we can safely infer other things, enough to make an indexical approach profitable. From the perspective of the textual world, we know that the tabernacle is God's abode; we often know the situation that precipitates the ritual and occasionally the end result. In the case of the חטאת offering of Leviticus 4:22–26, the text indicates that the offerer approaches the sanctuary, God's abode, to deal with his sin so that he may receive atonement and forgiveness. In turn, because the action appears within a specific ritual context, we can logically conclude that there is an indexical relationship between the offerer and God. Given a rudimentary understanding of the context, the physical actions can index relations that are not otherwise obvious (e.g., blood manipulation marks the point at which the priest's activity begins[96]). Thus, indexing is a profitable method when used in tandem with the textual description of the system.

1.3.4. Modéus and Causa

The following two approaches apply aspects found in the text, upon which the indexical theory can build. For Martin Modéus, meaning inheres in the *causa*, namely "those circumstances, changes or events of nature or culture that are the ultimate reasons making the performance of the ritual desirable or necessary."[97] Indeed this *causa* is the reason for the ritual.[98] He isolates differentiation as the fundamental strategy to focus on the *causa*, for the major point of ritual is to make the *causa* experientially real to the audience.[99]

The situation prompting the ritual is certainly informative. If a sin precipitates a ritual, we can naturally assume that the ritual responds to the sin. In addition, the differentiated actions do in some way focus on the

---

[95] For a more humorous example illustrating the importance of context for understanding, see Grimes 1996:288: "If one does not understand the shit devil rites, one might assume that boys who stumble, defecate, and wear ragged clothes were mentally ill instead of engaging in ritual caricature."

[96] Gilders 2004:80.

[97] Id. 2005:38.

[98] Modéus distinguishes between the reason for the ritual, defined as the *causa*, and the meaning, defined as the intellectual interpretation of the purpose (2005:38–39).

[99] Ibid. 39, 43.

causa. For example, the people are made aware of the gravity of sin via the ritual enactment.

Unfortunately, Modéus offers little evidence why the *causa* should be primary in interpreting ritual or why differentiation primarily serves to make the *causa* experientially real. Focusing exclusively on the *causa* may divert attention from other aspects of ritual that better encapsulate meaning. Although the prominence of the *causa* over other interpretive factors remains unproven and is likely overstated, the situation that gives rise to ritual is obviously informative and can profitably be used in combination with other approaches to understand biblical ritual.

1.3.5. Gane and Systems Theory

While Modéus finds meaning in the beginning of the ritual process, the *causa*, Roy Gane turns to the end, to the interpretive statements that provide the goal of the ritual.[100] He brings systems theory to bear on biblical rituals.[101] Ritual, like other non-ritual systems, finds meaning in the goal attributed to it by the authority who commands the ritual.[102] Individual actions are ambiguous. They find concrete meaning only as part of the larger whole[103] and thus should not be imported from one context to the next.[104]

Although Gane's approach is a major step forward, it has several difficulties. First, Gane does not distinguish between the world of the text and the historical world. Gane is correct to assert that meaning can be found at the level of the text in the interpretive statements strewn throughout the text, yet it does not necessarily follow that this is true in the real world. Ritual actions may produce a result innately, a result that indeed diverges from that of the official interpretation, or the actual result may not be apprehended at all.

Furthermore, although Gane is correct in asserting that individual action has no single inherent meaning, meaning does inhere to some degree in individual actions. For example, even within a given culture, there are multiple ways of interpreting a man starting a fire. He could be cold or hungry. He could be disposing of something or preparing for a ritual. He could simply be having a family barbecue or he may need light. He could be sending smoke signals for help or be a deranged pyromaniac. The fire itself

---

[100] See esp. id. 2005:3–24; cf. id. 2004.

[101] He draws particularly from Wilson 1984, who examines non-ritual activity systems.

[102] Gane 2004:18–23, 50–60; id. 2005:7, 13.

[103] Gane 2005:19–20.

[104] This is one of the fundamental assumptions of his book, that חטאת offerings can function differently in different contexts and their purpose emerges only from reading their purpose statements.

carries no fixed meaning. We can only understand it by placing it in an appropriate context, accomplished most simply by asking the man.

However, this does not mean that each action stands entirely alone. The reader should expect some consistency, especially within the same ritual system, otherwise designators such as חטאת would be meaningless. While there is some variability, ritual activities like חטאת must have some common meaning. Even if the various rituals contain variable symbols chosen to corporately express a transcendent reality, these particulars were indeed chosen for a reason. Although fire itself has no inherent meaning, it performs certain functions – warming, burning and illuminating – that naturally communicate something to observers and can thus be co-opted to serve ritual meaning.

Focusing exclusively on a single theory likewise overlooks other possible meanings.[105] In other words, although enormously helpful, an explanation does not exhaust ritual meaning.[106] Further meaning may indeed be found in *causa*, indexing, and even in symbolism, although the latter remains unverifiable.

Finally, as Gane himself acknowledges,[107] this approach allows us to find meaning only in those places where an interpretation is given. Unfortunately, such explanations are rare indeed.[108] The other methods elucidated above can be profitably applied both when an interpretation is found and especially when it is absent.

1.4. The Cumulative Approach

As intimated above, a cumulative approach offers the greatest possibility for uncovering ritual meaning. Each approach has its merits, but, when applied alone, each offers a limited range of meaning. The theories are compatible and connectable. When connected, they balance each other, preventing one explanation from claiming undue attention at the expense of the others. They likewise fill in the gaps, warding off nihilism and giving the picture greater depth and clarity. In ritual theory as in ritual action, the whole is greater than the sum of its parts.

---

[105] Gane himself does not advocate such an exclusive focus, merely that the search for interpretative statements should be primary.

[106] "Even if we identify an explicit official or public interpretation of a ritual act ... we should not assume that this explanation exhausts what can be said about the ritual gesture" (Gilders 2004:141).

[107] Gane 2005:23–24.

[108] Gilders 2004:5.

1.4.1. How the Theories Address Multiple Levels of Meaning

Employing parts of several theories is not simply postmodern indecision; meaning, like signs, functions on multiple levels. Because each method addresses some aspect of meaning, connecting the methods and their findings provides a much richer whole than any individual method would alone. To help us sort through the many layers, we will employ Modéus' model, tweaked to fit our purposes. It is certainly not the only one, nor is it problem-free. It merely helps the reader to visualize several of the levels and how the various theories address them.

For Modéus, the ritual system functions on three levels: 1) structure; 2) use; and 3) ideology.[109] First, the level of structure[110] refers to the relations between people and places which can be derived from the very ritual itself.[111] "The most obvious example is probably the emphasizing of status and power relations through the positions in the ritual room."[112] At this level, meaning or function is often unconscious yet is internalized by all as natural.[113] Without being consciously aware of the situation within a given ritual,[114] people are aware of what they may do, where they may go, and how their limits are different from other actors. For example, the priest knows his role and how it differs from the layperson's. This approach is also verifiable given we have enough information about the context in which it appears.[115]

Gilders' indexical theory is a perfect example of a method that finds meaning at this level. In his examination of the burnt offering, the blood manipulation indexes differences in the participants (between priest and non-priest) based on where they are allowed to stand and what they may do. It also makes distinctions between places (the entrance to the tent of meeting from the bronze altar).[116]

Second, the level of use[117] can be described as the participant's view on why ritual is being done. Since success is measured by the consent of the participants, use is verifiable interpretation. For example, using a handshake as a greeting is successful because the participants concur that by

---

[109] Modéus 2005:128–135.

[110] Ibid. 132–134.

[111] It is "to some extent present in all human activity" (ibid. 134).

[112] Ibid. 132.

[113] Cf. Bell 1992:99.

[114] However, if asked, they may provide an adequate response. Even so, the question would likely seem nonsensical, yielding an answer like, "That's just the way it works. Everyone knows that!"

[115] Without this context, physical actions will not tell us much.

[116] Gilders 2004:78–84.

[117] Ibid. 131, 133–134.

this action they have greeted each other. In the biblical realm, agreement takes a different form. The author or authority behind the text gives the official, agreed-upon interpretation.[118] The text often presents the situation that gives rise to ritual, the *causa*, or states that the ritual action achieved its desired effect (as explained by the goal statements).[119]

Use examines the obvious meaning of ritual; instead of discovering why rituals use blood, the level of use examines simple and more accessible motives. It asks what concrete situation the ritual responds to (e.g., sin) and what the expected result is (e.g., forgiveness). Statements at the level of use are also more than verifiable interpretations. They may also be descriptive, as they describe the agreed upon instrumental effects of ritual action (e.g., correctly performing a חטאת ritual for sin leads to forgiveness). The approaches of both Modéus and Gane are at home at the level of use, yet at different ends of the process. Modéus finds meaning in identifying the situation that gives rise to the ritual and Gane finds meaning in identifying the (expected) outcome of the situation via the goal statements.

Third, ideology[120] examines the text's theoretical underpinnings and rhetorical implications. More than simply addressing the *causa* and agreed-upon outcome of ritual, ideology addresses the underlying rationale of the author. Ideological analysis examines why the ritual is being performed in such a way, what the author understands it to mean, and what he means to communicate to his audience. In other words, what is the text's ideological import, and what is the author's ideological agenda?

At this level we may speak of the transcendental and theological. For example, understanding the result of an offering as restoring order to a world threatened by chaos is an ideological explanation, as is understanding sacrifice as a gift or communion. We also may speak more concretely about the text's intended message and what ritual action accomplishes beyond the structural interplay, its *causa*, and stated purpose(s). For example, rather than simply declaring that blood manipulation cleanses, ideological analysis examines its non-explicit effects and, more fundamentally, why the ritual uses blood at all. Ideological analysis extends to questions of language usage (e.g., what does a word mean, why is it used, and what connotations does it carry?).

Statements at this level are implicit and non-verifiable, and interpretive rather than descriptive. Ideological interpretations do not often make truth claims; they express opinions. Thus, although different and often contradictory, the variance among interpretations often does little to detract from

---

[118] At least, it is agreed upon in the textual world.

[119] If the text is prescriptive, the goal statements reveal the expected (instrumental) outcome if the ritual is performed appropriately.

[120] For the level of ideology, see Modéus 2005:128–130, 133–134.

1.4. The Cumulative Approach

ritual efficacy, since "ideological interpretations are seldom articulated more forcefully than as opinions."[121] Individuals and groups both now and in the ancient past naturally think theoretically, making categories to understand how the world works and how individuals and groups fit into it. In biblical ritual texts, such interpretative statements are rare if present at all. Rituals are patently practical in responding to a situation, *causa*, through ritual to achieve a result. Although most would likely acknowledge that rituals have ideological connotations, such theories are not easily accessible to its participants. They "grow in and around" ritual, which is primarily understood to achieve practical results (e.g., sin removal).

Klawans' symbolic approach fits nicely into this category. He searches for unifying principles to explain the rationale for sacrifice, namely, *imitatio dei* and the desire to attract and maintain God's presence. His theory does not explicitly emerge from the text; instead it grows in and around it. It offers an unverifiable explanation, one option among many other unverifiable explanations, going beyond what is explicit in the text. Watts' rhetorical analysis is equally at home here since it addresses the text's nonverifiable persuasive purposes.[122]

Because the various approaches operate on different levels, they may give legitimate yet different interpretations of the same event. A sacrifice is a prime example. On the level of structure, the sacrifice defines relationships between people and places. On the level of use, the same sacrifice may result from sin (its *causa*) and lead to forgiveness (determined at the textual level by the goal statements). On the level of ideology, it could function as a payment, offered to restore good relations, as a substitute for human life, or a symbol for humble devotion.

With ritual theory in hand, we are now prepared to analyze the ritual texts. Before doing so, however, we will pause to examine the central figure in ritual, YHWH, and the nature of his presence in the textual world of the Priestly writers.

---

[121] Ibid. 130.

[122] See Watts 1999; id. 2007. We may compare the Priestly ritual texts to an instruction manual (see analogy in section 1.1.). However, these instructions are not merely informational; the Priestly writers also aim to persuade the audience to play the game and to ensure that they play by the Priestly rules.

Chapter Two

The Divine Presence

2.1. The Difficulty of Describing the Divine Presence

Divine presence, like divinity itself, is difficult to explain, much less envision, as one must describe in human terms what by definition transcends them. Such a quest remains an effort to grasp the ungraspable. The Priestly writers use the language and imagery at their disposal to describe YHWH in a way that accurately and approximately reflects him, yet not so definitively that the description becomes a distortion. Said another way, the Priestly writers seek to ensure that YHWH is comprehensible, yet not so comprehensible that he is misunderstood.

The Priestly texts describe YHWH using analogical language so that Israel may know enough of YHWH to properly serve him. At the same time, they are judicious in their language so that YHWH retains his transcendent mystery instead of becoming too familiar, too human, and, hence, no longer a source of appropriate fear and reverence.

Given the difficulties of divine description, the Priestly portrait of divine presence is more complicated than is often assumed. Although the Priestly writers clearly contend that YHWH dwells in the tabernacle (Ex 25:8; 29:45–46),[1] they are circumspect in describing his manifest presence. References to YHWH's indwelling appear only before the tabernacle is constructed, explained, and ritually inaugurated.[2] During this process, the language of divine presence is more elusive.

---

[1] On the durative aspect of the verb שכן, see Mettinger 1982:90–97 and references cited therein; see also the continual references to actions in the sanctuary being before YHWH, which logically implies that he is physically present [*pace* Milgrom 1990:375]). In other words, God's dwelling in the tabernacle is both the cause and the result of the tabernacle construction, dedication, and inauguration.

[2] Num 5:3 mentions YHWH dwelling in the midst of the camp yet does not specifically refer to the tabernacle. Alongside references to divine dwelling, we find multiple references to God's meeting with the people, particularly Moses (Ex 25:22; 29:42–43; 30:6, 36), leading some (e.g., Milgrom 1990:373–375) to assume that this implies a temporary and unpredictable presence. However, God's meeting with the people says nothing about the duration of his stay in the tabernacle; it merely indicates the temporary nature of the various encounters with God (see also Lev 16:2, where God appears [נראה] on the כפרת,

First, the Priestly writers are careful to distinguish between the ark and כפרת and YHWH himself, such that the ark is not like a divine statue and YHWH is not like the other gods. Although the ark and כפרת are clearly connected to the divine presence, the כפרת, and by extension the ark upon which it rests, explicitly serve only as the location where YHWH manifests his presence (Ex 25:22) and in no way partake of the divine essence.

Second, when describing the divine presence, the Priestly writers use glory (כבוד) and the seemingly connected concepts fire (אש) and cloud (ענן). This shift seems to be an intentional device to explain what it means for YHWH to be present, in light of his ineffability. In other words, having established that YHWH will dwell among them, the Priestly writers proceed to carefully describe what divine dwelling looks like. The dwelling they envision is different from and more transcendent than both human and other ANE divine models, and thus designed to be superior to them.

How then are we meant to understand the divine presence in the Priestly texts? In answering this question, we will focus on the divine glory, since glory and the fire and cloud associated with it are most closely allied with YHWH himself. Although it is clear that YHWH's presence is related, if not identical, to YHWH's glory,[3] the exact nature of this relationship is difficult to determine.[4] Although many simply conclude that YHWH's glory is a technical term for YHWH's presence,[5] the evidence points to a more nuanced position. In the following pages, we will examine this nuanced position and what it conveys about the nature of YHWH's presence.

2.2. Linguistic Context

We begin with a foray into the larger literature to provide כבוד יהוה with a field of reference. The noun כבוד appears 199 times in the Hebrew Bible.[6]

---

i.e., is visible, requiring Aaron to shroud that presence with an incense cloud while approaching [16:13]).

[3] Lev 9:4 mentions that God will appear. 9:6 seems to anticipate the same appearance, which is later described as the appearance of God's glory (23). God also speaks from the midst of cloud-encased glory (Ex 24:16; Ex 40:34–Lev 1:1).

[4] The options are myriad. The glory could simply be how God manifests himself on earth; it could be a visible aura, like a halo, which surrounds and locates his invisible presence; it could even be his clothing; it could be part of his presence, used as a metonym for the whole; like the cloud, it could be a veil of sorts that at once hides and locates his true presence.

[5] E.g., NJPSV and Levine (1989) translate כבוד as 'presence' and 'glorious presence' respectively. Mettinger argues that the כבוד is "God himself," כבוד serving as a divine name (1982:107).

[6] Weinfeld *TDOT* 7 (1995):24.

The primary meaning roughly corresponds to the English 'honor' or 'glory,'[7] which may be subdivided into several categories:[8] 1) dignity, high position; 2) respect or reverence; 3) an object of respect; 4) a means of self-reference; 5) כבוד יהוה. In these usages, honor is inherent or ascribed. One may ascribe honor to an object or to oneself, likely as a means of self-respect. Synonyms include הוד, 'majesty,' הדר, 'splendor,' and תפארת, 'beauty,'[9] and express the (often visible) importance of the referent.[10] In all, כבוד and its synonyms express honor or importance in their various forms.

The use of כבוד in Ezekiel is particularly helpful,[11] as it equates the glory with the bright and fiery radiance (נגה) that visibly surrounds YHWH (1:28). In this case, the form of the throned presence, presumably YHWH, is described anthropomorphically amid the radiance (1:26). From the waist up, he looks like glowing metal and, from the waist down, like fire (1:27).[12] Thus, in Ezekiel the glory emanates yet differs from YHWH. Instead, the glory seems to be YHWH's visible honor that surrounds his presence, expressed tangibly as pulsating brilliance.

ANE material offers additional comparative evidence. In Akkadian, the words *pul(u)ḫ(t)u* and *melammu* mean roughly 'terror' and 'majesty'[13] and express the divine clothing visible in a theophany. They describe respectively the supernatural "garment of flames" and the "dazzling aureole or

---

[7] *HALOT* (cf. Weinfeld 1995) includes 'heaviness' as a meaning, referring to Isa 22:24 and Nah 2:10. However, although present in the verbal form, such a meaning is uncertain for the nominal form even in these passages, which can perhaps be better understood to be referring to wealth (cf. Collins *NIDOTTE* 2 [1999]). In turn, if present at all, the sense 'heaviness' is either secondary or a rare alternative.

[8] Collins 1999, who simplifies the senses given in *HALOT* and *BDB*. Alternatively, Weinfeld divides the usage into 1) substance, quantity, power; 2) honor and dignity; 3) glory; 4) glorified objects (1995:25–29).

[9] Collins 1999; cf. Weinfeld 1995:28.

[10] For example, "clothed in majesty and splendor" stands in apposition to "covering yourself with light as with a cloak" in Ps 104:1–2. כבוד and 'beauty' are use to describe the visible majesty of the priestly garments (Ex 28:2, 40), a majesty that reflects their high position.

[11] Nonetheless, we must be careful not to uncritically ascribe all the characteristics of Ezekiel's glory to that of the Priestly writers because 1) the two were written by different hands and, as such, are not necessarily in agreement and 2) even if the two are in agreement, it is dangerous to compare dream imagery to an event described as occurring in real space and time.

[12] The image of Ashur in his solar disk from the time of Tukulti-Ninurta II (Mettinger 1982:105, fig. 5) resembles that of God in Ezekiel 1:26–27. Ashur's head and torso "exhibit recognizably human features, while his lower parts seem to consist of flaring fire. The figure is surrounded by an aura comparable to the rainbow in Ezekiel 1:28" (ibid. 105; cf. Mendenhall 1973:43–53; Keel 1977:260–263).

[13] Oppenheim 1943:31; cf. *CAD* M.2: 9–12; P:503–504, 505–509.

nimbus [that] surrounds the deity," usually like a crown.[14] Often expressed as a hendiadys, *pulḫu* and *melammu* of the Assyrian god or king[15] overcome their enemies in battle.[16] Like כבוד, *melammu* is characterized by a wealth of synonyms,[17] among them *namrirrū*, 'radiance,' and *šalummatu*, 'brilliance.'[18] Egypt may offer an additional parallel, as the Egyptian crown too is something like a fiery diadem[19] and is deified as the goddess Isis.[20] It too is a "source of awe and terror that overthrows the enemy."[21] The fiery sun-disk, most prominently of Egypt, yet also present in Mitannian and Assyrian art, likewise resembles *pulḫu* and *melammu*.[22] Another notable aspect of the *melammu* is that its pulsating light can render its wearer unrecognizable.[23] The sun-disk may also share in this function by identifying the divine presence yet hiding its true form behind the fiery 'mask.' Most commonly associated with Re in Egypt, the sun-disk may also serve as a shorthand symbol for the deity himself, as it identifies him using the image of his manifestation in nature, without revealing his true form.[24] Thus, in Mesopotamia, and potentially in Egypt and elsewhere, when gods appear on earth, they are resplendent in fiery and brilliant attire, which at times is so luminous that it obscures their true identities.

---

[14] Oppenheim 1943:31; on the *melammu* as a crown or tiara, particularly in Assyrian literature, see further ibid. 31–34; Cassin 1968:9ff; Römer 1975:308.

[15] Both are representative of divinity or divine sanction. When adorned with these attributes, the king carries the favor and power of the deities with him into battle, which naturally terrifies and overwhelms the enemy (Oppenheim 1943:31).

[16] Weinfeld 1995:30; see *CAD* M:41 for references to this phenomenon. Kings and gods are also clothed in synonymous expressions like *namrirru* and *salummatu* (Römer 1975:307; Weinfeld 1995:28).

[17] Weinfeld 1995:28; cf. Cassin 1968; Oppenheim 1943; Römer 1975:145ff.

[18] Weinfeld 1995:28; cf. *CAD* N:237–238; Š:283–285.

[19] Weinfeld 1995:28. As in Mesopotamia, "radiance is what betrays the presence of Egyptian deities" (Hornung 1983:134).

[20] Frankfort 1948:107–108.

[21] Weinfeld 1995:28.

[22] Waldman 1984:615; see further, Mendenhall 1973:32–66.

[23] Oppenheim suggests that the *melammu* may be a mask that renders its wearer invisible (1943:31–34). Cassin, however, rejects this notion, instead identifying it as vital force in the form of pulsating light (Waldman [1984:614–615] provides a clear and concise summary of the various options). Cassin is right to identify the *melammu* as pulsating light, yet this conclusion does not entirely negate the force of Oppenheim's argument. Although not in the sense suggested by Oppenheim, the *melammu* does indeed mask its bearer by surrounding him with pulsating light.

[24] Roth 2006:37. We may also be able to discern a similar masking in the name Re, which means 'sun.' This may be a 'paraphrastic' name that conceals the god's true identity, a suggestion bolstered by a myth that describes Isis learning Re's secret, true name (ibid. 36–37; for the text, see *ANET* 12–14).

On the heels of this survey, we stand better equipped to interpret the
כבוד יהוה in the Priestly texts. Like the fire used to describe it (Ex 24:17),[25]
YHWH's glory functions like a simile, as it is connected to yet distinct
from YHWH himself. In particular, although nowhere explicit in the Priestly texts themselves, כבוד יהוה seems to describe YHWH's surrounding radiance. This radiance may naturally be identified with YHWH; for, even
more than with the ark, the presence of the divine effulgence ensures the
presence of the divinity. As such, the כבוד יהוה is an especially appropriate
metonym for YHWH himself. However, although the glory is inextricably
linked with the divine presence, the glory does not encapsulate that presence. It is instead the visible aspect of that presence, which both ensures
the presence of YHWH himself and highlights his power and high-
standing. In a sense, like the *pul(u)ḫ(t)u* and *melammu* in Mesopotamia,
the glory is YHWH's clothing.[26] More specifically, the glory is YHWH's
cloak,[27] for, while it reveals the importance and location of its bearer, it
simultaneously conceals him in its radiant folds.

2.3. The Varying Intensity of Glory

YHWH's presence in the tabernacle emits a fiery refulgence, and YHWH
himself controls the location and intensity of this emanation. In this way,
the glory functions similarly to a modern light with a dimming switch that
controls its brightness. The potency of the glory and the consequent access
of Moses and Aaron demonstrate the glory's flexibility. YHWH's glory
fills the tabernacle after its erection (Ex 40:34–35), barring all access to
the holy precincts. With the inauguration of the priesthood and the tabernacle (Lev 8–9), Moses and Aaron may then enter the tabernacle structure
(9:23). However, access into the inner sanctuary is prohibited, except for
Aaron's annual entrance armed with an incense cloud as a shield.

---

[25] In the expression "like a consuming fire" (Ex 24:17), like (כ) indicates both approximation and relative separation, since the glory is both like its referent and distinct from
it (Garr 2003:111).

[26] One finds support for this idea in the priestly garments, made "for glory and for
beauty" (Ex 28:2, 40). The materials themselves, even the forbidden mixture of these
materials in one garment, clearly demonstrate the importance of the wearer and the otherness of his task. In the same way, the divine aura showcases the importance and otherness of God.

[27] Cf. Weinfeld 1995:31.

It seems logical then to conclude that the glory recedes[28] (i.e., that YHWH uses the dimmer on the light switch). At first, YHWH's glory shines so brightly that none can enter the tabernacle. This light show serves both a practical and a didactic purpose. Practically, YHWH's glory must first consecrate his tabernacle (Ex 29:43–44) before it becomes a suitable dwelling. Didactically, the effulgent glory is a visible display of presence, indicating that the deity has come to reside and that his manifest presence is awesome. Once it has served its purposes, the glory may then withdraw into the inner sanctuary, leaving in its wake the cloud and fire as a perpetual reminder of presence, so as to allow the proper interchange between human and divine. After the glory recedes, the priests and Moses can enter the outer sanctuary to serve YHWH and receive oracles respectively. The presence of pollutants and the need to purge them from the sanctuary necessitates further access. However, YHWH's glory can recede no further without leaving his house. Thus, the priest is forced to bring his own 'dimmer,' the incense cloud that shields the divine presence from view (Lev 16:13).[29]

At other times, YHWH intensifies the display of glory. In Lev 9:23, the one-time inauguration of the tabernacle and its priesthood merits a special revelation of YHWH's glory, which provides tangible proof of God's approval of his home, the system designed to preserve it, and his servants the priests. It also offers assurance of his residence and suggests that the system will work if the people follow the proper protocol. At other times, the glory becomes more tangible in crisis management situations (Num 14:10; 16:19; 17:7; 20:6) when it is necessary to assure YHWH's presence and assert his authority, often to protect Moses and Aaron from the people.

2.4. The Divine Form Beyond the Glory

Although the glory ensures divine presence, it is unclear what form, if any, stands behind this effulgent veil. This circumspection is especially pronounced when discussing the divine presence in the inner sanctuary. YHWH himself appears between the cherubim to meet with the people, and unless properly screened, his presence is fatal to those who approach

---

[28] So Rashbam. It is also possible that the priesthood conferred on Aaron and his sons enabled them to enter the outer extremities of God's glory. However, this does not account for Moses' newfound access.

[29] It is possible that God provides an extra dimmer – namely, he appears wrapped in cloud (Lev 16:2). If this is true, then dimming the divine presence is a cooperative effort, as both God and Aaron provide their own shielding clouds to protect Aaron from YHWH's lethal presence.

(Lev 16:2, 13). From this evidence, two questions emerge: 1) What form does this presence take? 2) Why is an encounter with this presence fatal, while viewing YHWH's glory is not?

Regarding the terrestrial divine form, the text is silent. YHWH's presence in the inner sanctuary may be either the glory itself and/or an invisible, anthropomorphic, or some undetermined form. One can muster arguments both for and against each of these proposals, yet ultimately a definitive answer is purposely elusive. The divine form must remain undefined since it cannot be seen and lest an approximate description misrepresent it.[30] Thus, while the glory may be described as like fire, the divine presence itself may not be described at all.[31]

Too close an encounter with this undefined presence will prove fatal. However, it seems clear that viewing the glory itself is not fatal. In Leviticus 9:23, it seems the people may safely behold the glory without an attendant cloud, whereas elsewhere, even with the cloud, the people can still see God's fiery presence (Ex 24:16–17; cf. Ez 1). What then makes an encounter with YHWH lethal in the inner sanctuary unless protected by one, perhaps even two, cloud covering(s)?[32] Again, the Priestly language is purposely elusive. The Priests may only speak of the lethal danger of too close an encounter with YHWH.[33] The nature of that encounter, like the form of the deity, must remain a mystery because it can neither be described nor approximated.

2.5. The Glory and the Fire

Having examined two tiers of divine presence – YHWH himself and his glory – we now move to the third, the fire by night and the cloud by day that hover over the tabernacle. The fire outside the tabernacle is compatible with YHWH's presence inside. Like the glory it too is similar to yet distinct from regular fire (Num 9:15, where it is described as כמראה־אש).[34] In

---

[30] Even if the divine form is understood to be human-like as in Ezekiel 1, there is no benefit in describing it as such, since doing so would only narrow the gap between God and his human servants.

[31] In fact, the Priestly writers' abstraction extends even further, as they do not describe YHWH at all, neither his form nor his character. They mention only his words, actions, and attendant features (like the glory, fire, and cloud).

[32] The divine cloud would then be like a storm cloud, a visual sign of danger lurking within.

[33] Omitting a description of the divine form also serves a rhetorical purpose to P's audience. If what the people can see, the fire and cloud, is imposing and safe, how much more formidable must the divine presence be in the sanctuary in its lethal potency?

[34] In P proper, it is simply called fire (Ex 40:38), perhaps used metaphorically.

fact, the fire outside is an 'emanation' of the glory within,[35] distinct from it in several respects. In general, the fire seems to function like Moses' shining face. It is merely an effect of the glory that illustrates its presence and potency. The glory, which appears selectively and with noticeable effect,[36] surrounds YHWH's immediate presence, both revealing and concealing it. In contrast, the fire at night seems to be the mass-marketed version of glory, a nightly reminder to all that YHWH is present.[37] While the cloud and fire clearly indicate YHWH's presence, they are more mundane, always available for all to see and thus not inspiring the same notice and awe as appearances of glory.

Whereas YHWH's glory shrouds his immediate presence in light, the fire itself only illumines YHWH's proximate presence in his home. When inside the tabernacle, YHWH's visible presence is functionally invisible behind the tent curtains. The fire then serves to visually assure the people that YHWH is still present in their midst.[38] In essence, having the light on indicates that YHWH is at home.

Like the fire that surrounds the tabernacle at night, the fire that consumes the offerings in Leviticus 9:24 and Nadab and Abihu in 10:2 also seems to be an emanation of divine glory. Both serve as tangible signs that YHWH's presence is more than simply bright lights; like the fire it resembles, the fiery aura is also dangerous, able to burst forth and consume at a moment's notice.[39]

2.6. The Glory and the Cloud

The cloud that covers the tabernacle during the day does not mask YHWH's visible presence. Instead, it serves as a visible sign of YHWH's

---

[35] Mettinger 1982:89; id. 1998:15; cf. Schmitt 1972:224, who uses the term "*Hervorscheinen.*"

[36] Presumably the rest of the time it surrounds the divine presence perched between the cherubim.

[37] Analogously, the fire at night is like a light on a timer that comes on at the same time every day. Like the fire, it marks an occasion that is worth noting (the onset of night and the continual presence of God), yet one that does not draw special attention. On the other hand, the glory is like a stage light that focuses on the actor at certain times to draw special attention to him.

[38] This fire is either masked by the cloud during the day and intensified at night so that it pierces both the cloud and the darkness, or, more likely, the fire appears only at night, when a cloud would be an ineffectual sign of divine presence.

[39] It is unclear whether fire comes out from God's presence and his glory, or the fire itself is God's glory. In the end, there is little practical difference. In both cases, the fire comes out from before YHWH (מלפני יהוה), who is presumably present in the inner sanctuary.

hidden presence, this time concealed not by the cloud but by the tent itself. This cloud is the daytime indication that YHWH is at home. The cloud is a constant and tangible marker of YHWH's proximate presence, whether or not the glory, the sign of more immediate presence, is visible.

The cloud also seems to have a similar function to the glory,[40] to simultaneously locate and conceal the divine presence. When the glory is present, the cloud veils both the divine presence and the visible emanation of glory. However, the veil must be somewhat diaphanous, as the fiery glory is partly visible through the cloud (e.g., Ex 24:16–17). If the cloud performs a similar function to the glory, why then is it necessary? If necessary, why is it only a partial veil, allowing some of the glory to shine through?

In the ANE and elsewhere in the Priestly tabernacle, multiple coverings indicate the importance of the entity being covered.[41] The cloud covering may also be a concession for the benefit of the people. If Moses' shining face is too much to behold, how much more the effulgent glory that illuminates it in the first place?[42]

The partial shielding adds an air of mystery. A hint of the fiery glory is a reminder that something magnificent lurks intangibly beyond the cloudy veil. Similarly, it may indicate that, when at full blast, YHWH's glory is too brilliant to be covered, even by a divine cloud.[43]

2.7. Priestly Assimilation of Theophanic Elements

The Priestly texts co-opt traditional elements of a theophany, transforming them into part of the divine entourage and systematizing their roles. In Priestly hands, the attendant features of a non-Priestly theophany instead mark the three tiers of divine presence in the tabernacle: 1) YHWH himself; 2) the divine glory; and 3) the cloud and fire. Each adds definition to the non-Priestly portrait, ensuring that YHWH's presence is both assured and enigmatic.

---

[40] The cloud is clearly distinguished from the glory. It functions as a cover in which the glory appears (Ex 16:10; 24:15–18; 40:34–35; cf. Milgrom 1991:589).

[41] The covering of the ark for traveling adds further support (Milgrom 1990:25). With the sacred and most sacred coverings, the ark (and כפרת) as the locus of divine presence are marked as especially important.

[42] The cloud may also be for the people's protection in a similar way as the cloud protected Aaron's entry into the Holy of Holies. However, seeing God in the inner sanctuary brings death, while the glory is visible to all without immediate consequence.

[43] On the other hand, when God hits the dimmer switch, the divine aura may be concealed within the inner sanctuary of the tabernacle.

Elsewhere YHWH manifests himself in luminous majesty or fire[44] from which he speaks.[45] The Priestly texts add a degree of precision to this fiery, luminous presence, giving it the name 'glory' (כבוד) and associating it clearly and consistently with divine presence. Rather than merely being an attendant feature, the radiant glory functions as the cloak of YHWH's presence,[46] at once revealing and concealing him in its luxuriant folds. In addition, the Priests distinguish this fiery glory from its fiery emanation at night, giving each specific roles, and distinguish both the glory and the nightly fire from mundane fire.

Whereas elsewhere the cloud serves as merely one of many natural signs of divine presence, the Priestly texts assign it a specific role.[47] The cloud becomes a partial cover of the divine glory that surrounds the divine presence serving as a boundary between humanity and God, as in the non-Priestly texts.[48]

The Priestly writers likewise absorb other non-Priestly uses of cloud and fire, in which they accompany YHWH's theophanic presence and guide his people in the wilderness. In the non-Priestly texts, the fire and cloud appear when God appears (Ex 19:16–18; Ps 97:2–3; Dt 4:11; 5:22) and serve to guide (Ex 13:21; Num 10:34; Dt 1:33; Ps 78:14; 105:39; Neh 9:12, 19) and protect the people (Ex 14:19–20).[49] In the Priestly texts, the cloud and fire hover over the tabernacle by day and night, serving both as a tangible sign of divine presence and a guide for the journey ahead.

The Priestly texts also assimilate the idea of mobility expressed elsewhere. The god who dwells in the mobile tabernacle must himself be mobile, along with his entourage. The elements of a theophany that come and go with YHWH[50] are a natural way of expressing this movement.[51] The

---

[44] Ex 19:18; Ps 18:9, 13, 14, 15; 77:19; 97:3; Isa 29:6; 30:27, 30; Hab 3:4, 11; Job 37:22. The text also uses the term הופיע to describe God's presence: Dt 33:2; Ps 50:2, 80:2, 94:1 (cf. Mettinger 1982:123 n. 20; for light in theophanies, see further Jeremias 1977:62–66, 172–173).

[45] Ex 19:21; Dt 4:33; 5:4, 24, 26.

[46] Ps 97 seems to present a similar picture.

[47] In Exodus 19:9 (cf. 16–17), previously ascribed to E (after Baentsch 1903), God descends in a thick cloud so that the people may hear his voice and recognize Moses' authority. Although by no means explicit, the cloud here could also serve as a cover, one which at once locates God's presence so the people may hear and believe, yet conceals God's real presence.

[48] For example, Lam 3:44 uses the cloud as a metaphor for impenetrability, expressing the distance between God and the exiles: "You have covered yourself with a cloud so that no prayer can pass through."

[49] Cf. Weinfeld 1995:32.

[50] See the frequent use of ירד in theophanic contexts (e.g., Ex 19:18; 34:5; Is 31:4). See other references to God leaving his dwelling and coming (Dt 33:2; Jdg 5:4–5; Mic 1:3; Hab 3:3; Mettinger 1982:120).

Priestly writers may also pick up on another nuance of the traveling cloud, namely its identification as YHWH's cloud chariot,[52] which may at once transport and conceal the divine presence.

For the Priestly writers, the divine presence seems to be a mobile, semi-permanent theophany.[53] However, rather than using movement as a sign of transience, the Priestly texts use movement to indicate permanence.[54] In the Priestly texts, the tabernacle follows the theophany, which moves by its own power. Instead of appearing as a temporary intrusion of heaven into earth, the Priestly theophany will remain on earth as long as Israel correctly serves YHWH. Thus, in the Priestly hands, the divine presence in the tabernacle is a semi-permanent intrusion of heaven into earth, of YHWH into human habitation.

2.8. Synthesis

In describing divine presence, Priestly language paradoxically mixes precision with ambiguity. Given the confines of human language, the Priestly writers are as precise as possible. They add specificity to the non-Priestly theophanies, transforming YHWH's attendant features into a three-tiered system of divine presence. However, at times precision is impossible, such as defining what it means for YHWH to dwell in the tabernacle; for, by definition, natural language cannot encapsulate the supernatural. As descriptions move ever closer to YHWH himself, precision becomes increasingly elusive. Instead of misrepresenting YHWH with anthropomorphic approximations, the Priests leave their language increasingly undefined. In pursuit of accuracy, the Priests tread carefully between precision and imprecision.

In the Priestly writings, YHWH's presence is both assured and enigmatic.[55] In the tabernacle, tangible presence intersects with intangible mys-

---

[51] The cherubim, elsewhere the divine chariot (Ps 18:10–11), may also imply mobility.

[52] Ps 104:3; Is 19:1; Ez 1:4. This idea finds an especially strong parallel in the Ugaritic material, where the storm cloud functions as Baal's chariot (see Green 2003:190–198). See also Smith (1987:49–55) for a comparison with theophanic elements in the Ancient Near East, especially Ugarit, where divine theophanies are accompanied by storms and convulsions of nature.

[53] Cf. Mettinger 1982:121. On the transience of divine presence in the non-Priestly texts, see, e.g., Ex 33:18ff.

[54] Movement also has the added benefit of not limiting YHWH to a single place.

[55] One may ask why the Priestly texts are so circumspect when describing God's presence when, elsewhere, they are characterized by greater precision than the non-Priestly texts. First, although suffused with mystery, their presentation seems to be more precise, assimilating and systematizing other expressions of divine presence into a concrete

tery.⁵⁶ The text expresses that YHWH intends to dwell in the sanctuary, while attendant signs – the expression 'before YHWH' and the glory, cloud, and fire – ensure his habitation. However, as our analysis indicates, the nature of his presence in his dwelling remains a mystery.⁵⁷ His true form and location remain hidden. Although he presumably rests between the cherubim, his whereabouts between appearances are unclear. The ambulatory nature of the theophanic elements hints that he may come and go.

In order to establish YHWH's preeminence, the Priestly texts replace both divine statues and the non-Priestly ark with glory as the locus of divine presence. Glory at once visibly marks YHWH's immediate presence and conceals that presence from closer scrutiny. Like the ANE cult statues and the non-Priestly ark, the glory ensures proximate presence and makes its benefits available to the people. At the same time, the deity himself is more elusive, more other, more transcendent than his ANE counterparts. In ANE terms, by establishing YHWH's supreme transcendence, the Priests establish YHWH's ultimate supremacy.

The glory ensures that the mystery of divine presence in the tabernacle is greater than that in the rest of the ANE. The Priestly texts do more than simply eliminate the divine statue; they also put something positive in its place, something that maintains, perhaps even enhances, the divine mystery. YHWH's aura veils his true form. Thus, YHWH is doubly transcend-

---

whole. Second, the remaining imprecision seems to serve their purposes. They specify at length the plan of God's abode and the details of his service because of the greatness of this God, a greatness that defies explanation. God's ineffability may either be an intentional device to preserve divine mystery or a necessity because no one knew how to adequately describe him.

⁵⁶ The mystery surrounding divine presence is likely the reason why scholars cannot agree on the permanent nature of the divine presence. Drawing on the ambiguity in the language to describe God's appearing, his meeting with Moses, and the presence of the fire at night (understood to be the glory, shrouded by the cloud during the day), Milgrom (1990:374–375) asserts that divine presence with the ark is "temporary, unpredictable, and symbolic." Others base their conclusions on an incorrect reading of שכן (see the summary and response in Mettinger 1982:90–97). Conversely, Mettinger (1982:83–97; id. 1998:15) draws on the glory filling the sanctuary with no hint of leaving, the precautions in approaching God, especially in the inner sanctuary (see also the use of לפני יהוה), and the use of שכן to suggest a permanent presence in the inner sanctuary. Both seem to be somewhat justified in their approaches, Mettinger for emphasizing the tabernacle as God's earthly abode, Milgrom for identifying some ambiguities that allow for divine movement.

⁵⁷ The texts clearly anticipate his dwelling. However, when it comes to God actually taking up residence, they are purposely circumspect. Such concrete anthropomorphisms – God dwelling like a man – would seem too crass and limiting. Instead, the Priestly writers describe his presence abstractly, thereby indicating that how God actually dwells on earth cannot be explained. In the end, God's presence, like his person, is ultimately elusive.

ent over the other ANE gods. He has no statue, and his real form, if such exists, is hidden behind impenetrable glory.

In addition, whereas ANE statues require daily intimate service, humanity cannot come into contact with YHWH's true presence.[58] This true form even transports itself in the cloud and fire. It does not need to be carried; indeed, it cannot be carried, nor can it be quantified. The most tangible sign of YHWH, his refulgent garb, is only described analogically – "like a consuming fire." If his aura may only be described analogically, how much less can YHWH himself be described?

Like a divine statue, yet unlike the ark, the glory seems to be a metonym that captures some of the divine essence.[59] Instead of being a human object, YHWH's glory emanates from his person. It is part of him, shining to express his greatness, and, as such, is a fitting representative. Because the divine aureole emerges from YHWH himself, its presence ensures YHWH's presence, yet does so in a way that preserves YHWH's mystery. In turn, while present, YHWH remains beyond description and understanding; we may only describe his radiance via analogy. Although we may speculate, what his true presence looks like (if it is visible at all) and how exactly it dwells in the tabernacle remain elusive. The Israelites must be content with the promise that YHWH does indeed dwell in the tabernacle, with the glory, fire, and cloud as the only visible signs that YHWH is keeping his promise.

In many ways the divine glory functions like a divine statue, yet with few of its potential weaknesses. It too locates the deity and inspires worship. In theory, one could distinguish between YHWH and his glory, as one could distinguish between a god and his statue. The visible aspect of a god, be it the statue or the glory, is not coterminous with the god himself. Practically, however, the two are indistinguishable. Within the Priestly texts, the glory as the visible aspect of YHWH is equated with YHWH himself (Lev 9:4, 6, 23).

Nevertheless, this amalgamation is far less problematic than the amalgamation of deity and statue. The glory does not bind YHWH to a human-made form, nor does it bind him to space, leaving open the possibility, seized upon in Ezekiel, that YHWH's glory may leave his home.[60] In addition, this form cannot be destroyed,[61] nor is there any real danger of

---

[58] Moses himself could only approach the glory to receive a revelation. He never pierced this shiny veil; for a non-Priestly approximation, cf. Ex 33:18–23.

[59] Bahrani refers to the ANE image as a "metonymy of presence" that captures some of the divine essence without encapsulating the whole (2003:205).

[60] The divine presence in the ANE may be disentangled from its statue, yet not without some problems. By separating God from a man-made receptacle, the Priestly writer avoids these problems.

[61] It also does not require human transport.

YHWH's visible effulgence usurping YHWH's identity.⁶² Likewise, if YHWH himself controls where he is present and the location and intensity of his glory, and he limits his dwelling to the tabernacle, there is no danger of multiplying YHWHs, thereby creating competing hypostasized forms. Although YHWH dwells on earth in a human-made structure, YHWH's presence remains undiluted. He condescends to reside with humanity without in any way limiting his form or essence, without (meta)physically joining with human objects. In the end, in order to establish preeminence, YHWH's glory jettisons unnecessary limits and misunderstanding while ensuring that YHWH is present to act on his people's behalf.⁶³

---

⁶² It is a natural emanation from him, controlled by him and not the product of human craftsmanship or manipulation. As such, there is no real harm in identifying it with him. Indeed, it seems that in some ways it was designed to be God's 'cult statue.'

⁶³ For the similar Deuteronom(ist)ic approach, see Hundley 2009.

Chapter Three

The Dedication and Inauguration of the Tabernacle and its Cult

"An intrusion of transcendence into the empirical, [YHWH's glory] is dangerous and volatile, a toxic and hazardous substance, as it were, requiring proper containment."[1] To this end, the Priests must fashion a miniature environment, clearly demarcated from earth functionally, spatially, and aromatically,[2] to recreate heaven on earth. Preparing the sanctuary and its servants for the divine residence is thus an especially important process.

A comparison of the dedication ceremonies[3] in the Priestly texts (Ex 28–30; 40; Lev 8) with analogous ANE ceremonies and with those in 1 Kings 8 places the Priestly account in sharper focus. First, much of the ceremony is roughly analogous to ANE temple dedication ceremonies and the dedication in 1 Kings 8, allowing us to situate the Priestly ceremony in its larger context and, by analogy, to help explain some of its elements. Second, certain elements are distinct, especially how the deity takes up residence in his new home, and thereby serve to differentiate the Priestly ceremony from both those in the ANE and that of 1 Kings 8.

In our analysis, we will start with a brief comparison of 1 Kings 8 with the ANE ceremonies. The bulk of the argument will then examine the dedication and inauguration of the tabernacle in light of its larger context.[4]

---

[1] Kawashima 2006:256–257; cf. Sommer 2001:61.

[2] See chapter 4.

[3] Dedication ceremonies follow the completion of the temple building and fall into three broad categories: preparation for the entrance of the deity, the entrance of the deity and the resultant celebrations. For simplicity, the dedication prayers of the ANE and 1 Kgs 8 will be omitted. Their absence in the Priestly texts invites many questions, most prominent of which is whether or not the tabernacle (or temple) was a "Sanctuary of Silence" (Knohl 1995).

[4] Our analysis will be selective, omitting many of the differences in details, while focusing on those that highlight the different worldviews and/or the different foci within the same worldview.

3.1. Temple Dedication in 1 Kings 8 and the Ancient Near East

The text of 1 Kings 8:1–11 and 62–66[5] has many affinities with typical ANE accounts, especially those of Mesopotamia, such that we may conclude that each conforms to a common ANE pattern.[6] Several points of comparison are of particular interest. The entrance of the deity stands at the heart of each rite[7] and is often accompanied by long ceremonies, characterized by offerings to the deity and a celebratory atmosphere.

Throughout the ANE, the duration of the ceremony highlights its importance. In the Hebrew Bible, Solomon celebrates the dedication of the temple for 14 days (1 Kgs 8:65). In Egypt, the temple dedication is accompanied by a month-long series of rituals.[8] "Dedication ceremonies in Mesopotamia were also multi-day events."[9] Among the Hittites, the duration of rituals is not mentioned explicitly. However, the Kizzuwatnan ritual for the establishment of a satellite temple for the Goddess of the Night lasts at least seven days and likely longer, since the ritual is still in full swing at the end of the first tablet and the second tablet has not survived intact.[10]

Offerings also feature prominently. In the biblical account, they are said to be uncountable (8:5; cf. 8:62–63). In Mesopotamia, references to offerings abound, at times approaching the biblical descriptions.[11] These offerings normally follow the installation of the deities in their temples.[12] In Egypt, often-sumptuous offerings follow the presentation of the temple to the deity.[13] Offerings and gifts also feature throughout the Hittite ritual mentioned above. The Baal epic, unearthed at Ugarit, also mentions sacrifices (VI 38–43).[14]

---

[5] Although presumed to be a composite text, the relevant verses are consistently assigned to the Deuteronomistic Historian(s) or earlier.

[6] Hurowitz 1992.

[7] For 1 Kgs 8 and Mesopotamia, see ibid. 266–267, 272–273. For Egypt, see Shafer 1998:7. This also seems to hold true in the Hittite world (e.g., at Kizzuwatna, where the animation and installation of the divine statue play a central role).

[8] Shafer 1998:7.

[9] Hurowitz 1992:276; the duration of the celebration is often left unmentioned in the inscriptions, yet enough examples exist to make a case for their longevity: e.g., Gudea celebrated the dedication of Eninnu for 7 days and Esarhaddon alloted three days to the dedication of Esharra.

[10] Collins 2005:29–32.

[11] Hurowitz 1992:276; see the inscriptions of Sargon (Lie 1929:78) and Esarhaddon (Borger 1956:5 V 37–VI 1).

[12] Especially in Neo-Assyrian accounts but also in Gudea and the Hymn to Enlil with a prayer to Ur-Nammu (Hurowitz 1992:56, 58).

[13] Wilkinson 2005:38.

[14] Hurowitz 1992:95.

Joy is another seemingly ubiquitous feature (e.g., 1 Kgs 8:66; cf. 2 Sam 6:14). In Mesopotamia, texts often speak of both the joy of the deity (who is brought in to the temple in 'joy and gladness') and the people in celebration. This joy even features in the mythological texts (e.g., *Enūma eliš* ll. 73–75 and Enki's Journey ll. 93–114). Joy features prominently in Egypt (such as multiple mentions of divine joy in the consecration of the NK temple of Abydos).[15] Although joy is not explicit in the few available Hittite inscriptions, the Kizzuwatnan ritual suggests divine joy in paragraph 24, where it mentions attracting the deity "to the city which she loves."[16] Indeed, since attracting (lit. 'pulling') the deity is a major element in the ritual complex, it seems natural that the ritual tradents would do so in a way that brings joy to the goddess. Joy also features in the celebration of the construction of Baal's palace (VI 38–59).[17]

This pattern is natural given the purpose of the ceremony. The presence of a temple is vital to an ANE community, as it signifies the presence and blessing of their god in their midst. In turn, the heart of the temple dedication ceremony is the entrance of the deity into his dwelling.[18] This naturally is a source of great joy for both the celebrants and the deity. Indeed, the whole ceremony aims to please the resident deity so that he will be favorably disposed to the community and continue to dwell and bless in their midst. Sacrifices and offerings are a requisite part of the process. Finally, the ceremony's duration reflects its importance and gives time for appropriate celebration and service.

Although similar, the deity's entrance also serves as the most significant point of contrast. In the ANE accounts, the entrance of the deity is equated with the entrance of his cult statue.[19] The Kings account is similar to yet purposely different from its ANE analogue. YHWH is not coterminous with the ark; it serves as the supports for an invisible throne, a pedestal, or simply a marker of divine presence. Nonetheless, although theoretically distinct, the two are so closely associated that the text often practically

---

[15] David 1981:116.
[16] *COS* I:176.
[17] Hurowitz 1992:102.
[18] Ibid. 266–267, 272–273.
[19] Given the nature of these texts, the association of deity with cult statue is not always explicit in the temple dedication texts. However, such a connection is hard to deny (see Hurowitz 1992:315 for Mesopotamia), as it is evident in certain texts (e.g., Ashurnasirpal II's inscription [King 1912: 164–165]) and features prominently in others (esp. mouth-washing, mouth-opening texts and procession texts and images in Mesopotamia and Egypt); for the return of divine statues to their cities and temples in Mesopotamia, see, e.g., Miller and Roberts 1977 (Nebuchadnezzar I); Streck 1916:262–69 (Assurbanipal); Borger 1956:88–89 (Esarhaddon).

equates them.[20] Thus, in many ways, the ark continues to function like a cult statue; it is elegantly adorned, elicits sacrifices, is the center of a grand procession, and signals divine presence.

Since so close an association between deity and dais is unpalatable, the text adds certain elements that strengthen the distinction between deity and ark beyond a theoretical level. Only after the ark makes its glorious entrance into the temple do YHWH's glory and cloud enter and fill it.[21] Although the ark is closely associated with YHWH's presence to such an extent that sacrifices can be legitimately offered before it, the ark is not YHWH himself. YHWH himself in the form of his glory and cloud comes later.[22]

Lest this distinction is lost on the reader, the Deuteronomistic History makes it more clearly. It stresses that YHWH's home is in heaven (1 Kgs 8:30; 39; 43; 49). His unnatural presence on earth does not negate his presence in his heavenly abode. By placing YHWH in heaven, the Deuteronomistic Historian ensures that YHWH is not understood to be coterminous with the ark. The Deuteronomistic Historian also uses YHWH's name to express divine presence in the temple. The term brilliantly implies practical presence – YHWH's attention and blessing – yet equivocates about physical presence. While clearly asserting that YHWH is present in heaven, the text suggests that he is also present on earth, a presence effectual yet shrouded in mystery.[23]

---

[20] In 1 Kgs 8:5, Solomon's sacrifice before the ark suggests God's presence with the ark (see more explicitly in 2 Sa 6, where sacrifices before the ark of YHWH also occur before YHWH himself).

[21] The Mesopotamian texts intimate that the arrival of the deity (i.e., the statue) makes the city luminous (e.g., Nabonidus' description of his rebuilding of Ehulhul in Harran [COS II:312], where Harran is "as brilliant as moonlight" [Hurowitz 1992:273]; cf. the much earlier Gudea cylinder A iii.10–12 [COS II:430], where brilliant moonlight illuminated the land when Ningirsu came from Eridu to enter the temple).

[22] It is possible that the glory and cloud emanate from the ark once it has been installed in the temple as a sign of divine approval. However, on the basis of other biblical parallels (Ex 40; 2 Ch 7; cf. 2 Ch 5:14, which like 1 Kgs 8:10–11 is ambiguous), it seems best to conclude that although YHWH is somehow present with the ark, YHWH comes more fully (from heaven) with the cloud and glory.

[23] See Hundley 2009.

3.2. The Dedication[24] of the Tabernacle in P

The Priestly account has many of the same constituent elements found in the ANE and 1 Kings 8, yet is significantly different in two respects. Like its analogues, the Priestly ceremony itself is long, joyous, and full of offerings. The initiation of the priesthood and tabernacle lasts seven days (Ex 29:37; Lev 8), while the dedication of the bronze altar lasts 12 days (Num 7).[25] Although likely a prominent feature, reference to joy appears only in Lev 9:24.[26] Offerings feature in the preparation for the deity's arrival (Lev 8), the inauguration of cult (9), and the dedication of the bronze altar (Num 7). However, 1) the nature of YHWH's entrance is especially distinct, and 2) the Priestly texts contain a ritual focus that is largely absent in the parallel texts.

First, the dedication of the tabernacle enhances the distinctions between deity and ark.[27] Unlike in 1 Kings 8, there is no equivocation in the Priestly texts. The ark enters the tabernacle without fanfare, sacrifice, or any association with divine presence.[28] In fact, it is installed merely as the first among many items of furniture before any ritual action occurs, distinguished from all others only by its place at the front of the list, its composition, and its position in the inner sanctuary. Unlike the ANE cult statues, it undergoes no unique preparation for its privileged role; like the tabernacle and all of its furniture, it is merely anointed with oil to consecrate it.[29] Once the tabernacle complex is set up and set apart for YHWH, YHWH's cloud-encased glory appears of its own accord (Ex 40:34–38), expressing divine approval and habitation. However, to ensure that the reader does not misconstrue the arrival of YHWH's glory as a divine animation of the ark, the glory later emerges from the inner sanctuary without the ark (Lev 9:23–24). Thus, the Priestly dedication of the tabernacle clearly distinguishes the ark from YHWH in a way that far exceeds its ANE analogues.

Furthermore, whereas in the ANE and Kings the entrance of the deity forms the heart of the ceremony, in the Priestly texts YHWH arrives before

---

[24] This term is somewhat misleading, since its Hebrew equivalent (from the root חנך) only appears in Num 7 in relation to the bronze altar. It is used here to describe the events from the final preparations for the entrance of the deity (Ex 40) to the inauguration of the cult (Lev 9).

[25] Hurowitz 1992:275; cf. 1985:23.

[26] In one word: וירנו, 'and they shouted for joy' (Hurowitz 1985:23).

[27] Here, we use the term ark to include the כפרת, which rests atop it and is more particularly the locus of divine revelation (Ex 25:22).

[28] Cf. Milgrom 1991:575. Earlier mentions of the ark as a meeting place (e.g., Ex 25:22) merely prefigure the role it will play in the functioning cult. There is nothing inherent in the ark that suggests such a role.

[29] Prescribed in Ex 30:25–32 and 40:9–11, and described in Lev 8:10–11.

the ceremony begins. More precisely, he appears after the tabernacle has been set up (Ex 40), yet before all ritual action to prepare and consecrate it and its priesthood for divine service (Lev 8). As we will see, this anomaly is rhetorically significant, both to differentiate it from its closest parallels and to indicate that ritual action in the tabernacle, particularly consecration, requires divine presence to be efficacious.

Second, the Priestly texts focus much more on purificatory rituals than either the parallel account in 1 Kings or other ANE depictions. 1 Kings 8 and the Mesopotamian dedicatory inscriptions either omit such rituals or mention them minimally.[30] However, rather than indicating that such actions were not performed, the omissions are simply a mark of the texts' emphases, which do not include purification.[31] 1 Kings 8, like many royal dedicatory inscriptions, particularly those of the Neo-Assyrian kings, instead "emphasizes the public procession of the ark, the royal blessings and prayers and the popular festivities."[32] Egyptian reliefs and their accompanying texts are less reticent, displaying purification scenes of the construction site before building using gypsum and of the completed temple using natron and a form of whitewash.[33] Although present, such reliefs are less

---

[30] 1 Kings 8 does not mention any rites of purification either for the participants (both priests and laypeople) or the temple itself (except for the brief mention of consecrating the court in v. 64 to explain how the king could have offered so many sacrifices). Many of the Mesopotamian accounts likewise omit such purificatory procedures.

[31] Mesopotamian texts often mention preparatory rites, including building only with with divine approval, according to the divinely approved model, starting the dedication on a propitious day, and occasionally with the celebration of a sacred marriage (e.g., in the Gudea Cylinder). Although not strictly purificatory, these rites serve to ensure a good destiny for the temple, its deity, and the surrounding populace (cf. Hurowitz 1992:271). We may also infer by analogy that purificatory rites did exist yet were simply omitted for stylistic reasons because of the general fear of demonic forces, the presence of purification in removal/renewal rituals like the *akītu* festival (which serves as a re-dedication of the temple) and in mouth-washing rituals both for the statue and its course through the city. In 1 Kings 8, verse 64 incidentally mentions purification for a practical purpose and suggests that, although not present in the text, purification procedures are a necessary prerequisite to the deity entering his abode.

[32] Hurowitz 1985:23.

[33] Černý 1952:114–115; David 1981:52; Shafer 1998:7; Wilkinson 2005:38. Although not strictly purificatory rituals, Egyptian temple builders, like their Mesopotamian counterparts, went to great lengths to ensure that the temple was fit for the deity by enlisting divine help in construction and through such rites as 'stretching the cord' and placing foundation deposits (Wilkinson 2005:38; for such rites and their NK provenance, see the lists of Thutmose III on the walls of the small temple at Medinet Habu). There is also evidence that the opening of the mouth ceremony was performed on every room at Edfu to give "the temple life and make it cultically operative" (Shafer 1998:7; see further Blackman and Fairman 1945:85). Although it is a late example, one may infer (as do

effusive than their Priestly counterparts. The Hittite Kizzuwatnean ritual is the only striking anomaly. As a ritual text, it describes in detail the rites necessary both to prepare a new temple and to animate its cult statue.

Unlike the Mesopotamian and Egyptian examples yet like the Kizzuwatnean text, the Priestly dedication of the tabernacle is a ritual text and, as such, is concerned primarily with the proper performance of ritual and the accompanying result. However, it is unique in combining the dedication of the tabernacle with the inauguration of the priesthood. In our analysis of the Priestly ritual, we will draw from a wide range of texts, beginning with the Hittite, Egyptian, and Mesopotamian dedicatory texts. Since these are of limited explanatory value, we will add priestly installation rituals from Emar, Mesopotamia, Egypt, and Anatolia.[34] Finally, as a general point of comparison, we will include the rituals to animate cult statues, which offer fruitful comparative material since they 1) often accompany the dedication of a new temple; 2) explicitly prepare for divine habitation; 3) serve as a point of comparison with the installation of the ark and arrival of the glory; and 4) are detailed enough to illustrate the complexity of ritual praxis and thereby serve as a fitting analogue to the Priestly ritual.[35] Instead of examining each text individually, we will focus on the Priestly rituals, mentioning the ANE analogues as they illumine our text.

3.3. Tabernacle Dedication and Priestly Installation

Exodus 29 prescribes the various rituals to be performed relating to the purification and consecration of the tabernacle, the altar, and the priests.[36] Exodus 40 both prescribes and describes the final preparations for the di-

---

Černý 1952:115; David 1981:52; Shafer 1998:7) that such a rite was also common in earlier periods.

[34] With the installation rituals of Baal's high priestess, the Emar texts provide our strongest and most elaborate parallel (for a detailed analysis of this ritual in comparison with other rituals from Emar, see Fleming 1992; for a detailed comparison of this ritual with Lev 8, see Klingbeil 1998). The Mesopotamian parallel comes from several broken Sumerian tablets and describes the ordination of a priest of Enlil (see Borger 1973; Reiner 1985:1–16). The Egyptian and Hittite examples will be drawn from a number of sources.

[35] However, although analogous, we will postpone an analysis of the purificatory (damage control) rites until chapter 6.

[36] According to the order in Leviticus 8 (the fulfillment of Ex 29), Moses washes and dresses Aaron and his sons, anoints the tabernacle and all its furnishings, and pours anointing oil on Aaron's head. Moses then offers a חטאת and an עלה, places the blood of the ordination ram on the priests' extremities, and takes the oil and some of the blood from the altar and applies them to the priests. The ritual process lasts seven days, during which Aaron and his sons are forbidden from leaving the entryway of the tabernacle.

vine presence.³⁷ Moses erects the tabernacle, lights the lamps, burns the incense, and offers the burnt and grain offerings. YHWH then fills the tabernacle with his glory so that none may enter. Leviticus 8 describes the ritual prescribed in Exodus 29, while Leviticus 9 describes the inauguration of the cult, at the end of which YHWH's glory appears and fire comes forth from him to consume the offerings.³⁸

Scholars have traditionally had difficulty reconciling certain elements in Lev 8 with Ex 29. Most resolve the difficulties by attributing the texts to different hands, written at different times. Since Wellhausen,³⁹ the majority of scholars attribute (much of) Lev 8 to a later hand than Ex 29.⁴⁰ Nonetheless, some maintain the opposite perspective.⁴¹ Others, most notably Nihan,⁴² attribute the bulk of both chapters to the same hand as command and fulfillment and consign the most troublesome bits to later additions (e.g., Lev 8:10aβ–11). Instead of addressing the likely complex compositional history, we will attempt to make sense of the ritual in its present form. The ritual depicted in our analysis will be an amalgam of the two texts with elements of Ex 28 and 30 serving as complements. Although it is integrally related to the dedication and inauguration, Ex 40 will primarily be incorporated after the ideology section, since it takes on special meaning in the context of the larger dedication and inauguration process.

3.3.1. Structure

The ritual's structure in Exodus 29 and Leviticus 8 informs the reader of the relationship between persons and objects.⁴³ Aaron and his sons clearly stand out from the rest of the congregation in that they are the only people who receive ritual action. The presence of the congregation both shows that the ritual is public and serves to differentiate the priests from it. Aaron and his sons are brought forward, washed,⁴⁴ dressed in special garments, anointed with oil, daubed with blood, and they lean their hands on all of the sacrifices (Ex 29:4–10, 19–21, 41; Lev 8:2–14, 23–24, 30).⁴⁵

---

³⁷ It also includes a prescription for anointing the tabernacle, altar and priests, which remains unfulfilled until Lev 8.

³⁸ In Leviticus 9, Aaron offers a חטאת and an עלה for himself and the people (and a מנחה for the people), and concludes by offering a זבח שלמים.

³⁹ Id. 1963:142–144 (1899 original).

⁴⁰ E.g., Milgrom 1991:513–516, 545–549.

⁴¹ E.g., Levine 1965:310–318; Janowski 1982:215 n. 168; Péter-Contesse 1993:36.

⁴² Id. 2007:124–147; cf. Rendtorff 1985:268.

⁴³ We will not examine Moses' role here other than to mention that he acts as a necessary cultic officiant, mediating between human and divine, since the priests are not yet priests until the end of the seven days.

⁴⁴ The fact that there is a washing at the beginning but no recorded washing at the end of the ritual (as in Lev 16) may indicate the permanence of the priestly status, i.e., there is no need for another entry ritual; once a priest, always a priest (Gorman 1990:117).

⁴⁵ Hand-leaning clearly identifies the offerer with the offering. Any additional implications of this connection are not explicit.

At the same time, the ritual distinguishes between Aaron and his sons. Aaron's better and fuller ritual treatment occurs before that of his sons, sometimes with a significant time lag that clearly establishes a hierarchy between them. For example, Aaron is clothed first and in more and finer garb;[46] his sons are clothed only after Aaron and the sancta are anointed (8:7–13). He is anointed first, his sons are anointed much later in the ritual (after the elevation offering), and Aaron alone is anointed twice (8:12, 30).

Although not explicit or indexically implicit, the distinction between priestly garments appears significant. Like the tabernacle curtains and appurtenances, Aaron's garments alone are made of mixed fabrics and adorned with gold (Ex 28).[47] Aaron's apparel both privileges him over his sons and identifies him with the tabernacle, while the regular priestly garments are of equivalent workmanship and thus of equal status with the courtyard.[48]

The ritual actions also serve to privilege the various anointed items. Each item is already connected to YHWH's domain and, after anointing (Ex 29:36; 30:26–28; Lev 8:10), is set apart further from the mundane sphere because it receives the oil exclusively reserved for YHWH (Ex 30:25). The bronze altar is a special case in that blood is applied to it alone (Ex 29:12, 16; Lev 8:15, 19), the potential implications of which will await the ideology section.

The application of the same anointing oil at the same time to both the high priest and the sancta indexes a relationship between the two (Lev 8:10–12, 30). Each is set apart from its surroundings and set apart to the resident deity. In fact, as is clear from a comparison with other Priestly rituals, the anointing oil sets the bounds of the cultic domain and of the high priestly activity in it.[49] In other words, the anointing oil ritually marks the tabernacle, the bronze altar, the basin, and the high priest as part of God's domain. When in this domain and in the apparel befitting it, Aaron belongs to and serves YHWH as high priest.

The application of the same blood and blood-oil mixture at the same time to all of the priests and to the bronze altar indexes a special relationship between the two groups (Ex 29:21; Lev 8:30). The ritualized action of applying blood to the extremities of the priests after two applications of

---

[46] This distinction is significant as only Aaron's garments are made of mixed fabrics (Haran 1978:171), a blend forbidden outside the cultic sphere (Lev 19:19; cf. Dt 29:9, 11). The text also allots much more space to the description of Aaron's garments to enhance the distinction (Lev 8:7–9 vs. 8:13; Ex 28:4–39 vs. 28:40–43) (Houtman 2000: 466). The number of garments is yet another point of distinction (eight for Aaron and only four for his sons) (ibid.; see more fully Haran 1978:165–174).

[47] Haran 1978:165–174, esp. 171.

[48] Ibid.

[49] Cf. Gorman 1990:118–119.

sacrificial blood to the altar highlights the importance of the action by distinguishing it from normal procedure.[50] Like the altar, the priests are marked with sacrificial blood and oil and thus are set apart for God's domain and, by extension, YHWH.[51] This shared action indicates that the altar is a primary place of priestly activity.

In addition, the structure implicitly communicates the transitional nature of the ritual. Aaron and his sons are restricted to the entrance of the tent of meeting (Lev 8:33, 35), between the divine abode and world around it.[52] The blood manipulation of the חטאת corresponds to that of a leader of the community or a commoner rather than that of a priest.[53] The priests-to-be are never the subject and always the object of ritual actions. Until the seven-day ordination period is complete, the priests occupy a liminal state, having been set apart from the populace yet not fully set apart to YHWH, a liminal state made evident by the setting and the actions that occur in it.

The ritual in Leviticus 9 moves forward the action in Leviticus 8, and hence the connections between actors and those acted upon. Aaron and the people each bring their respective offerings to the sanctuary, thereby indexing a relationship between themselves and their offerings (2–4). As before, the blood manipulation both privileges the priests over the rest of the Israelites and distinguishes between them, yet it does so in a way that pushes the narrative forward. Instead of being the recipients of ritual actions, the priests now perform them. In other words, they may now function as priests. Nonetheless, even as priests, the hierarchy remains. The priests alone handle the blood, yet Aaron's sons merely bring the blood to him at the altar, while Aaron performs all of the blood manipulations (9, 12, 18).[54]

Since the priests and YHWH alone partake of the חטאת and עלה, the priests are further distinguished from the populace and indexically connected to YHWH. The people, however, are also indexically connected to YHWH in that they both partake of the זבח השלמים (4, 24; cf. Lev 3). Finally, the divine fire (Lev 9:24) connects YHWH explicitly with the offerings, and by extension with the offerers, while simultaneously expressing his approval of both offerings and offerers.

---

[50] Cf. Gilders 2004:101. Although embedded in a textual representation, if such a ritual were practiced, it would not be lost on the audience. Like a "plot twist" (ibid.), it would elicit a dramatic response from the audience and thus garner attention.

[51] Noth 1977:72; Houtman 2000:541; Gilders 2004:101.

[52] Cf. Gorman 1990:115. Aaron enters the tent of meeting only after offering the first sacrifices of the inaugural cult (Lev 9:23). For an Egyptian parallel, see Gee 1998:288.

[53] Gorman 1990:122. The offering may not even be for the priests (see section 3.3.3.1.c.1.). In this case, the distinction would not be decisive.

[54] Gilders 2004:121–122.

3.3.2. Use

The dedication of the tabernacle and the installation of its priesthood bridges the gap between the construction of the tabernacle and its inauguration as a fully-functioning divine abode. Since the tabernacle materials and the priests are not inherently holy or fit for divinity, they must be made so through ritual so that YHWH may dwell in the midst of Israel. In short, the ritual prepares the area and its furniture for God's residence and the priests for his service.[55]

While the structure gives hints of how this is to be done, the purpose statements add specificity.[56] The first interpreted ritual action, washing in water, prevents death (Ex 30:21). The next, robing in holy garments (28:2, 4; 29:29), is both "for glory and beauty" (28:2, 40) and to consecrate Aaron to be a priest (לקדשו לכהנו־לי) (28:3). The application of the holy anointing oil (30:25), which is YHWH's exclusive property (30:31–33), makes the tabernacle, the altar, and Aaron holy (30:26–30; Lev 8:10–12). The first offering, the חטאת (Ex 28:10–14; Lev 8:14–17), decontaminates (חטא) the altar and makes it holy to effect clearing[57] on or on behalf of the altar (ויקדשהו לכפר עליו) (Lev 8:15).[58] The עלה ram serves as a pleasing aroma, a (food) gift to YHWH (Ex 29:18; Lev 8:21),[59] as does the ordina-

---

[55] The introductory goal statements in Ex 28 and 29 (cf. the concluding purpose statement in 28:41) seem to only reflect one aspect of this *causa*. They explicitly indicate that the rituals serve to make Aaron and his sons priests (לכהן). However, other purpose statements seem more expansive. The end of Ex 29 tacks on the divine consecration of the tabernacle, the altar, and the priests since YHWH will dwell among them and be their God (43–46). Elsewhere goal statements include the consecration of the tabernacle (Lev 8:10) and various rites related to the altar. For a resolution of this difficulty, see the ideology section below.

[56] Although straightforward in most contexts, some of the goal statements require clarification, which does not explicitly arise from the text. See the ideology section.

[57] Or by effecting clearing.

[58] In translating כפר as clearing, I follow Propp (2006:466–467) in an attempt to preserve some of the multivalence and ambiguity of the Hebrew expression (see further section 7.3.3). Regarding על, there is precedent for understanding it as either 'on' or 'on behalf of' (for arguments, compare Milgrom 1991:255–256 and Propp 2006:317 with Kiuchi 1987:93 and Gane 2005:130–131). The difference is largely immaterial since, whether clearing is done on or on behalf of the altar, most agree that the altar is the beneficiary of the clearing (in Ex 29 and Lev 8) in the same way that it is the recipient of decontamination or sanctification (the decontamination appears alternatively with the direct object [ויחטא את המזבח in Lev 8:15] and with על [וחטאת על־המזבח in Ex 29:36]). Leviticus 8:15, however, remains a point of contention (for an interpretation, see the ideology section).

[59] On the translation (food) gift as opposed to the traditional translation 'fire-offering,' see Milgrom 1991:161–162. For its derivation, see Ehrlich 1909:5; Hoftijzer 1967; Driver 1969:181–184. The appellation 'food' appears because biblical examples of the אשה

tion ram (Ex 29:25; Lev 8:28). The application of the ram's blood to the priestly extremities is left uninterpreted in both texts. The subsequent application of blood and oil to the priests and their garments makes them holy (Ex 29:25; Lev 8:30). On each of the seven days of priestly ordination (Ex 29:35; Lev 8:33–35), Moses offers the חטאת concerning clearing (על־הכפרים) (Ex 29:36)[60] and decontaminates the altar when (or by) effecting clearing on (or for) it and anoints it to make it holy, effecting clearing on (or for) the altar and consecrating it so that it is most holy and contagious to the touch (29:36–37). Like the first, the priests' last ritual action, staying by the doorway of the tabernacle, prevents death (Lev 8:33–35). Finally, YHWH's glory makes holy the tent, the altar, and the priests (Ex 29:43–44).

The ritual in Leviticus 9 follows the tabernacle dedication and serves as a grand opening with the intention of securing divine presence. Before the ritual begins, Moses commands the people to bring their various offerings since (כי) YHWH will appear to them (2–4). The חטאת and עלה offerings effect clearing for (על) Aaron and the people (7).

In amassing the various goal statements, it immediately becomes clear that multiple (and often repetitive) actions are assigned the same function. The עלה and the ordination offering both serve as a pleasing aroma, a (food) gift to YHWH, as do the daily עלה offerings introduced in Exodus 29:38–42. Each daily חטאת effects clearing, after which, on the inauguration day, both the עלה and חטאת effect clearing (Lev 9:7).[61] Most strikingly, anointing oil, חטאת offerings (both used repeatedly), garments, blood and oil, and YHWH make persons and/or objects holy.

These multiple means of accomplishing the same end clearly establish ritual purpose – e.g., to effect clearing, to present YHWH with a gift, and to make his place and people holy so that he may dwell among them and

---

always involve foodstuffs, and the expression appears in the longer form לחם אשה in Lev 3:11, 16 (Milgrom 1991:162). On the translation 'pleasing aroma,' see ibid. 162–163.

[60] Rashi and Ehrlich (1899:194) suggest that the phrase על־הכפרים expresses the purpose of the חטאת. Since there seems to be no other example of על to express purpose, it is perhaps better to translate the phrase more generally, 'concerning' clearing (Propp 2006: 469).

[61] It is also a distinct possibility that the ordination offering and the left-over bread effect clearing (Ex 29:33; so Milgrom 1991:1083). When Moses tells the priests to eat those things by which clearing was effected at their ordination and consecration, he refers back to verse 32, which mentions the ordination and the remnant of the bread from 29:23–5 (Ibn Ezra), called the elevation offering. Thus, it is logical to conclude that the combination of the bread and ordination ram effect some sort of clearing.

they may serve him. However, it is unclear why the text employs multiple actions to accomplish the same purpose.[62]

Regardless of its compositional history, there are roughly three options. The final text 1) forms a coherent whole; 2) does not form a coherent whole; 3) is somewhat coherent, even though some of its parts do not entirely cohere. We will attempt to make sense of the composite text, appealing to redactional layers only secondarily.[63] Although such an approach may seem harmonistic, it is pragmatic for three reasons. 1) The ritual tradents with the composite text before them would not be looking for discrete layers; they would perform the whole ritual, since, as we will see, ritual practice is more important than ritual understanding.[64] 2) Deciphering redactional layers is a difficult and often subjective enterprise.[65] 3) Even if much of the data is interpolated, it is worth addressing the logic of the interpolators instead of simply removing the troubling bits from consideration by calling them later additions or fossilized vestiges of earlier practices.

3.3.3. Ideology

Before analyzing the system, three preliminary remarks are in order. First, the western uneasiness with using multiple means to accomplish a single end simply is not a concern in the ANE world.[66] In fact, in the ANE, multiple or repeated actions are seen as more effective than a single action.[67]

---

[62] Although differing ritual orders in the different texts are also problematic, an analysis of them will not figure prominently.

[63] For a complex and plausible solution to the problem of compositional layers in Lev 8 and Ex 29, see Nihan 2007:124–147.

[64] Instead of trying to uncover the authentic ritual and the subsequent additions, participants would be much more concerned with performing the ritual as dictated, so that they could receive the full benefits. However, with two texts before them, one prescriptive and one descriptive, ritual tradents would have to decide if the two were compatible and, if not, which to follow (in making this argument, I assume that the rituals were performed or at least written to be performed).

[65] Like Propp, "on principle, I dislike arbitrary assumptions of secondary interpolations, the first recourse of too many critics for far too long" (2006:464).

[66] Milgrom, as well as many other before and after him, seems to expect the Priestly system to conform to modern sensibilities (or more precisely in his case modern and rabbinic sensibilities). Thus, multiple means of accomplishing a single end expressed in the text are an embarrassment for his systematic approach that must be minimized (see, e.g., his treatment of the anointing of Aaron and his sons in Lev 8; cf. Nihan 2007:127, who uses the altar's two-fold consecration in Lev 8 as a criterion for identifying vv. 10aβ–11 as a later insertion).

[67] See in this respect the rituals for the activation of the cult statues in Egypt, Mesopotamia, and Anatolia. The Egyptian ritual, for example, entails three actions that help to quicken the divine statue: two presentations of a bull's foreleg and heart as well as touch-

Conversely, using a single means often means that the desired end is relatively unimportant.[68]

Second, in such a complex ritual system, each individual element contributes and is essential to the efficacy of the whole.[69] Although it is not always clear how each element functions within the larger system, it is clear that each element is necessary for the system to function. As observed, the purpose of the system is to prepare the tabernacle and the priesthood for divine service. In the minds of the ritual tradents, if any element were absent or misapplied, the ritual system would fail to achieve its desired end. Thus, although it is possible to identify the discrete function of an individual act when a purpose statement is present, it is not always profitable to extract that element from the system in which it is embedded; for an element often shares its 'discrete' function with other elements and, regardless of the importance of its stated function, is only one of many necessary actions.[70]

Third, in most cases, correct performance of a ritual is much more important than understanding how or why it works.[71] If the ritual tradents believe that God ordained the ritual as a means of responding to various situations, performing the ritual exactly ensures the desired result, while understanding the role of the constituent parts is secondary at best. For example, although purpose statements do appear in the text for individual elements, Moses does not explain them to the assembled Israelites. He merely speaks of what YHWH commanded them to *do* (Lev 8:5; 9:6). Thus, although they may be rhetorically insignificant,[72] actions without goal statements cannot be ignored.

---

ing the statue's mouth with various implements. By repeatedly quickening in different ways, the elements make the quickening more thorough and more secure.

[68] While we may claim that the rituals did not originally exist in such complex forms, ritual authorities clearly welcome and thrive on complexity, regarding the rituals as fuller and more effective in their aggregate forms.

[69] For the application of systems theory to ritual, see Gane 2004; id. 2005:3–24.

[70] Once again, because of his exhaustive work and well-deserved lofty status, Milgrom will be our parade example. He too often focuses on certain elements in a ritual complex and derives meaning from them at the expense of the larger ritual complex (see, e.g., his focus on the blood manipulation of the חטאת as the sole instrument of כפר [1991:254–261]; cf. the helpful critique of Gilders 2004:137–138).

[71] See Bell 1992:69–93; id. 1997:159–164. Too often scholars focus on the mental activity at the expense of the ritual action (Bergen 2005:25); cf. Gilders 2004:98: "P seems remarkably unconcerned with explaining or interpreting ritual actions. P's concern is with the actual execution of the rites, which is typical of ritual specialists in a variety of cultures, for whom it is the correct performance of the rite itself that is 'meaningful.'" Again, my position assumes that the described ritual was practiced or was written to be practiced.

[72] E.g., they do not help to explain the purpose of the ritual.

These three principles have implications both for the overall ritual complex and for the individual actions within it. Further support abounds in the ANE.[73] The temple dedications, the rituals to animate a divine statue and install it in the temple, and the rituals to install a new priest are especially illustrative. In Egypt, the opening of the mouth ritual involves two presentations of a bull's foreleg and heart and the application of various tools to the statue's mouth. Each serves as equally valid means of quickening inert matter, and each builds on the one before to make that quickening more thorough and more secure. The foreleg and the heart, respectively, give strength and consciousness to the statue, while the tools give the statue human faculties, especially the ability to open its mouth.[74] The second presentation of the foreleg and heart endows the statue with strength and consciousness in a new setting (after the use of tools), enhancing the presentation of strength and consciousness to ensure the presence of both. The second presentation also seems to be a first meal, in which the newly enlivened divine statue partakes of strength and consciousness before partaking of its normal daily fare with its newly opened mouth.[75] Conversely, the absence of any of these elements would render the ritual incomplete and the assurance of divine presence more precarious. In addition to being the result of complementary and comprehensive means, the statue's quickening also seems to be a joint effort of human and divine. The rituals stress the human element, while the hymns and mythological texts stress divine action.[76] The human actions (which in a sense are also divine actions, since the priests perform them in the guise of deities) appropriately prepare the statue for divine presence, provided by the deity.

This multifaceted approach also features in the Egyptian temple dedication and installation of the priests. Before construction, the temple site is purified with gypsum. Once completed, the temple is purified again with natron and a form of whitewash before it is presented to the deity.[77] The purifications before and after construction make purification more complete, as does the use of different and complementary means. Again, all of the elements are essential to ensure success. Once sufficiently purified, the temple may then be enlivened and handed over to the soon-to-be resident deity. Similarly, priestly installation includes presentation in the temple,

---

[73] The following is built on more extensive research.
[74] Lorton 1999:165, 173.
[75] Ibid. 174–175.
[76] Ibid. 185.
[77] Černý 1952:114–115; David 1981:52; Shafer 1998:7; Wilkinson 2005:38. There is also some evidence that, after purification, the opening of the mouth is performed on every room in the temple to enliven the temple (Blackman and Fairman 1945; Černý 1952: 115; David 1981:52).

purification, and beholding the deity.[78] Various elements contribute to and complete the priests' purification process – washing, censing, robing, and anointing.[79] Each action contributes different elements, none of which is sufficient alone, so as to ensure that the cumulative effect is sufficient.

In Mesopotamia,[80] the washing and opening of the mouth rituals (*mīs pî* and *pīt pî* respectively) and the priestly installation rite employ a multiplicity of means to accomplish the desired end.[81] For example, mouth-washing and mouth-opening recur throughout the *mīs pî* and *pīt pî*, marking the stages of the statue's transition and building on previous actions to make the transition more complete and secure. Even the initial purification of the statue involves three elements: a censer, torch, and holy water basin. As in Egypt, the animation process involves both divine and human initiative. The various human actions help to bring about change and provide a conducive environment for the gods to play their (more important) role. The priestly installation also includes multiple purifications accompanied by various incantations aimed at effecting perfect purity in the priest-to-be (he may not enter the temple until he is "as pure as a golden statue"). In addition, purification requires human and divine cooperation, as Marduk is repeatedly mentioned as the one who enables purification.[82]

Instead of positing a single solution, the Mesopotamian rituals put forth multiple solutions, as if realizing that none alone will do, and using as many as possible to cover all the bases.[83] To produce such a cumulative effect, repetition naturally occurs[84] as a way of enhancing the meaningfulness of the words and actions. As a result, the ritual functions on multiple levels that, although often interrelated, do not always coexist peacefully.[85] How-

---

[78] Sauneron 2000:48–49.

[79] Gee 1998:288–311. The preceding list describes the daily entry requirements for priests. Although not identical to the priestly installation, where the data is sparser, it is hard to imagine that purification for installation is less involved than daily purification for service.

[80] Although complex actions also form a central part of rites of removal and purification, we will postpone our discussion of them until chapter 5.

[81] See a transliterated and translated copy of the mouth-washing ritual in Walker and Dick 2001.

[82] For temple construction narratives, see, e.g., Hurowitz 1985; id. 1992; Jacobsen 1987:386–444; Linssen 2004:92–109, 252–305.

[83] The "duration, expenditure and complexity" of the ritual also signal its importance (Berlejung 1997:45; see further Hurowitz 1989:48–51, 53–57; Berlejung 1998:182–185; Walker and Dick 2001:10–15). In anthropological terms, the special and multiple means ritualize the actions, thereby differentiating the ritual from and privileging it over other more ordinary rituals.

[84] Especially in the wording of incantations.

[85] E.g., the statue is both born and self-created (IT 4.A:23–33; STT 199:1–5).

ever, in an ancient context, such tensions are far preferable to a consistent yet simple and thus simply ineffective ritual.[86]

The Hittite bent for comprehensiveness finds clear expression in the Kizzuwatnean ritual for dedicating a new temple and enlivening its new cult statue, which abounds with action and repetition regarding both the temple itself and its statue. As in Egypt and Mesopotamia, the multiple actions and repetition are simply part of the nexus of ritual. The various actions serve as a multiplicity of means to ritually accomplish the desired end, means that naturally function on various levels.[87] In other words, since no single action is sufficient, the Hittites seem to employ every means at their disposal to achieve the desired end. Repetition naturally appears alongside these multiple actions to produce a cumulative effect, enhancing the function of any one action.[88] The concentration of actions and the repetition of those actions in various settings marks the ritual as important and the desired effect as difficult to attain. As in Mesopotamia, the human role seems to be limited mostly to providing a conducive environment for the divine investiture. The officiants set the stage and create the mood, while the deity does the work.[89]

The installation of the high priestess at Emar both predates the emergence of Israel and is more complex than its Priestly counterpart.[90] The nine-day ritual[91] marks the priestess' gradual transition from her father's house to the temple of Baal, through daily processions to the temple and back to her father's house.[92] In the course of this transition, the text employs multiple means to accomplish the desired end. For example, the priestess' consecration involves two anointings and a head shaving, the

---

[86] Naturally, the absence of any one element would render the whole less secure and thus each element would remain essential in the minds of the ritual tradents for full efficacy.

[87] These means likely forge similar and similarly multiple connections to those in the Mesopotamian ritual. One such level may be the mythological birth of the deity (Collins 2005:31–32). The spatial dimension likely has a role to play as well, as the ritual progresses from the old temple out into the world and to the riverbank before settling in the new temple.

[88] By repeating the same actions in different settings, these repetitions seem to make what is done more of a reality. As in the rest of the ANE, each element makes an essential contribution to the efficacy of the whole.

[89] The actors perform various actions to coax the deity to be present, and, once that presence is assumed, they merely ask the deity to divide herself in order to inhabit the new temple. The presence of the goddess Pirinkir may also serve to strengthen the connection with the divine sphere.

[90] Hurowitz 2002:605.

[91] Fleming 1992:292. Since the chronology is ambiguous, the ritual could last up to 10 days.

[92] Ibid.

gods' consecration involves two sets of offerings on two different days, and the ritual complex includes multiple purifications and offerings as well as two presentation ceremonies (*kubadu*).[93] In sum, the multiple processions and the events and actions that accompany them increasingly prepare the high priestess for service. Such a "delicate process" cannot be completed sufficiently in "one motion with full assimilation achieved on the first visit" to the temple.[94] Instead, multiple and often repeated actions are required for cumulative effect.

Likewise, in the Priestly dedication of the tabernacle, multiple and often repeated actions work together and are necessary to bring about the desired results,[95] highlighting their importance and helping to ensure their permanency. This holds true for both the ritual as a whole and its constituent parts and can be established both explicitly and by analogy.

3.3.3.1. Ideology of the Individual Elements

Only some of the many elements in the dedication rituals are ascribed a purpose, and we will examine them in more or less sequential order under the categories of washing, consecration, clearing, pleasing gift, and uninterpreted acts.

a) Washing

For the priests, washing with water is a prerequisite for approaching and serving YHWH in the tabernacle complex (Ex 30:17–21). Elsewhere it often serves as a prerequisite for encountering YHWH in a theophany or redresses impurity (in combination with the passage of time and possibly an offering) so that the worshiper may again access the tabernacle complex [96] In each case, washing prepares the worshiper to access the divine presence, either in response to uncleanness or in advance of special access to YHWH.[97] Although it is clear that washing averts death and allows for tenuous access, it is unclear what change it effects in the priests.

Perhaps it serves to purify the priests, thereby granting them special access to YHWH. Elsewhere in the Priestly writings, washing is part of a process to remove impurity with the end result that the one washed be-

---

[93] Regarding the interpretation of the latter, see ibid. 166.

[94] Ibid. 117.

[95] I.e., the preparation of the tabernacle and priests for YHWH's presence.

[96] For a list of references and a brief discussion, see Lawrence 2006:26–32, 222–230.

[97] If the impurity is severe enough, two washings may be necessary, the first to reinstate the individual into YHWH's special community and the second to renew his access to the cult (such as the מצרע in Lev 14). Cf. Milgrom 1991:967, 993–994.

comes clean (טהור).⁹⁸ In the priestly installation, however, as well as in preparation for theophany, the text mentions no prior impurity or subsequent state of cleanness.⁹⁹ It seems then that although the worshiper is already in a clean state, such a state is not clean enough for special access to the deity, whether in theophany or cultic service. In short, approaching YHWH requires an elevated state of purity. Washing is the most tangible, visible, and physical means of achieving this end. In the priestly installation ritual, it seems to symbolically and/or physically remove impurity inherent in the mundane sphere, as the priest who approaches and serves YHWH must be purer than the common Israelite.¹⁰⁰ Nonetheless, here as elsewhere, understanding the ritual function is not as important as correctly performing the ritual action.

The necessity of washing immediately brings to mind the possibility of ritual failure. What may seem like a minor action has major consequences if omitted. Not only would the entire ritual fail to be effective, but the offending priests-to-be would also be killed.¹⁰¹ Human participation in the ritual ends with the command to remain by the doorway of the tabernacle and, like the preparatory washing, is accompanied by the death penalty for noncompliance (Lev 8:33–35; 10:7). By situating the death penalty on either side of the ritual – from washing to remaining seven days by the tent of meeting – the Priestly writers make clear that the ritual must be performed correctly from beginning to end.¹⁰²

b) Consecration

In the Priestly texts, including H and Numbers*, קדשׁ is a multifaceted root, used in roughly three ways. First, holiness may be understood in an absolute sense; one is either holy or not. When used of YHWH, holy refers

---

⁹⁸ The non-Priestly theophanic passages use התקדשׁ, which Milgrom calls "the non-Priestly technical term for purification through bathing in preparation for receiving the presence of the Lord" (1991:965).

⁹⁹ Cf. Lawrence 2006:32.

¹⁰⁰ Cf. Propp 2006:460, commenting on the חטאת: "To commune with God, humans must first be in a state of maximal purity (e.g., 19:10, 14–15)." The ANE evidence seems to support this proposition, in that worshipers must wash before entering the sacred complex and performing ritual action in it, regardless of their prior state (for a helpful summary of some of the data, see Milgrom 1991:958–963; for Egypt in particular, see Gee 1998:291–301; for Ugarit, see Levine 1963:105–107; id. 1983).

¹⁰¹ Other fatal ritual missteps are Aaron failing to wear the golden bells and pomegranates (Ex 28:35), the priests failing to wear linen breeches (28:42–43) or to remain at the entrance of the tent of meeting for seven days (Lev 8:35), and Nadab and Abihu's misuse of incense (Lev 10).

¹⁰² Nadab and Abihu's failure soon thereafter highlights that the priests who officiate before YHWH are never entirely out of danger.

to God's status as wholly other, "altogether separate from the created world."[103] When used of persons or objects, being holy means belonging to the deity and thus the divine sphere.[104]

Second, since no more suitable term exists, holiness is also employed relatively to express the hierarchy within the divine realm.[105] As wholly other, YHWH naturally rests atop the hierarchy. For everyone and everything else, holiness is a derived quality, whose relative value, as we will see, is determined by several factors.

Third, in the Holiness Legislation, holy is also used to express fitness for the divine sphere, which is achieved through obedience. In other words, the people's "holiness depends on [their] compliance with the entire range of commandments."[106] This obedience may be social, ethical, religious, ritual, or divine imitation, all of which are undergirded by a simple reality: the behavior and welfare of the people have a direct impact on their deity's reputation. Thus, to adequately reflect the greatness of the God in their midst, the Israelites must obey so that others can see them manifesting YHWH's principles and receiving divine blessing as a result.[107]

How then does a person or object become holy and how is this holiness reflected in the hierarchical grid? YHWH's presence exudes holiness.[108] This contagious holiness may be absorbed[109] by proximity, ritual action and pre- and post-requisite obedience.

In H, laypeople absorb divine holiness from afar through obedience.[110] In Numbers, disobedience is not necessarily fatal unless it is done ביד רמה (Num 15:30). However, it becomes so when one approaches the deity.[111]

---

[103] Schwartz 2000:48, drawing on the definition of holy by Rudolf Otto. Joosten refers to God's 'unspeakable nature' (1996:123).

[104] E.g., presenting offerings to YHWH makes them holy, and, as such, the remnants of those offerings may be consumed only by holy people (i.e., the priests).

[105] Ironically, although his study addresses graded holiness, Jenson's definition of holiness does not allow for gradations (Wilson 1994:87).

[106] Schwartz 2000:59; see more fully 55–59. Schwartz cites Lev 20:7–8 and Lev 19, where obedience and holiness appear as bookends to the chapter, between which stand 34 verses with a "sampling of all types of commandments"; cf. Zimmerli 1980:493–512; Joosten 1996:132.

[107] YHWH brought them out of Egypt to be their God, logically effecting a change in ownership from one master to the next. Their obedience to the God in their midst enables divine holiness to be manifest and protects against profaning his name (Lev 22:31–33; cf. Ex 29:45–46; Schwartz 2000:57; cf. Joosten 1996:132, 134).

[108] Joosten 1996:128, Schwartz 2000:54–55.

[109] If the altar is contagiously holy (Ex 29:37), how much more so the deity who sanctifies it?

[110] Joosten 1996:128–132; Schwartz 2000:53–59.

[111] Since they are forbidden to approach the deity, such an act alone merits the death penalty (Num 1:51; 3:10, 38).

3.3. Tabernacle Dedication and Priestly Installation

The priests absorb greater holiness by ritual action and by proximity to and service of the deity. In P proper as well as in H and Numbers, obedience plays a vital role. The priests must fulfill all the ritual requirements from their inauguration onwards so that they are suitable both for divine service and to absorb divine holiness. If, however, they inappropriately approach YHWH, absorbing divine holiness will kill them.[112]

People's hierarchical holiness is determined by both ritual and proximity. The high priest stands above the other priests since he is doubly anointed and has annual access to the divine presence in the adytum. The other priests stand above the rest of the Israelites because they are anointed and are granted greater access. The priests' greater holiness has a direct bearing on their behavior, since with greater holiness comes greater responsibility. For example, because of greater access and function, the high priest must observe stricter rules of purity than the other priests, who, in turn, must observe stricter rules of purity than everyone else.[113]

Objects absorb holiness by ritual action and proximity to the deity. Each object receives the same ritual action,[114] anointing, yet is plotted on the holiness grid based on proximity.[115] Unlike people, objects are not in danger of being destroyed by divine holiness.[116] Instead, they may lose effectiveness by accruing too much pollution. To counter such a possibility, the altar, for example, is re-consecrated through ritual action so that it may function again as intended.

Consecration in Exodus 29 and Leviticus 8

Over the course of the tabernacle dedication ritual, Aaron's priestly garments, the anointing oil, the חטאת offerings, blood and oil, and YHWH are said to make persons and objects holy. Of the list, the garments seem to be the oddest choice for an instrument of sanctification (לקדשו לכהנו-לי [Ex

---

[112] A person can become holy safely only by following the proper procedures. The person who inappropriately contacts the contagiously holy or approaches the deity dies (regarding the latter, see, e.g., Korah [where the misused censers are also reassigned for divine use] and Nadab and Abihu; cf. 2 Sa 6:3–7; see also the fatal missteps listed above (section 3.3.3.1.a.) and the usage of the term חרם). Nonetheless, there seems to be some room for priestly error (Lev 4:3–12). Where the line falls between fatal and expiable remains open for debate.

[113] Cf. Joosten 1996:129–130.

[114] As we will see, the bronze altar receives more elaborate treatment than the other items.

[115] Assuming God is present in the adytum, those objects which are closest to him in it are especially holy. The holiest objects, the ark and כפרת, are not inherently holy. They are most holy because of their proximity to the deity. Their elaborateness and hiddenness merely reflect their special place and ascribed status.

[116] E.g., Num 16:38.

28:3]). Two possibilities present themselves: either the garments are merely the clothes Aaron must wear for his consecration or they in some way help to bring about his consecration. Although the two choices seem at odds, one need not distinguish between them. It is clear that wearing the priestly apparel cannot consecrate alone. It is also clear that Aaron cannot be adequately consecrated without them. The robing is an integral part of the ritual that cannot be ignored. It is also necessary later in the ritual when Moses applies the blood and oil to both Aaron and his garments to consecrate him (29:21, 29).[117] Thus, regardless of whether or not they consecrate, the priestly attire forms an integral part of the consecration process, one which, if extracted, would ruin the whole. To say that one element alone consecrates is to misunderstand both the complexity and interconnectedness of the ritual.

What then does the priestly apparel add to the consecration process? As Houtman asserts, "Clothes make the man."[118] What a person wears determines his status. Dressing in an official capacity transforms an individual into an "office bearer."[119] Aaron's garments are integral to his office. First, they are holy (Ex 28:2; 4; 29:29; 31:10; 39:41; 40:13),[120] and as such are consecrated with a blood-oil mixture. Second, they are made up of elements that mark this distinction. They are crafted from the finest materials, materials reserved for the high priest and the tabernacle alone. Third, the specialness of the garments, and by extension those who wear them, is visible for all to see. "For glory and beauty" (Ex 28:2, 40), the visible majesty of the priestly garments, like that of the divine glory, reflects the importance of the one wearing them. Aaron's adornment in front of the entire congregation (Lev 8:3–4) serves as a visible sign of his elevation in status, one which would be lodged in the minds of the onlookers. Although they may not be able to recognize the high priest's face, they would always remember the elaborate clothes that mark his office.[121]

In the ANE and in the Bible, anointing with oil, like one's outfit, "ceremonializes an elevation in legal status."[122] Anointing an individual to be-

---

[117] Cf. Propp 2006:431.

[118] Houtman 2000:466. In support of his position, he points to Gen 37:3; 2 Sam 13:18; Is 61:10; Dan 5:16; Zec 3:3, 5; Ps 45:14; 104:1; Est 8:15.

[119] Ibid., citing Gen 41:40ff; Num 20:26, 28; 1Kgs 19:19; 2Kgs 2:13–14; Isa 22:21ff.

[120] Cf. Ex 29:6; 39:30, where a specific element of the priestly apparel, the crown (נזר), is also called holy.

[121] This holds true throughout the ANE. For example, one can often only identify the individuals depicted in reliefs from their adornments. Robing is also an essential part of the purification process in Egypt (see Gee 1998:303–305).

[122] Milgrom 1991:553–555.

come a priest is merely one of its many applications.¹²³ The Priestly writers co-opt this practice, attested both in the ANE and in the Bible outside the Priestly sphere, and adapt it to serve their purposes. Like the priestly garments, the anointing oil itself is holy, and thus its specific configuration is reserved for YHWH alone (Ex 30:23–33). When Moses applies YHWH's personal oil to the priests, the tabernacle and its furniture, YHWH marks them as his possession and thereby elevates them to a special sacred status.

The חטאת offerings are most commonly associated with clearing (כפר). However, in Leviticus 8:15 and 16:19, they are also explicitly identified with (re)consecration.¹²⁴ On the face of it, the חטאת consecrates because the text and the ritual authority that stands behind it say that it consecrates. Furthermore, nothing in ritual syntax prevents the blood of the חטאת from serving a dual role, one of which is consecration. Instead of resting on such tautological laurels, we are better served by examining why and how the חטאת has such an unusual function. As will be argued below,¹²⁵ the repeated חטאת offerings seem to effect a maximal state of purity in the altar.¹²⁶ Although purity does not itself make something holy, it is a prerequisite for the consecration that does produce holiness.

In loose terms, decontamination then may be understood as part of the larger consecration process (Ex 29:1, 33).¹²⁷ Although decontamination and clearing do not consecrate, they move forward the consecration process. Decontamination and clearing prepare the altar to be set apart to the divine sphere (i.e., consecrated) by setting it apart from all vestiges of mundane imperfection (i.e., purifying it). Moreover, as we saw in the previous section for H, obedience is part of the consecration process, of absorbing divine holiness. Here in P, Moses' obedient clearing makes the altar suitable for consecration and divine service. More specifically, clearing makes the altar perfectly pure as God is perfectly pure.

---

¹²³ For the voluminous ANE evidence for anointing priests from Egypt, the Levant, Anatolia and Mesopotamia, see, e.g., Fleming 1998 and the literature cited therein, which focuses on the Emar material but also includes other ANE evidence.

¹²⁴ Milgrom views the reference in 8:15 as a "summary statement recalling vv 10–11" and/or a "vestige of the original reference to the altar (and sanctuary's) consecration" (1991:523–524) (he seems hard-pressed to explain the role of the חטאת in 16:19 [1991:1037–1039]). Even if it is a remnant of an earlier form of the ritual, in the present context, the statement refers to the consecrating function of the חטאת as does the reference in 16:19.

¹²⁵ Section 3.3.3.1.c.

¹²⁶ Cf. Propp 2006:460.

¹²⁷ The first text uses לקדש אתם לכהן לי as shorthand for the entire ritual (which includes other elements including clearing). The second text speaks of Aaron and his sons eating the food by which clearing was made למלא את־ידם לקדש אתם. In other words, clearing is part of the larger ritual purpose defined in short as ordination and consecration.

How do we account for such a loose distinction between purity and holiness in the Priestly texts, which are otherwise marked by great precision? Instead of castigating the Priests for their carelessness, we should applaud them for their overall precision. Although at times they equivocate, they nonetheless add precision to the ANE and other biblical conceptions of holiness and purity.

In Egypt, for example, there appears to be a significant overlap between pure and holy. "The Pharaonic verbs *w'b* 'to be pure' and the causative *sw'b* 'to purify' as well as *ḏsr* 'to be holy' and *sḏsr* 'to sanctify' are all used to designate objects that are pure."[128] *Ḏsr* can mean either clean or holy, depending on the context, and at times means both in the same context (so too *sḏsr*).[129] On occasion, "to say 'cleared' [i.e., purified] and 'holy' is saying one and the same thing," since to be wholly other – i.e., holy – means to be separated from "the profane world with its defiling forces."[130] In other words, being free from pollutants is requisite for holiness. Purity and holiness are thus so closely connected in the Egyptian mind that the two may be described by the same word.

In Akkadian, *qadāšu* and its derivatives likewise blur the cultic distinction between holy, as pertaining to the divine realm, and pure, as free from pollutants. When used in a cultic context, the verb *qadāšu* in its various forms means to be clean, to cleanse, and (perhaps secondarily) to consecrate or dedicate to the divine.[131] Its derivatives appear "almost without exception in religious-cultic contexts where they qualify objects, places, and persons that as a prerequisite have been 'cleansed, purified' and thus 'consecrated,' i.e., dedicated to the deity."[132] Likewise, the Akkadian has no precise equivalent for Sumerian KU_3, which "has a primary meaning of 'pertaining to the realm of the divine.'"[133] It regularly uses *ellu*, along with its verbal and nominal forms. However, *ellu* means 'free from physical pollutants,' with a possible derived meaning of belonging to the divine realm.[134] Thus, it seems that in Akkadian thinking, holy and pure overlap. Although purity seems to be of primary importance (since there are far more words to describe it and none that exclusively or even primarily describes holiness), purity and holiness seem to be part of a single continuum. Once pollutants are removed, the object may be fit for and dedicated to the divine, and therefore described in one word as both pure and holy.

---

[128] *WbÄS* 4:66; 5:610; Gee 1998:6–7.
[129] Hoffmeier 1985:165.
[130] Ibid. 70, 229.
[131] *CAD* Q 46–47.
[132] Kornfeld and Ringgren *TDOT* 12 (2003):524.
[133] Wilson 1994:65.
[134] Ibid. 67, 83.

3.3. Tabernacle Dedication and Priestly Installation

In the Hebrew Bible, in addition to its normal usage ('to consecrate'), the non-Priestly קדשׁ at times "refers to washing, laundering and refraining from sexual activity in order to achieve a state of bodily cleanness, and by extension to the removal of idolatrous objects metaphorically thought of as 'pollutants' in order to 'purify' the Temple and its precincts."[135] Rather than understanding קדשׁ as consecration and קדשׁ as purification as unrelated yet identical roots,[136] it is better to see them as part of a single continuum. Characterized by greater precision for the most part, the Priestly texts consistently differentiate consecration from purification. However, as expected from those with less intimate access to the cult, the non-Priestly texts use the term קדשׁ less carefully, at times referring to holiness and at other times to purity. For example, Chronicles seems to use the roots טהר and קדשׁ almost interchangeably.[137]

Nonetheless, actions in the second category (קדשׁ as purification) overlap with the Priestly understanding of קדשׁ, and can be understood as an imprecise outflow of קדשׁ as consecration. In both instances, consecration often involves being in the divine presence. In the Priestly texts, consecration means belonging to the divine sphere, and, thus, often being in proximity to the deity. Being in proximity to the deity, at least in part, also brings about consecration as the person or object absorbs YHWH's emanating holiness (in H).

This usage of קדשׁ as purification relates to divine presence in that it is often a prerequisite for an encounter with God (e.g., Ex 19:10, 22; Num 11:18; Dt 23:15; Jos 3:5; 7:3; 1Sa 16:5; 1 Ch 15:12, 14; 2 Ch 5:11; 29:34; 30:3, 15, 17, 34; 35:6). It usually appears in the *hithpael* (and thus התקדשׁ can be called "the non-Priestly technical term for purification through bathing in preparation for receiving the presence of the Lord"),[138] yet it may also occur in the *piel* (Ex 19:10) as well as adjectivally (Dt 23:15).

Actions in the second category of קדשׁ "do not consecrate, that is they do not confer any lasting status of belonging to the divine sphere."[139] Instead, they purify, which in P is a prerequisite for consecration yet not consecration itself. Rather than keeping the distinction intact, the non-Priestly texts recognize that the two are intimately related – i.e., often part of a single process – and thus at times conflate the terms. Realizing that consecration is often necessary for a close encounter with God (e.g., priestly service), they sometimes use קדשׁ more generally to refer to preparation for

---

[135] Schwartz 2000:48.
[136] Ibid. 47–48.
[137] Ibid. 48 and n. 7.
[138] Milgrom 1991:965.
[139] Schwartz 2000:48.

an encounter with God, which the Priests describe as purification (טהר).¹⁴⁰ Thus, for the non-Priests, it is no great leap of imprecision to incorporate obedient preparation for a (proximate) encounter with God into the semantic field of קדש, which normally includes belonging to the divine sphere (and absorbing YHWH's holiness through proximity, ritual, and obedience). Since such preparation includes washing, it may also be termed purification (טהר).¹⁴¹

Ultimately, we may forgive the Priests for an occasional, and rhetorically meaningful, indiscretion, which communicates that every element is interconnected and contributes to the efficacy of the whole. Furthermore, as we will see, the Priests could not entirely disentangle purification from consecration. Since YHWH alone may consecrate, human consecratory acts (8:15) effect purity to elicit divine consecration.¹⁴²

The oil and the blood of the ordination ram also make the priests holy (Ex 29:21; Lev 8:30). As for the altar and for Aaron, anointing oil consecrates, elevating Aaron's and his sons' status from common to holy.¹⁴³ However, it is unclear why the blood also has a consecratory role. Even if its specific role remains a mystery, the text makes clear that it partners with the oil to make the priests holy and thus must be included in the ritual performance.

It is possible, although unlikely, that the consecratory power comes from the oil alone.¹⁴⁴ Milgrom appeals to Exodus 29:37, where all that touches the altar partakes of its holiness, and argues instead that the blood consecrates because it picks up the altar's holiness, which it then may impart to the priests.¹⁴⁵ This is certainly possible. However, if this were true, it does not adequately explain how the blood in Leviticus 8:15 consecrates. Blood that touches the anointed altar and is sanctified by it would then in turn sanctify the altar.¹⁴⁶ It seems odd that the blood that in 16:19 has been sanctified by "being aspersed inside the adytum and shrine of the Tent" would then be "qualified to consecrate the sacrificial altar when sprinkled upon it."¹⁴⁷ Indeed, although the blood comes from the same animal(s), it is hard to imagine that Aaron asperses the bronze altar with

---

¹⁴⁰ In some ways, H's use of holiness is closer still to קדש as purification, in that it calls for consecration through obedience, which may even include appropriate purification rites.

¹⁴¹ It is then possible to understand the appearance of קדש in texts like 2 Samuel 11:4 even when there is no hint of an encounter with God. Having lost sight of its original non-Priestly meaning, the author simply replaces טהר with קדש, its imprecise synonym.

¹⁴² Although the human actions (with divine supervision) purge the altar of imperfections, P calls their activity 'consecration' because divine consecration is the ultimate goal of their activity. See further the following pages and sections 3.4. and 7.3.3.

¹⁴³ Cf. Milgrom 1991:533.

¹⁴⁴ Propp 2006:463.

¹⁴⁵ Id. 1991:534.

¹⁴⁶ Milgrom's claim that v. 15 refers back to 10–11 is a possible way out, yet it does not seem to adequately account for 16:19.

¹⁴⁷ Ibid. 534, 1037–1039.

3.3. Tabernacle Dedication and Priestly Installation

the same 'sanctified' blood that he uses inside the tabernacle. In 8:15 and 16:19, it seems more logical to assume that, by effecting כפר, the blood removes all vestiges of human impurity, leaving it in a state of maximal purity and making it fit for divine use. The blood in 8:30, however, comes from the ordination ram and thus does not (explicitly) have the same purificatory effect. If Milgrom and Gilders are correct that daubing of the blood on the extremities of Aaron and his sons has a purificatory effect,[148] then the same blood could also contribute to the consecratory effect of the anointing oil by making the priests maximally pure. Even so, it seems odd that one would have to reapply the blood to produce the secondary effect of making the priests holy. Perhaps it is best not to over-analyze the instrumentality of the ritual, since, in an empirical sense, the ritual actions do not instrumentally achieve the stated end. Instead, the action may be present for rhetorical effect, made practical and effectual by YHWH who is believed to have ordained and completed the ritual (Ex 29:43–44). The use of the blood from the altar highlights the connection between the priests and the altar through the blood applied to both. The mixture of the blood with the oil and the similarity of its application to both the priests and the altar furthers this connection (especially as daubing the blood on the priestly extremities seems to mimic daubing it on the altar horns). As the altar is holy, separated exclusively for divine use, so are the priests when they serve in an official capacity. Thus, the altar is identified with the priests, the holy instrument that is the primary means of serving God and redressing pollution that prohibits such service with the holy ones who are responsible for its care.

The apparent dual consecration of Aaron is another point of contention,[149] yet one that can be more easily resolved. Aaron's double anointing, like that of the high priestess at Emar, indicates that sanctification of a person, like that of the altar (Ex 29:36–37), is a process.[150] Through the course of the ritual, Aaron becomes increasingly holy until, at the end of seven days, his holiness is sufficient for him to serve YHWH in the inauguration of the cult (Lev 9).[151] Aaron's dual anointing also elevates his status over his sons. As his garb is especially elaborate and holy, so too is his anointing and

---

[148] Ibid. 528–529; Gilders 2004:100–103.

[149] Milgrom tries to limit Aaron's consecration to a single instance. He identifies the anointing sequence in Ex 29 and Lev 8 with different traditions, with Ex 29 reserving consecration for v. 21 alone, while Lev 8 does the opposite: after being consecrated in v 12, Aaron need not be anointed again (1991:532–533). Although clever, such gymnastics are unnecessary and overlook that consecration can be a process (e.g., the daily anointing of the altar to consecrate it over the course of 7 days [Ex 29:36–37]) and that both texts mention double anointing (Ex 29:7, 21; Lev 8:12, 30).

[150] In claiming that purification is a process, I am not arguing that either ritual was necessarily twofold in origin, only that they cohere in their present form.

[151] Milgrom himself contends that "each day's rites will remove them farther from their former profane state and advance them to the ranks of the sacred, until they emerge as full-fledged priests" (1991:538). Would not the dual anointing and consecration be part of this process?

consecration. Such extreme holiness is necessary to enter the inner sanctum on the Day of Atonement and even to wear the high priestly attire.[152]

YHWH then finishes the consecration process.[153] As in the rest of the ANE,[154] the deity has a crucial role to play. As ritual texts, Exodus 29 and Leviticus 8 both focus on the human end, detailing what the people must do (at the divine behest) to fulfill their role. God's role bears scant mention because it is somewhat of a mystery and lies beyond the control of human participants.[155] This textual reticence does not, however, mean that God's role is minimal. Changing a person or object's status from mundane to holy is a difficult and unnatural transition, requiring multiple stages and methods to ensure maximal holiness. Making the tabernacle and the priests fit for divine service requires divine intervention from beginning to end. First, God (is believed to have) prescribed the ritual in its present form. Second, he enables it to function properly outside of normal empirical categories[156] (as we will see, the present ritual is impossible without the divine presence). Third, in addition to outlining and overseeing the process, he brings it to completion by sanctifying the priests and the tabernacle with his glory. In effect, as in the ANE, human and divine both have a role to play; humans obey the deity's ritual instructions, thereby providing a conducive environment for YHWH to do the heavy lifting.

The placement of God's role at the end of the prescriptive text provides a well-placed reassurance of the efficacy of the whole process, as long as

---

[152] Ex 29:29–30 seems to imply that moving from the status of a priest to that of the high priest requires an additional elevation ceremony.

[153] Propp 2006:473; cf. Houtman 2000:598.

[154] See section 3.3.3. See also the *akītu* ceremony, where an initial purification by human agents is followed by setting up a golden canopy and the recitation of an incantation to dispel demons from the temple, in which the gods are said to purify the precincts (line 374, according to the text in Linssen 2004:215–237) "This seems to imply that after one level of exorcism has exhausted its power during the earlier stage of purification, the gods complete the task by dealing with any 'great evil demon' (line 382) that remains to haunt the premises. So the goal of the human activity is to promote divine purification activity" (Gane 2005:374).

[155] The Egyptian texts offer the best available parallel. The ritual texts seem to indicate that humans are the primary impetus for the statue's construction and quickening, while the hymns and mythological texts tend to ignore the human element, instead attributing the statue's creation and animation solely to the deities (Lorton 1999:185). The ritual texts naturally focus on the human element, what role the ritual tradents must fulfill, leaving the deities alone to fulfill their role. The hymns and mythological texts focus instead on the deities and their (more important) role in the process. Juxtaposed, the two sets of texts provide a fuller picture, as one details the necessary human element while the other extols that of the divine.

[156] For example, in the חטאת ritual for expiable sin (Lev 4), following the prescriptions laid out by YHWH leads to clearing. After the process, the offerer achieves his ultimate goal; he is forgiven by God (נסלח).

3.3. Tabernacle Dedication and Priestly Installation 81

the people correctly play their part. It also serves as the purpose for bringing Israel out of Egypt; YHWH completes the consecration process so that he may dwell among them and be known, honored, and served by them as their God (29:43–46).[157]

c) Clearing

Before analyzing how the elements effect clearing, we must first examine the enigmatic expressions that describe clearing, since the clearing function of the חטאת, and of the passage as a whole, is not as explicit or straightforward as one might expect, especially from the English translations. For example, in Leviticus 8:15, the blood manipulation of the חטאת on the altar decontaminates (חטא) the altar rather than effecting clearing on it, while the blood at the base enigmatically consecrates לכפר עליו. In Leviticus 8:34, YHWH commands the participants to do as they had done on the first day to effect clearing for the priests. Exodus 29:36 refers to offering a חטאת concerning (על) clearing, another enigmatic construction, before commanding Moses to decontaminate the altar בכפרך. How then should we understand these diverse and enigmatic expressions?

Here, we present only a cursory examination, as a full analysis of the term כפר will be postponed until the final chapter with all the data finally available. Provisionally, כפר connotes clearing, broadly understood as the removal of unwanted impediments. First, there is a significant overlap between כפר and חטא and טהר.[158] More specifically, when present together חטא or טהר often add specificity to כפר and vice versa. Leviticus 16:30 specifies that the purpose of clearing is לטהר, i.e., in this case the clearing specifically cleanses from sins. Numbers 8:21 functions similarly, as clearing cleanses the Levites. Ezekiel 43:20 uses חטא and כפר together to specify the effects of the חטאת. Verse 43:26 adds specificity to the כפר function of the altar with both cleansing and ordination; in this instance clearing brings about cleansing, both of which occur so that the altar may be ordained and fit for service. In 2 Chronicles 29:24 one decontaminates (חטא) the altar to effect clearing on behalf of the people. In Ezekiel 45:18 and 20, חטא and כפר even seem to be used synonymously.

Second, within the dedication rituals, כפר seems to be shorthand for a much larger process as are other expressions elsewhere in the ritual. Levit-

---

[157] Cf. Blum 1990:297.

[158] Cf. Kiuchi 1987:97–99. Although they may theoretically be distinguished, חטא and טהר are often used interchangeably (Lev 14:7, 49, 52; 16:30; Num 8:21; 19:19; Jer 33:8; Ez 36:33; 37:23; Ps 51:4, 9). While clearly related, חטא and טהר nevertheless describe the operation of pollution removal from opposite directions. חטא expresses the negative side of the operation, the removal of the problem, while טהר expresses the positive outcome of the operation, the restoration of purity.

icus 8:34 abbreviates the purpose of the first day's proceedings with לכפר עליכם, which, as we have seen, includes many other elements (of which consecration is the most prominent and most anomalous). Leviticus 8:15 invites a similar conclusion. Blood manipulation both decontaminates and consecrates the altar, the purpose of which is לכפר עליו. Again, clearing seems to be a way of summing up the process, a process that does not logically include consecration.[159] Exodus 29:33 is another interesting case where eating food may even effect clearing that leads to consecration and ordination. The food which contributes to the clearing process seems to contribute to the efficacy of the larger ritual, here summed up as consecration and ordination (as in 28:41). Furthermore, in Exodus 28–29, three different purpose statements seem to be describing the same process (28:1, 41; 29:1). In the first, the purpose of bringing forward Aaron and his sons is simply to make them priests. The second adds specificity to the process, including some of the steps to bring about making them priests, namely anointing, ordination, and consecration. The third refers to the same process as consecrating them to make them priests. In each case, the complementary terms serve as a shorthand for the entire process, making priests, as they provide some specificity for how the entire process is to be achieved. In each case, the constituent parts do not logically produce the stated purpose and/or the goal described does not logically include some of the constituent parts. Consecration does not effect clearing; clearing does not produce consecration. Nonetheless, with their shorthand expressions, the Priests implicitly make such connections.

Why are the otherwise precise Priests here so maddeningly imprecise? Carelessness and the presence of multiple layers are potential culprits. However, the Priestly imprecision has a clear rhetorical effect (and may even be purposeful). The inexact shorthand that binds together otherwise discrete elements communicates that the ritual elements are interconnected and that each, in some way, contributes to the efficacy of the whole and the various subsystems that comprise it.

Clearing in Exodus 29 and Leviticus 8[160]

We may conclude that during the tabernacle dedication ceremony the daily חטאת offerings, the ordination ram, and the grain offering effect clearing,

---

[159] One may also interpret the phrase as a future-referring shorthand, one that describes the purpose of consecrating the altar, summing up that multifold purpose with effecting clearing on it (cf. Milgrom 1991:493, 524–525). This, however, is less likely since, as opposed to Ex 29, Lev 8 seems to focus exclusively on the narrative present.

[160] In Leviticus 8:15, decontamination is a synonymous subset of clearing. In Exodus 29:36, the altar is decontaminated by clearing or when clearing is effecting on it. In either

while the חטאת and עלה offerings for the priests and the people perform the same function during the inauguration of the cult.[161] How do these offerings do so, and who or what benefits from them?

In addition to marking it as holy, a primary purpose of the overall ritual is to prepare the altar for holy use. Since its primary role is to remove pollution, whether from impurities or sins, the חטאת offering is a natural choice to make the altar maximally pure. In the present ritual, it functions especially like the mouth-washing ritual in Mesopotamia,[162] in which multiple mouth-washings effect perfect purity in the divine statue.[163] Such purity is a mark of the divine realm (especially in the cultic sphere) and, thus, prepares the statue to commune with and be endowed with the divine.[164] With these enlivened faculties, the statue can fully serve as the divine presence on earth, a presence that will partake of the human offerings and respond with divine blessing.[165]

In our ritual, the multiple חטאת offerings likewise effect perfect purity in the altar.[166] Since purity (being טהור) is necessary to enter the tabernacle complex to sacrifice, it is only natural that the instrument upon which the

---

case, decontamination and clearing are intimately connected and together provide greater specificity than either could alone. In Exodus 29:33 the offerings eaten by the priests are explicitly an instrument of clearing. Leviticus 9:7 is a clear case of clearing on behalf of the people.

[161] We will not analyze the clearing function of the entire ritual (Lev 8:34), since it has already been explained sufficiently.

[162] So also like the mouth-opening ritual in Egypt and the animation ritual from Kizzuwatna. However, the purification in the Priestly dedication ritual is much simpler and more straightforward than the Mesopotamian mouth-washing ritual, which in addition to the multiple mouth-washings in multiple different contexts is surrounded by many other elements likely used to impart purity.

[163] The emphasis on purity is strong throughout the ritual. The preparation of the 'holy water basin of mouth-washing,' for example, contains elements of a purificatory nature (see further section 3.3.3.). On this interpretation, see Berlejung 1997:45; Hurowitz 2003:147; for comparative material, see Hurowitz 1989.

[164] While mouth-washing purifies the statue, thereby opening the divine conduit, mouth-opening seems to activate the divinity's faculties. The texts accompanying the ritual stress the importance of enlivening the statue's faculties. "This statue without its mouth opened cannot smell incense, cannot eat food, nor drink water" (STT 200:42–44, translation from Walker and Dick 1999:99; IT 3:70–71). Similarly, since the completion of the ritual and the very fate of the deity lay with the great gods (Ea, Shamash, and Asalluhi), the priest implores them to grant the statue the ability to eat and to hear (IT 3:6–25, 33–37 in Walker and Dick 2001:148–149).

[165] The statue can smell the incense and eat the food (Berlejung 1997:45; Hurowitz 2003:147), yet it does so in a transcendent anthropomorphic way. The participation of the statue in the rituals in some way ensures their efficacy. If the god appreciates his care, he will remain enthroned in the temple and continue to bless and protect his people.

[166] Cf. Propp 2006:460.

sacrifices are offered and through which they are accepted be especially pure to ensure its efficacy. The various חטאת offerings perfectly purify the altar in preparation for its consecration so that it can both be holy and suitably pure for divine use. Once sufficiently cleared, the altar is then prepared to be sanctified and used as a primary means of commerce between humanity and the holy divine, whereby people present offerings and YHWH responds favorably.

What then does the חטאת clear and who or what benefits from the clearing? In many instances the preposition מן follows the verb כפר, after which the text identifies the expelled pollutants.[167] Here and in Leviticus 9:7, however, the construction preposition + pollutants is missing. Although not a hard and fast rule, its absence may stem from the fact that the חטאת is not clearing any specific sins or impurities.[168] Instead, the חטאת seems to clear the altar of all traces of the mundane sphere so that it is perfectly pure and suitable for divine use.[169] The sanctification process completes the transaction from common to holy, from a piece of bronze to God's holy and effective altar.[170]

---

[167] Gane 2005:106–143; for a list of the references, see the chart on 110–111.

[168] It is also possible that the specific pollutants are simply omitted. Although his position seems less likely, Milgrom (1991:521–522) could be right in asserting that the חטאת effects clearing from unavoidable impurities of the priests. The daily clearing may even be a safeguard against possible uncleanness to ensure that the priest and altar are free from pollutants during each stage of the ritual.

[169] What other offering would be appropriate for such a task?; cf. Kiuchiv 1987:42, followed by Hartley 1992:113; Jenson 1992:156–157. S. Driver 1911:131 contends that "the altar, prior to its consecration, is regarded as affected by the natural impurity of human workmanship, which must be removed." Gane (2005:132 n. 52) rejects this proposal on the grounds that only the altar receives such decontamination. However, his critique is not decisive for several reasons. First, the offering may be functioning *pars pro toto*. By purifying part of the tabernacle complex from human impurity, the ritual in effect purifies all of the tabernacle complex. Alternatively, the divine glory may both purify and consecrate the tabernacle. Second, the altar is the primary locus of commerce between human and divine, and as such requires a heightened state of purity. Third, the altar's purification may also be somewhat prophylactic in that it receives the most human traffic and will thus be subject to the most human pollution. Fourth, it serves a rhetorical effect beyond the instrumental effect of clearing. The multiple purifications of the altar visually concretize (in a way that multiple purifications of the tabernacle interior would not) the arduous process required in making the tabernacle sufficiently pure for divine service.

[170] This may also find a parallel in the Mesopotamian mouth-washing ritual. The rituals by the river and in the orchard are clearly purificatory in nature, yet they mention no specific impurities to be removed. Since perfect purity is requisite, the ritual may be removing the impurities of human contact, after which the mouth-opening carries the process one step further.

3.3. Tabernacle Dedication and Priestly Installation

The altar is clearly the primary beneficiary of the clearing in the tabernacle dedication ritual,[171] yet it may carry additional benefits. While clearing makes the altar suitable for divine service, it seems to have a secondary effect on the priests.[172] As it becomes increasingly fit for service through clearing and consecration, the altar becomes increasingly effective in removing priestly pollution. The clearing may then progressively purify the priests so as to make them increasingly fit for divine service – i.e., free from pollutants as YHWH is free from pollutants.[173]

In Leviticus 9:7, the חטאת offerings seem to perform a similar function as in the tabernacle dedication. However, the priests and the people are the stated recipients (using בעד). Although specific sins and impurities may be in mind, it seems better to assume that the offerings enact an initial pure state sufficient to enter the tabernacle complex, which must be maintained by vigilance and sacrifice.[174] In other words, clearing removes (past) pollutants in one fell swoop so that the people may appropriately access YHWH. Where before the priests were the secondary recipients of clearing, here they move to the forefront. While their clearing may also enable a sufficient ground state, it clearly serves a precautionary function. In Leviticus 9 as in 16, when presenting an important calendric offering for the people,[175] the priests must first make sure that they are sufficiently pure to officiate so as not to annul the benefits of the people's offering. Where before the altar was the primary recipient of clearing, here it seems to benefit at most secondarily.[176] Thus, through the course of the ritual there is a transition in beneficiaries. During the initial purification and consecration stage, as it transitions from a simple object to an altar fit to effect human and divine commerce, the altar was the primary recipient of clearing. Once properly equipped for divine service, the altar could function properly and the people could receive the primary clearing benefits.[177]

---

[171] Since it is the identified recipient of clearing (using על).

[172] The priests' hand-leaning, which elsewhere identifies them as the offerers and the recipients of the ritual's benefits, provides the strongest support. The Day of Atonement, where the altar is cleared and re-consecrated is another helpful parallel, since the people and priests share the benefits with the altar (16:6, 11, 17, 33 and 18–19). Finally, something has to be the instrument of priestly clearing (Lev 8:34). The חטאת is the most logical choice (though cf. Ex 29:33).

[173] As in H, the priests' obedience in purifying themselves may contribute to their absorption of holiness.

[174] This purification may also remove expiable sins that had not been dealt with before the sacrificial system was implemented.

[175] Calendric refers to offerings that occur according to a fixed schedule.

[176] For a fuller examination of the חטאת, see chapters 6–7 below.

[177] When the altar was re-purified and re-consecrated on the Day of Atonement, it again becomes the primary recipient, with the people deriving a secondary benefit, so that it could again function properly and effect clearing on behalf of the people.

In Leviticus 9:7, the עלה contributes to the clearing function of the חטאת. As a gift, the עלה evokes the proper response from YHWH, which outside of the tabernacle context may approximate כפר.[178] When in combination with the חטאת, the gift nature of the עלה stresses that כפר (and, in the case of sin, the resultant forgiveness) is ultimately the gift of God.[179] In other words, the gift adds to the efficacy of clearing in that it elicits an appropriate response from YHWH, for without a cooperating deity, the ritual would be useless.[180]

Exodus 29:33 presents an enigmatic case of clearing.[181] At first glance, the offerings seem to function like the עלה[182] As a gift[183] both the ordination ram and grain offering seem to contribute to the clearing process by eliciting a proper response from YHWH.[184]

d) Pleasing Gift

As indicated above,[185] the עלה, the ordination offering, and the daily עלה offerings explicitly serve as a pleasing aroma (ריח ניחח), a (food) gift (אשה). Each offering adds to the efficacy of the aromatic gift, which itself adds to the efficacy of the larger ritual. As the gift of a pleasing aroma, the עלה and ordination offering evoke a favorable response from the deity.[186] As elsewhere in the ANE, it is natural to offer such 'house-warming' gifts to make the deity comfortable in his new environs, pleased with his new cadre of servants, and thus more apt to respond with blessing and secure presence.

The עלה is particularly apt in this regard. Outside of the tabernacle,[187] the עלה functions as a gift to make an entreaty, prompted by any of the

---

[178] For details, see the next section. The clearing function of the עלה is also present alone in Lev 1:4 and 16:24 and in combination here and in 14:20.

[179] See Lev 1:4, where the עלה is an acceptable gift to elicit divine clearing.

[180] For example, without a resident deity, such offerings would stop (see, e.g., the situation faced by Judaism with the destruction of the Second Temple).

[181] Milgrom 1991:1083.

[182] Whether or not the ram and the grain specifically effect clearing, they contribute to the clearing process as the priestly garments contribute to the consecration process.

[183] Ex 29:25=Lev 8:28 and Lev 2:2, 9 respectively. As we will see in the following section for the burnt offering, the grain offering also seems to "duplicate the manifold purposes of the burnt offering," likely including expiation (Milgrom 1991:196; cf. 195–202).

[184] For an alternative solution, see the following pages.

[185] Section 3.3.2.

[186] Cf. Milgrom 1991:149.

[187] It is traditionally understood to be the oldest Israelite sacrifice (for the biblical evidence, see Thompson 1963). It also has strong parallels among the Canaanites and Hittites in the latter half of the 2nd millennium (for a summary with references, see Watts 2006:134–135; cf. Milgrom 1991:174–175) and even finds its way into Assyria in the 8–

needs an individual brings before his deity.[188] As a gift, it elicits a favorable divine response (e.g., Gen 8:21). Although it does not have the same range in the Priestly texts,[189] there too it seems to function as a gift intended to elicit a favorable response. In reference to the tabernacle dedication, it functions on a general level to make YHWH favorably disposed to his new residence and his people, thereby prompting YHWH to stay and to bless the people. More specifically, it invites divine participation in the ritual. The gift of a pleasing aroma prompts YHWH to ensure that the ritual is a success, that the tabernacle and the priests are suitable for him by consecrating them with his glory (Ex 29:43–44).[190]

While the burnt offering seems to be a gift intended to elicit divine favor to ensure the efficacy of the entire ritual complex, the goal of the ordination ram seems to be more specific – to prepare the priests for divine service.[191] Like the עלה, the ordination offering, as a pleasing aroma and a gift, invites God's participation in and blessing on the ritual.

e) Important Uninterpreted Acts: The Priests and the Ordination Blood

Whether or not we can pin down the specific role of the application of ordination blood to the priests, its rhetorical effect is clear. The ordination offering (Ex 29:19–28; Lev 8:22–29) is the third sacrifice involving hand-leaning, slaughter and blood manipulation, in a sequence said to be witnessed by the populace. In each of the two previous offerings, Moses applies all of the blood to the altar. In the ordination offering, the first two elements are the same, but Moses applies the blood to the extremities of the priests before sprinkling the rest of it on the altar. Such a ritual action would have a dramatic effect on the audience,[192] which the people would notice and associate with the installation of the priests. The people would see that the priests are somehow being changed and that this change is im-

---

7th centuries (Berquist 1993:25–26; Lambert 1993:194) and into Egypt by the 4–3rd centuries (Quaegebeur 1993:329–353).

[188] Cf. Milgrom 1991:176. These include "homage, thanksgiving, appeasement and expiation" (ibid. 175; see more fully, Thompson 1963).

[189] Nonetheless, in some circumstances, it continues to effect clearing alone (Lev 1:4; 16:24) or in combination (Lev 9:7; 14:20). Even so, as a gift, it does not seem particularly appropriate for sanctifying or purifying the altar, unless it inspires God to do so himself.

[190] However, unlike at Kizzuwatna, there is no need to lure the god from elsewhere, for, according to the text, YHWH institutes the tabernacle plan, dictates the ritual, and chooses to dwell among Israel of his own initiative. Instead, the offerings appropriately honor and welcome him.

[191] As expected, ordaining the priests is the manifest purpose of the ordination offering.

[192] Gilders 2004:101.

portant, unnatural,[193] and intimately connected to the altar. In short, it would communicate that making people holy and fit for divine service requires complex and extreme means.

Both the larger and more immediate contexts provide clues to the specific function of the ritual action. When blood is applied to persons in a ritual context, it indicates a change in status,[194] in this case from common men to holy priests. More specifically, the blood is applied to the priests' extremities, which most closely resembles the application of the חטאת blood to the extremities of the altar (i.e., its horns). This visual and physical parallel suggests that the two might share a common function. Since the חטאת blood effects clearing on behalf of the altar (and elsewhere the offerer), the application of the ordination offering's blood may also effect clearing, this time on behalf of the priests.[195] The following ritual action adds support to this proposal. The application of ordination offering blood from the altar mixed with the anointing oil to the priests explicitly makes the priests holy. The ordination then follows a natural sequence in ordaining the priests. The blood applied to their extremities makes them sufficiently pure, and the blood and oil make them sufficiently holy to serve YHWH.[196]

The clearing function attributed to the ordination ram and grain offerings in Ex 29:32–33 may also be illuminating. Instead of referring to its nature as a gift, the clearing effected by the ordination ram may refer to the purification effected by applying the blood to the priestly extremities. The grain offering would then be a complementary gift that adds to the efficacy of clearing, like the עלה alongside the חטאת in Leviticus 9:7. The altar's marginal status over the course of the ritual – its gradual purification and consecration for its intended function – may provide yet another clue. If it remains unfit to be the instrument of sufficient priestly purification until it is sufficiently purified and consecrated itself, another means would be necessary. The application of the ordination offering blood to the priests may then be a substitute חטאת of sorts, which purifies in place of or in addition to the חטאת, one whose clearing ability is bolstered by the gift of the grain offering. Even though such an interpretation is highly speculative, the ac-

---

[193] Its uniqueness points to its importance and unnaturalness.

[194] Here, the blood is part of the ordination ritual, which is explicitly part of the priestly ordination. In Lev 14, the application of the blood of the אשם to the מצרע is part of the process of readmitting him into the community with access to the sanctuary. In Ex 24:4–8 (outside of the Priestly corpus), the application of blood to the people is part of the ceremony in which Israel enters into covenant with YHWH as a vassal (cf. Propp 2006:308–309).

[195] Gilders 2004:101. Milgrom arrives at the same conclusion by a more circuitous route (1991:528–529).

[196] Lev 8:34 may also have the blood ritual with the ordination ram in mind when speaking of clearing.

tion's effect is not. It makes full use of its opportunity to communicate visually and viscerally the importance and unnaturalness of the priests' change in status as well as their inextricable link to the altar in a way that no חטאת offering could.

3.3.3.2. The Cumulative Effect

Over the course of the dedication ritual, multiple and repeated actions gradually achieve the intended effect: a functional tabernacle with a functional priesthood. Washing with water and remaining at the entrance of the tent of meeting, both necessary on pain of death, bookend the ritual, thereby demonstrating the importance of correct procedure and the potential perils of approaching the God in their midst. As part of the system, even the uninterpreted actions play an essential role and hence may not be omitted from ritual performance.

The multiple interpreted actions testify to the complexity, interconnectedness, unnaturalness, and importance of the ritual system. The high priestly garments, the anointing oil, the חטאת offerings, the blood and oil, and YHWH himself each in their own ways contribute to making the tabernacle and its priests holy. Similarly, the daily חטאת offerings, the ordination ram and the remnant of the bread, in their individual ways effect clearing, so as to present the priests and the altar as perfectly pure and fit for divine consecration and contact. The חטאת and עלה offerings for the priests and people on the eighth day likewise effect clearing so that the offerings and those who present them are acceptable and effective before YHWH. The עלה and ordination offerings each serve as a pleasing aroma, a gift to YHWH, that educes a favorable response from him and his necessary participation in the ritual.

Instead of being redundant, multiple repeated actions produce a cumulative effect, making the result more complete and secure. Although not explicit, it is possible that "all rites of the first day were repeated during the entire week of consecration" to enact the gradual transition necessary to make the tabernacle and priests perfectly pure and maximally holy.[197] Even if each action is not repeated, it is clear that some do occur multiple times. The daily חטאת gradually effects clearing on behalf of the altar (and the priests), while the daily anointings gradually consecrate it, so that at the end of the seven day process the altar is sufficiently ready to function as intended and able to sustain the divine fire (Lev 9:23–24).[198] The twofold (daily?) anointing of Aaron demonstrates the gradual and maximal holiness

---

[197] So Milgrom (1991:537–540), with the possible exception of consecration of the sanctuary.

[198] Cf. Propp 2006:460.

necessary to serve God as high priest. At the end of the ritual, the multiple and repeated actions ensure that the priests and the altar are maximally pure and holy and that YHWH is maximally satisfied. YHWH's consecration of the priests and tabernacle with his glory marks both his approval and the necessity of his cooperation.[199]

3.3.3.3. The Ideology of the Tabernacle Inauguration

After the tabernacle and its priests become suitable for divine service, the inauguration of the cult serves as a preparation for YHWH's appearance (using כי [9:4]). In other words, although he has already moved into the tabernacle, chapter 9 assures the people that he will emerge from his new home to act. To elicit his visible presence, the newly ordained priests perform various offerings on the newly consecrated altar, two of which, the חטאת and עלה, effect clearing. This time the fully-functional altar may perform its intended role. It may effect clearing on behalf of the people, until the Day of Atonement when it must be re-purified and re-consecrated. Only at this point is the joyous זבח שלמים suitable.

After the tabernacle has been fully dedicated and inaugurated YHWH makes a special appearance in his glory (9:23–24). In addition to expressing God's approval of the whole process, his new home, and his new servants, the appearance of YHWH establishes a pattern. Although he will not always appear to the people in a blaze of glory to devour offerings with his flames, his appearance sets a precedent that assures the people that if they properly perform the appropriate rituals, he will make a functional appearance.[200] God will both approve of the offering and respond as promised (in the case of the חטאת, with clearing and forgiveness or cleansing). Since the larger purpose of the rituals is to maintain God's presence and blessing, his visible appearance and approval provide reassurance that God will continue to dwell among them and bless them as long as they fulfill their roles.

---

[199] This Priestly ritual is not a lone expression of such complexity. (Even in all its complexity, the Priestly ritual is more straightforward than its counterpart at Emar and the rituals animating divine statues in Mesopotamia, Egypt, and Anatolia.) For Priestly analogues, see esp. the gradual cleansing of the skin-diseased person (14:8, 9, 20). Although complex, the reinstitution of the skin-diseased person is far simpler than the tabernacle dedication. Its relative simplicity indicates its relative unimportance.

[200] I.e., even if he does not physically appear each time, he will ensure the ritual's efficacy.

3.4. Ritual Sequence and Function in Exodus 29, 40, and Leviticus 8–9

Thus far various questions remain unanswered. Why do the priesthood and altar[201] feature so prominently in Leviticus 8? Why does the tabernacle feature so minimally? Is there no fuller dedication of the tabernacle? Why does YHWH arrive before the dedication ceremony, whereas elsewhere the deity's arrival is the ceremony's centerpiece? When does YHWH's glory consecrate? What role does Exodus 40 play? Why is the altar deemed most holy?

One can first appeal to a diachronic perspective. It is possible that the ritual prescribed in Exodus 29 and described in Leviticus 8 was originally concerned with the institution of the priesthood (as reflected in the goal statements). Since the priestly institution and service are inextricably linked with the altar, it should come as no surprise that the altar figures prominently in the ritual. For whatever reason, the dedication of the tabernacle itself and its altar are not preserved or never existed. Redactors, in turn, add elements that make the priestly institution include the dedication of the tabernacle complex. More specifically, they add purpose statements relating to the altar (some even may have been embedded in the original ritual in a secondary role) and the anointing and consecration of the tabernacle and altar.[202] Thus, over time, the installation of the priests is made to include the dedication and consecration of the tabernacle complex. The other anomalies can likewise be explained as casualties of the textual amalgamations and redactions.

Unfortunately, such solutions are speculative. We may instead endeavor to explain the composite ritual and all its elements as the final (Priestly) writers envisioned it. The purpose statements in Exodus 28–29 inform the ritual, in that they serve as a meaningful shorthand for installing the cult and its functionaries.[203] In other words, when the priests speak of making priests, they mean, more expansively, making a functioning priesthood that includes a resident deity and a functioning altar. Purpose statements con-

---

[201] Appearing 11 times in Leviticus 8 (Klingbeil 1998:315).

[202] Because ritual action on the altar is already integral to the installation of the priesthood, the Priestly redactors could have easily added (more) purpose statements relating to it. However, since the tabernacle itself did not feature in the 'original' ritual, mentions of it have to be inserted and are thus kept to a minimum. This could explain why the altar features much more prominently than the tabernacle.

[203] The Priestly texts speak of instituting the priesthood, of which preparing the altar is a necessary and constituent part. In a similar process, Ezekiel speaks exclusively of ordaining the altar once the divine glory has arrived (43:18–26) since there is no need to re-ordain the priests.

cerning the consecration of the tabernacle and the clearing and consecration of the altar then are perfectly in order.

Exodus 40 serves a dual role in the process. First, divine presence is necessary before ritual consecration and clearing can be effected.[204] In the Priestly account, ritual is not automatically efficacious. YHWH must approve of and be present in some form for ritual action to achieve its desired ends. Since the priests cannot make the divine abode, its altar, and its priesthood holy,[205] Exodus 40 may only prepare for YHWH's presence by getting the house ready in terms of both structure and comfort.[206] Second, the arrival of the deity seems to be the first stage of the consecration envisioned in Exodus 29:43–44. Although not explicitly stated, we may assume that the glory consecrates the tabernacle when it fills it.[207] Such an act would then be the primary consecration of the tabernacle, since YHWH alone can suitably consecrate his house.

Although seemingly misplaced, anointing the tabernacle in Leviticus 8 logically follows the arrival of the divine presence. With the divine presence in house, Moses may meaningfully perform a consecration ritual on it,[208] thereby marking the space as divine. The tabernacle anointing at this point in the ritual has two important corollaries. First, it further differentiates the ark from YHWH, since Moses is given access to it to anoint it, yet none are given immediate access to YHWH. Second, such an anointing has a powerful effect on the onlookers. By placing the same anointing oil on Aaron and the altar as he has just placed on and inside the tabernacle, where YHWH visibly manifested his glory, Moses stresses the extreme importance of the priesthood and the cult, while establishing the bounds of his holy domain and the priestly activity in it.[209]

The institution of the cult begins in this dramatic light. With a consecrated tabernacle and God's necessary presence and cooperation, Leviticus 8 may focus on getting the cult up and running. The priesthood and the al-

---

[204] We find some evidence for the fact that the deity must be present to actualize the rituals in the locative expression mentioned repeatedly above (לפני יהוה).

[205] I.e., belonging to and suitable for the divine realm.

[206] Although they would be meaningless without divine presence, these actions do not require divine activation.

[207] Although the former is in the *piel* and the latter in the *qal*, there may be a word play here between the priestly ordination (יד מלא) and the divine glory filling (מלא) the tabernacle.

[208] His access seems to break the sequence, whereby none may enter the tabernacle from the divine arrival (Ex 40) until the cult is fully functional (Lev 9) (Nihan 2007:232–234). However, *pace* ibid. 127, it is certainly possible that Moses was granted temporary access for this function.

[209] The curtain to the court separates that domain from the world around it and serves as a boundary, where ingress is barred to the unclean but available for the clean Israelite.

3.4. Ritual Sequence and Function in Exodus 29, 40, and Leviticus 8–9

tar are inextricably linked since neither could function meaningfully alone, and thus must both receive ritual attention. Since the bronze altar is shared space and the priests are shared personnel, the dedication and inauguration of both require greater human-divine cooperation. In other words, since humanity meets with the divine at the altar and the priests mediate between the two parties, they have the shared responsibility of preparing and preserving the space for this interchange.[210] The people's participation in the ritual also stresses the importance of honoring the God in their midst through obedience.

The altar's label as most holy requires further comment. Such a descriptor naturally differentiates the altar from its surroundings, yet, in the present context, probably refers most directly to its contagious holiness. Calling the altar most holy is a warning. It stands within reach of both the people and priests yet is off limits to the former and must be accessed carefully by the latter. When improperly approached, its contagious holiness is fatal.[211]

Leviticus 9 is a fitting conclusion to the ritual complex. In addition to marking the beginning of the sacrificial cult, YHWH's approval of it and his blessing to those who make proper use of it, the appearance of glory may be a final act of consecration. The fire that emanates from his presence serves to make the altar sufficiently holy. Even if this is not the case, God's glory (anticipated in Exodus 29) nonetheless appears as bookends for the ritual sequence in Exodus 40 and Leviticus 9. By putting glory on both ends of the ritual, the text stresses YHWH's essential participation throughout. By omitting it from the rest of the ritual, the nature of his participation remains a mystery.[212] Thus, after the events of Exodus 40 to Leviticus 9, the deity is at home and satisfied, the cult is operative, and the people are blessed, at least for the present.

---

[210] E.g., in 8:15, their shared actions bring about consecration of the altar, as YHWH turns a rite that would otherwise effect clearing into an act of consecration.

[211] It seems unnecessary to refer to the most holy or contagious quality of the rest of the tabernacle since it is off limits to the people (seeing the tabernacle furniture is fatal even for the Levites [Num 4:20]).

[212] Presumably, although unmentioned, the divine consecration of the priests occurs somewhere in (or even throughout) the process.

Chapter Four

Regular Divine Service

Divine presence and divine service are inextricably linked in the ANE. After luring the deity into his earthly abode, the people seek to preserve his presence. Such maintenance often takes the form of regular (anthropomorphic) service that is both a primary duty of humanity and a primary way of eliciting divine blessing. The Priestly texts are no exception to this rule. However, the Priests cull from and adapt the common practices in such a way that their system is truly unique, both akin to and distinct from its counterparts.

4.1. Ancient Near Eastern Background

Before analyzing the Priestly solution, we will sketch the daily temple services in the surrounding cultures, from which Israel emerges and to which it responds. In the ANE, daily service addresses the care and feeding of the gods.[1] This daily cult ritual naturally follows on the heels of the animation of the divine statue and the dedication of its new home, serving to maintain the newly enshrined divine presence. In each culture, the daily care and feeding is anthropomorphic in nature, in many ways resembling the care and feeding of a monarch.[2] As the royal court exists to please the king, the divine cult exists to please the deity, including such elements as bathing, clothing, feeding, purifying, entertaining, and praising the divinely-imbued statue. Such service is not altruistic; in each culture, people serve their deity in order to elicit blessing.

In Egypt, the ritual serves as the deity's daily care, which consists of awakening, feeding, bathing, anointing, clothing, embracing, purifying, and enlivening various elements (*ba, sekhem,* and *ka*).[3] In Mesopotamia, regular service features twice-daily sumptuous meals,[4] and washing, dressing, and adorning the statue with multiple and magnificent outfits and jew-

---

[1] Oppenheim 1977:183.
[2] For a brief summary, see McCarthy 1969:167–168.
[3] Lorton 1999:131–147.
[4] Each consists of two courses, the 'main' and the 'second' (Oppenheim 1977:188).

elry.⁵ Among the Hittites, divine statues were periodically "clothed, fed, bathed (usually prior to a ritual service), entertained and their festivals were celebrated according to a regular calendar."⁶ The Syro-Palestinian evidence is sparse, yet enough hints exist to infer a similar daily ritual.⁷

4.2. How do the Israelites Maintain YHWH's Precarious Presence?

The Priestly portrait likewise features the anthropomorphic care and feeding of YHWH intended to elicit blessing, yet it does so in response to the other systems' perceived shortcomings, hoping to ensure presence and blessing while preserving divine majesty and mystery. We will begin with an overview of the Priestly attempt to maintain divine presence on a daily basis, followed by an analysis of the individual elements of regular service, according to the order in Exodus 40, with appropriate ANE parallels, and conclude with a synthesis of our findings.⁸

To understand how to maintain YHWH's precarious presence, we must return in more detail to the purpose of the divine presence and the cult that exists to serve him. In H, YHWH emancipates Israel so that he can be their new master and they can serve him in his sanctuary.⁹ Exodus 29:43–46 offers a similar rationale. The installation of the priests and dedication of the tabernacle are necessary so that YHWH may dwell among them, which is

---

⁵ Bottéro 2001:132–133.

⁶ Collins, 2005:13, 24. Although the daily regimen is less well-preserved than in Egypt and Mesopotamia, certain references point to a daily meal and make some of its elements explicit (see, e.g., Goetze 1957:162–163). For example, the Instructions to the Priests and Temple Officials refer to both daily bread and a morning divine meal (*COS* I:217, 220). At Nerik, there is even a brief text listing prescriptions for the daily rite of the temple (*KUB* 31.113; see Haas 1970 for text and translation; for commentary see Weinfeld 1993).

⁷ For example, many textile products presented to deities at Ugarit seem to indicate that either the statue was clothed and his clothes were changed frequently or that the fabrics were intended for priestly apparel (Pardee 2002:226). *KTU* 1.39 may even refer to a daily ritual.

⁸ Although festivals are also important in (pre)serving the divine presence, an analysis of them will not feature, since they serve a secondary role to the regular service and also are directed toward the people as much as (or more than) toward YHWH. Likewise, festivals as a whole do not feature in the core Priestly texts.

⁹ Joosten 1996:132, 134; Schwartz 2000:58. This is distinct from the still-popular communion model in which offerings are a means of establishing and maintaining relationship (cf. Marx 2003:111). Likewise, the tabernacle is not designed as a gathering place for an adoring congregation. The tabernacle and cult exist to serve the resident deity; relationship, blessing, and adoration are merely the benefits of this service.

4.2. How do the Israelites Maintain YHWH's Precarious Presence?

the very purpose of their deliverance from Egypt. The preceding verses add further specificity. Verses 38–42 seem to be both a purpose statement for the installation of the cultic system prescribed in verses 1–37[10] and a condition of the divine presence that arrives in verses 43–46.[11] Putting the two passages together, Israel exists to serve God in the tabernacle, and this service is typified by the twice daily food offerings. In other words, daily service of YHWH is a, if not the, primary purpose of the cult.[12]

Exodus 40 provides additional information about the all-important daily service, as it alone puts together the various elements (each a תמיד)[13] that appear piecemeal throughout the Priestly texts and connects those elements with presence. As part of setting up the tabernacle, Moses puts the bread on the table (40:23), lights the lamps (25), burns the incense (27), and offers the burnt and grain offerings (29). The subsequent appearance of divine glory serves both as a sign of approval of the construction of the tabernacle and an encouragement that if Israel regularly and rightly serves God, he will continue to dwell in their midst.[14] Thus, the various regular elements are directly related to YHWH's continued presence.

Divine presence is not the only benefit of the new servitude. With God's presence comes the possibility of blessing through obedience both by absorbing his holiness and receiving the benefit of his rule.[15] In short, the cult exists to serve YHWH, service encourages presence, and presence enables blessing. Thus, as in the rest of the ANE, regular service is of the utmost importance.[16]

This service carries with it many of the anthropomorphic elements of ANE cults; it occurs in a divine dwelling place with the appropriate furniture: a table for meals, a lampstand, and an incense burner.[17] However, instead of portraying YHWH as a transcendently anthropomorphic god like

---

[10] With special reference to the altar (cf. Houtman 2000:550).

[11] Cf. Marx 2003:105.

[12] In Exodus 25, "Israel's first task after witnessing the revelation was to build the Tabernacle." Thus, "Israel can be assured by God's presence only through his sanctioned cult and sanctuary" (Milgrom 1990:237).

[13] On the meaning of the term, see Haran 1978:207.

[14] The glory in Ex 40 sets a similar precedent to that in Lev 9. In the latter, God's glory assures the people that if they perform the proper sacrifices, God will respond appropriately. In the former, God's glory suggests that if the people correctly perform the daily service, God will continue to dwell among them.

[15] Regarding the latter, see particularly Lev 26.

[16] Its loss would be calamitous since it would signal the cessation of the cult and all benefits derived from it (cf. 2 Chr 29:5–8; Dan 8:11–13; 11:31; 12:11).

[17] Cf. Haran 1978:216–220. "It is these [ritual acts], performed regularly and continually, that give the tabernacle-temple its character of a dwelling place of the deity" (218).

the other ANE cultures,[18] the Priestly writers carefully adapt their language to minimize anthropomorphisms so that YHWH is portrayed as more transcendent than his ANE counterparts.

Ambiguity is the primary means of both ensuring the divine presence and protecting it from misunderstanding. Although often precise, the Priestly texts resort to selective ambiguity, perhaps even ambivalence, when describing the intersection between human and divine.[19] Recognizing the limits of human language in describing the divine, the Priestly writers use ambiguity, lest they misrepresent YHWH. This ambiguity is expressed by omitting certain expected elements of divine service (e.g., meat to accompany the bread on the table) and by inserting simple purpose statements without embellishment (e.g., the purpose of the bread is to set it before YHWH for seven days). Without symbolic purpose statements, with minimal anthropomorphic ones, and without certain key elements, YHWH's service, and thus YHWH himself, is distinguished from ANE royal and divine analogues.

This ambivalent language is especially pronounced the closer one gets to YHWH's presence, since his presence and the service in his abode determine how he is understood.[20] As we have seen with descriptions of the divine presence and the dedication of the tabernacle and as we will see with the divine service, the Priestly writers take great care in describing these elements in order to portray YHWH as accurately as possible. Since YHWH, by definition, bursts the confines of human language, accuracy paradoxically requires ambiguity. Concrete enough to be meaningful, descriptions of divine service are not so concrete that God is conceived of as like a human or, worse yet, a human-made statue. The language is thus practical enough to detail the people's service and the deity's response, yet equivocal enough to preserve his transcendence. Such equivocation yields a wholly other God who precariously overlaps with humanity instead of a human-like deity at home with, yet above, his human servants.

This ambiguity also has a pragmatic rhetorical effect for the deity and his priests. In ritual contexts, ambiguity is a powerful device. The presence of simple purpose statements – e.g., the purpose of a ritual action is to obey the deity – without elaborating on its effect reinforces ritual authority and ritual necessity. With only a simple tautological goal statement, the

---

[18] The transcendently anthropomorphic ANE deities are depicted like humans but in a transcendent way, thereby establishing their superiority (over both each other and their human subjects).

[19] Even in their ambiguity, they are often more precise than their non-Priestly counterparts in the Bible and the ANE, as we have seen. The Priestly writers are careful in their language, whether that language is concrete or ambiguous.

[20] Although the people's role is precisely enumerated, the Priestly writers are unwilling to presume to understand the divine role or, worse still, to misrepresent it.

ritual will never fail to meet its goal. Without an ideological or even instrumental explanation, the ritual is likewise difficult to challenge and its interpretation is open to debate. Although, or perhaps even because, interpretations vary,[21] all of the participants will agree that the ritual is necessary since there are no grounds to challenge its efficacy. Thus, the deity is served and the priests keep their important status as his servants.

4.3. The Individual Elements

4.3.1. Bread of Presence

4.3.1.1. Structure

The bread indexically connects three parties hierarchically: YHWH, the priests, and the people. The bread is placed before YHWH (the privileged recipient), by the priests (the privileged servants), and merely supplied by the people. The offering of the frankincense as a gift to YHWH parallels the consumption of the bread by the priests (Lev 24:7, 9), thereby indexing a special connection between YHWH and the priests while privileging both over the ordinary Israelites. When juxtaposed with 'before (לפני) YHWH,' the name itself (לחם ה[פנים]) also seems to specify proximity to the deity.[22] Whereas the offerings on the outer altar are simply called food (לחם) (Lev 3:11, 16; 21:6, 8, 17, 21, 22; 22:25; Num 28:2, 24; cf. Ez 44:7), the bread placed on the golden table is called bread (לחם) of presence. Other than the material and method of presentation, the major difference is location – the outer altar versus the table in the outer sanctuary. However, despite the difference, both are simply located before (לפני) YHWH. The appellative 'presence' then serves as a descriptor, specifying the greater proximity of the bread of presence to the deity inside the divine abode.[23] Alongside the bread, there is at least a hint of an accompanying drink offering, yet unlike the bread there is no explicit connection between the drink and the deity. Finally, the use of 'pure' to describe the frankincense (זך) and the table (טהור) highlight the extreme importance and requisite purity of the materials in the outer sanctuary (Lev 24:6–7).[24]

---

[21] The purpose may be ascribed to ineffable divine mystery or to often competing arcane theories.

[22] Gane 1992:180–182.

[23] Ibid.

[24] The appellative זך occurs only with items used exclusively inside the sanctuary and, as such, seems to be a status marker (cf. Haran 1978:164 n. 30; Milgrom 2001:2086–2087). טהור may be interpreted both literally and figuratively; the table is made of unalloyed gold and its purity is a status marker, since only the best, purest metal befits the home of the holy God (cf. Propp 2006:380 in reference to Ex 25:11).

In Exodus 25:29 and 37:16 (cf. Num 4:7), the last two items mentioned are libation vessels.[25] However, it is unclear where they may have been used since Exodus 30:9 explicitly forbids pouring a drink offering on the incense altar and golden vessels are used exclusively in the tent.[26] We may appeal to a diachronic solution that minimizes anthropomorphisms in stages: 1) a drink offering was originally performed on the incense altar (especially if one reads Num 28:7b as referring to such an offering in the outer sanctuary); 2) the drink was merely placed before YHWH and imbibed by the priests; 3) the libation vessels remained empty.[27] It is also possible that the vessels, at least in their final textual form, were meant to carry other liquids, either water for washing or the oil for the lamp.[28] Gane offers a harmonistic solution in which he interprets the preposition ב in the phrase אשר יסך בהן as "into," thus rendering the entire phrase "into which shall be poured." Drawing from Numbers 28:7, he interprets the שכר in the second half of the verse as a daily accompaniment of the libation on the outer altar in the first half of the verse.[29] Although there are no (other) examples of non-functioning cultic equipment,[30] it is even possible that the libation bowls were intended (in their final form) to make a point. The empty cups would visually communicate better than the absence of such cups that YHWH is different than the other gods and does not require a drink. In the end, the existence and meaning of the drink offering remain a mystery.

4.3.1.2. Use

The *causa* for the bread-laying itself is unclear, although, as outlined above,[31] it is one aspect of the regular service aimed at maintaining divine presence. The people offer it and the priests bring it into the tent for the purpose of setting it before YHWH on a weekly basis (Ex 25:30; Lev 24:8). The accompanying frankincense is YHWH's token portion of the bread,[32] his (food) gift (Lev 24:7). The bread is an eternal covenant related to the people (24:8) to be consumed by the priests as their portion of the deity's (food) gifts (24:9).

4.3.1.3. Ideology

In the ANE, divine meals are transcendently anthropomorphic in that they resemble and transcend human, particularly royal, meals. In Mesopotamia, for example, texts often use the term *naptanu*, meaning "a big formal meal," to describe both divine and human meals.[33] At the same time, the meal is not consumed by the deity in the traditional sense. In the ANE,

---

[25] Cassuto 1967:339.
[26] Milgrom 1990:26; id. 2001:2092–2093.
[27] Milgrom 2001:2093; cf. Haran 1978:216–217.
[28] Propp 2006:397.
[29] Id. 1992:183–189.
[30] Ibid. *apud* Milgrom.
[31] See section 4.2.
[32] Regarding the translation of אזכרה, see Levine (1989:10 and n. 7) and Milgrom (1991:181–182) who arrive at a similar conclusion from different directions.
[33] Lambert 1993:194.

since a deity often exists beyond the realm of human perception, he consumes the food in a way that humans cannot perceive.[34] Once the deity is finished with his meal, his servants are permitted to eat the leftovers. Instead of building on this foundation, the Priestly writers challenge the basic assumption that YHWH requires such a meal so as to limit anthropomorphisms. Thus, although anthropomorphisms necessarily remain, the Priests limit them to such an extent that YHWH is more transcendent than the other ANE deities.

As in the ANE, a table[35] with food placed inside the divine dwelling-place suggests that it is intended as a divine meal. Although nowhere explicitly denied, various factors militate against so facile a comparison. Here, ambiguity is the primary means of doing so. The present text is both concrete enough to identify the food as a gift to YHWH, thereby establishing his presence and the regular service required to maintain it, and ambiguous enough to minimize the ANE anthropomorphisms, thereby preserving his mystery.

If consumed daily by YHWH, the bread would be substantial in quantity, roughly 3.5 times the normal human meal.[36] However, such a meal would not be of substantial quality, with none of the luxury, variety, or frequency of its ANE counterparts. In Mesopotamia, the divine repast includes the four elements of a worthy meal in Mesopotamian 'society' – beverages, grain products, fruit, and meat – all in gargantuan portions.[37] The presence of meat from the herd, the most valuable foodstuff in Mesopotamian society,[38] highlights the importance of the god being served. In Egypt, texts and reliefs testify to the ample quantity, rich variety, and excellent quality of the food and drink offerings.[39] Hittite meals likewise are rich in quantity, quality, and variety. As in Mesopotamia and Egypt, the presence of rare meat is a clear sign of status.[40] Among the Israelites, while other sacrifices require expensive meat, the bread of the presence is simply bread, the staple food (and thus can simply be called 'food' [לחם]). As a meal, it has none of the grandeur or variety of its ANE counterparts and, if a meal, might imply that YHWH is less important than his divine rivals.

---

[34] In Mesopotamia, his consumption of the food takes place behind a curtain, hidden from human eyes; cf. Oppenheim 1977:192.

[35] Elsewhere in the Bible, tables are associated with altars to such an extent that tables may be called altars and altars called tables (Gane 1992:182).

[36] Contra Milgrom (2001:2096), the deity's daily portion would be approximately (.2 ephah per loaf x 12 loaves)/7 days or ~.34 ephah per day (Lev 24:5), ~3.5 times the size of a normal human portion of .1 ephah (Ex 16:16, 36).

[37] Bottéro 2001:128.

[38] Sigrist 2004:330–331.

[39] Englund 1987:57; cf. Willems 2004:327.

[40] Beckman 2004:337.

Moreover, the bread is never said to be consumed by the deity. The presence of the libation vessels would add weight to the meal theory, yet there is scant evidence that they are ever used for libations, let alone as a drink to accompany the bread.[41] Without a complementary beverage, the bread would not be a fit meal even for a common Israelite. Thus, although the text is ambiguous enough that we cannot rule out the possibility that the bread is intended as a divine meal, it is concrete enough to demonstrate that, whatever the bread presentation may be, it diverges from a traditional ANE divine meal. Instead of building on the model of a royal meal and making it better to accommodate the deity, the Priestly bread presentation co-opts certain elements of a meal while calling into question whether it can be conceived of as a meal at all.

Even if not a full divine meal, is the bread still consumed by the deity? As a (food) gift to YHWH presented before him in his home, the bread is clearly connected to the deity.[42] However, it is unclear if the bread is anything more than a gift. The priests consume the bread, yet it is unclear if YHWH partakes of it first like the other ANE deities. The token portion, also present in grain offerings, is burnt to YHWH while the priests eat the rest. Since the token portion is frankincense and not bread, it would seem that the bread is presented to and before YHWH for seven days and then given by him to the priests for their consumption. More than simply being a ritual divested of some of its anthropomorphic overtones, the bread also plays a positive role as an eternal covenant between YHWH and the people.[43] Even so, although we may argue that YHWH does not eat the bread, we cannot eliminate the possibility; for the text is silent about what happens to the bread over the seven days, and it is explicitly YHWH's food gift. Indeed, if the text wanted to demonstrate that the bread was not eaten by the deity, it could simply say so. The fact that it does not implies that

---

[41] Whether or not they were offered at all, it seems clear that libations were never offered in tandem with the weekly bread of presence (Gane 1992:189), thus putting additional distance between the requisite elements of a meal.

[42] Although a bit of a stretch, the phrases לפני יהוה and לחם פנים(ה) may also add to the ambiguity. Interpreted literally the phrases can be translated 'to YHWH's face' and 'face bread' and hence may be connected with the divine visage. As the glory conjures up a concrete yet mysterious presence, YHWH's face may indicate a partial presence that does not necessarily encapsulate the whole (cf. Ex 33:11, 14–15, 20). It could be a "projection of his anterior aspect into our three-dimensional realm" (Propp 2006:619; cf. 687). Thus, the terminology may at once ensure some form of divine presence and leave the nature of that presence a mystery.

[43] Gane 1992:192. The number twelve also connects the loaves to the twelve tribes, and thus the bread offering is a "pledge of the covenant between the twelve tribes and the Lord" (de Vaux 1961:422, followed by Milgrom 2001:2094).

the ambiguity serves a different purpose than to deny divine consumption.[44] As above, we may only conclude that, whether or not it is eaten by the deity, the presentation of the bread before YHWH deviates from the standard ANE divine meal.

The ambiguity of the drink offering further muddies the waters. It is never connected with the bread, and it is never poured out before YHWH. However, if the drink is presented to YHWH in a cup, one may argue that he partakes of it in an immaterial sense. Again, all we may conclude is that presentation of a drink, if it exists at all, is not a libation and thus differs from most ANE drink offerings.

In the end, although clearly a divine gift, it is unclear whether the bread is a divine meal. Such selective ambivalence serves a dual function. The bread as gift highlights YHWH's practical presence and the priestly service necessary to maintain it, while the ambiguity of the meal protects YHWH from unnecessary anthropomorphisms and preserves divine mystery.[45] Although similar to a divine meal, the Priests omit key elements of such a meal and any specific reference to divine consumption in order to differentiate the bread presentation from human and divine analogues. In other words, the bread presentation connects YHWH to other deities, while the presentation's otherness highlights God's transcendent otherness.

At the same time, although clearly distinguished from a typical meal, the bread is placed in the divine dwelling before YHWH himself. Thus, although undefinable, the bread highlights the presence of the deity and the need to serve him in his abode. Below,[46] after examining the daily offerings on the bronze altar, we will return to the question of YHWH's need for and consumption of food with more resources to offer a more comprehensive explanation.

4.3.2. Light

4.3.2.1. Structure

Like the bread, the lamp and its oil indexically connect the same three parties hierarchically. The people bring the oil to the tabernacle wherein the priests tend to the lamps that burn before YHWH (Ex 27:20–21; Lev 24:2–

---

[44] It is also possible that the Priests assume the anomalies are sufficient to prove that the bread is not a divine meal. However, this is unlikely because the default position in the ANE is to consider a food gift as a divine meal. To refute this position would require more than mere insinuation. Finally, it is possible that later (Priestly) redactors minimized the anthropomorphic statements of their source text yet were not bold enough to overtly deny that the bread was consumed by YHWH.

[45] Both the nature of the deity's presence and the nature and fate of his food gift remains a mystery.

[46] Section 4.4.

4). Like the frankincense and the table, the oil is pure (זך) as are the lampstand and its utensils (טהור) (Ex 25:31, 38–39; 27:20; 31:8; 39:37; Lev 24:2, 4), thereby marking the superior quality of the materials in the divine abode and the superior importance of their owner.[47]

4.3.2.2. Use

The *causa* for the lamp is clearly associated with the regular service and the divine presence. More specifically, the purpose of the lamp and its oil is to light the outer sanctuary[48] before the presence of YHWH (Ex 25:37; 27:20–21; Lev 24:2–4). The people's and the priests' roles, bringing the oil and tending the lamps so that they burn from evening until morning respectively, are a perpetual statute (Ex 27:20–21; Lev 24:2–3).

4.3.2.3. Ideology

While their explicit purpose is to provide light, it is unclear whether the lampstand and its light carry additional ideological freight. The intricate design of the lampstand suggests such an interpretation, yet the text nowhere makes this explicit or even implicit. To fill in the gaps, various proposals have been made that fall roughly into two categories: astral and botanical.[49] While such elaborate theories may fail to convince, it is hard to deny the connection between the light and divine presence.[50] Although there is no clear archaeological parallel to the Priestly lampstand,[51] the use of light in the divine abode is pervasive in the ANE.[52] This should come as no surprise since, in P and the ANE, a suitable home, i.e., one where the deity resides, needs light. More than that, the lit lamp indicates that YHWH is at home, and may even indicate that he remains ever-watchful.[53]

---

[47] The oil is also כתית, 'crushed,' and thus of the finest grade (Cassuto 1967:369–370; Durham 1987:379; Propp 2006:427). In addition to its rhetorical effect, the quality of the oil may also serve a practical purpose, namely the elimination of impurities so as to minimize smoke damage to the curtains (Stager and Wolff 1981:97).

[48] More specifically the space in front of the lampstand (Ex 25:37).

[49] For a summary of these possibilities and the possibility that both could be operative at once, see Propp 2006:510–512. Gerstenberger (1996:356), followed by Milgrom (2001:2088), alternatively suggests that "God forfeits none of his power, even if the sun itself 'goes down.' The lamp before the holy of holies extends this daylight symbolically through the darkness, signalling thus God's unbroken life: in this sense, it is an 'eternal light.'" Although they have some merit, none of the theories are ultimately convincing.

[50] Ex 25:37, 27:20–21 and Lev 24:2–4 make the same connection indexically.

[51] Propp 2006:509–510.

[52] For example, in the Hittite temple of Nerik, the priests also light the lamp from evening until morning (Milgrom 2001:2089).

[53] Cf. Gen 1:3.

4.3.3. Incense

4.3.3.1. Structure

As above, the incense indexes a hierarchical relationship between God, priests, and people. The priests bring and burn it before YHWH in his sanctuary (Ex 30:6–8, 36; Lev 4:7), while the people have no explicit contact with the incense.[54] Again, as above, the incense is pure (זך) as is the altar it is burned on (טהור), thus highlighting the extreme importance of the deity and his tabernacle. In addition to being pure, the incense is also called סמים, perhaps meaning 'fragrant,'[55] which is likely another way of illustrating its importance.[56]

4.3.3.2. Use

As above, the *causa* for the incense is clearly associated with the regular service and the divine presence.[57] The purpose of the altar is to offer the prescribed incense (Ex 30:1), namely the fragrant incense (7) whose composition is described in verses 34–36 and whose use is restricted to the divine realm (37–38). Aside from the application of the חטאת blood (30:10; Lev 16:18), the altar has no other use.[58] Aaron is commanded to burn this holy incense (30:35–37) every morning and evening (7–8). Since the effect of the incense is here unstated, we turn to other explanations in the Priestly literature to help fill in the gaps. In Leviticus 16:13, the incense covers the כפרת when Aaron approaches to prevent his death. In Numbers 17:11–15, incense effects clearing (כפר) on the people's behalf.

4.3.3.3. Ideology

a) Incense in the ANE

In general, like the Priestly עלה, incense is a pleasing gift to the gods intended to evoke a favorable response and thus has multiple uses. In Egypt and Mesopotamia, incense may be purificatory, apotropaic, propitiatory, or

---

[54] Moses is commanded to make the incense (Ex 30:34–38), while Bezalel is credited with having done so (37:29). However, the text does not specify where the ingredients come from. As elsewhere, we may assume that the people provide them.

[55] So most major translations.

[56] Although (*pace* Haran 1960) the fragrant incense does not seem to be exclusive to the tent (Nielsen 1986:69–70; Heger 1997:88–96), the term סמים, as well as the incense's status as YHWH's exclusive property, highlights its importance (cf. Nielsen 1986:70).

[57] Cf. Houtman 1992:463; 2000:463.

[58] Burning meat, meal, or strange incense and pouring liquid on the altar are all strictly prohibited (Ex 30:9).

mediatory.⁵⁹ Its unique nature and accompanying connotations also add contour to its various uses.

In the ancient world, odor is important.⁶⁰ The aroma of incense both attracts the gods⁶¹ and invites a favorable divine response to human entreaty. If the deity is angry, incense appeases his wrath, e.g., leading to forgiveness of sins. If the supplicant is in need of direction, it evokes a positive oracle.⁶² More than simply being pleasant, incense is also divine air.⁶³ Like the gods, incense is free from (olfactory) impurity, and, hence, its odor is associated with divinity. In Egypt and Mesopotamia, for example, by shrouding himself in incense, the priest becomes god-like and thus fit to enter the divine presence.⁶⁴ Lest humanity's relative impurity come into contact with the pristine deity, those who approach then must be cloaked in the divine aroma.⁶⁵ The people are thereby purified of their bad odors⁶⁶ so that they may access the divine presence. At the same time, the deities are protected from bad (human) odor by the surrounding cloud of incense.⁶⁷ Similarly, incense purifies the environment to ensure that the divine presence is safe from evil influences.⁶⁸ In short, incense serves to purify people and places, in order to protect the deity from pollutants and to please the

---

⁵⁹ Nielsen 1986:3–15, 25–33; id. 1992:3:405–406.

⁶⁰ Houtman 1992.

⁶¹ For a Mesopotamian example, see the Atrahasis (III.iii.31; iv.21–22) and the Gilgamesh epics (XI.159–161).

⁶² Nielsen 1986:30 regarding Mesopotamia.

⁶³ Houtman 1992.

⁶⁴ Cf. Nielsen 1986:9, 31. Egyptian wordplay demonstrates this reality: "burning 'incense' (snṯr) for the god could 'deify' (snṯri) the king" (Bell 1998:174).

⁶⁵ In the Egyptian pyramid texts, incense ensures that, upon death, the king takes his place among his divine brethren since his "scent is as their scent, [his] sweat is as the sweat of the Two Enneads" (Utt. 412). Similarly, the king says, "my sweat is the sweat of Horus, my odour is the odour of Horus" (Utt. 508; Nielsen 1986:9).

⁶⁶ Or at least these odors are masked, which by ANE standards is practically equivalent.

⁶⁷ Thus, it is no wonder that in Mesopotamia, "incense burners always are placed between the deity and the suppliant" (Nielsen 1986:32). In Canaanite temples as well, it seems that incense burners stood before the cellae or niches that housed the divinity (Propp 2006:512–513).

⁶⁸ In the Egyptian daily ritual, it purifies the cult statue as the deity awakens and is enlivened (see, e.g., the text from Medinet Habu in Nelson 1949:221). It is also especially associated with processional festivals, acting to purify the environment, thereby protecting the deity (and the populace) from rampant impurity and clothing him in the appropriate scent (cf. Nielsen 1992:405). In the Mesopotamian akītu festival, it purifies Marduk's temple on the fifth day in preparation for his arrival, cloaking it in good air that dispels evil influences, including the corruption of bad smells (cf. Nielsen 1986:32).

deity to produce a favorable response to entreaty.⁶⁹ "Most important, incense is simply to be enjoyed,"⁷⁰ and is thus a necessary luxury in the deity's abode to ensure his pleasure.⁷¹

b) Incense in the Tabernacle

The incense of the tabernacle does not explicitly have any of the above ANE uses. Instead Aaron is simply commanded to offer it to YHWH as part of the regular divine service, a command that, if improperly followed, has dire consequences.⁷² However, although nowhere explicit, we can draw inferences from elsewhere in the Priestly texts and by comparison with ANE practice.

Most simply, the incense is burnt to ensure YHWH's presence and pleasure. As in the ANE, it seems to be aimed at pleasing YHWH so that he responds favorably to whatever ritual action the people perform. However, although such a use seems straightforward, it is puzzling to note that the incense (קטרת) used in the tabernacle is never called a gift (אשה) or a soothing aroma (ריח ניחוח), whereas offerings on the bronze altar are frequently called both.⁷³

As in Mesopotamia and Syria-Palestine, the placement of the incense altar between priest and deity suggests that it serves as a mediatory bridge between the two. On the rare occasion when the priest moves beyond the incense altar, the incense must accompany Aaron so that he does not die. As in the ANE, the incense seems to provide a cloak of 'good air,' one whose scent, unlike in the rest of the ANE, is exclusive to the divine realm. On one hand, the incense protects the supplicant by adorning him in the

---

⁶⁹ Nielsen repeatedly contends that incense carries human prayer to the gods. Although an Egyptian pyramid text speaks of the dead king ascending to the sky "on the smoke of the great censing" (Utt. 267; Nielsen 1986:9), it seems better to conclude that incense draws the gods to human prayer – i.e., its scent attracts their attention and puts them in a favorable mood to receive entreaty – and protects the human and deity from each other (esp. when incense is offered in a temple, where the deity is already assumed to be present).

⁷⁰ Propp 2006: 513; cf. Nielsen 1986: 89–100. Conversely, approaching the deity, like anyone else, with a foul smell is simply bad manners (cf. van der Toorn 2004b: 500–501).

⁷¹ Incense was a luxury item in wealthy ANE households (Houtman 1992:463; id. 2000:582).

⁷² "In Leviticus 10, the right people (the priests Nadab and Abihu) use the wrong materials and die; in Numbers 16, the wrong people (Korah the Levite and his followers) use the right materials and die" (Propp 2006:475; cf. 2 Ch 26:16–21).

⁷³ The frankincense (לבנה), an ingredient in the incense (קטרת), however, is referred to as a gift (אשה) and a soothing scent (ריח ניחוח) when offered with the grain offering (e.g., Lev 6:8). The frankincense of the bread of presence is also a gift (אשה) (Lev 24:7).

divine aroma, in a sense purifying him from his relatively impure odor.[74] On the other hand, it protects YHWH from bad odors by ensuring that he only inhales his divinely chosen perfume.[75] In essence, the fragrance forms a miniature atmosphere that separates YHWH from the world around. To preserve that atmosphere, one entering must be shrouded in his fragrance. More than simply being an olfactory shield, the incense cloud also forms a visible barrier that at once shrouds and locates the divine presence (Lev 16:13), thereby assuring presence while protecting the priest from too close an encounter with that presence.[76]

Although anomalous in the Priestly texts, the use of incense in the Korah incident and its aftermath has some strong affinities with its ANE counterparts. Elsewhere in the Priestly texts, incense never effects clearing nor is it used outside of the tabernacle context. As such, the use of incense in Numbers 17 appears to be the Priestly solution to the need for clearing outside of the tabernacle.[77] Since offerings are not acceptable without the tabernacle altar[78] and clearing is anomalous, if not impossible, without the tabernacle and its resident deity (from a Priestly perspective), Aaron's incense burning brings the tabernacle to the problem.[79] In doing so, the Priestly texts seem to draw from the ANE processionals in which bringing the divine aroma outside of the divine abode purifies the environment. By placing a curtain of the pleasant divine aroma between the living and the dead, Aaron appeases the divine wrath and wards off the plague. Thus, the incense in the tabernacle, like that in the ANE, seems to be mediatory, purificatory, apotropaic, and propitiatory. Why then are these ideological uses never made apparent? Why is the tabernacle incense never called a soothing scent or a gift?

As above, the text seems to be laconic to avoid unnecessary anthropomorphisms in the sanctuary.[80] The Priestly writers are careful with their use of language so that their audience understands YHWH's use of incense,

---

[74] The perfect purity achieved by the priestly dedication is insufficient. To approach the deity, the priest must also smell like him (cf. Houtman 1992:464).

[75] Ibid. 463–464.

[76] Perfect purity and perfumed scent are likewise not enough to approach the deity unobstructed. The incense cloud too must serve as a visual barrier to allow the wholly other God to encounter his holy priests. The cloud also carries with it the connotations of the divine cloud (see chapter 2).

[77] Milgrom translates כפר here as "make appeasement" (1991:142).

[78] Cf., however, the Red Heifer in Num 19 for an anomalous חטאת.

[79] The use of incense is also a form of poetic justice, since the same incense that brings destruction when used by unauthorized personnel averts destruction when used by the authorized priest (Midrash Aggadah).

[80] As we will see, such anthropomorphisms are more acceptable outside of the tabernacle, since they are not as closely associated with divine presence.

like his presence, to be different, both assured and beyond adequate explanation. The text clearly states that incense must be burnt appropriately before YHWH to ensure presence and prevent disaster. However, YHWH's connection with the incense remains unstated so as to avoid the implication that YHWH is like an ANE noble or an ANE god. By making the incense a divine command, the Priestly writers suggest that incense cannot be used to manipulate the deity.[81] Instead, offering incense is simply a form of obedience. Its effect upon YHWH likewise may be inferred, yet the offerers may not presume to fully understand it lest they limit him.

In addition to being less anthropomorphic, the Priestly understanding of incense also makes YHWH more transcendent than his ANE counterparts. In the ANE texts, incense at times protects the deity from evil influences.[82] In the Priestly texts, since YHWH will not tolerate a rival, the incense instead protects the people from YHWH. It explicitly effects clearing on behalf of the people to avert YHWH's wrath (Num 17:11–13) and covers the כפרת to save Aaron's life (Lev 16:13).[83] In the end, the presence of incense suggests divine presence and pleasure yet does so in a way that preserves YHWH's transcendence, a transcendence that exceeds that of the other ANE gods. Instead of having divine rivals or evil influences to ward off, incense protects the divine atmosphere from the natural smells of this world, which are an affront to his nostrils.

4.3.4. Burnt, Grain, and Drink Offerings

4.3.4.1. Structure

The offerings index a hierarchical relationship between the people who bring the offerings (Num 28:2), the priests who offer them (Ex 29), and YHWH who receives them (Ex 29:38–46; Num 28:1).[84] Like the oil for the lamp, the oil for the grain offering (מנחה) is of the finest quality (כתית). By implication, since the regular מנחה as described in Leviticus 2 does not have the same descriptor, the oil for the daily offerings is of a higher quali-

---

[81] Although it is only natural to assume that YHWH inhales its fumes, the text does not make this explicit, since such a connection, especially in the divine home, would "drag the deity down on a human level which P could not accept" (Nielsen 1986: 76; cf. Dt 33:10 for such an anthropomorphic association).

[82] E.g., incense wards off evil influences in the *akītu* festival and the divine enemy, Seth, in the Egyptian pyramid texts (Utt. 29; Nielsen 1986:8).

[83] In the latter case, although the priest is maximally pure, God's extreme otherness is such that Aaron may not behold his presence nor may he enter the inner sanctuary without an olfactory shield of the divine fragrance.

[84] As indicated above, the burnt, grain, and drink offerings are connected with presence. They are offered before YHWH, where he will meet with them (Ex 29:42–43) and where he will dwell among them (45–46).

ty,[85] thereby highlighting the importance of the mandated regular service over that of individual offerings. The absence of frankincense further distinguishes the daily grain offering from that described in Leviticus 2.[86]

4.3.4.2. Use

The purpose of the bronze altar is to offer lambs, grain, and drink twice daily (Ex 29:38–41). These offerings are God's offering, food, soothing aroma, and (food) gift (Ex 29:41; Num 28:2),[87] and they must be offered at the appropriate times (Num 28:2).

4.3.4.3. Ideology

In the ANE world, burnt offerings seem to be largely a West Semitic and Hittite phenomenon that eventually found its way into Mesopotamia and Egypt.[88] However, the analogous West Semitic rites do not have much explanatory power beyond establishing the antiquity of the practice.[89] Thus, the investigation of the complex of rites at the bronze altar will be largely internal to the Priestly texts, with broad comparisons by analogy.[90]

In the Hebrew Bible, the Priestly texts combine two offering systems – derived from a cult place and a divine abode, respectively – into one interconnected whole.[91] Nevertheless, the union is not entirely seamless. With

---

[85] So Milgrom 1990:239.

[86] If Milgrom is correct (1991:389–391) that there is no priestly prebend, which seems reasonable especially in comparison with the priestly grain offering (Lev 6:16), this would indicate another difference from the individual's grain offering.

[87] Individual burnt and grain offerings also function as a pleasing aroma, a (food) gift (Lev 1:9, 13, 17; 2:2, 3, 9, 10, 16).

[88] For the antiquity and dispersion of the practice, see section 3.3.3.1.d. n. 187; Watts 2006:134–135. This discrepancy could perhaps be explained by the nature of the West Semitic cultures. The Mesopotamian and Egyptian communities had long had centralized power and a centralized cult. However, in the more precarious West Semitic societies, it would be more necessary to attract divine attention and favor without a temple. Thus, the West Semites developed the burnt offering whose pleasant aroma wafted to heaven and attracted the deity. Since this was so prevalent a form of worship, it was also incorporated in temple worship. Although not mentioned in the texts, such sacrifices nonetheless may have been offered in Egypt and Mesopotamia outside of the royal cults for the same reasons as their West Semitic counterparts. Either way, burnt offerings are not entirely alien to the Mesopotamian culture (cf. the starving gods in the Gilgamesh Epic gathering around the offering like flies [XI:161]).

[89] E.g., the lack of interpretive statements. Instead, the evidence from the biblical texts has often been used to fill in the gaps in ANE practice, especially regarding method and function (cf. Weinfeld 1983:106–109).

[90] In many ways, the closest counterpart to the rites performed at the bronze altar is to be found in the 'care and feeding' of the gods in the temples.

[91] Cf. Haran 1978:219.

the two systems also come two spheres of activity,⁹² whose respective rites overlap.⁹³

Often identified as the oldest Israelite sacrifice,⁹⁴ the עלה continues to be offered at shrines throughout the land down to the time of Hezekiah or Josiah.⁹⁵ Rather than entreating God in his dwelling, the altar is a "pipeline to heaven."⁹⁶ Along with the grain offering, it aims to attract the deity's attention and approval so that he will respond favorably to human entreaty.⁹⁷ If accompanied by a drink offering, it constitutes a full meal.

When attached to the divine abode, however, the altar takes on a horizontal as well as a vertical dimension. In addition to being a pipeline to heaven, the bronze altar is a liminal zone between heaven (the divine presence in the inner sanctuary) and earth (the Israelites and their camp).⁹⁸ Likewise, although the Priests truncate the range of meaning of both עלה and מנחה, the offerings made at the bronze altar continue to function as a gift intended to elicit a favorable divine response.⁹⁹

Whereas the bread of presence is clearly food and a divine gift, yet not necessarily divine food, the daily offerings on the bronze altar are explicitly YHWH's food (Num 28:2; cf. Lev 3:11, 16; 21:6, 8, 17, 21, 22; 22:25; Num 28:24; Ez 44:7). Likewise, whereas the incense is curiously never referred to as a pleasing aroma or a gift, burnt and grain offerings are called both. What then accounts for the distinction between the inner and outer

---

⁹² Ibid. 206; see, e.g., Ex 28:43, 30:20, and 40:32.

⁹³ Instead of simply being the unwanted consequences of an unnatural amalgam, the overlap of rites and functions serves a practical purpose. Whereas the regular service inside the sanctuary takes place beyond the reach of the ordinary Israelite, the common person could watch and vicariously participate in the daily service at the bronze altar. He would thereby have access to and be able to take ownership of the regular divine service. These regular, tangible offerings naturally came to signify divine presence and a functioning cult. In turn, as long as they were offered, all was presumed well in the divine abode (cf. Dan 8:11).

⁹⁴ See section 3.3.3.1.d. n. 187.

⁹⁵ Haran 1978:15–16, 64–65, 132–135, 219.

⁹⁶ Propp 2006:499; cf. Jdg 13:19–20; Levine 2000:371.

⁹⁷ See section 3.3.3.1.d. pp. 86-87 and n. 188. In essence, the עלה was a "signal directed at the deity, residing in heaven, in an effort to get him to respond and to approach his worshipers, or to do their bidding from the distance of his heavenly abode" (Levine 1974:22).

⁹⁸ Cf. Propp 2006:501. Although not necessarily intentional, the juxtaposition of these two directional orientations lends an additional air of mystery, or at least another layer of complexity, to the divine presence, as offerings are at once sent upwards to God in heaven and westward to God in his earthly sanctuary. Thus, it would seem that in P, as in Zion-Sabaoth theology and D and Dtr, God is present on earth and in heaven simultaneously.

⁹⁹ See sections 3.3.3.1.c.1 and 3.3.3.1.d, esp. nn. 183, 188–189. Its function with regard to the daily ritual remains to be determined.

rites? It is possible that the reference to divine food is merely a fossilized vestige, a remnant of a ritual practiced at a shrine whose practitioners were less careful in their language, or simply believed the deity needed nourishment.[100] Although this theory may account for the origin of the term, it does not account for its use in the present context, in the complex Priestly adaptation of various discrete elements to form a coherent whole.[101]

The nature and location of the two zones and their respective rites provide the interpretive keys. Because the 'food' at the bronze altar is distanced from the deity in form and space, there is less danger in calling it 'food,' or a soothing aroma or (food) gift. It is not offered inside the divine abode, nor is it consumed in anything resembling a normal sense (i.e., it is vaporized rather than laid out before royalty). Offered in the court, the burning meal ascends to YHWH in heaven and in his dwelling, who presumably partakes of the smoky vapor through inhalation.[102] The divine inhalation of the immaterial food both signals divine acceptance of the offering and differentiates the food offered from a normal meal; inhalation also identifies both the manner in which YHWH partakes of it and that it is YHWH himself who does so. Likewise, albeit a full meal, the divine meal is "restricted to the essential staples of the Israelite diet:" the most affordable meat and the three most abundant crops, wheat, wine, and oil.[103]

By contrast, excising 'feeding' and 'inhaling' language from the sanctuary, whether or not such practices are implied, preserves the mystery of the deity in his abode. Outside of his dwelling place, at the bronze altar, divine mystery is not as threatened by anthropomorphic identifications, rendering such language comparatively innocuous. However, even in this realm, the Priests are careful in their use of language. As vapor, the divine repast cannot be confused with a human meal. As vaporized simple fare, it cannot be considered a sufficient meal for the deity.[104] Instead, as we will see, it is a meal of ambiguous nature that carries with it ideological freight.

---

[100] So Milgrom 1991:213 and *passim*.

[101] It is unpalatable to simply excise troublesome texts without sufficient evidence by labeling them fossilized vestiges; it is equally troubling to resort immediately to a symbolic interpretation (e.g., the midrash concludes about the pleasing aroma that "it is not because I eat or drink that I told you to offer sacrifices, but on account of the aroma which should remind you that you must be sweet and pleasing to me like a pleasing aroma" [*Num. R.* 21:19, implicitly condoned by Milgrom 1990:238]).

[102] Although not explicitly inhaled, the odor of burning flesh and meal is a pleasing aroma that the deity naturally smells. "What else would ethereal beings...eat, if not translucent, intangible, gravity-defying vapors (see Jdg 13:9–23; Iliad 8:550–52)" (Propp 2006:499; cf. Levine 2000:402).

[103] Milgrom 1990:487; so already Abravanel.

[104] If it were considered YHWH's daily meal, then it would fail to differentiate YHWH from the people. Moreover, it would differentiate YHWH from the other deities in that the other deities would have better food.

4.4. What is YHWH's Relationship to His Food?

Elsewhere in the ANE, the gods partake of the food prepared by their servants. However, this food is of a different kind and consumed in a different manner from human food. It is not 'eaten' as such, but consumed in an immaterial sense, beyond the purview of human perception.

Although each culture agrees that the gods consume the meals, it is less clear that the deities need the meals to survive. In Egypt, divine meals are both a requirement and source of divine nourishment that enables the divine *ka* to inhabit his earthly body. Instead of signaling death, a failure to meet these basic needs would precipitate a withdrawal from the statue in the same way that Tutankhamun alleged that the deities abandoned Egypt when their cult was neglected by Akhenaten.[105]

In Mesopotamia, humanity exists to serve the gods, a primary responsibility of which is to provide food. The mythological and literary epics, most particularly Atrahasis (III.iii.31; iv.21–22) and Gilgamesh (XI.159–161), suggest the potential starvation of the gods without the proper human sacrifices.[106] However, as is often the case, hymns and cultic literature seem to paint a different picture. Although these texts do not address the deity's need for human nourishment directly, their language and content suggest that the deities have no such trivial needs.[107] Given that the latter texts are prone to flattery, it seems preferable to conclude that Mesopotamians believed that the deity requires nourishment. However, if humanity fails to provide such nourishment, the deity will not wither and die. Instead, he will be forced to abandon his opulent lifestyle and literally work for a living.

In the Priestly texts, the bread in the tabernacle and the meat, grain, and wine offered in the courtyard seem to be two complementary meals. Nevertheless, since the divine food is divested of many of its anthropomorphic associations and associations with ANE temple practice, one wonders why the Priests mention food at all. Why not bring some other gift to the deity to ensure his presence?

Although nowhere stated explicitly, the Priests' food offerings are appropriate in context and as a point of contrast. Because YHWH's service in

---

[105] See the Restoration Stele of Tutankamun (Urk. IV 2027; Schlögl 1983:86). While away, if the deity needed nourishment of some sort, he would have to see to it himself.

[106] See also the widespread fear of starvation among the deities at the threat of a strike by the lesser gods (Bottéro 2001:99).

[107] They express henotheistic tendencies, addressing the subject of the hymn or the object of worship as if he is the only and all-sufficient god. Such expressions are expected, as one is most likely to receive blessing from a deity if one extols that deity in the warmest terms.

the tabernacle resembles so closely its ANE counterparts, Priestly adaptations of that service are a particularly effective way of distinguishing YHWH from his divine counterparts. Likewise, in a farming and herding society, what better way to serve God than with produce and livestock?[108] The concept 'feeding' likely functions on multiple levels, beyond establishing his presence and eliciting his pleasure. From one perspective (for example that of Ps 50:12–13), likely not alien to the Priestly writers, all of the world's bounty already belongs to God (cf. 1 Chr 29:10–22). Thus, in offering sacrifices people are not giving him something he does not already have.[109] Perhaps then God accepts human gifts as a token of devotion to him as a king would accept gifts from his vassals, a token that, even though it is rightfully God's already, costs people something to give. On another level, gifts to God may also be a simple act of daily remembrance, harking back to God being the one who feeds and sustains them.

If such food is the primary means of service, it follows that YHWH would recognize their service by 'eating' the food in some way. Perhaps such a meal is a divine condescension similar to a parent eating a "simple meal prepared and proudly presented by [his] child."[110] The presence of food, light, and incense may also serve another ideological agenda.[111] The elements in the outer sanctuary may be a way of expressing hospitality (cf. Gen 18). Given the limited resources at their disposal, these elements take on greater meaning, as they are all the people have to give and what they cannot survive without (with special reference to bread). Even though God does not need bread, light, or incense, he will accept offerings in human language, the only language available to his worshipers. These mundane actions thus may transcend the mundane and reach the divine.

While YHWH consumes the pleasant fumes of the burnt, grain, and drink offerings, he may even deign to offer the bread of presence to the priests lest he be confused with other (anthropomorphic) deities. Whether or not he eats the food, the Priestly language is ambiguous enough for him to preserve his transcendent mystery. In other words, although YHWH accepts and enjoys the offerings, thereby establishing his presence and suggesting his blessing, he does so in a way that keeps his majesty and mystery intact.

While YHWH seems to consume his people's offerings, it is clear that he does not need them to survive. In other words, although YHWH may

---

[108] Cf. Marx 2005:50, 77–80, 86–87, 202–204.

[109] Cf. Gane 2005:321.

[110] Propp 2006:507; cf. Janzen 1997:198.

[111] Assuming they communicate analogically to try to approximate a transcendent reality, it follows that these elements may communicate multiple messages, especially given the limited and purposive choice of resources.

need nourishment of some sort, he does not need it from his people. There is no hint that YHWH went hungry before he built the tabernacle, nor is there a sense that he needs to dine off the substances of this world, for he predates the earth's creation (Gen 1).[112]

4.5. Access for Divine Service

In the ANE, access to the temple and the deity present within it seems restricted to the privileged few. However, those few have regular access to the divine presence and are charged with his care and feeding, much like (yet differentiated from) service to a human king.

In Egypt, common people have access to the courtyards but not the temple interior.[113] In principle, the king oversees the daily care and feeding of the gods; in practice, however, he delegates most of the officiating to the priests. The priests who officiate must be pure and covered with an aromatic shield of incense. In Mesopotamia, "only the priests and, within limits, the ruling family and highest officers of state would be allowed to enter and participate in" the daily care and feeding of the deities.[114] Although entrance is restricted, priests with daily access are nonetheless numerous.[115] Among the Hittites, access is granted exclusively to the king and queen, the priests and the priestesses, all of whom must be especially pure.[116]

In the Priestly tabernacle, clean common people may access only the courtyard, the liminal zone between the divine abode and the Israelite camp. They cannot, however, touch the altar, since it is most holy and serves as a boundary, both vertically and horizontally, between heaven and earth. The priests alone, who have become holy through ritual action and proximity to the deity, can officiate in the most holy realm and access the divine abode (heaven on earth). The high priest may encounter the divine presence in the inner sanctuary only once a year to effect clearing, with extreme caution, perfect purity, and a dense cloud of incense.

---

[112] Cf., e.g., Psalm 50:12–13: "If I were hungry, I would not tell you; for the earth ands its fullness are mine." Likewise, offerings offered by those with displeasing conduct or intentions may not be accepted (Isa 1:10–17; Jer 6:20; Amos 5:21–27; Pro 15:8), thus suggesting that offerings are not necessary for divine survival.

[113] Bell 1998:163–172; Gee 1998:29–32.

[114] Lambert 1993:193. "A general term for the temple clergy is ērib bīti (enterer of the temple), a person authorized to enter (all parts of) the temple" (Westenholz 2004:293), thereby distinguishing them from the general populace.

[115] The most numerous group of priests "was that of the purification specialists, charged with maintaining the holiness of the statues, the sacred objects, and the sacrosanct area of the temples; they also offered sacrifices and libations" (ibid.).

[116] Haroutunian 2004:299–300.

Although similar in some respects to ANE conceptions, the intersection between human and divine is governed by stricter regulation in the Priestly texts. As in the ANE, those who approach must be pure and cloaked in the divine aroma. However, unlike in the ANE, none may directly access the divine presence in the tabernacle. Priestly service is generally restricted to the bronze altar and outer sanctuary. When the high priest enters the inner sanctuary, he may neither touch nor behold the divine presence lest he die. His only role is to effect clearing for the sanctuary (Lev 16:16). Thus, the Priestly texts control and restrict contact with the deity much more than their ANE counterparts, rendering YHWH more transcendent, more untouchable, more dangerous, and less needy.

4.6. Synthesis

In the Priestly conception of Israel, as in the rest of the ANE, regular divine service is paramount. Israel exists as a nation to serve YHWH, and the cult is the locus of this service. Proper service encourages presence, which in turn facilitates blessing.

As elsewhere, cultic service consists of the care and feeding of the deity. However, in the Priestly texts, care and feeding is more distant than its ANE counterparts both spatially and conceptually. On a spatial level, none have direct and intimate access to the divine presence; the priests are merely responsible for keeping his home in order. What YHWH does within his sanctuary remains hidden.

On a conceptual level, the simple, and at times circular, purpose statements and the lack of key elements obscure the meaning and nature of the service in the sanctuary. The text informs us that the purpose of the bread is to set it before YHWH on a weekly basis; the purpose of the lamp is to provide light; the purpose of the incense altar is to offer incense. It never mentions why YHWH wants or what he does with the bread, the light, and the incense. In essence, when asked why, the text answers, "Because YHWH says so."

When we attempt to overcome the lack of purpose statements and put the pieces together, our efforts are frustrated. Too many pieces are missing, and those that we have provide conflicting evidence, such that we cannot reach concrete conclusions. The bread is a prime example. It is a gift to YHWH, yet, although large in quantity, it lacks diversity and quality. Furthermore, the text is silent about whether or not YHWH consumes the meal, while explicitly stating that the priests eat it at the end of the seven days.

4.6. Synthesis

In each case, the text speaks of what the priests must do to maintain the divine abode and keep YHWH satisfied. However, what YHWH does in his own space on his own time with his own things is his business. On a practical level, the servant must simply obey his master; he does not have the right to invade his master's space or to fully understand his purposes.[117] Likewise, although holy, the priests must keep their distance lest YHWH's extreme holiness destroy them. In turn, YHWH has significantly more privacy than the other ANE gods, rendering him more otherworldly and less conceptually accessible.

On a conceptual level, the text is concrete enough to ensure proper service and to indicate that YHWH makes his home among his people, yet abstract enough to prevent misunderstanding and misinterpretation.[118] At the bronze altar in the courtyard, there is less danger of anthropomorphic misunderstanding than in the sanctuary, especially since smoke carries YHWH's food heavenward for immaterial divine consumption. Given the anthropomorphic elements already present in the sanctuary, the well-adorned double-roomed tent with bread on a table, a lamp, and incense, the Priests must tread more cautiously. In order to accurately approximate YHWH and his appropriation of human service, they must render both irrevocably enigmatic. More than simply being laconic, P seems to intentionally frustrate attempts to reach any conclusions regarding YHWH and his nature beyond those that they explicitly communicate. Since in P, selective ignorance of YHWH is far preferable to misunderstanding him, the Priests both present the audience with a mystery and ensure that it is unsolvable. The mysterious deity they depict thus seems superior to all ANE rivals precisely because he is more elusive.

---

[117] This factor may be used explain why biblical and ANE texts about temples are preoccupied with human behavior, even though the temple is primarily conceived of as the divine abode. Because the tabernacle is the divine abode, the Priests may not presume to regulate what YHWH does within his own home, especially since he is superior to them both socially and ontologically. Instead, the rules of the house in the Priestly texts and the ANE naturally focus on the appropriate way for guests to access divine space and to interact with the resident deity. Since they are in his space, they must follow his rules. What YHWH and the ANE gods do inside their homes is their business. Since humans may not presume to understand, regulate, or enumerate divine actions in divine space, divine conduct is commonly mentioned only when it is necessary to ensure that the guests behave appropriately.

[118] Ironically, it uses misunderstanding (i.e., mystery) to prevent misunderstanding YHWH. While the text necessarily employs human terms, it renders YHWH ineffable so that he cannot be encapsulated by those terms.

Chapter Five

Damage Control in the Ancient Near East

As we have seen, the Priestly writers render YHWH less accessible and more mysterious than his ANE counterparts. He transcends the created world; thus, his presence in it is unnatural. Maintaining this presence requires recreating heaven on earth or, more accurately, the closest approximation of heaven given the available materials, according to his exact specifications. Those who serve him in it must obey stringent requirements, including maximal purity, i.e., being without any imperfection. Even then, physical distance must remain between deity and human servant. Like the dwelling place itself, the language used to describe YHWH and his tabernacle is merely an approximation. As in the spatial realm, this language must be used carefully without any hope of encountering or encapsulating the divine in all his plenitude.

What place, if any, is there for human frailty in this precarious system? The mixture of absolute, otherworldly perfection with human imperfection is both unnatural and perilous. In the textual world, this danger is not merely theoretical. For Nadab and Abihu, YHWH's holy priests, it is all too real (Lev 10:1–2). How then can the system continue to function without dissolution, without breaking up the carefully established paradigm of service → presence → blessing? Is there any hope for 'sinners' or a 'polluted' sanctuary? In other words, how does damage control function for both individuals in the system and the system itself?

Although intimately connected, our analysis of damage control nonetheless will be divided into three chapters. To provide an appropriate contextual foundation, chapter 5 will investigate damage control within the ANE before we turn to the the Priestly texts. Chapter 6 will address individual and communal sin (Lev 4–5) and impurity (12–15) removal rites, followed by an investigation of Clearing Day (Lev 16).[1] Chapter 7 will conclude with an analysis of the rhetoric and implications of the Priestly system, an examination of its key terms, and a synthesis of the Priestly and ANE systems.

---

[1] Rather than continuing to employ the traditional rendering 'Day of Atonement,' I henceforth translate the ritual complex in Leviticus 16 as 'Clearing Day,' from יום הכפרים, lit. 'day of clearings' in Lev 23:27 (the plural כפרים is alternatively interpreted as a superlative, complete purgation [Snaith 1967; Milgrom 2001:2022; cf. GKC 124e]).

5.1. The State of Scholarship on ANE Damage Control

In my research, I have not encountered an exhaustive study on any one ANE culture, let alone all.[2] When they have been undertaken, systematic studies rarely have addressed both temple and community rituals. Likewise, most studies on community rituals have been selective, examining only aspects of the system. In Egypt, for example, many studies have focused on incantations and the relationship between 'magic' and medicine, but few have tackled ritual actions.[3] Much work also remains to be done with regard to the many Hittite rituals.[4] In Mesopotamia, studies have largely focused on the various ritual series instead of pursuing a more systematic account.[5] Although based on a fuller investigation, space will allow only an unnaturally synthetic summary of the ANE material due to the breadth, complexity, and variety of the material, and the relative lack of systematic scholarly examination. Nonetheless, despite its limitations, the following sketch yields important results that help to better illumine the Priestly material.

5.2. The Gods' Relationship to Creation and its Inhabitants

Two factors particularly influence ritual practice throughout the ANE: the deities' relationship 1) with humanity and 2) to the world. First, while there is a functional interdependence between human and divine, intimacy is not built into the equation. In Mesopotamia, for example, humans are created solely to serve the gods and meet their basic needs.[6] The gods, for

---

[2] Wright's work (1987), for example, addresses the individual rites that most closely resemble Israelite rituals, instead of focusing on the Hittite and Mesopotamian systems as a whole (he does, however, provide a helpful survey of Hittite purification techniques [31–44]).

[3] One reason for this is that most of the data about ritual procedures comes from other sources, textual and archaeological (Borghouts 1978, VIII–IX). For an attempt to redress this situation, see in particular Ritner 1993; cf. Sauneron 1966.

[4] Laroche (1971) lists 111 different rituals, which do not include numerous other cultic texts; for an overview of 'magical' rites with texts, see Ünal 1988:71–85.

[5] For the *Šurpu* series, see Reiner 1958; cf. Reiner 1956; for the *Maqlû* series, see Meier 1937; for a convenient English summary, see Abusch 1987–1990; for the *Bît rimki* series, see Læssøe 1955; see Caplice 1974 for the *namburbû* texts.

[6] This position finds abundant expression in "hymns, prayers, historical texts, royal inscriptions, and art, but it appears most unequivocally in a number of Sumerian and Akkadian myths" (Wiggermann 2000:1859; cf. ibid. 1860–1861; Bottéro 2001:38). In fact,

their part, provide a measure of protection and provision in order to ensure continued service. Among the Hittites and in Syria-Palestine, as in Mesopotamia, a master-slave relationship best characterizes the divine-human intersection.[7] In Egypt, despite the mutually beneficial cult, there is significant separation between humanity and the gods.[8] Thus, throughout the ANE gods are not obliged to provide remedies for human ills, nor even to enumerate their wills.

Second, although the ANE gods possess great power and are shrouded in considerable mystery, they are part of the created world, and thus subject to its vicissitudes. In Egypt, for example, although they remain superior and often inaccessible spatially and conceptually, the gods nonetheless are confined to the ordered world.[9] They are thus embroiled in the struggle to maintain its order against the various chaos forces that encroach upon it.[10] As part of the cosmos, its fate determines their own. As part of a polytheistic hierarchy, preserving the cosmos is a constant and joint venture, one in which humans have a role to play. In Egypt, chaos is the ever-present enemy of human and divine alike threatening to topple world or-

---

the creation of humanity is a secondary solution, initiated to relieve the lesser gods of the burdens for which they go on strike (see, e.g., the summaries in Wiggermann 2000:1859–1861; Bottéro 2001:97–103).

[7] Regarding the Hittites, see Furlani 2000:1935, 1938, based primarily on the text 'Instructions for Temple Personnel' (*CTH* 264; *ANET* 207–210; *COS* 1:217–221); Gurney 1977:2; Beckman 2000:531; McMahon 2000:1989. This is especially clear in the *Plague Prayers of Murshili II* and the *Instructions for Temple Personnel* (Popko 1995:131–132; McMahon 2000:1988; Collins 2007:177). Regarding Syria-Palestine, see Wright 2004: 175; cf. Gröndahl 1967:150; Korpel 1990:306.

[8] In order to explain the current disarray on earth, Egyptian mythology claims that, although human and divine originally dwelt together, evil in creation (attributed to human rebellion or Seth) brought about separation (Meeks 1999:120; Assmann 2001:6, 17–19, 113–116). This separation is mitigated by the presence of the divine *ka*-spirit in the king (Bell 1985; id. 1998:137–144), who is often depicted in intimate commerce with the deities, especially from the New Kingdom onward. However, the average citizen is far removed from this reality, for whom the gods are distant and other (cf., however, the increased intimacy with the gods beginning in the New Kingdom [Assmann 2001:189–244]). Indeed, "Egyptian temple religion remained, for the most part, a series of performances for the elite" to which the commoner had minimal access (Spalinger 1998:260).

[9] Hornung 1983:166–170, 186–196. At times, however, Amun gains a degree of transcendence (Tobin 2002a:18–20); see further Akhenaten's anomalous Aten.

[10] Although they may withdraw to locales inaccessible to (living) humans, gods may not withdraw from the ordered world. Only chaos may be truly called transcendent, since it dwells outside of the ordered cosmos and ever seeks to infiltrate it (cf. Hornung 1983: 195). Regarding the Mesopotamian gods, see Kawashima 2006. According to Wright (2004:179), Syro-Palestinian deities are also immanent in creation.

der.[11] In the divine realm, for example, Re has to nightly overcome the serpent Apep (Apophis), his chief enemy, who is one of the primary threats to order.[12] Within the human sphere, the king helps to preserve order by serving the gods and presenting them with the eye of Horus and *maat*, both representing what is "sound and perfect."[13] In Mesopotamia, the rule of the gods is especially contested beyond the nation's borders by such inimical forces as demons, monsters, rebellious mountains, dangerous seas, and barbarians.[14] Although there is room for significant strife in the Mesopotamian divine community,[15] too much upheaval of the divine hierarchy has cosmic consequences.[16] Humans, in turn, may influence the divine sphere primarily through the cult. In Ugarit as well, the gods at the center clash with monstrous powers at the periphery in a perpetual push-and-pull exchange, the outcome of which determines the fate of humanity.[17] Among the Hittites, as in Egypt, Mesopotamia, and Ugarit, preservation of the cosmos requires the cooperation of its deities.[18] Withdrawal of any god's services leaves the entire system in turmoil.[19] Redressing this rift often requires the joint efforts of both humanity and the gods.[20] Thus, the fate of the world remains an ever-relevant issue for both humanity and the ANE gods that requires constant attention.

---

[11] Hornung 1983:172–185, 195, 212–216; Quirke 1992:70; Tobin 2002b:239–246; Robbins 2005:1.

[12] Tobin 2002b:242–243, 245.

[13] Englund 2002:279–280; see, e.g., Quirke 1992, chapter 3, entitled "Preserving the Universe: Kingship and Cult."

[14] Wiggermann 2000:1857; on the issue of and interchange between gods of the center and inimical forces of the periphery, see further id. 1996:207–220. Although the threat of monstrous enemies in Mesopotamia, like Tiamat, largely has been averted in the past (unlike Yamm and Mot in the Ugaritic Baal Cycle, who continue to plague Baal), some danger nonetheless remains, from these divine foes and especially from internal strife.

[15] As most Akkadian myths attest.

[16] Excessive turmoil naturally invites encroachment by divine enemies. Disaster from within, however, is perhaps the greater threat (see esp. the myth of Erra and Ishum [*COS* I:404–416], in which Erra's rebellion against Marduk threatens to unsettle the world order [cf. the title given by Foster 1995:132ff : *How Erra Wrecked the World*].

[17] See, e.g., Smith 2006. As in Mesopotamia and Egypt, humans participate in this cosmic interchange by means of the cult.

[18] McMahon 2000.

[19] Ibid. 1982; id. 1989; Collins 2004a:404; cf. Beckman 1989:105.

[20] Collins 2007:178.

5.3. Damage Control in the Ancient Near East

Because of divine and human vulnerability, removal of various evils is naturally important for both parties. However, sanctuary removal rites are seldom related to individual rites.[21] Human imperfection is anathema to the divine realm, lest it offend or infect the deity. Likewise, given the nature of their relationship, deities are not bound to help free their servants from various evils, much less allow those evils into the divine sphere. Instead, human imperfection must be dealt with before contact with the deity or simply denied.[22] Thus, although necessary, human purification rituals are usually absent from, perhaps even inimical to, the temple system.

Although such rituals are not part of the temple system and, as such, do not ensure divine attention or assistance, the participants still often require the god's help to ensure the removal's success. Since a ritual is not automatically efficacious, it often requires divine participation,[23] which has to be elicited outside of temple channels. The method of communication hence differs inside and outside the temple. In a temple context, there is no need to invoke the deity since he is already presumed to be present, nor does he need to be especially coerced to fulfill his role, since ritual action in the temple is explicitly for his benefit.[24] Outside of this sphere, however, the gods may not be present and so need to be both invoked and convinced to act. Thus, the same hymns that are performed inside the temple as a greeting to an already present deity serve, in the domestic realm, as a means of coercing an absent deity to appear and respond favorably to human entreaty.[25] In turn, the efficacy of the ritual depends to a large extent

---

[21] The only significant overlap between purification in the human and divine spheres is the regular purification of temple officials before an encounter with the divine, so as to increase the purity of those who approach to a level suitable for the divine sphere. Various forms of purification are mandated and performed in the temple precincts (as a sort of liminal rite) before entry into the divine abode. Thus, although connected, human and divine purification are clearly differentiated.

[22] More than simply removing imperfection through purification, at times it is necessary to deny it altogether. Such denials (negative confessions) are not uncommon, yet confessions of guilt seem to have little place in temple rituals. See the Mesopotamian king's negative confession in the *akītu* festival. In Egypt, see the negative confessions from the *Book of the Dead* 125, which takes place during the final judgment where it is determined whether or not the deceased may enter into the divine sphere, and in daily cult ritual (*COS* 1:56–57). The Hittites seem to borrow negative confessions from Mesopotamia (Popko 1995:133); cf., however, the Akkadian penitential prayers that may have been recited during temple liturgies (Seux 1976:169–201).

[23] See, e.g., Maul 1999:126 for Mesopotamian evidence from the *namburbû* rituals.

[24] Cf. Borghouts 2000:1775.

[25] Cf. Assmann 2004:350–351 regarding Egypt. However, in the so-called magical incantations (*Beschwörungen*), the gods are not always directly invoked. Instead, in Egypt,

on the strength of the suppliant's case.[26] In other words, the suppliant has to convince the deities that it is worth their while to help, and, in the process, must take great care to avoid infecting the divine with his pollution.[27]

5.3.1. The Nature and Source of Evils

Before outlining the various ANE removal rites, we will sketch the nature and sources of the evils. In the temple context, imperfection cannot be tolerated. It acts as a malevolent force that affixes itself to sancta and must be removed for the system to work. The source and nature of such evils are often left unstated (at least in the ritual texts), as many of these rites are simply blanket removals that are prerequisite to the larger purpose of the rituals, whether installation, service, or celebration. In addition to being more laconic, there are far fewer texts describing temple rituals than individual rituals (perhaps because temple rituals are more esoteric[28] and simply because of the sheer number of human problems). Nonetheless, we may infer from the texts that the sources of pollution in the temple are similar to those in the communal sphere, i.e., human, demonic, and divine.[29]

As in the temple, regardless of its source, evil is a destructive force that attaches itself to and afflicts the individual. In Mesopotamia, for example,

---

the ritual actor may take on a divine role himself (his words are said to be the 'emanations of Re' [Ritner 2002a:194]). Such divine circumvention cleverly "expresses the (binding) will of supernatural powers by impersonating them" (Borghouts 1978:x), and thereby co-opts their coercive powers. Even then, the ritual practitioner could not profitably act without knowing the divine will. In Mesopotamia, the *āšipūtu* (the ritual actions and incantations to be performed by the *āšipu* [ritual specialist; alternatively physician (Scurlock 1999; cf. Avalos 1995:157–167)]) are understood to be the instructions of Ea/Enki to his son Marduk (cf. Lambert 1962), which priests could then imitate. Nonetheless, although they are divine decrees, such incantations often retain a petitionary tone (see, e.g., Reiner's summary of the *Šurpu* series [1958:1–2]; while they are cast as instructions of Ea to Marduk [tablets V–VII], the series remains plaintive; cf. the similar interplay in the *Maqlû* series). In the end, the 'magical spells' are simply another way of securing divine participation and power.

[26] See, e.g., Lebrun 2004:359 for Hittite evidence; Maul 1999:126 for Mesopotamia; regarding Egypt, cf. Borghouts 2000:1775.

[27] Because a high level of contact with the divine is necessary to convince the deity to reverse a portentous omen, the suppliant in the Mesopotamian *namburbû* rites must be especially careful in keeping his impurity separate from the gods (e.g., he cannot touch the purified earth; he stands instead on a carpet behind the offering altar at a safe distance from the deities, which serves to channel impurities into the ground after a favorable judgment [Maul 1999:127]).

[28] See, e.g., the statement that the ritual is a secret of the temple in ll. 33–35 of the *akītu*; line numbers according to the composite Babylonian text in Linssen 2004:215–237.

[29] Milgrom (1991:256–267) unnecessarily reduces the evil influences to the demonic sphere, likely to clearly differentiate the Priestly system from its ANE counterparts.

an omen does more than refer to a future evil. The object bearing the omen itself is already imbued with evil energy that afflicts its recipient.[30] Likewise, sin is both an act that leads to evil and an evil stain that must be removed.[31] In Egypt, *bwt* refers to both evil itself and the actions that lead to it (including sin and contact with anything labeled *bwt*).[32] Among the Hittites as well, actions may lead to pollution (*papratar*).[33] Evil is a (necessary) result of certain actions, whose effects must be reversed.

Suffering, whether presently felt or anticipated (usually through omens), physical, emotional, or economic, is evidence that one is afflicted. Sources of affliction include human sin, contact with impurity, and/or the displeasure of the divine, the demonic, the dead, or other humans exercising witchcraft.[34] In Mesopotamia, for example, illnesses entail a state of impurity, and mental disturbances, such as a nightmare, are likewise defiling.[35] Although derived from different sources, sin and impurity, which feature in the Priestly system, have functionally the same result: evil affixes itself to and afflicts the person.[36]

5.3.2. Removal Rites

Given their injurious nature, much attention is devoted to removing these evils. Although there is some variance, the goal of such removal rites is the return to a state of (relative) wholeness, often translated as purity. In Egypt, purity (*wab*) is the absence of *bwt*. That is, the pure individual or object is free from any of the various manifestations of evil, "whether this-

---

[30] For example, in an evil omen borne by a dog, "the evil (*lumnu*), which according to the omen would later harm the person, already inhabited the dog (sent by the angry gods) and the dog then infected the person and his surroundings by means of the sinister energy that emanated from it. The danger of infection was considered to be so great that the evil (*lumnu*) penetrated into a person even if he had not touched the dog or animal or object, but had only seen it" (Maul 1999:124).

[31] Van der Toorn 2004b:500.

[32] Frandsen 2004:497; cf. id. 2000.

[33] Beckman 1989:106; Collins 2004c:504; id. 2007:178; cf. Popko 1995:82; *CHD* P 103–106.

[34] See, e.g., Abusch 2004a:355, id. 2004b:457 for a similar list from Mesopotamia; for Egypt, see Sternberg 2004:455, though there is little evidence for witchcraft (Borghouts 2000:1782); for the Hittites, see Beckman 2004:336; Collins 2007:178–179. Among the Hittites, there is less evidence of the demonic than in Mesopotamia (Wright 1987:261–263).

[35] Van der Toorn 2004b:501.

[36] In many cases, evil is equated with impurity. In Egypt, purity (*wab*) is explicitly the absence of *bwt* (roughly translated evil) (Frandsen 2004:498). Thus, impurity (*abw*) entails *bwt*, both the evil stain itself and the act that causes it (see van der Toorn 2004b: 499–500 for similar Mesopotamian evidence). Among the Hittites, *papratar* is translated variously as pollution or impurity (see Collins 2007:178–179).

worldly or other worldly, social or cosmological."[37] In Mesopotamia, purity (most often *ellu*) "stands for perfection and integrity – moral, physical, spiritual, and social."[38] Purity also involves a brilliant, shining quality[39] that visually demonstrates a person or object's freedom from imperfection, much like a glistening floor shows that it has been freshly cleaned.[40] Among the Hittites, the adjective pure *(parkui)* refers to an object being unalloyed, namely, free from any imperfections, and to a person who is free from contaminants, and thus physically clean and/or ritually pure.[41]

In Egypt, removal rites seek to co-opt and apply *heka*, the "all-pervading coercive power" responsible for creating and maintaining the world, to the situation at hand to achieve wholeness.[42] Although expressed differently (and often less clearly) elsewhere, the principle is largely the same; Mesopotamian and Hittite rites seek to harness the various, often divine, powers in the world that may be potent enough to redress their problems.[43] Naturally, there are multiple means of enlisting these powers to achieve wholeness, often even within a single removal ritual. Thus, as in other ANE rituals, practitioners often adopt a maximalist approach to ensure ritual efficacy.[44]

5.3.2.1. Temple Removal Rites

Temple removal rites generally operate according to a fixed schedule; maintenance rituals occurring as the need arises and crisis management rites are the primary exceptions.[45] Fixed temple rites aim to achieve perfec-

---

[37] Frandsen 2004:498

[38] E.g., "the candidate for the priesthood must be pure in the sense that he should be of noble descent and have no chipped teeth, bruised limbs, or other physical imperfections" (van der Toorn 2004b.500). In both Mesopotamia and Egypt, the proper scent is also necessary for purity.

[39] Ibid. 499.

[40] Thus, it is no surprise that the Priestly writers use such imagery to describe the divine glory.

[41] *CHD* P 163–166.

[42] Assmann 2004:350. Such coercive power in Egypt and elsewhere is often translated as magic. Here, we avoid such a term because of its different and often negative modern connotations and the problematic dichotomy commonly drawn between ancient religion and magic.

[43] For example, in Akkadian, the Sumerogram ME ('divine power, divine order') is occasionally used for *parṣu* ('rite, cult') (Linssen 2004:19), suggesting that rites employ divine power and may enact divine order.

[44] Cf. Avalos 1995:227.

[45] For example, in Mesopotamia, the restoration of a temple and the repair of its kettledrum takes place when necessary (the text merely specifies 'in an auspicious month, on a favorable day'), and involves various protective rites. The temple restoration ritual contains lamentations, offerings, and libations to appease the anger of the gods whose

tion befitting the divine sphere, so that its occupants (the gods) and their representatives (the kings) may continue their unfettered rule and humans and deities may continue their mutually beneficial commerce. Such rituals are obviously in the best interest of the gods, so there is no need to coerce them to participate. The removal of imperfections forms a regular part of, and is often a necessary prelude to, temple rituals. In Egypt, the daily cult ritual involves continual purifications of the divine statue, especially with water, incense, and natron.[46] In fact, every stage in the god's care – i.e., every time a human makes contact with the deity – requires purification.[47] In Mesopotamia, although the evidence is not as extensive,[48] it is clear that purification occurs. For instance, there is some evidence that the statues are ritually washed periodically.[49] The daily ritual itself also involves smearing the entry points to the cella with various substances[50] and using water for washing and fumigation (which elsewhere serve as the primary means of purification).[51] The awakening of the temple ceremony (*dīk bīti*), which is performed regularly, if not daily, from Neo-Assyrian to Hellenistic times at the start of the ritual day, includes lamentations to neutralize any (unknowingly) committed offenses.[52] Among the Hittites, there is less evidence of the daily service. However, it seems clear that the preparations

---

temple was being torn down (Cohen 1981:48–49), a purification of the city (likely since the ceremony continues away from the temple area), and a final purification of the temple (see Linssen 2004:100–109, 283–305 for transliterations, translations, and comments on Hellenistic texts with probable antecedents). The kettledrum ritual includes a washing of the mouth ceremony to ensure the perfect purity of the bull and later of the drum, purifications along with incantations and lamentations (ibid. 92–100, 252–282 for transliterations, translations and comments on Neo-Assyrian, Neo-Babylonian, and Hellenistic texts). Other non-fixed rituals seem to be in response to crises. Although not attested earlier, Hellenistic Mesopotamia has a rite to neutralize the negative effects of a lunar eclipse (ibid. 109–117, 306–320). For what seems to be a Hittite emergency rite (peeling an onion and twisting a cord to the left appear to remove evil by reversing the analogical actions taken to effect a curse on the temple and its deity; cf. *KUB* 17.27 ii 28–41 [= *ANET* 347]); see Wright 1987:43 and n. 95. See also waving the temple with various animate and inanimate objects and accompanying purifications with consecrated water as a potential emergency rite (Collins 2004b:462; *KUB* 30:31 4,36–40 + *KUB* 32.114 rev 4'–8'). These counterexamples seem to be the exception rather than the rule (cf. Wright 1987:73). Nonetheless, one may surmise that such elimination rites were performed more regularly (as in the private sector) and simply not preserved.

[46] See David 1981:59–60, for an outline of this ritual.
[47] Cf. ibid.
[48] E.g., the daily cultic texts are late and less forthcoming (Bottéro 2001:126–132).
[49] Ibid. 132; cf. Cohen 1993:332, who asserts that deities have their cults purified periodically.
[50] AO 6460 line 10.
[51] Van der Toorn 2004b:501.
[52] Linssen 2004:27–36.

for offering rituals usually include purification and/or consecration of the divine image, sancta, setting, offering, and offerers.⁵³ In short, purgations enable the various systems and their rituals to work by removing any threats to their carefully preserved order. Rituals also are adapted as necessary for special occasions, such as installation rites and festivals.

As expected, removal of imperfections features in installation rites, and often occurs on multiple levels. In the installation of new cult statues, such complexity is necessary to enact the transformation from image to fully functioning locus of the divine presence. In Mesopotamia, the mouth-washing ritual involves multiple and multi-layered means with two aims in mind: the removal of all vestiges of imperfection and the endowment of the statue with divine faculties. In addition to the regular purification of the statue with censer, torch, and holy water basin, the multiple mouth-washings effect perfect purity in the statue, while the mouth-openings endow the perfectly pure statue with divine perfection.⁵⁴ The ritual also employs various other means, which, at every step, seek to maximize the divine role at the expense of the human (e.g., the tools are thrown into the river, the participants swear that they had no role in the process, and the gods are continually encouraged to bring about the transformation from object to enlivened statue). The Egyptian ritual features the same purificatory elements as the daily cult service as well as a stress on the divine and a disavowal of the human roles. As in Mesopotamia, the emphasis on the divine role aims to overcome the limitations of having a human-made statue as a divine locus. The deities imbue the statue with their perfection, while removing the taint of human contact. The Hittite ritual employs water and oil. Uniquely, it also employs blood to purify the sancta and sanctuary, including the divine statue.⁵⁵ Like its cultural counterparts, the Hittite ritual seems to stress the divine role and minimize that of the human craftsmen; much of the ritual is aimed at securing divine presence, while the craftsmen disappear from the scene after finishing their craft. In each context, the human role seems to be to provide a conducive environment for divine presence and divine action.

Festivals, especially those involving processionals, form another special case. As the deities travel, purification rites must take place out of the temple context. Thus, the deity is often purified at various locales on the way. In Egypt, for example, fumigations and libations feature at bark stations, where the deity rests during his journey.⁵⁶ In the Hittite Telipinu ritual, as a prelude to offerings, priests purify the sancta on day four by washing

---

⁵³ Collins 2007:165; such purifications employ water and occasionally aromatic substances (Beckman 2004:338).
⁵⁴ Cf. Berlejung 1997:45; Hurowitz 2002:147.
⁵⁵ For a helpful summary, see Collins 2005:30–31.
⁵⁶ Thompson 2002:66.

them in the river.⁵⁷ In Mesopotamia, during the mouth-washing ritual, the priests cleanse the city with holy water as the deity processes to his temple.

One oft-cited temple removal rite deserves special mention. During the *akītu* festival,⁵⁸ priests purify Marduk's temple in Babylon, the Esagila, as well as Nabû's guest quarters, the Ezida. The purification of the Esagila is rather straightforward. After simple prayers to Marduk and his consort Zarpanitu to get their attention and ensure participation, the priests sprinkle water, sound a copper bell, and carry around a censer and torch to dispel any lingering evils.⁵⁹ The purification of the Ezida is more complex. In addition to the various purgations,⁶⁰ the ritual involves the transfer and disposal of evils and an incantation.⁶¹ In fact, it seems that one ritual is not enough, as the priests then set up a canopy called the 'golden heaven' to cover the Ezida and recite an incantation to remove evil, including the 'great evil demon' (ll. 369–383), a text in which the gods are explicitly said to purify the temple.

Rather than being merely an aberration, the elaborate nature of the Ezida purification is both necessary and illustrative. Since Nabû is absent, a greater purification is required.⁶² All sorts of evils may accumulate during his absence. Because of their potential severity, a transfer rite and incantations are necessary in addition to the use of water, fire, and aromatics. The plea for divine purgation particularly illuminates other temple rituals. In a temple context, the gods participate with their human servants to keep evil at bay. However, since it is obviously in their best interests to do so, the text does not need to make this explicit.⁶³ In the present ritual, Nabû is ab-

---

⁵⁷ Gane 2004:246, 261–278; they also sing a song that may add to the purification; cf. Popko 1995:148.

⁵⁸ See, e.g., *ANET* 331–334; *TUAT* 2:223–227; Thureau-Dangin 1921:86–111, 127–154; van der Toorn 1991; Cohen 1993:400–453; Pongratz-Leisten 1995; Sommer 2000; Bidmead 2004; Gane 2004:199–243; Linssen 2004:71–86, 184–237.

⁵⁹ See Wright 1987:63 n. 135 for the use of percussion to effect purgation. However, no one may enter Marduk's private quarters, presumably because he is present (Gane 2005:226).

⁶⁰ The priests perform the rituals in Nabû's room, presumably because he is not yet there, with an additional smearing of the door of the room with cedar oil (l. 350) and without the copper bells.

⁶¹ Ibid. 231–232. The priest wipes (*kapāru*) the room with the ram carcass before throwing the carcass into the river (ll. 353–354, 357–360). Although it is left unstated, the incantation (355) likely has something to do with the ram rite.

⁶² Gane 2005:365. As elsewhere, instead of being redundant, multiple means of removal make the removal more effective and highlight the situation's complexity and the ritual's importance.

⁶³ When human pleas are present, they are instead often aimed at preserving human safety in the presence of the divine (see, e.g., the lamentations in the awakening of the temple ceremony mentioned in the previous section).

sent. Thus, divine participation may not be assumed. Instead of resorting to a simple prayer, the priests must then petition the gods to ensure ritual efficacy, especially since no one has been protecting the Ezida from evil throughout the year.

Although elaborate, the temple purifications serve as a prelude to the rest of the ceremony. Thus, in a temple context, like the purification of the participants, the purification of sancta is generally embedded in a larger ritual and is performed to remove all possible encumbrances so that the larger ritual may proceed smoothly.

5.3.2.2. Individual and Community Removal Rites

Removal rites of individuals and the community usually occur in response to a crisis, and are aimed at returning the individual to a state of wholeness, expressed as freedom from any sort of affliction, whether present or portended. Since these rituals are performed for the benefit of the afflicted individual, not the temple, the gods, or the cosmic order, they often occur in non-temple locales[64] and stand alone rather than forming a subset of a larger ritual. Although some removal rites are straightforward, simply involving water, aromatics, and/or medicine,[65] many are complex like the rites in the Ezida because of the complexity of both the problem and its solution. Since the rituals occur away from the divine abode, are not for the divine benefit, and do not require divine presence, much less protection, individuals must cover all possible bases, using multiple means to procure divine aid and power and to ensure a favorable result.[66]

---

[64] Abusch 2004a:354; Avalos 1995:226; Beckman 2004:337; cf. Frantz-Szabó 2000: 2008; Ritner 2002a:194–195; id. 2002c:204. The home is a natural place for such rites (Avalos 1995:226). In some cases, it is sufficient to simply remove imperfections from the afflicted. In others, the pollution is disposed of in far away locales to ensure that it does not return. Thus, other rites occur or the pollution is disposed of in areas separated from human habitation, which serve as suitable dumping grounds (e.g., the underworld, the wilderness, the river, or enemy lands; see Wright 1987:248–271 for Mesopotamian and Hittite disposal spots). The river has a dual function and, thus, bears special mention. In addition to being a channel from the afflicted to the underworld (ibid. 252–255, 266), running water is also the primary means of purification (see next note).

[65] Water is the primary means of removal in Egypt, while natron and incense are also common (Meeks 1975:9.430–452; Frandsen 2004:499). In Mesopotamia, both running water (to wash away dirt and stains) and perfume (to take away unpleasant odors) feature (van der Toorn 2004b:501). Among the Hittites, running water is primary, and is occasionally accompanied by fragrances (Popko 1995:105; cf. Collins 2007:165). In most cases medicine is inextricably linked with 'magic' (see the summaries in Johnston 2004: 454, 457, 463 and *CANE* 582–583, 1777, 1787, 1901, 1908, 1911, 2007–2008).

[66] Instead of being alone in their quest, people do have some recourse to divine aid, particularly in the form of their personal gods (see e.g. Vorländer 1975; Jacobsen 1976: 145–164; cf. id. 1970:73–101; Albertz 1978; van der Toorn 1996; Assmann 2001:189–

Many of these rituals involve a complicated interplay of ritual words, actions, objects, and actors. Such rites serve as an attempt to do something tangible in the face of an intangible problem, to bring about restoration by connecting the afflicted to the divine realm and its power. Individuals may directly beseech the gods for their aid with well-constructed cases that employ such elements as confession, flattery, gifts, and promises. Confession acknowledges the problem, whether the sin is known or not,[67] in the hopes that the deity will redress the situation either directly or through ritual.[68] While largely unacceptable in the temple sphere, confession often features in individual rites. Because the individual is afflicted, something clearly has gone awry. Rather than upholding the perfection of the divine realm, the individual acknowledges his imperfection in an attempt to attain the wholeness that results in freedom from affliction. Confession then is often a necessary step in the process. Flattery, gifts, and promises seek to increase the odds of a positive divine reply. Flattery naturally serves to make the deity favorably disposed to the supplicant. In addition to eliciting a favorable response, gifts and promises function on the principle *do ut des*; the afflicted gives or promises to give something of value to the deity in order to coerce the deity into responding with the gift of divine power and aid.[69] The Hittites and Egyptians even employ threats to coerce divine cooperation.[70]

To make their efforts more successful, gifts may be expressed in contractual terms.[71] The supplicant may offer food, precious objects, and/or worship to the deity, who, upon acceptance would be contractually obligated to remove the affliction.[72] Alternatively, people may secure divine pow-

---

244; for Mesopotamian prayers to their personal gods, see Lambert 1974; for Hittite evidence, see Güterbock 1974). They are likely a concomitant response to the spatial and emotional absence of the gods in the temples and the need for divine attention in a dangerous and complicated world. However, such attention is not a panacea. Personal gods could become angry or absent, withdrawing their protection, or worse yet, causing affliction. In addition, personal gods are often on the second tier of the hierarchy. Thus, certain evils are beyond their abilities to counter; to bring about change, they often have to serve as intermediaries with the great gods (see Abusch 1999; van der Toorn 2004a:427).

[67] When the sin is unknown, supplicants often make blanket confessions in order to cover all possible infractions.

[68] See, e.g., the Egyptian texts from Deir el Medina (Lichtheim 1976:104–110), the various confessions in the Mesopotamian *Šurpu* series, and the Hittite plague prayers of Muršili II.

[69] Cf. Mauss 1990.

[70] E.g., King Muršili II reminds the deity that continuance of the plague will mean no divine service, particularly no food. For Egypt, see, e.g., Assmann 2001:69.

[71] See the use of Akkadian *šullumu*, which refers to completing a sacrifice, completing a transaction (paying in full), and pacifying an angry deity (*CAD* Š.1 219–229).

[72] See, e.g., Scurlock 2002a:395–397(cf. 2006b:241–244) for Mesopotamian evidence.

er somewhat indirectly via analogy, imitation, and/or impersonation. Suppliants may take on the persona and power of the gods through analogy with mythic precedents (in essence re-enacting the myths for their own benefit). By comparing the present situation with a favorable parallel in the divine realm, the afflicted hopes to link his fate with a divine prototype and thereby confer divine authority on the rite.[73] Alternatively, the suppliant may use analogy from the mundane world to add efficacy to ritual action.[74] Analogy, thus, mixes ritual action with words that link the action to the desired outcome.[75] However, an analogy does more than simply encourage a deity to act; it is in some way also connected to and helps to bring about that outcome. Imitation is a more direct form of divine coercion than analogy, through which individuals echo the divine will. Impersonations (for example, speaking as and on behalf of a god) are even more direct. As such, they are often replete with blame-shifting, apologetic statements asserting that the speaker is simply reciting the divine will with divine authority, not his own.[76]

These words and gifts are usually accompanied by ritual actions that may involve concretization, analogy, transference, substitution, banishment, destruction, and protection. Through concretization, the petitioner makes his afflictors and affliction concrete in the form of images and objects.[77] As we have seen elsewhere, such images are connected to and contain some of the essence of their referent. Thus, when the ritualist manipulates the images during the course of the ritual, he likewise manipulates the referents.[78] The ritualist may use these or other elements in analogical action. For example, in the Hittite *Tunnawi* ritual, the old woman takes off a man's black clothes, thereby removing blackness or sin.[79] Alternatively, a Hittite male could counteract impotence by removing female attributes (spindle, distaff) and replacing them with masculine attributes (bow, arrows).[80] In both cases, the objects are especially efficacious since

---

[73] In Egypt, e.g., the afflicted typically aligns himself with Horus (Ritner 2002a:198; id. 2002b:201); cf. Lambert 1968; Beckman 1989:104; Imparati 2000:583.

[74] E.g., in both Mesopotamia and Hatti, ritual words and actions link peeling an onion to peeling away affliction (e.g., *Šurpu* 5–6.52/53, 60, 70; *Samuha* 36–41; see *ANET* 346; Lebrun 1976:117–143).

[75] Collins 2007:182.

[76] Many Egyptian incantations include such apologia (see Borghouts 1978:x and the multiple texts that follow); for a Mesopotamian example, see Foster 2005:177–178.

[77] In Mesopotamia, images are also made of protective deities (Abusch 2004b:457).

[78] Cf. the bound prisoner motif in Egypt (Ritner 1993:113–136).

[79] Wright 1987:41.

[80] Collins 2007:182.

they are like and in some ways the same as their referents.[81] Like most of the temple rites, some individual rites simply remove the pollutants (such as sin and femininity); others, like the Ezida ritual, transfer the evils to another object or area. In Mesopotamia, for example, a goatskin is placed on or near the suppliant, which, with the help of Ishum, absorbs the evil. The skin is then deposited in the street, signaling the evil's return to the underworld.[82] The skin is therefore the instrument of transferal from the individual to the underworld. In some cases, the instrument of transferal also acts as a substitute.[83] At times, banishment and substitution are not enough; the evil must be destroyed to ensure that there is no chance of it wreaking havoc again. In the Egyptian execration texts[84] as in the Akkadian *Maqlû* series, the image of the enemy, whether a foreigner or a witch, must be destroyed so that the enemy himself would bear the fate of his image and, hence, be unable to cause additional harm. Likewise, the substitute king is often killed to ensure that he alone bears the full penalty portended in the omen, thereby keeping that penalty permanently away from the king himself. Finally, various rites and objects are also used to protect the suppliant from evil influences, whether present or future. Amulets feature in Egypt, Mesopotamia, and Hatti,[85] functioning as bearers of divine power and, thus, protectors against evil.[86] In Egypt, circumambulation is "perhaps the most common ritual technique" used to "enclose and defend sacred space."[87] With divine help, such actions serve to concretely remove imperfections so that the individual can return to wholeness and prosperity.

5.3.3. Synthesis

Thus, in both the ANE temple and community, rituals are a joint venture of humans and the divine. In the temple, both parties are willing and able. In the individual rites, however, the gods must be convinced to participate; for, although willing, the individuals are not able without divine aid. Nevertheless, procuring divine assistance away from the divine abode is often

---

[81] See section 5.3.1. p. 124-125 and n. 30, where the dog in the *namburbû* rite both represents and carries within itself the portended evil.

[82] Wright 1987:65–67.

[83] E.g., the Mesopotamian king substitution rituals (Parpola 1970–1983), where an individual takes the king's place as a substitute so that he may then bear the predicted suffering in the king's stead.

[84] See Ritner 1993:136–153.

[85] See respectively Sternberg 2004:454–455, Abusch 2004b:457, and Collins 2004b: 462.

[86] Cf. the incantations in *Šurpu* IX, which serve to empower various objects.

[87] Ritner 2002a:197; cf. 1993:57–67.

far from easy. As a result, individual rites often are complex because of both the problem itself and the difficulty of securing divine aid.

Chapter Six

Damage Control in the Priestly Texts

Unlike in the ANE, the Priestly damage control system, comprised of Leviticus 4–5, 12–15, and 16, integrates individual and sanctuary pollution removal into a single all-encompassing system, concerned with safeguarding both the divine presence and the integrity of its community.[1] Chapters 4–5 and 12–15 prescribe rites for the removal of sins and impurities from individuals,[2] and chapter 16 primarily prescribes the annual removal of all pollutants from the sanctuary itself.

We will begin with an analysis of Leviticus 4–5 and 12–15, yet only offer limited conclusions in anticipation of a more thoroughgoing assessment of their position in the larger damage control system and of their central concepts and relationship to their ANE counterparts in chapter 7. Our study will then focus on Leviticus 16, the Priests' ultimate solution for keeping heaven on earth.[3] After our analysis of Clearing Day in Leviticus 16, the final chapter (7) will present the results of the analysis. We will first examine the Priestly damage control system's ideological thrust. Then, with the data in front of us, we will analyze key Priestly concepts: sin and impurity, the חטאת and אשם offerings, and clearing (כפר).[4] Finally, with a fuller understanding of the Priestly damage control system, we will compare that

---

[1] Leviticus 1–7 also includes a general summary of the עלה, מנחה, and זבח שלמים offerings (1–3), and additional information about the various offerings, especially their disposal (6–7). As we have seen, 8–9 address the dedication and inauguration of the cult, while 10 focuses on the sad fate of Nadab and Abihu. Chapter 11 enumerates the clean and unclean animals. For the sake of simplicity and because Leviticus 1–16 forms a complex system in its own right, we will leave aside discussion of the so-called Priestly texts in Numbers.

[2] See section 6.2. for a justification.

[3] Leviticus 16 is a fitting conclusion to our study since it is an annual re-dedication of the tabernacle (see chapter 3) that enables continued presence (chapter 2) and divine service (chapter 4).

[4] This delay prevents us from applying a definition before we have examined the terms that are meant to be defined by it. As a preliminary distinction, clearing refers more broadly to the removal of unwanted impediments, while cleansing refers more specifically to the removal of impurity. The ultimate goal of impurity removal is being clean, namely free from impurities, while the ultimate goal of sin removal is forgiveness.

system with its ANE counterparts in order to better illumine the Priestly agenda in chapter 7.[5]

6.1. YHWH's Relationship to the World and His People in P

As a bridge to the previous chapter and a general point of reference, we begin with YHWH's relationship to the world and its inhabitants. Unlike the ANE gods, YHWH is transcendent in that he is not derived from nor bound to creation. His essence transcends it[6] and his presence in it is unnatural, an intrusion into space and time.[7] In turn, the world's fate does not determine his own.[8] Instead, the world's state determines his presence in and his actions toward it and is determined by the behavior of its inhabitants.

As with other ANE gods, YHWH is the master of his people, going beyond his ANE counterparts by requiring an absolutely exclusive relationship with them. Even so, he opts for a degree of intimacy by emancipating them from Egypt for the purpose of dwelling in their midst as their God. YHWH further distinguishes himself from his ANE counterparts by providing explicit remedies for infractions and imperfections. Thus, unlike in the ANE, where the divine will must be secured or mimicked, YHWH himself decrees the rituals via Moses, thereby practically ensuring their efficacy if properly performed.

6.2. Individual and Communal Removal Rites (Leviticus 4–5 and 12–15)

Schwartz has conclusively differentiated between sins and impurities, noting that they produce similar yet distinct defilement that often must be removed by חטאת offerings.[9] Once properly differentiated, we may separate chapters 4–5 from 12–15. Leviticus 4–5 primarily, if not exclusively, pre-

---

[5] By doing so, we are allowing the Priestly system to emerge in its own terms before comparing it to its ANE counterparts.
[6] Cf. Kawashima 2006:237.
[7] Ibid. 256.
[8] As seen in the creation account in Gen 1, he also has no rival in it.
[9] Id. 1995. As we will see, חטאת is a multivalent term that describes a sinful act, its contaminating effect, and the offering to remove it and to remove impurity from both the afflicted and the sanctuary. As will be demonstrated below, אשם too is polysemous, referring to guilt, its consequences, its reparation, and its reparation offering.

scribes the procedures for removing general and specific sins from people that includes both חטאת and אשם offerings.¹⁰ In fact, Leviticus 4–5 is the only section in the Priestly Sinai pericope that specifically addresses sin.¹¹ By contrast, chapters 12–15 alone prescribe the procedure for removing impurities from people,¹² yet never mention sin, only the so-called 'sin' offering (חטאת) as a primary means of impurity removal. Thus, we will examine chapters 4–5 and 12–15 separately under the headings of offerings for sin and remedies for impurity respectively.¹³

Milgrom in particular has argued that all חטאת offerings only purge the sanctuary.¹⁴ However, his theory is untenable for several reasons. First, there is no mention of effecting clearing for the sanctuary or sancta in Leviticus 4–5 and 12–15, only clearing for (כפר על) people. Second, when it modifies כפר, the preposition מן is privative (e.g., 4:26; 5:6; 5:10; 15:30), indicating that ritual action removes pollutants from the individuals in 4–5 and 12–15 just as it removes pollution from the sanctuary in Leviticus 8 and 16. Third, all חטאת offerings need not be interpreted identically. Specifically, Milgrom is not justified in applying the explicit clearing function of the חטאת offerings in Leviticus 8 and 16 to 4–5 and 12–15 without justification.¹⁵ While it is clear that the חטאת offerings in 4–5 and 12–15 remove pollution from individuals, it remains unclear if they have any effect on the tabernacle itself.¹⁶

---

¹⁰ The cases in 5:2–3 are somewhat anomalous. Although they, like all offenses prompting חטאת and אשם offerings in chapters 4–5, are related to sin, they also address impurities. Touching anything unclean (טמא) naturally renders one unclean (טמא). However, such offenses normally fall under the legislation in chapters 11–15 and Num 19 and merely require the individual to purify himself, not bring a sacrifice (Milgrom 1991:298–299, 310–311). The offenses in 5:2–3 require a חטאת offering because the individual 'sinned' by failing to undergo the proper purification procedures in the allotted time (ibid. 310–313; Gane 2005:150–151, 199). The offerer must then bring a חטאת offering as his reparation (אשם) in order to be cleared מן his sin (5:6), not from his impurity. Thus, although prompted by impurity, the offenses in 5:2–3 require חטאת offerings for sin removal, and hence fit comfortably within the general ethos of chapters 4–5. By contrast, the presence of sin and sin removal renders them inappropriate for chapters 12–15.

¹¹ 6:18–7:7 does, however, address more generally the proper preparation and disposal of the offerings for sins enumerated in chapters 4–5.

¹² Leviticus 5:2–3 also address impurity to some extent, but is primarily concerned with remedying the sin of improper purification (see n. 10). 7:19–21 simply expresses the danger of contacting the holy in an impure state.

¹³ The term 'remedies' is employed instead of 'offerings' because offerings are only one of the many remedies for impurity.

¹⁴ Id. 1991:254–258.

¹⁵ For a fuller critique, see Gane 2005:106–143, 273–274; 2008; cf. Eberhart 2002: 240–243; Nihan 2007:178–179.

¹⁶ Compare Gane 2008 with the more prevalent view in Nihan 2007:186–187.

6.2.1. Structure

6.2.1.1 Offerings for Sin (Leviticus 4–5)

From the beginning, the language of Leviticus 4–5 differentiates it from 1–3 in its specificity and its specific focus on damage control. Unlike chapters 1–3, which use vague language, chapters 4–5 specify what situations require חטאת and אשם offerings and stress both sin (חטאת) and its consequence, guilt (אשם).[17] As such, like the tabernacle dedication and regular service, textual detail in chapters 4–5 is sufficient to inform the reader of the relationships between people and objects. Although similar, the specific structural aspects also distinguish the offerings in 4–5 from the other texts.

Ritual action indexically connects the offerer, priest, offering, the tabernacle complex, and the deity. The people are indexically linked with the altar, upon which the blood of their offerings is manipulated (4:25, 30, 34; 5:9), while the priests are connected with the outer sanctuary (4:5–7). Specifically, Aaron enters the outer sanctuary and applies the blood of his offering on the incense altar and before the veil. During the offering for the entire congregation, the people, as part of the congregation, are also connected to the outer sanctuary in the same way as the priests (4:16–18). Regarding YHWH, offerings are presented to him (e.g., 4:3; 5:6–7, 15, 25; 7:3–5),[18] while ritual action occurs before him (e.g., the expression לפני יהוה occurs 9 times in Lev 4 alone) in his abode. When performed correctly, the חטאת and אשם offerings[19] in 4–5 bind these elements to clearing (כפר) and forgiveness (סלח). The rituals also indexically bind the three parties, including YHWH, to the sin in some way, since the rituals in the tabernacle complex are concerned with the clearing and forgiveness of those very ills (4:20, 26, 31, 35; 5:10, 13, 16, 18, 25).

In addition to their linking function, ritual actions simultaneously serve to distinguish between people and objects, namely offerers, priests, offerings, altars, and the deity. The offerers' activities are limited to bringing, slaughtering, and performing hand-laying on their offerings (4:15, 23–24, 28–29, 32–33; 5:6, 7, 11). The priests are privileged above the offerers in that they perform all ritual actions at the bronze altar and inside the tent

---

[17] Watts 2007:84, 91–92. Chapters 4–5 also especially emphasize that the offerings are divinely decreed. Chapters 1–3 only mention divine sponsorship at the beginning of the ritual legislation (1:1–2). By contrast, chapter 4 begins with a mention of divine sanction and chapter 5 includes two such mentions (4:1–2; 5:14, 20). Language of divine supervision is even more prevalent in chapters 6–7, where it occurs five times (Watts 2007:91–92). The general term guilt here includes objective guilt, an awareness of guilt, guilty feelings, and suffering (cf. Sklar 2005:39–41)

[18] Lev 6:17–7:7 is included in our analysis since it comments on sacrificial procedure and the disposal of sacrificial remains for the חטאת and אשם offerings.

[19] Traditionally rendered 'sin offering' and 'guilt offering' respectively.

(4:5–12, 16–21, 25–26, 30–35; 5:6, 8–10, 12–13). YHWH naturally rests atop the hierarchy as the recipient of the offerings. The priests are further connected to YHWH and distinguished from everyone else because both partake of some part of the offerings.[20]

The unblemished nature of the offerings (4:3, 23, 28, 32; 5:15, 18, 25), their divine recipient, the locale of ritual action, and the ritualized actions themselves distinguish the offerings from other normal activity, such as a meal. The offerings likewise differentiate the various offenses to be cleared. The חטאת offerings in chapter 4 are distinguished from those in Leviticus 5:1–6, as the offenses in the latter are enumerated, include a confession, and omit the root שגג (expressing inadvertence).[21] There is a similar distinction within the אשם legislation; unlike those in 5:14–19, offenses in 5:20–26 are enumerated and do not mention the root שגג.[22]

The value of the offerings also differentiates hierarchically between offerers. Ranging from a bull to flour (4:3, 14; 5:11), חטאת offerings for sin distinguish between priests, the entire congregation, leaders, and individual Israelites, who are subdivided according to their economic means.[23] Offerers and their offerings are further separated by the disposal of sacrificial remains and the location and extent of blood manipulation. In each context, the leftover blood is poured at the base of the bronze altar (4:7, 18, 25, 30, 34; 5:9). For priestly and communal offerings, two separate blood manipulations occur inside the tent and the remains are burned (4:5–7, 12, 16–18, 21), whereas, for everyone else, the rites involve only a single manipulation at the bronze altar (4:25, 30, 34; 5:9; 7:2) and the remains are consumed by the priests (6:19; 7:6).

The location, the offering itself, and the ritual actions necessary to offer it distinguish the אשם offering from the חטאת. Unlike the חטאת, the אשם offering is an unblemished ram regardless of the crime.[24] Unlike the חטאת offerings, each אשם offering includes a reimbursement for damages plus

---

[20] The fat of the offerings is burnt to YHWH on the altar and the blood is applied to his furniture (4:6–10, 33–35), while the priests consume the flesh of the non-priestly offerings in both חטאת and אשם offerings (6:19; 7:6).

[21] Cf. Milgrom 1970:124–125 n. 13. However, while Lev 5:1 clearly refers to an intentional sin, verses 2–4 mention נעלם, which seems to suggest something like inadvertence (see further 6.2.3.1.a.).

[22] The אשם pericope is likewise divided into two divine speeches starting in 5:14 and 20 (Nihan 2007:245).

[23] 5:7–13, which addresses offerings for individual Israelites scaled to their economic means, seems to apply to all of 4–5:6 (Nihan 2007:244–245). However, it is also possible that Milgrom, following rabbinic exegesis, is correct that it only applies to 5:1–6 (1991: 307–318). For an explanation of privileging the male goat over the female, see Scurlock 2006a:18; Nihan 2007:253 n. 666.

[24] The חטאת is never a ram in Lev 4–5. However, at times a burnt offering ram is required (e.g., Lev 8; 9; 16).

1/5 extra (5:16, 21).²⁵ The blood manipulation for the אשם is likewise different, as the blood is spread around on the altar (7:2), not on the horns, and every blood manipulation occurs at the bronze altar.

Nonetheless, there is some common ground between the two categories, as they both cover unintentional and (potentially) intentional sins and as the more serious offenses require a reparation (אשם). More specifically, the חטאת offerings in Leviticus 4 and the אשם offerings in 5:14–19 both redress crimes committed inadvertently (בשגגה), while the חטאת offerings in 5:1–6 and the אשם offerings 5:20–26 do not (i.e., there is some intentionality). Like the more serious crimes in the חטאת legislation of chapter 5, the offenses in the אשם legislation of 5:14–26 require a reparation (אשם),²⁶ taking the form of a חטאת in Leviticus 5:1–6, and an אשם offering, repayment plus an additional fine in 5:14–26.

Finally, in Leviticus 4–5, there is an especially strong connection between the roots חטא and אשם. The former, commonly associated with sin, expresses the improper act, the performance of that act, and the penalty for it. The latter, commonly associated with guilt, refers to the consequences of an act (suffering guilt's consequences, which includes objective guilt),²⁷ the required compensation, and the offering that forms (part of) that compensation. Each root occurs in the passages relating to both the חטאת and אשם offerings, yet as the text moves from the חטאת to the אשם, the proportion gradually swings from חטא to אשם.²⁸

6.2.1.2. Remedies for Impurity (Leviticus 12–15)

Although both offerings are called a חטאת, result in clearing, and index similar connections between people and objects,²⁹ חטאת offerings for impurity (טמאה) are in many ways different from those for sin. First, חטאת offerings for impurity are connected with clearing and cleansing (טהר) (12:7–8; 14:20, 31, 53; cf. 15:15, 30) rather than clearing and forgiveness. Second, there is a good deal more variability and complexity when redress-

---

²⁵ Lev 5:17–19, however, seems to require only a sacrifice. This is to be expected since it is difficult to pay appropriate damages when the crime remains unknown (see further section 6.2.3.1.a).

²⁶ Although the same word is employed, this reparation (אשם) is not the same as a "reparation" offering (אשם) (Milgrom 1991:303).

²⁷ Translating אשם as suffering guilt's consequences (Sklar 2005:39–41, followed by Nihan 2007:237–239) is flexible enough to allow for objective guilt, awareness of guilt, guilty feelings, and suffering as the (perceived) consequence of guilt.

²⁸ See Watts 2007:88.

²⁹ At times, only the individual to be cleansed and water are involved (YHWH is also involved by proxy as the one who prescribed the rite). However, when a sanctuary offering is necessary, all three participants have the same roles as above for the offerings for sin.

ing impurities than when addressing sin. Unlike the חטאת offerings for sin, those for impurity never stand alone; they always include a burnt offering (12:6, 8; 14:19, 22, 31; 15:15, 30).[30] In addition to חטאת and burnt offerings, cleansing rites include other elements, most notably washing clothes, bathing, and waiting. On certain occasions they also may require two birds, wood, string, hyssop, oil, shaving, a grain offering, and an אשם offering (Lev 14:1–20). In some cases such as menstruation the offerings are even unnecessary (15:19–24), and in others the object of cleansing varies, as the text addresses garments and houses in addition to people (13:47–59; 14:33–57). Third, unlike sins, (some) impurities are explicitly contagious to persons (e.g., 15:2–12).

Like the offerings for sin, offerings for impurity seem to hierarchically distinguish between offerers. However, rather than by social status, this distinction is made according to the severity of the affliction and the relative complexity of the cleansing process. Less severe impurities merely require washing, bathing, and waiting;[31] more severe impurities require additional time and offerings. The most severe impurity requires banishment from the community, additional time, multiple courses of washing, shaving and bathing, the ritual with two birds, oil, an אשם, and finally a חטאת and a burnt offering (14:1–20). We may also distinguish between the various impurities that require offerings by the price of those offerings. The parturient's impurity seems to be more severe than the man or woman with a discharge as she offers a lamb and a bird instead of two birds.

The application of the oil and blood to the skin-diseased[32] person (14:14–18), like the priests in Leviticus 8, breaks normal protocol and thereby marks the ritualized action as an abnormal (and important) ritual procedure. The identification of the oil and the אשם as an elevation offering (14:12)[33] likewise indexes a connection between the two items and suggests a shared purpose (this is also reinforced by the placement of the oil on the blood of the אשם [14:17]). However, while similar, the details differentiate the two rites; as, unlike in the priestly ordination, the oil and blood are not said to be put on the altar.[34]

---

[30] חטאת offerings for sin in chapters 4–5 include a burnt offering only when an individual cannot afford a more expensive offering (5:7, 10).

[31] At times, aspects of washing clothes and bathing are left unstated. However, it seems best (and simplest) to conclude with Milgrom (1991:667, 746, 919, 986–987) that when waiting is mentioned alone, it functions as a shorthand for all three activities, or at least for bathing the body.

[32] See Avalos 1995:311–316 for a possible identification of what constitutes skin-disease.

[33] For this translation, see Milgrom 1991:461–473.

[34] Although elsewhere the אשם blood is explicitly applied to the altar (7:2), its absence here seems to minimize the connection between the offerer and the altar.

6.2.2. Use

6.2.2.1. Offerings for Sin

The rites described in Leviticus 4–5 serve as damage control, aimed at removing the damage caused by certain sins so that the system can continue to function as intended. In particular, the unspecified inadvertent sins and specific potentially intentional sins that bring with them guilt's consequences (אשם) prompt ritual action.[35]

Supporting goal statements add further specificity to the overarching purpose. In Leviticus 4–5:13, a single חטאת offering for sin[36] is the instrument of clearing (כפר) and the ultimate goal of forgiveness.[37] Both the unspecified unintentional and specified (potentially) intentional sins may be redressed via a חטאת offering manipulated by the priests before YHWH.[38] However, clearing is expressed in different ways. It most often appears with forgiveness; alternatively clearing is followed by מן or על + the offense, or it simply stands alone. More specifically, the priest effects clearing with the חטאת offering for the leader "from his sin" (מחטאתו) (4:26), for the common person "concerning his sin which he sinned" (על־חטאתו אשר חטא) (4:35; 5:13), "from his sin" (5:6), and "from his sin that he sinned" (מחטאתו אשר חטא) (5:10). In one case, clearing is even missing (4:1–12), while, in another, forgiveness is absent (5:6). In a third case, the fat of the offering is given additional significance as a soothing scent (ריח ניחח) (4:31).

Although describing a different kind of ritual procedure prompted by different offenses, the purpose statements in the אשם pericope of 5:14–26 nonetheless resemble those in the חטאת pericope. The goal of the אשם legislation, like that of the חטאת, is clearing and forgiveness. More specifically, the sacrilegious crimes (מעל) in 5:14–26, whether intentional or not, may be redressed through a sacrificial and monetary compensation (אשם), taking the form of an אשם offering and repayment plus a fine, so that clearing may be effected for the individual responsible and he may be forgiven. Thus, in the אשם legislation as with the חטאת, a single offering manipulated by the priests before YHWH (with the help of monetary compensation) may redress both unspecified inadvertent sins against sancta (5:14–16) and

---

[35] The sins in 5:14–26 are specifically called sacrilegious acts (מעל); for this translation, see Milgrom 1991:345–356.

[36] The two birds (5:7) provide an exception to the single offering principle; one serves as a חטאת and the other as a burnt offering.

[37] Forgiveness' place as the end result of clearing indicates that it is the ultimate goal; cf. the remedies for impurity, where clearing is only occasionally necessary to secure the ultimate goal of cleansing.

[38] For the specified (potentially) intentional sins, the חטאת offering explicitly serves as a reparation (אשם).

specified (potentially) intentional sins (5:20–26).³⁹ Like Leviticus 4–5:13, 5:14–26 expresses clearing and forgiveness in different ways. Clearing always appears with forgiveness and alternatively is followed by עַל + the sins committed or it simply stands alone.⁴⁰ Forgiveness for the offender usually stands alone, yet once it is followed by עַל + the offense that brings with it guilt's consequences. In 5:26, the offerer is forgiven for any of the things he does to bring guilt's consequences on himself (ונסלח לו על־אחת מכל אשר־יאשה לאשמה בה). In one case, the fat of the אשם is given additional significance as a (food) gift (אשה ליהוה) (7:5), which resembles the designation of the חטאת as soothing scent.

6.2.2.2. Remedies for Impurity

Like the offerings for sin, remedies for impurity in Leviticus 12–15 serve as damage control, this time aimed at removing the damage caused by certain impurities. In particular, they serve to cleanse people with various impurities, i.e., to remove the effects of impurity from them.

While the חטאת and אשם offerings for sin express clearing and forgiveness with a single purpose statement, the rituals for impurity use more variable and often more complex formulae. Cleansing is the ultimate goal,⁴¹ but, over the course of a single ritual, it is often expressed multiple times and with various complementary goals. Each ritual expresses cleansing and its complementary actions and goals differently. Redressing the parturient's condition includes two cleansings and one clearing (12:1–8); the skin-diseased person's situation calls for five cleansings, three clearings, and two installments of washing, bathing, and shaving (14:1–32); the restoration of the man with a discharge speaks of two cleansings, one clearing, and one washing (15:13–15); and restoring the woman with the irregular discharge mentions two cleansings and one clearing (25–30). The man with a seminal emission (16) and the woman with menstrual impurity (19) are anomalous cases, as neither mentions clearing or cleansing.⁴² Where present, the formulation of the purpose statements varies. Clearing either stands alone or is followed by מן + the evils to be purged. Verses 15:15 and 30 are the only clear instances of clearing + מן. In 14:19, מן + impurity may be the object of either clearing or the one to be cleansed

---

³⁹ 5:17–19 deals with inadvertant, unknown sins that require an אשם, but no monetary compensation, to effect clearing and elicit forgiveness.

⁴⁰ In 5:18, the priest effects clearing for the individual concerning his inadvertent sin that he committed inadvertently (על שגגתו אשר שגג).

⁴¹ In that it is always the (at times implicit) final goal of remedies for impurity; by contrast, clearing is only occasionally necessary.

⁴² Those contaminated by the corpse of an unclean animal are also abnormal in that time alone is prescribed to remedy their impurity (e.g., 11:27).

(המטהר). Likewise, cleansing either stands alone or is followed by מן + the evils to be cleansed. In 12:7, the parturient is cleansed מן her flow of blood. In 14:19, the priest effects clearing for the one to be cleansed מן his impurities, while both 15:13 and 15:28 describe cleansing מן the impurities even before the ritual activity begins.

6.2.3. Ideology

6.2.3.1. Offerings for Sins

Whatever their actual setting may have been, the regulations in Leviticus 4–5 appear to be cast as new, or at least important, legislation for the tabernacle. With YHWH now present amid the Israelites, the חטאת and אשם offerings are instituted as damage control. By contrast, "the offerings described in Leviticus 1–3 seem to reflect long-established rituals in Israelite culture."[43] Since there is no need to reestablish them, they are simply applied to the tabernacle setting with rather generic language.[44] As new legislation, the text identifies the situations requiring the חטאת and אשם offerings, the ritual actions necessary to offer them, and their effects.[45]

However, while Leviticus 4 requires a חטאת for unintentional sins against any of YHWH's commandments, it nowhere identifies these commandments. How then are we meant to understand them? Are the priests assuming that the reader will know the laws, perhaps in the form of a pre-existing code ([partially] preserved in another source)? Or might they have another motivation? It seems that here as elsewhere the Priestly texts "resort to the widest possible generalization in order to cover every future contingency."[46] In other words, the omission allows their legislation to adapt to new circumstances and to always cover all possible inadvertent sins. The חטאת legislation in chapter 5 expands the already wide net to include certain potentially conscious sins.[47] Once again, the scope of these sins is undefined, as the cases listed may be exhaustive or merely a sampling. Likewise, the situations requiring an אשם in Leviticus 5:14–19 are described as broadly as possible. 5:14–16 does not list the unintentional

---

[43] Watts 2007: 83.

[44] Perhaps their place at the head of the legislation in Leviticus serves to reinforce the Priestly text's "credibility as the authoritative source of ritual instructions" (ibid).

[45] The lack of detail in chapters 1–3 may signal their relative unimportance or, more likely, their importance is assumed.

[46] Milgrom 1991:351.

[47] Milgrom (ibid.) argues that the legislation in 5:1–4 refers to doubtful cases. However, since the inadvertent nature of the offenses in Leviticus 4 seems to exclude the potentially conscious sins of 5:1–4, it is better to refer to 5:1–4 as an expansion of 4 (or, perhaps, as a list of anomalous cases). See the following section for a short explication of the nature of the offenses in 5:1–6.

sacrileges against sancta, while 17–19 speaks of an אשם for unknown sins, which may be brought to remedy any (perceived) hardship or guilty feelings. Verses 5:20–26 are again somewhat ambiguous.[48] The list may be a sampling of sacrilegious acts requiring an אשם or either an exhaustive or partial list of additional cases of sacrilege against YHWH that do not involve sancta. Finally, as it is concerned with describing the remedy for expiable sins, Leviticus 4–5 neither mentions inexpiable sins nor where the line between the two lies. This omission also serves the practical function of encouraging more offerings, as it leaves open the possibility of forgiveness for more serious offenders.

Together, the open-ended identification of expiable sins signals that all sins that may be remedied require a tabernacle offering. Thus, all sinners, whether individual or communal, must come before YHWH in his earthly abode if they hope to be freed from sin's consequences, even if only their suffering leads them to suspect that they have sinned.[49] The fact that the remedy is clearly outlined and decreed by God, and thus its outcome is all but guaranteed, provides further incentive to bring offerings to the tabernacle instead of seeking alternative means.

Clearing and forgiveness are the Priestly terms that describe the removal of sin and its consequences. Here, we will limit our discussion to their instrumentality and modifiers. In each instance, the priest is the subject of clearing, while the offerer is the object (וכפר עליו/עלהם הכהן is typical).

Although unusual, there may be a couple of reasons why the text opts for על instead of the direct object marker, את. First, על is appropriate because there is no direct contact between the blood and the offerer.[50] Second, the expression carries with it ideological import.[51] Elsewhere, in what Levine calls religious and politico-legal texts, כפר most often takes a direct

---

[48] See the following section for a brief explanation of the nature of the offenses in 5:14–26.

[49] The ambiguity likewise serves priestly self-interest as it encourages offerings and makes priests an indispensable part of the expiatory process.

[50] In contrast, clearing of places and objects may be expressed either directly or indirectly, perhaps because the blood makes direct contact with them (Milgrom 1991:254–256).

[51] Milgrom offers a third possibility, arguing that the indirect object indicates that the offering does not result in purification for the individual, but only for the sancta upon which the blood is manipulated. In making his case, he seems to have two (noble) goals in mind: 1) to combat the traditional interpretation that חטאת blood manipulation is primarily, if not exclusively, symbolic (see Gese 1977; Janowski 1982; Schenker 1991; cf. the response of Eberhart 2002:262–263) and 2) to harmonize biblical Israel with postbiblical Judaism (Milgrom 2001:2452–2453; cf. Hurowitz 1994:221). Nonetheless, his conclusions cannot be sustained (see above section 6.2. for a critique).

object and roughly means wiping away sins and transgressions.[52] By opting exclusively for the indirect object, the Priestly writers may seek to remove the element of causation. While the benefits still accrue to the individual, the priests' actions do not automatically bring about clearing; they are merely a prerequisite activity whose consequence is clearing.[53] על then indicates that the priest's actions alone do not cause clearing. YHWH is the silent partner before whom the rites are performed and by whom clearing is ultimately effected.[54] At the same time, the presence of על indicates that the priests do not necessarily compel the silent partner to act; YHWH does it of his own volition.[55]

The *niphal* used to express forgiveness (ונסלח לו) functions similarly. The construction leaves the forgiver unspecified, who we logically deduce is YHWH.[56] The lack of a subject and the passive voice indicate that, although forgiveness follows as a consequence of the ritual action, the priest does not himself confer pardon.[57] It simultaneously suggests that, although YHWH grants forgiveness, he is not bound to do so.[58]

The multiple modifiers of clearing and forgiveness also seem to follow a purposeful progression. 4:1–12 introduces the חטאת legislation by describing the ritual process.[59] In the next instance (4:20), the text adds clearing and forgiveness as the result of proper performance of the חטאת ritual. The following case (4:26) adds even more detail, indicating that clearing occurs for the offerer "from his sins" (מחטאתו). Chapter 4 returns to the basic formula of clearing and forgiveness (4:31) before concluding with

---

[52] At times, the indirect object with על appears as well (Levine 1974:64). The Akkadian *kapāru/kuppuru* (in the D stem) also tends to take the direct object (ibid. 63).

[53] Ibid. 65–66. The use of *piel* instead of the causative *hiphil* כפר may also be indicative of Priestly reticence.

[54] Cf. ibid.; Propp 2006:467. This principle finds support outside of the Priestly texts, where YHWH is often the subject of clearing (Dt 21:8; 32:43; Ez 16:63; 2 Chr 30:18; Ps 65:4; 78:38; 79:9; Jer 18:23). The Priestly system seems to simultaneously uphold the non-Priestly position while giving the people, and especially the priests, a more direct role in the clearing process, i.e., a clear course of action through which divine clearing may be elicited.

[55] The fact that YHWH prescribes the rituals also militates against priestly coercion.

[56] See Gane 2005:51 and the references cited therein.

[57] Propp 2006:467–468.

[58] That the offering itself is not automatically efficacious, that YHWH himself empowers it, is supported by the fact that lesser substitutes (e.g., flour in 5:11) are acceptable.

[59] Although it is possible that the lack of explicit clearing and forgiveness for the priest suggests that the priest received clearing only on Clearing Day (Rendtorff 1985:160; Kiuchi 1987:129; Nihan 2007:187 n. 342), it is more likely that the expression is implied and was (purposely) omitted. Throughout the חטאת legislation, various elements are omitted yet clearly implied (e.g., forgiveness in 5:6).

another way of expressing clearing and forgiveness; the offerer is cleared "concerning his sin that he sinned" (על־חטאתו אשר חטא) (4:35).⁶⁰ In other words, instead of stating that clearing leads to sins being removed from the offerer, the expression is more general, stating merely that clearing addresses the offerer's sins. In turn, the modifiers progressively add more and/or varied detail. By putting all of the expressions in the same section, the Priestly writers establish that the different expressions describe the same process. In each instance, regardless of the exact wording, sins are being cleared from the offerer with the result that he is forgiven by YHWH.

Chapter 5 introduces additional חטאת legislation. The first instance (5:6) mentions clearing from sin, thereby indicating that the חטאת in chapter 5 performs the same function as that in chapter 4. However, it neglects to mention forgiveness. Lest we assume that forgiveness is not implied, it appears in the following parallel examples along with clearing from "the sin that he sinned" and clearing "concerning the sin that he sinned" (5:10, 13). Once again, the presence of multiple expressions indicate that there are various ways of describing the same process.

Chapter 5:14–26 introduces the אשם legislation. In the first instance (5:16), the text provides the details of the new offering with the simple result of clearing and forgiveness. The Priestly writers thereby suggest that, although the sins and the ritual procedure differ, the goal and result are functionally the same. The next example (5:18) adds another wrinkle to the result clause, as clearing is effected concerning the offerer's inadvertent sin that he inadvertently committed (על שגגתו אשר שגג). The final example (5:26), which addresses specifically enumerated cases, adds more detail by specifying what is forgiven, namely, doing any of the things that bring guilt's consequences (ונסלח לו על־אחת מכל אשר־יעשה לאשמה בה).

a) The Nature and Function of the חטאת and the אשם Offerings for Sin in Leviticus 4–5

From the above analysis, it is clear that the חטאת rituals in Leviticus 4–5 remove sins from (מן) the offerer.⁶¹ Sin removal is described by the verb to effect clearing (כפר) and its ultimate purpose is forgiveness. However, although the results are the same, the text indicates that the crimes in 5:1–6 are more serious than those in chapter 4, or at least different. The legisla-

---

⁶⁰ Cf. Gane 2008:219–220; contra Milgrom 2007:162; Sklar 2007.

⁶¹ It remains to be seen if removing sin from the individual has any effect on the sanctuary. However, that investigation will have to wait until after Clearing Day is examined.

tion in 5:1–6 includes intentional sins, such as failing to testify (5:1), and requires a confession and compensation (אשם) in addition to sacrifice.[62]

The complex and confusing nature of the offenses in 5:1–6 also requires comment. In 5:1, a person fails to testify after hearing an imprecatory oath. To avoid the consequences of his guilt for not testifying, he must bring an offering.[63] In 5:2–3, a person fails to perform the appropriate cleansing ritual after contacting impurity from touching an unclean carcass or any human uncleanness. His action may be a conscious act that he either forgets about committing[64] or whose implications he does not fully grasp.[65] In 5:4, he makes an oath without being fully aware of its implications or which he forgets to fulfill.[66] In each of these cases, the text mentions a reparation (אשם) that takes the form of a חטאת offering.[67] It seems that such a term is necessary since all sins in 5:1–6 constitute an offense against YHWH. However, since they are only the indirect consequences of the crime itself, the reparation does not need to be an אשם offering.[68]

The burning of the חטאת fat in chapters 4–5 is also given a concomitant purpose to clearing and forgiveness; it is a soothing scent (ריח ניחח) (4:31) that serves as a complement to the clearing process. Although YHWH has bound himself to effect clearing and forgiveness, he is bound to do so only by his promise. By providing him with a pleasing aroma, the offerers acknowledge this fact and reward him for his benevolence. However, the fat's complementary role is mentioned only once lest the reader confuse the חטאת with the עלה, whose primary role is as a pleasing gift, and forget the mandatory remedial nature of the ritual.[69]

It is likewise clear that the אשם offerings of Leviticus 5:14–26 redress sin by means of a clearing ritual whose ultimate purpose is forgiveness.[70] While analogous, the text demonstrates that violations requiring an אשם offering are more serious, as the offense is labeled מעל (5:15, 21) and requires a more expensive animal than the חטאת for common people, as well as monetary compensation and a fine.

Although it is apparent that the sin's effects are cleared from the offenders, the nature of their offenses is not entirely clear. 5:14–16 clearly speaks

---

[62] Cf. Milgrom 1991:301–303; Schenker 2000:119.

[63] See esp. Wells 2004:57–59.

[64] Kiuchi 1987:28–29; Milgrom 1991:299, 312–313.

[65] Nihan 2007:239–241.

[66] Ibid. 241 and Milgrom 1991:299–300 respectively.

[67] Here, reparation (אשם) is a broad category, indicating the penalty for 'sinning,' which may include either a חטאת or an אשם offering.

[68] Nihan 2007:243–244; cf. Schenker 1999; id. 2000:108–109, 111, 118–120.

[69] Cf. the Temple Scroll, which calls the fat of the חטאת an עלה (22:04). Its authors seems to connect the fat as a gift with the gift-nature of the עלה, which serves to entreat divine favor and may contribute to clearing (e.g., Lev 9:7).

[70] In 5:14–26, the text does not mention sin removal (expressed with מן + the sins). It seems to be implied by comparison with the חטאת section. However, this is not stated explicitly, so we should not be overhasty in making such an assumption across rituals.

of sacrilege against sancta. The remaining cases are more difficult to pin down. Leviticus 5:17–19 addresses an unknown sin that requires an אשם either because the offerer's ignorance is an aggravating factor[71] or because he simply brings the most expensive sacrifice to cover all possible expiable offenses.[72] In 5:20–26, the offenses clearly address trespasses against property.[73] However, this does not seem to be enough to justify the label sacrilege and the need for an אשם offering. Instead, the major offense in 5:20–26 appears to be lying under oath in YHWH's name.[74]

After assembling the data, it seems best to conclude that the אשם offering addresses potential sacrilege, and sacrilege against sancta and YHWH's name.[75] Remedying such a direct offense against the deity requires a reparation (אשם), while its sacrificial portion may be translated as a reparation offering (אשם).[76] Furthermore, by including offenses that belong to the legal sphere (5:20–26), the Priestly writers extend the priestly purview even further.[77]

In addition to the clearing function, the burning of the offering's fat serves the complementary role of being a (food) gift to YHWH (אשה ליהוה) (7:5). The fat of the אשם plays a parallel role to that of the חטאת, providing YHWH with something pleasant during the clearing process. However, here, the gift language is more problematic, threatening to blur the line between a mandatory reparation and a voluntary gift. Thus, to minimize the confusion it appears only once, in the supplemental section to the various offerings.

6.2.3.2. Remedies for Impurity

Like the offerings for sin in Leviticus 4–5, remedies for impurity in 11–15 are cast as new legislation and may also function as an adaptation of old

---

[71] Nihan 2007:248–249.

[72] Cf. Milgrom 1991:332–333. In the end, there is little practical difference between the two positions.

[73] Marx 2003:118.

[74] The clause ונשבע על־שקר in 5:22 and the equivalent clause in 5:24 seem to refer to all preceding cases. See further Milgrom 1983:84–128; id. 1991:365–373 (cf. already Stade 1887–1888:2/256; Bertholet 1901:17); followed now by Rendtorff 1985:207; Levine 1989:32–33; Hartley 1992:83–84; Schenker 2000:120; Wells 2004:138–141; Nihan 2007:250–252; for the nature of such oaths see Westbrook 1994.

[75] Milgrom 1991:348–349.

[76] Milgrom 1976; id. 1991:327–328, 339–345, a position now accepted by most commentators.

[77] This is especially the case if Schenker (2000:120) and Nihan (2007:250–251) are correct that these verses serve as a supplement to the covenant code.

legislation to the new tabernacle/Priestly setting.[78] In the text's present form, the offerings for impurity are centralized in the sanctuary and the legislation governing them is synthesized and stressed. In each context, the unclean person must bathe, launder, and wait in order to become clean. Under special circumstances, he must also present offerings to be cleared and cleansed. Although anomalous in many respects, the purification of the skin-diseased person also includes washing and ends with clearing and cleansing. In each context, the one being cleansed moves progressively toward the sanctuary and, in the more severe cases, finishes his cleansing with sanctuary offerings. Lest the offender neglect his responsibility, the text emphasizes that refusal to deal appropriately with the impurity signals death.[79] Thus, as with the offerings for sin, offerings for impurity have become imperative sanctuary offerings.

Whereas 4–5 is rather general in its definition of what behavior prompts an offering for sin, Leviticus 11–15 enumerates various specific cases. However, as with the enumerated cases in Leviticus 5, it is unclear if the examples given are intended as a sampling or an exhaustive list.[80] As it stands, the text gives those suffering with certain afflictions a clear means of removing the final vestiges of impurity and re-entering the worshiping community. The afflicted are thus encouraged to follow YHWH's precepts and, as needed, come to his sanctuary for the final removal of the effects of impurity or face the fatal consequences.[81]

The goal statements add to this centralizing function. While the offerings for sin are rather straightforward, requiring a single offering and a single purpose statement with two elements (clearing and forgiveness), the offerings for impurity are both more complex and more variable. Nonetheless, there is a strong commonality across rituals, as in each context, the ultimate goal is cleansing. The necessary steps leading to this ultimate goal include healing, washing, bathing, and waiting, and may include sanctuary offerings that effect clearing and a final cleansing. In the most extreme case, cleansing the skin-diseased person requires an earlier ritual with two birds outside the camp, a second ablution, and another ritual with oil and an אשם offering in the sanctuary are necessary to reach its goal. In addition, since statements of clearing occur only in relation to tabernacle rituals in Leviticus 12–15, as in 4–5, clearing appears to be a tabernacle matter.

---

[78] See Nihan's diachronic solution (2007:270–301, esp. 299–301) for a possible reconstruction, wherein the Priestly writers adapt a pre-existing composition to fit the new Priestly corpus.

[79] The presence of this warning at the end of the impurity legislation provides a fitting conclusion, by stressing the importance of obedience (15:31).

[80] Since Num 19 feels free to append corpse impurity, the former seems more likely.

[81] The number and location of the steps in the progression from affliction to the sanctuary also indicates the severity of the affliction.

6.2. Individual and Communal Removal Rites

While cleansing is the ultimate goal, it is nevertheless said to occur more than once during the cleansing process. As we have seen elsewhere, multiple rites are another way of indicating the severity of the affliction and the importance and thoroughness of its removal. This oddity may have another cause as well, arising from the fact that Hebrew lacks incremental and variable language for cleansing. In other words, no words adequately indicate that cleansing is a process nor is there any way to appropriately express that different elements in the process contribute to cleansing in different ways.

Nonetheless, although the text uses the same root (טהר) to express the various aspects of cleansing, the context helps us to differentiate those aspects.[82] The first instance of cleansing designates the removal of the physical effects of the impurity, also called healing (expressed with the root רפא).[83] In each of the enumerated cases, there is a second stage of cleansing involving waiting, bathing, and washing. The presence of a second stage indicates that, once the physical impurity has been removed/cleansed, pollution/impurity remains. In order to remove enough impurity to access the sanctuary, one must also bathe and launder his clothes before being admitted the following day.[84] In the case of the seminal emittant and menstruant, this second stage is the final stage of cleansing, after which the effects of impurity have been removed and the person may re-enter the worshiping community.[85] For the others, the offender must bring an offering the following day when he accesses the sanctuary to achieve a final cleansing; this third cleansing, involving a חטאת and an עלה, is identified explicitly with clearing. For the skin-diseased person, there are two additional cleansings inserted before and after the first washing, bathing, and shaving: one as a consequence of the bird ritual outside of the camp and the other as a result of the second washing, bathing, and shaving.

In this extended ritual, the text offers indications of what the various stages of cleansing achieve. The second and third stages, the bird rite and

---

[82] Milgrom convincingly argues that each purification stage reduces the toxicity of the impurity by one degree (1991:983–1000). It is unclear whether each rite simply chips away at impurity or is designed to target a specific aspect of it.

[83] Cf. the parallel descriptions of the skin-diseased person in 13:13, 17 and 14:3. In the case of a seminal emission or menstrual impurity, although not explicitly stated, the initial cleansing naturally follows the conclusion of the defiling flow. Since these impurities are so common and so finite, mentioning the initial cleansing would be unnecessary.

[84] Ablutions occur one day before one is admitted to the sanctuary (Milgrom 1991: 966–967).

[85] This final stage is left unstated for both cases. In each, the statements imply that he will be unclean until evening or she will be unclean for seven days. From this, it follows that the individual is now clean, and the absence of any further legislation indicates that the impurities' effects have been removed fully.

the first washing, allow the offender to re-enter the camp, yet he must remain outside of his tent.[86] By inference, the next stage of cleansing, namely the second ablution, allows him to enter his tent. However, as elsewhere, he must wait until the following day to access the sanctuary.[87] The three sanctuary rituals then occur in succession, each of which is said to effect clearing.[88] After the final ritual, the presentation of the burnt offerings, the offerer is clean, i.e., he is free from the effects of his impurity and he is free to resume normal activity.

Within these rites, the Priestly writers are inconsistent in expressing their goal statements, at times omitting certain elements. The cleansing of the parturient mentions two cleansings, related to healing and clearing. However, the second stage related to washing and laundering is missing. The cleansing of the man with a discharge mentions two cleansings, related to healing and washing and waiting. However, the text fails to mention cleansing with clearing. The cleansing of the woman with a discharge mentions two cleansings, related to healing and waiting (washing and laundering are omitted), but fails to mention cleansing with clearing. Finally, aspects of bathing, laundering, and waiting are omitted in various places. These omissions may be explained by the complex history that lies behind the text, by the writers' economic language, by their rhetorical purpose, or because of simple carelessness. Regardless, in the present context, the variable actions and the various means of expressing them connect each ritual process to the common goal of cleansing.

In turn, to accurately reconstruct the envisioned rituals, my conclusions necessarily build upon the explicit purpose statements.[89] By filling in the informational gaps, three categories of removal emerge.[90] In each case, the complexity and amount of ritualized actions indicate the severity of the pollution. The first category includes the rites for the seminal emittant and the menstruant and involves two stages, initial healing (i.e., the impure flow has stopped) and bathing, laundering, and waiting. The second group, including the parturient and the man or woman with an impure discharge, involves three stages: initial healing; bathing, laundering, and waiting; and sanctuary offerings. The skin-diseased person constitutes the third category. His cleansing involves five stages: initial healing, a bird ritual outside

---

[86] These extra stages are necessary since the skin-diseased person's impurity was severe enough to necessitate banishment from the camp.

[87] This finds support in the parallel case in Leviticus 12:4, where the parturient is barred from the sanctuary before presenting her offerings.

[88] Although not explicitly said to cleanse, these three ritual sequences do effect clearing. Their presence in the larger ritual complex and their role as vehicles of clearing thus contribute to the overall goal of cleansing.

[89] Compare my conclusions with the results at the end of the use section.

[90] Cf. Milgrom 1991:976–1000.

6.2. Individual and Communal Removal Rites 153

the camp, two bathing, laundering, washing, and waiting stages, and a final sanctuary offering stage (which itself is divided into three sub-stages involving oil and an אשם, a חטאת, and an עלה). In each removal rite, access is granted to the sanctuary after bathing, laundering, and waiting. Pollution in the second and third categories are severe enough to require sanctuary offerings to redress impurity and allow the individuals to resume normal life.[91]

The potential for contagion adds complexity to impurities and their cleansing processes. To begin with, it is unclear which impurities are contagious, since the animals in chapter 11 and the afflictions in chapter 15 alone are described as contagious. The element of contagion may be implied for the other categories or else must be limited to genital discharges and impure animals.[92] Despite the dearth of solid evidence, the former conclusion seems more feasible.

Perhaps the strongest evidence for the contagiousness of all impurities may be adduced from Leviticus 5:2–3, where contact with (minor) human and animal uncleanness requires cleansing and/or forgiveness, depending on how it is redressed. However, it is possible that human uncleanness refers to the genital discharges in Leviticus 15, while animal uncleanness refers to chapter 11. The individual texts are likewise ambiguous. While pregnancy itself is not contagious, it is possible that the impurity generated by childbirth may be contracted. Finally, skin disease is a particularly complicated example. It seems clear that the skin disease is in some way contagious since the infected must be isolated from the community. However, it remains unclear if the contagion refers to the skin disease itself or merely the pollution it generates. Contra Milgrom,[93] the former possibility is supported by the legislation for 'skin' disease in garments, which concerns itself explicitly with the spread of the infection (in addition, there is a difference between actual and perceived contagion). If both the disease and its pollution are contagious, skin disease, in addition to being closely associated with sin,[94] may also be especially serious because of its dual contagion. It is likewise possible that skin-disease pollutes by overhang,[95] i.e., anyone under the same roof is infected. However, this seems less likely since Milgrom's case is based on a comparison with the infected house. Because part of the house is visibly infected, the whole house is infected and thus contagious. In the same way, although the infection manifests itself on part of the infected individual, the whole individual is infected and hence contagious. There is, however, no indication that the individual's contagion extends to the whole house. Thus, overhang does not seem to apply.

---

[91] The skin-diseased person's severe condition mandates expulsion from the camp and thus requires a special ritual for re-entry. The severity of the condition necessitates two stages of laundering, washing, and waiting and includes a new element, shaving, in each stage. It likewise requires a more elaborate sanctuary ritual to redress the impurity and re-institute the individual into normal society.

[92] Since contact with the corpses of impure animals renders one impure, the impure animal is, in effect, a living disease, whose negative effects – i.e., uncleanness – may be contracted.

[93] Id. 1991:805, 815–818.

[94] Ibid. 363–364.

[95] Ibid. 992–993.

It is perhaps most likely that skin disease is considered so severe because of its visible association with death.[96]

Regardless of the severity of the initial impurity, cleansing of those secondarily afflicted requires a single stage of laundering, bathing, and waiting (15:5–11, 21–23, 27).[97] The afflicted does not need to be healed/cleansed from the disease since he never contracted it himself. He merely absorbs the negative consequences of the physical impurity by contact. Thus, it seems that regardless of the severity of the initial affliction or its power to pollute the afflicted, the affliction affects all others equally.[98]

The instrumentality of the removal rites for impurity is similar to those for sin. The priest is the subject of clearing and the individual its indirect object. As with the offerings for sin, the indirect object marker, על, indicates that there is no direct contact between offering blood and offerer and that the priest alone does not cause clearing. YHWH's participation is necessary, and he cannot be compelled to offer it.

Cleansing is expressed in an analogous way to forgiveness. In most instances, the offender is the subject of the stative טהר, indicating that he becomes clean as an automatic result of the cleansing process.[99] Thus, the priest is not the (sole) instrument of cleansing. If the impurity is severe enough, the remedy requires the participation of the offerer, the priest, and deity in a tabernacle ritual. When less severe, the priest is excluded from the cleansing process; the offerer must perform the appropriate washing rituals himself and wait, while YHWH is implicitly involved in that he prescribes the ritual remedy.

Although they do not follow a clear progression like the offerings for sin, the modifiers of clearing and cleansing are also illustrative. The gen-

---

[96] Ibid. 819

[97] The discrepancy, lying with a woman during menstrual impurity, may be explained by the close proximity to the 'disease.' Such an intimate encounter is akin to contracting the 'disease,' and thus bears a similar penalty.

[98] Although a bit of a stretch, this principle may even help to explain the different levels of quarantine. For most cases, regardless of whether or not they require a sanctuary offering, the pollution itself is the only contagion. Thus, the individual is isolated from the sanctuary while others are warned of the effects of his impurity. If both the disease and its pollution are contagious, the individual with skin disease must be isolated from the sanctuary and isolated from the community.

[99] The priest is at times said to pronounce the afflicted clean (טהר) (e.g., 13:6, 13, 17, 37), which in each context means that he is clean (טהור). Pronouncing him clean is not, however, the same as making him clean. The priest merely judges the condition of the disease. If it is sufficiently healed, he merely labels the afflicted clean (it is also possible that the priest is pronouncing the disease [נגע] clean, which would have the equivalent result). 14:7 and 11 may share the same meaning or represent an exception. In the latter case, the priest would cleanse the skin-diseased person by performing the bird ritual with the implicit participation of YHWH who prescribes the ritual.

eral expression that the offerer is cleared concerning (כפר על) his impurities does not appear. Instead, we find simple clearing and clearing from (כפר מן) impurities. Cleansing, as well, either stands alone or is modified by מן. The presence of both formulations in parallel cases indicates that each describes part of the same process, namely removing impurities from the offerer so that he becomes clean.

The location of the expressions, clearing and cleansing, and their modifiers is also illustrative. Clearing appears with the parturient and the people with impure discharges following the חטאת and עלה offerings. In the case of the skin-diseased person, it follows the oil and אשם ritual, the חטאת ritual, and the עלה ritual. Thus, in the context of offerings for impurity in Leviticus 12–15, like those for sin in 4–5, כפר is the result of sanctuary rituals.[100]

Although it appears numerous times alone, cleansing is modified by מן only after the disease is healed (12:7; 15:13, 28) or after כפר is mentioned (14:19). This may serve to express that cleansing from impurity is the same as initial healing, while clearing from the impurity (or in the case of 14:19, clearing for the individual to be cleansed from the impurity)[101] means the same thing as final cleansing. Thus, both ends of the process involve removing impurities, in the first case the physical affliction and in the second the residual results of that affliction.

a) The Nature and Function of the Rituals for Removing Impurity

Cleansing rites clearly remove impurities from the afflicted individual. However, the summary in 15:31–33[102] muddies the interpretive waters by suggesting that the Israelites pollute (טמא) the sanctuary with their impurities, thereby suggesting that the people's impurity has an effect on the sanctuary. Cleansing rites naturally result in the individual being clean and require clearing only under certain circumstances. The presence of clearing and the length and complexity of the cleansing rites serve to indicate the severity of the affliction. Various elements, including the אשם and חטאת rituals, contribute to the overall purpose of cleansing. We will return in chapter 7 to the function of clearing and the role of אשם and חטאת in achieving it. For the present, our comments will focus on the anomalous bird rites and the oil and אשם rites for the individual being cleansed from skin disease.

---

[100] Cf., however, 14:53.

[101] Again note that it is unclear if the object of clearing is the impurity or the individual.

[102] Summarizing either all of 11–15 or at least 15 (vv. 32–33 suggest the latter but do not rule out the former).

In the bird ritual, the priests seem to incorporate a pre-existing removal rite into their new sanctuary system. In the Priestly hands, the rite still seems to remove impurity from the one being cleansed.[103] Nonetheless, it is one of many steps since serious impurities like skin-disease require multiple means to achieve the ultimate end.[104] As the various rites combat impurity, the offender moves closer to the sanctuary. In addition to its incremental effect, the rite serves a rhetorical purpose, indicating that the boundary between the camp and the outside world is similar to that between the sanctuary and the camp. In other words, serious impurity (i.e., imperfection) is not welcome in the camp and requires serious steps to reinstitute anyone who has been afflicted with it.

At first glance, the אשם offering in 14:12–17 appears misplaced.[105] Nevertheless, whatever else it may mean, it too has a rhetorical role to play in the cleansing process. Everything about the offering suggests that it is different from other אשם offerings, while it shares substantial common ground with the priestly ordination offering and some common ground with the bird rite in 14:4–7. Unlike the other אשם offerings, the אשם offering in Leviticus 14 is a lamb instead of a ram, the offering occurs first in the ritual sequence, its blood is applied to the person, and the blood is mixed with oil. As in the ordination rite, blood and oil are applied to the right ear, right thumb, and right big toe. However, the two rites differ in that the oil and the offerings that supply the blood are not the same,[106] the אשם rite minimizes the connection between the offerer and the altar,[107] and while the ordination offering and oil consecrate (Lev 8:10–15), the text implies no

---

[103] The sprinkling rite seems to transfer impurity from the offerer to the living bird. The offerer is then declared clean since the impurity has been transferred from him and the live bird is then sent away so that the impurity stays away.

[104] If we subdivide the cleansing rites, we may conclude that, together, the bird rite and first ablution remove enough impurity for the person to enter the camp. However, it is perhaps more natural to conclude that each rite simply attacks the impurity until it is eventually eliminated, and that as the rites are performed the one being cleansed moves closer and closer to the sanctuary.

[105] Milgrom argues that the priest offers the אשם to account for the possibility that the one being cleansed committed sacrilege and/or that he violated one of the prohibitive commandments unknowingly as in 5:17–19 (1991:363–364). However, as we will see, various ritual elements differentiate this אשם from the others recounted in chapter 5, suggesting that it may have a different function. Also, if Milgrom is correct that the אשם is the central rite in the cleansing process, it seems odd that the central rite would only be precautionary.

[106] In the אשם rite, the offering blood naturally comes from an אשם and the oil is simply a log of oil (לג שמן אחד), whereas in the ordination rite, the blood comes from the offerings manipulated on the altar, which do not include an אשם, and the oil is the special anointing oil.

[107] In that there is no mention of applying the blood or oil to the altar.

such purpose for the אשם and the oil. Both the bird rite and the אשם in Leviticus 14 are abnormal and involve the application of blood to persons.

In context, the אשם in 14:12–17 suggests that drastic, even unnatural, measures are necessary to reinstate the offerer into the worshiping community. This re-institution is akin to yet distinct from his reintroduction into the camp and the priest's inauguration into his sacred priestly role.[108] In short, each procedure in its own way indicates the seriousness (and unnaturalness) of being in community with YHWH and especially of accessing his home.

The choice of an אשם offering may also be a matter of necessity since no other offering would suffice. The blood of the חטאת is never applied to persons and features elsewhere in the tabernacle ritual.[109] The ordination offering is only suitable for ordaining priests, while the עלה, מנחה, and זבח שלמים likewise seem inappropriate. The מנחה has no blood, the עלה already appears in the ritual, the זבח שלמים does not seem to fit the occasion, and the presence of both the עלה and the זבח שלמים might confuse the cleansing rite with the non-Priestly covenant inauguration of Exodus 24. Thus, the priests are left with the אשם offering to restore the offerer's status. More than simply being the least problematic option, the אשם also plays a positive role as a reparation, repairing the damage caused by severe impurity and reintegrating the offerer into the sacred realm without making him holy.

While it is clear that the offerings for impurity remove impurity, it is unclear if there is a unifying rationale to these regulations. Various scholars have sought the unifying principle with varying degrees of success.[110] The most palatable harmonizing principle seems to be that the Priestly impurities represent an "intrusion of the biological into the social sphere."[111] However, it is not without shortcomings. The theory is general enough to cover the enumerated elements, but perhaps too general to be overly illus-

---

[108] It is also possible that the author has in mind the non-priestly application of blood to the people (Ex 24). The Priestly authors may then be differentiating the rites. Whereas an עלה and זבח שלמים may suffice to inaugurate a covenant, skin disease is an offense that requires a reparation (אשם), namely an אשם offering (the Priests may only have meant to indicate that the re-admittance of the former skin-diseased person is not the same as rejoining the covenant community).

[109] The red heifer's blood is the only exception (Num 19), and it is possible that it stems from another hand (either H or the theocratic revision).

[110] See the helpful summary and critique by Nihan (2007:301–317, 324–339), who separately describes the attempts to unify chapters 12–15 and 11 respectively.

[111] Nihan 2007:307–323, after Dumont 1967:85. For him, Lev 11 introduces the rest of the legislation and connects it with the restoration of creational order, i.e., systematic control of intrusive biological forces contributes to re-creation (Nihan 2007: 338–339), or perhaps more specifically to an environment suitable for YHWH to dwell on earth.

trative. While it is of course true that the impurities mentioned are biological forces and that such forces are considered disruptive, this theory does not tell us why other 'impurities' are not included. Likewise, it is somewhat misleading, since the primary focus is the integrity of the sanctuary, while the social order is important only as it affects and reflects the resident deity. It thus seems more appropriate to conclude that the legislation serves to protect the sacred sphere, and by extension the community that reflects it, from physical imperfections that separate humanity from YHWH. Leviticus 11 would then be an appropriate introduction, serving to illustrate that God's people must avoid physical imperfection, whether animal or human, if he is to profitably live among them.[112] Although helpful, this definition is nonetheless too general, failing to account for various omissions. In the end, the quest for a more precise theory may be futile, and, worse yet, misleading; for, if the legislation reflects or even dimly resembles real practice, it undoubtedly has a complex genesis. In ancient times as today[113] purity regulations, like etiquette, are complex phenomena governed by and arising from multiple factors.[114] To reduce them to a single principle is to distort them.

6.2.4. Synthesis of Leviticus 4–5 and 12–15

As in the ANE, Leviticus 4–5 and 12–15 address the removal of sins and impurities from individuals, which naturally benefits the individuals involved by returning them to a state of relative wholeness and granting them access to the tabernacle complex. Such rites are also a boon to the sanctuary since removal rites prevent individuals from physically carrying their pollution with them into the sacred sphere. As elsewhere in the Priestly cultic system, ritual roles are clearly defined. The offerers present, lay their hands upon, and slaughter their offerings, the priests exclusively officiate at the bronze and incense altars; and offerings are presented to YHWH,[115] while ritual action occurs before him.

The Priestly writers use clearing (כפר) to express this removal process, which in the individual rites is a sub-goal of forgiveness and cleansing in Leviticus 4–5 and 12–15 respectively. In contrast to the ANE, this clearing for the full removal of individual sins and severe impurities must be effect-

---

[112] Cf. Houston 2003:159, who contends that Leviticus 11–15 informs "Israel how they may live in such a way as to be in conformity with Yahweh's ordering of the cosmos."

[113] Compare Fox's *Watching the English* (2005), which examines the complex factors that determine acceptable social behavior in modern England.

[114] Alternatively, the impurities may have been culled from a larger list of real impurities to serve a single rhetorical purpose. Either way, greater precision is elusive.

[115] E.g., 4:3; 5:6–7, 15, 25; 7:3–5.

ed in the sanctuary. Without it, the ultimate goal of forgiveness and cleansing cannot be secured from YHWH in the Priestly system. However, the pollution accrued in the sanctuary itself also must be cleared to preserve the system, to keep heaven on earth.

6.3. Clearing Day

Although integral to the system, the damage control rites in Leviticus 4–5 and 12–15 alone are insufficient. While these rites may remove individuals' pollution, thereby halting its spread, they do not redress the pollution that has affixed itself to the sanctuary, whether from people's forgiven sins, cleansed impurities, or other sins and impurities that either have not been or cannot be remedied.[116] To safeguard the divine presence, to effect full and final removal of pollution from the sanctuary, Clearing Day is necessary.

6.3.1. Structure

Like the tabernacle dedication, regular service, and individual and communal removal rites, the structure of Leviticus 16 informs the reader about the relationships between people and objects and does so in a way that differentiates this day from all others. On Clearing Day, ritual action casts a broader net than ever before, encompassing in one ritual the major aspects of the Israelite community including YHWH and the three significant spaces of his tabernacle complex,[117] the animals, natives, aliens, and priests. It also introduces foreign elements in Azazel and the wilderness.[118] In addition to being indexically connected to more entities, objects, and locations, the people and priests are more connected to YHWH than ever before. Aaron accesses the inner sanctuary and therein manipulates the blood of his and the people's חטאת offerings.[119] Each element is also connected to clearing and the pollution being cleared. In fact, YHWH's sanctuary and, by extension, YHWH himself are more closely associated with sin and impurity on Clearing Day than during the rest of the year. In Levit-

---

[116] I.e., pardonable offenses that have not been pardoned or unpardonable offenses that cannot be pardoned.

[117] Namely, the inner and outer sanctuaries and the bronze altar.

[118] The identity and meaning of Azazel (עזאזל) remains uncertain (see, e.g., Janowski 1999:128). Of the various possibilities, Azazel as a (demonic) entity best fits the evidence available at present (see, e.g., Nihan 2007:351–353, esp. n. 379, for a recent summary).

[119] Unlike elsewhere (e.g., in Leviticus 4 and 12), on Clearing Day, there is no distinction between non-priestly offerers, as all share the same חטאת offering.

icus 4–5 and 12–15, sin and impurity are indexically connected to YHWH and his sanctuary, since rites in his sanctuary effect their removal. Leviticus 16:16 makes this connection more concrete, since these pollutants must be removed from the sanctuary. Thus, in addition to being involved with clearing pollutants, YHWH's home is also afflicted by them.

The ritual actions that join people and objects also separate them from each other and differentiate this day's rites from all others. While the blood of the priest's and people's offerings have equal and unprecedented access, ritual roles of the offerers are more polarized. The people have less ritual responsibility, since the priest usurps the people's ritual actions such that a single priest is the lone ritual actor.[120] Whereas in Leviticus 4–5 and 12–15 the individual brings, lays his hand on, and slaughters his offering, in Leviticus 16 the priest slaughters the animal, and, instead of a single hand, lays both his hands on the second goat's head, confessing את־כל־עונות בני ישראל ואת־כל־פשעיהם לכל־חטאתם. The people's only ritual role is to provide their offerings, which the priest then takes and officiates with.[121] To fill the space left by their diminished role in the offering rituals, the people pick up the new responsibility of self-abasement and abstention from work. By contrast, the priest's ritual action is more elaborate and far-ranging than anywhere else in Leviticus 1–16. Instead of remaining in the outer sanctuary and at the bronze altar, he enters the adytum and applies blood on and before the כפרת, the locus of divine presence and the heart of sacred space. Aaron's actions are also more elaborate at the bronze altar. In addition to the normal application of blood to its horns (compare 4:30 with 16:18), the priest sprinkles blood on the altar seven times (16:19). Furthermore, although he himself does not lead the second goat away, he places the people's pollution upon it and banishes it to the wilderness. Thus, priestly influence extends beyond the sacred sphere. In turn, the complexity of the ritual action, its differentiation from other rites, and the prominence of the priest's role in performing it mark Clearing Day as special and intimate that it is especially important.

This complex activity is also governed by a clear spatial trajectory. Beginning in YHWH's inner sanctuary, activity progresses outward until it

---

[120] The identity of the main ritual actor is unclear; it seems to be Aaron in 2–28 or his successor in 29–34. This discrepancy may be due to different textual layers, or it simply could be expressing continuity (i.e., Aaron's descendants will continue to officiate after him) (compare, e.g., Nihan 2007:347–348 with Gorman 1990:71). Regardless of how we resolve the difficulty, there is only one priestly ritual actor at a time.

[121] However, individuals do have some role to play. An unknown man (איש עתי) leads away the second goat (21–22, 26), while other unidentified people burn the sacrificial remains (27–28).

6.3. Clearing Day

ends in the wilderness with Azazel.[122] The evils addressed follow the same trajectory. At first, the people's pollutants are attached to the tabernacle complex. Soon thereafter, they are successively cleared from its three layers.[123] The people's pollutants are then removed from the community by means of the second goat and end up in the wilderness with Azazel. This removal also serves to reinforce the boundaries of most sacred space[124] and to distinguish that space clearly from the wilderness. The evils that are progressively cleared from the tabernacle complex through ritual activity in its three zones are cleared to the wilderness, where they presumably remain.

The ritual further distinguishes between YHWH and Azazel. YHWH receives all the offerings and evils are cleared from his sanctuary. The goat for Azazel is brought before YHWH in order to effect clearing on it by sending it to Azazel with all the Israelites' pollutants.

Priestly bathing and robing (4, 23–24) connect the intervening ritual actions and separate them from the rest of the ritual. The חטאת bull and goat and their blood manipulations in the three sacred spheres as well as the ritual with the goat for Azazel fall within the inclusio. Burning the fat of the חטאת offerings, offering the burnt offerings, the disposal of remains, the clean-up for the handlers of Azazel's goat and the sacrificial remains, and the people's self-abasement and abstention from work fall outside of it. Although they fit into the same ritual envelope, the offerings in the sanctuary complex and the banishment of the second goat are nonetheless distinguished from each other. First, the offenses removed from the sanctuary (impurities and sins) are different from those loaded onto Azazel's goat (עונות and sins).[125] Second, 16:20 speaks of finishing effecting clearing for the three tiers of the sanctuary before the priest performs the main elements of the ritual for Azazel's goat.

---

[122] While the general movement is clear, it is unclear if the outward progression is uninterrupted, since the specific application of verse 16, וכן יעשה לאהל מועד, is ambiguous.

[123] In each layer (comprising the bronze altar and the outer and inner sanctuaries), clearing likely involves two blood manipulations (see previous note for potential complications in the outer sanctuary). However, the manipulations at the bronze altar differ from those inside the tent, as, in the second blood manipulation, the blood is sprinkled on the altar seven times instead of on the ground.

[124] I.e., the tent and the bronze altar in the courtyard, the places that indexically connect the three ritual actors (priests, people and YHWH) and involve blood manipulations.

[125] There is also some variability of expression within both sections. In 16:19, Aaron cleanses and consecrates the altar from Israel's impurities (וטהרו וקדשו מטמאת בני ישראל), while in 16:22 the goat bears the עונות of the people to the wilderness.

6.3.2. Use

The *causa* for Clearing Day does not emerge clearly from the context. Chapter 16 opens with divine counsel to Aaron on how to approach YHWH in the adytum to prevent his death after the deaths of Nadab and Abihu (2, 13), yet there is clearly more to the day than entering the divine presence. The purpose statements pick up the slack, identifying the day as the annual clearing of the people's corporate pollution from both the tabernacle complex and the community.[126] The individual purpose statements add specificity to this larger goal.

Whereas the ultimate goal for offerings for sin and impurity are forgiveness and cleansing respectively, the ultimate goal of Clearing Day naturally is clearing. In Leviticus 4–5 and 12–15, clearing is effected for the people so that they may be forgiven and cleansed, respectively. In Leviticus 16, the ritual components are aimed at effecting clearing, with no mention of forgiveness or cleansing from impurity.[127] This clearing on Clearing Day appears multiple times with multiple objects, instruments, and prepositional modifiers. It occurs 15 times in the chapter and is effected for the priests, people, the adytum, the tent of meeting, and the altar (6, 11, 16–18, 20, 30, 33–34). The bull, the two goats, and the burnt offerings are the explicit agents of clearing,[128] while the people's self-abasement and cessation from all work seems to contribute to the clearing process.[129] In one case, a single element, the bull, is the instrument of clearing for the priests, and, with the first goat's blood, the sanctuary, the tent, and the altar. Its blood and the goat's blood also cleanse (טהר) and consecrate (קדש) the bronze altar from Israel's impurities (מטמאת בני ישראל) (16–19).

Because of its anomalous nature, the second goat receives the fullest explanation. It is presented alive before YHWH for the purpose of effecting clearing on it by sending it to Azazel in the wilderness (לכפר עליו לשלח אתו לעזאזל המדברה) (10). The text also provides a hint about the manner in which the goat achieves clearing, namely the priest confesses over it את־כל־עונות בני ישראל ואת־כל־פשעיהם לכל־חטאתם so that it may

---

[126] 16:29 and 34 express the annual nature of the rite. However, it seems that 29–34 and their purpose statements were appended to an earlier ritual that lacked them (attributed by Milgrom 1991:1064–1065 and Knohl 1995:27–29, e.g., to H). Rather than trying to uncover the likely complex genesis of the chapter, we will analyze its present form as a coherent ritual text (cf. Gane 2005:25–42).

[127] However, clearing does appear anomalously with cleansing from sin (30).

[128] The recipient of the second goat's clearing is unstated. Nonetheless, it seems best to assume that the goat effects clearing for the people since their pollution is confessed over the goat and sent into the wilderness.

[129] Whether they effect clearing themselves, form a necessary part of the clearing process, or are simply the appropriate response to clearing, it is clear that humility and refraining from work are a requisite part of the larger ritual (29–31).

bear them into the wilderness (21–22). Although the text only mentions the goat bearing the עוונת of the people, we may assume that this is a shorthand expression, meant to encompass all three categories.[130]

6.3.3. Ideology

Leviticus 16 introduces important legislation.[131] Clearing Day demonstrates how to ensure that the precarious balance that is God's presence on earth does not tip in an unfavorable direction. More specifically, it communicates how the priest may approach YHWH annually to effect clearing for both the sanctuary complex and the people, so that divine presence and divine service remain undeterred.

An examination of the purpose statements gives us our first clue as to how Clearing Day functions. On one hand, statements about effecting clearing for people are sparsely adorned. Although clearing is effected for the priests and the people, this process does not result in forgiveness or cleansing from impurities. In fact, the purpose statements describing the effects of clearing for people are entirely unadorned, except in the concluding statements in verses 29–34.[132]

On the other hand, the purpose statements relating to the sanctuary, tent, and altar are rather robust. This is especially striking since Exodus 29 and Leviticus 8, referring to the dedication of the cult, list the only other instances of sancta clearing. In those texts, there is no mention of clearing from sins or impurities. Clearing is simply effected for the altar to prepare it for effective use, likely removing vestiges of the mundane sphere so that the altar can be perfectly pure as YHWH is perfectly pure. By contrast, effecting clearing for the adytum removes from it both sins and impurities (מטמאות בני ישראל ומפשעיהם לכל־חטאתם) (16a). Performing the same actions (כן) in the outer sanctuary seems to serve the same purpose (16b), while unique blood manipulation on the bronze altar effects clearing for it, cleanses it, and consecrates it from Israelite impurities (18–19).[133]

---

[130] Cf. Milgrom 1991:1043.

[131] In its literary context, with the other legislation in 4–5 and 11–15, it introduces damage control, a Priestly answer to how flawed Israel is meant to live profitably with their God. In its historical context, it explains what went wrong and, perhaps, what is necessary to secure a better future.

[132] In vv. 29–34, we find the enigmatic statement that clearing is effected for the people to cleanse them from their sins (30) and another declaring that clearing is effected for them from all their sins (34). In fact, there is no indication in the main body of the text that clearing is effected at all for the people at large.

[133] Although impurities and sins are different entities, impurities here likely serves as an inexact shorthand for the pollutants described in v. 16.

The Azazel goat also plays an unprecedented role as the vessel upon which clearing is effected.[134] Because of its aberrant nature, the text provides further specificity. The purpose of presenting the goat before YHWH is to effect clearing on it by sending it to Azazel in the wilderness (10).[135] Verses 21–22 identify its cargo. The priest confesses over the goat את־כל־ עונת בני ישראל ואת־כל־פשעיהם לכל־חטאתם, and the goat bears the עונת (and presumably the other elements as well) to an inaccessible area.[136] In short, clearing is effected by means of the expulsion of specific pollutants.

Thus, something different is occurring on this special day. Here and nowhere else, on Clearing Day, pollutants are cleared (i.e., removed) from the sanctuary and cleared (i.e., removed) from the community on the goat for Azazel. This departure from regular practice is mirrored in the spatial dimension. On Clearing Day, activities move ever outward, matching the trajectory of pollutants from the holy-of-holies to the wilderness, outside of both God's kingdom and human habitation.[137]

6.3.3.1. Pollutants Removed

טמאות, which are cleared from the sanctuary alone, is the most straightforward term, referring naturally to impurities arising from certain physical conditions.[138] The term פשע is more elusive, as it occurs only here in the Priestly texts (16:16, 21).[139] Elsewhere, the verb and noun refer to disen-

---

[134] It parallels the bird rite for the house (14:34–53) in that an animal is the instrument of clearing by removing and expelling impurity. However, the Azazel goat alone is presented before YHWH as a חטאת that removes and expels human sins (on its identification as a חטאת and the translation 'clearing upon,' see Milgrom 1991:1018, 1023; Gane 2005:246–261).

[135] "The final phrase of this verse, 'by sending it to Azazel into the wilderness,' is in apposition to 'to make expiation by it' in order to define how expiation will be accomplished with this particular goat" (Hartley 1992:236; cf. Heinisch 1935:74).

[136] עונת, as above (see previous page), seems to be an inexact shorthand for the three pollutants. Such inexactitude is also rhetorically significant as bearing עונת is a way of expressing guilt, more specifically, the responsibility for and effects of Israelite sins (cf. Schwartz 1994; 1995). Since guilt has been literally carried away, it no longer has any effect on the community or its God. The phrase, bearing עונת, powerfully expresses this proposition.

[137] Jenson 1992:201–203.

[138] Schwartz (1995) has conclusively differentiated between sins and impurities, noting that they produce similar yet distinct defilement that must be removed by חטאת offerings.

[139] Perhaps because the Priests are adapting an earlier text or interacting with the Prophets, who frequently employ the term.

gaging from a social partner or his property, and can be roughly translated as 'rebel' and 'rebellion' or 'commit a breach' and 'breach' respectively.[140]

The mention of the Nadab and Abihu incident at the beginning of chapter 16 provides another clue. Elsewhere, the Priestly texts in Leviticus describe expiable offenses, since they focus on the damage control process wherein the sin and impurity are ritually removed from the individual. The death of Nadab and Abihu in Leviticus 10 clearly fits in another category. While the effect on Nadab and Abihu is obvious enough, the text does not enumerate the consequences for the community and sanctuary. By connecting the Nadab and Abihu incident to Leviticus 16, the Priestly writers suggest that Clearing Day provides the solution. Since sins (חטאת) are a general category that includes expiable offenses, the Priests need another term to specifically describe inexpiable sins. פשע as a breach against YHWH, roughly akin to high-handed sins in Numbers 15 (ביד רמה), is the Priestly word of choice.[141]

The phrase לכל־חטאתם is also problematic. Outside of the Priestly texts, חטאת refers to sins in general, whether expiable or not. In Leviticus 1–15, the term is restricted to expiable offenses because these are the only offenses discussed.[142] However, in Leviticus 16, חטאת should revert to its normal meaning, all kinds of sins, expiable and inexpiable.[143] How then does לכל function? The ל specifies what precedes it, whereas כל expresses the totality of what follows.[144] Together לכל clarifies the term or terms[145] that precede it with the term or terms that follow it.[146] In the end, we are

---

[140] Cf. the clarifications of Knierim (1965:176–184; id. *TLOT* 2:1033–1037). More than simply rebelling, the perpetrator of פשע "breaks with [YHWH], takes away what is his, robs, embezzles, misappropriates it" (ibid. 1036). Carpenter and Grisanti identify its fundamental sense as covenant treachery (*NIDOTTE* 3:707).

[141] Cf., e.g., Gorman 1990:82; Milgrom 1991:257; Wright 1991:163; Nihan 2007:189 n. 347.

[142] As the lone exception, Leviticus 10 obviously describes an inexpiable sin, but does not label it as such; instead the fatal consequence identifies it as inexpiable.

[143] *Pace* Gane 2005:292–293. This general meaning is reinforced by the usage in the Holiness Legislation, where certain sins (חטאת) are inexpiable (Lev 26:18, 21, 24, 28).

[144] Kiuchi 1987:187 n. 50.

[145] Although the term following לכל often clarifies a list of terms, there is no reason why it could not clarify just one.

[146] Gane (2005:285–291) suggests that עונת, פשעים, and חטאת are distinct categories, drawing from the presence of ולכל in Leviticus 11:46 to introduce a new item. Although his perspective has the benefit of the LXX translation, καὶ πάσας τὰς ἁμαρτίας αὐτῶν, it is ultimately unconvincing. Wherever ולכל appears, often in context of a list, the ו as in English is decisive. It renders לכל which follows as a separate item in a list, rather than a clarification of what precedes it. As far as I can tell, there is no other example without the ו that does so. Although it is technically possible that חטאת could be used to summarize both preceding terms, this is also unlikely since impurities may not be subsumed under the general category חטאת. It is also possible that חטאת is in apposition to פשעים, but

left with two basic options: only inexpiable sins or expiable and inexpiable sins. The presence of impurity removal weighs in favor of the second option.[147] More specifically, the removal of impurities (טמאות) from the sanctuary, which have elsewhere been removed from the offerers (Lev 12–15), suggests that sins, which have elsewhere been removed from the offerers (4–5), are here being removed from the sanctuary as well.[148] Thus, we translate לכל־חטאתם loosely as 'including all their sins.'

Although the second two terms are the same, כל־פשעיהם לכל־חטאתם, the goat for the Azazel rite (16:21) introduces a new term in place of the first, טמאות, namely עונת. Once committed a sinful act naturally brings accompanying guilt and leads to punishment. Of all the Hebrew lexemes, עון seems to best capture this process. In turn, עון is most commonly understood as referring to any part of the sin, guilt, and punishment process.[149] In the Priestly texts, עון appears regularly in the phrase נשא עון, a term with juridical implications defined as sin-bearing.[150] It speaks of the offender being burdened with the consequences of sin, i.e., guilt that leads to punishment.[151] From this, it is natural to conclude that עון means something like 'culpability.'[152] However, since it appears here without נשא for the only time in Leviticus 1–16, it could also indicate sin.

Originally, עון may have stood alone in 16:21 as it does in 16:22.[153] The phrase כל־פשעיהם לכל־חטאתם may then serve as an explanatory gloss, indicating what sort of עונת are intended: all kinds of sins including rebel-

---

again this is unlikely since חטאת and פשעים are not identical. If our interpretation of חטאת is correct, we may also eliminate the exclusive use of לכל since פשעים is a subcategory of חטאת.

[147] See also the presence of sin removal from the people in 16:30 and 34. Schwartz (1995:18) argues for the genitival use, in line with Milgrom's model, where only defiant sins penetrate into the adytum. However, since he rightly differentiates impurities from sins, his theory does not explain how the impurities penetrate into the adytum.

[148] Our position holds even if we are talking about different impurities and sins than had previously been removed from the offerers or potentially even if we posit the same impurities and sins that had implicitly been removed from the sanctuary elsewhere. In either situation, it would be odd for impurities and inexpiable sins to be removed without inadvertent sins.

[149] So *BDB* 6866 p. 731; *HALOT* 799–800; Knierim *TLOT* 2 (1997):864; Gane 2005: 294; *DCH* 6.307–311.

[150] Schwartz 1994; id. 1995; for its juridical nature, see esp. Wells 2004:79–82.

[151] Milgrom 2000:1488–1490, who claims that punishment always follows even if that punishment is an offering; Wells 2004:73–78, drawing on Neo-Babylonian legal documents; Sklar 2005:20–23; Nihan 2007:242.

[152] So Gane 2005:294. It is possible that since the longer phrase נשא עון does not fit in context the author inserted the shorter עון, intending it to carry similar connotations. This is especially likely when read in tandem with נשא עון in 16:22.

[153] See Löhr 1925:3–4; Elliger 1966:206; Wright 1987:18–19; Nihan 2007:192–193.

lious acts.[154] Perhaps more likely, whether or not it stems from a later revision, the phrase כל־פשעיהם לכל־חטאתם expands the bounds of the removal rite, while simultaneously clarifying the use of עונת.[155] If our interpretation is correct that the ו connecting טמאות and פשעיהם is a simple ו,[156] then the ו here connecting עונת with פשעיהם should be similarly understood.[157] עונת and כל־פשעיהם לכל־חטאתם would thus fall into two separate categories. The latter, indicating all kinds of sin, would necessitate that עונת means something else entirely. Therefore, by the process of elimination, we conclude that עון refers to the culpability associated with sinful acts.[158]

Before moving on, we must identify which particular sins and impurities are removed and why the two Clearing Day rites list different pollutants. Given the scope of the ritual, the explicit purpose statements,[159] and the (ANE and) Israelite bent for comprehensiveness, it seems best to conclude that the Priests meant all the sins and impurities of the previous year. Since the rebellious acts are inexpiable, the text refers to all of them. Because it removes all the pollutants that have affixed themselves to the sanctuary, the ritual naturally removes sins and impurities that have not been previously addressed. Likewise, the same sins and impurities that had been removed from the offerers must now be removed from the sanctuary. Even if these sins and impurities have also been removed from the sanctuary earlier in the year, a second, final removal is not unlikely. As in the ANE, it would stress the importance and thoroughness of the removal process. Finally, given its scope and purpose, to effect clearing, the ritual covers all its bases by removing every conceivable pollutant, namely all sins and all impurities.

Why then do both clearing rites include sins, while impurities appear only in the first and culpabilities only in the second? The differences may

---

[154] Its insertion also more closely allies the expelled pollutants in Lev 16:16 and 21. Similarly it is possible that impurities originally stood alone in 16:16 as in 16:19 (see references in the previous note).

[155] When the two terms appear together, but not in parallel, חטאת clarifies עון; cf. the phrase עון חטאתי in Psa 32:5, which Koch translates "the culpability of my sin" (*TDOT* 10 [1999]:553, 559).

[156] Schwartz 1995:7.

[157] Gane 2005:257.

[158] This conclusion is supported by the observation that Lev 1–16 does not mix עון with חטא(ת) or פשע. Although present elsewhere, even in H, Lev 1–16 does not use the near synonym, נשא חטא(ת), alongside נשא עון, nor does it employ עון without נשא alongside חטא(ת) anywhere else but 16:21. Thus, whenever עון is present, whether or not it appears with נשא, it should be differentiated from חטא(ת).

[159] The purpose statements simply mention sins and and impurities (and, in the case of 16:21, all culpability, rebellious acts and sins). Since the Priestly writers were certainly capable of qualifying this expression, the fact that they chose not to do so militates against limiting its scope.

simply be the product of the text's multiple layers. Originally, impurities may have been removed from the sanctuary complex as a purification rite for sancta,[160] while sins (עונת) may have been removed from the community as a clearing rite for the people.[161] The Priestly redactor(s) may then have added all sins to both equations, in order to make both rituals more comprehensive and synonymous. Synchronically, the different terms differentiate between sins, impurities, and culpabilities. At one level, impurities are conditions in the body that often result from life's natural processes, while sins are evil actions, whether or not the sinner is aware of them. These actions may then carry a greater cost. When committed, one acts against the will of God, whether intentionally or not. Unlike bodily impurities which may fade with time, these actions cannot be undone and must be expelled. On another level, moral faults call into question one's loyalty to God. As such, any threat to loyalty must be expunged from the community.

Although we may only conjecture about the specifics, we may comment with greater certainty about the rhetorical effect that serves to distinguish sins from impurities. Since impurities only appear in the חטאת blood ritual, it would seem that they are less potent than sins. Removing impurities from the tabernacle then simply eradicates them, removing the last vestige of their pollution.[162] In contrast, sins' pollution lingers even after being removed from the tabernacle complex. Both the pollution and the culpability for it must be banished. Only then will they have no future bearing on the Israelite people and their God.

Impurities may also be omitted for another rhetorical purpose, namely to deny Azazel any responsibility in creating the problem.[163] While sins are clearly committed by the Israelites, certain impurities (such as skin-disease and irregular discharges) do not have a stated cause. To ensure that they are not attributed to Azazel and to suggest that the goat for Azazel is not an offering, they are omitted from the list of pollutants sent to him.

6.3.3.2. The Clearing Process

Clearing of the sanctuary complex and on the goat for Azazel are bracketed together by priestly robing and bathing (4, 23–24) and are explicitly separated by the text (20). In turn, they serve distinct functions in the same ritual sequence. Much like the dedication of the cult (Ex 29, Lev 8), the חטאת bull and goat offered in the sanctuary complex primarily effect clearing for the sanctuary. This clearing likewise seems to effect a sufficient ground

---

[160] Cf. the *akītu* festival.

[161] Nihan 2007:192–193; cf. the various examples in Wright 1987.

[162] Cf. Schwartz 1995. The afflicted have been cleansed and their impurities have been cleared from them and the sanctuary and, thus, pose no further threat.

[163] *Pace* Levine 1989:252; Gorman 1990:99; Gane 2005:261–265.

state, making the sanctuary complex perfectly pure as YHWH is perfectly pure.

However, rather than simply mirroring 'Dedication Day,' clearing on Clearing Day is more comprehensive and carefully directed. In addition to effecting clearing for the altar, clearing is effected for both the inner and outer sanctuaries, this time from all the people's sins and impurities. Instead of simply removing the last traces of the mundane sphere from the altar, Clearing Day removes the most serious pollutants of the mundane sphere from each zone of the divine sphere. Thus, Clearing Day serves as a re-dedication of sorts, one that requires much more serious and specific clearing rites to address the people's pollution so that the tabernacle complex becomes suitably pure again. After its purgation, the altar(s) may again receive offerings and remove the people's pollutants.

The expelled goat expands the scope of Clearing Day even further beyond that of Dedication Day. Rather than simply disappearing into thin air, or potentially being retro-absorbed into the animal carcasses, sins' effects are severe enough that they must be banished.[164] Removing them to Azazel in the wilderness serves both a negative and positive purpose. Negatively, sending the pollutants to the wilderness gets them as far away from the community as possible. Positively, the expulsion puts the pollutants in the realm where they belong, outside of God's ordered community that represents, albeit imperfectly, heaven on earth. In the wilderness, the pollutants lodge where chaos prevails so that the chaos they embody no longer affects God's community.[165]

If sancta clearing is primary on Clearing Day, how then does effecting clearing for individuals function? The text is unclear on this point. Perhaps, in removing the people's pollutants from the sanctuary, clearing is effected on behalf of the priests and people. While the blood of the people's חטאת goat is never said to effect clearing for them, this result seems to be implied. The bull is explicitly for the priests (6, 11), while the goat is for the people (15). Since the bull for the priests effects clearing for the

---

[164] While the goat explicitly carries away the sins and culpabilities of the people from the community, it is unclear if these are the sins just removed from the tabernacle complex, sins removed from the people, or both. It seems best to understand the term as broadly as possible, such that any vestiges are removed from both the tabernacle and the community. The placement of the expulsion ritual after the tabernacle clearing also appears significant. Only after the pollutants have been removed from the tabernacle can they be removed on the goat (Schwartz 1995:17) along with any vestigial pollution of the community (this includes the removal of inexpiable sins from the community; however, the individual offenders must still bear their load).

[165] *Pace* Gorman 1990:99 and Gane 2005:261–265, this is not the same as returning sin to its author, thereby mirroring, or perhaps prefiguring, the New Testament conflict between God and Satan. In this instance, the people themselves are the authors of sin.

priests, it seems logical to assume that the goat for the people effects clearing for the people. The goat's clearing function may also be implied in vv. 30 and 33–34. In short, the priests and people benefit from the removal of their pollutants from the sanctuary.[166] Although less likely, we cannot rule out the possibility that pollutants are simultaneously removed from both people and sancta.

Clearing pollutants on the חטאת goat for Azazel seems more straightforward. Clearing is effected for the people on a corporate level by removing their pollution from their community (10, 30, 33–34), including God's sanctuary. More than just banishing sins, the expelled goat banishes the responsibility for sin. The text describes this process as clearing to cleanse (טהר) from sins (16:30).[167] By juxtaposing clearing with cleansing from sin, the authors clarify the nature of clearing, albeit in an unusual way.

Cleansing from sin is an aberrant phrase, appearing nowhere else in Leviticus 1–16;[168] sins are normally forgiven, not cleansed.[169] However, since the people's sins have already been forgiven, the authors need to use another term. By opting for cleansing, they communicate their message both imprecisely and purposefully.[170] Cleansing suggests that all vestiges of pollution have been removed from the polluted individuals. In turn, cleansing from sins suggests that any final complications, including responsibility for sins, have been removed, so that the people may no longer be affected by them. Thus, cleansing from sins communicates that the people are free from their sin and its culpability, having permanently transferred them to Azazel.

---

[166] See Milgrom 1991:258–261; Gane 2005:231. This secondary clearing fits with the secondary role ascribed to clearing on behalf of the people in the sanctuary blood rites.

[167] Milgrom (1991:37, 62–63, 1064–1065; with Knohl 1995:27–28, 105) attributes this verse to H and interprets it as referring to moral purity in opposition to P's forgiveness.

[168] The oddity of this phrase may simply be explained by the relative imprecision of H's language, if indeed we ascribe v. 30 to H. However, instead of examining the compositional history of the text and interpreting the text diachronically, we will analyze the logic of the composite ritual.

[169] If the author meant to speak of sin removal, he could have more naturally used the *piel* of חטא or כפר + מן (although the former does not explicitly refer to sin removal in P, it is etymologically connected to it and thus a more logical choice).

[170] They also implicitly connect the cleansing and forgiveness processes, indicating that, although different, the processes significantly overlap. In addition, by opting for טהר instead of חטא, they choose the positive side of a similar process, i.e., making pure instead of removing the pollutants.

6.3.3.3. The Loose Ends

In addition to effecting clearing, the blood manipulation of the חטאת bull and goat are also said to cleanse (טהר) and consecrate (קדש) the altar (16:18–19). Through this association, cleansing and consecration add (imprecise) definition to clearing. Cleansing indicates that impurities (and presumably sins) are being removed from the altar.[171] Consecration indicates that clearing is effected to make the altar perfectly pure, namely to set it apart from human imperfection so that it can be set apart for divine perfection (i.e., consecrated).[172] In other words, once suitably cleared, the altar is ready to function appropriately again.

Why then is the altar alone consecrated and why is this consecration inexactly expressed? As in the tabernacle dedication, only YHWH can suitably consecrate his home. Although most holy, the altar stands at, even as, the intersection between human and divine spheres. Thus, it is only natural that the people must contribute to the consecratory process of shared space.[173] However, the only other way they have of consecrating divine space is with the anointing oil, which marks that space as holy. Since the altar has already been marked as holy, there is no need to mark it again. Therefore, the people only have recourse to clearing and cleansing that can be said to consecrate since it contributes to the consecration process finished by YHWH.

In addition, the burning of the חטאת fat and the clean-up process (16:25–28) stand outside of the ritual envelope (4–24).[174] Although unstated here, the fat seems to provide YHWH with something pleasant during the clearing process (cf. the use of the חטאת and אשם fat in Leviticus 4–5). Here, it stands apart to mark its secondary role. Only after clearing has been finished, does YHWH enjoy his portion.[175] Likewise, the fat serves to re-open normal lines of communication after the damage control process.[176]

---

[171] The text here seems to be imprecise in that it only mentions the removal of impurities, and speaks in terms of impurity removal (using טהר). Although there is some overlap in the use of טהר and חטא, in P the former usually refers to the removal of impurities, while the latter appears to be a more general category etymologically related to sin removal (in P, sins are cleansed [טהר] only in Lev 16:30).

[172] Although cleansing and clearing do not consecrate, they move forward the consecration process, similarly to Lev 8:15 (which uses חטא and קדש). Thus, they may be said to loosely effect consecration (for a fuller analysis, see chapter 3 on Lev 8:15).

[173] Although the priests enter YHWH's space, they do so at his behest to serve him therein. Priestly service in the tabernacle is an intrusion of the human into the divine sphere, while the bronze altar is the intersection of the two spheres.

[174] According to Nihan's diachronic reconstruction, the burning of the fat on the altar makes the original sancta purification rite into an offering (2007:179–180).

[175] In legal language, the fat is YHWH's payment for services rendered.

[176] Cf. Marx 2003:117.

Similarly, after clearing has been effected, the people tie up the loose ends so that the result is in no way nullified and that normal commerce may recommence.

Finally, although the people's role in clearing the sanctuary is minimal, they have a significant role to play in ensuring that the benefits of this clearing accrue to them. In the Holiness Legislation, obedience results in blessing and absorbing divine holiness. At the end of the Clearing Day legislation, obedient self-denial and cessation from work is the means of receiving blessing, namely the full removal of pollutants from the community.[177]

---

[177] Contra Milgrom (2000:2021), כִּי, which begins verse 30, indicates that "the purification of the people provides the motivation for rather than being the result of the people's self-denial" (Gane 2005:126–127). In other words, self-denial does not itself purify. It merely gives the individual access to the purification already performed on his behalf.

Chapter Seven

Damage Control: Evaluation

With the data before us, we are now ready to present the results of our examination of the Priestly damage control system, beginning with an analysis of its rhetoric and implications, followed by an investigation of its key terms,[1] and concluding with a comparison of the ANE and Priestly systems.

7.1. The Rhetorical Trajectory of Leviticus 1–16

Exodus prescribes the dedication of the cult and describes YHWH's arrival, enacting a sufficient ground state for YHWH's profitable presence. As expected, Leviticus 1–3 follows with a list of the basic offerings, which serve as a primary means of interacting with the resident deity. Leviticus 4–5 then indicates that elaborate preparations and regular offerings alone provide insufficient means of ensuring divine favor. The people's sins are an affront to God, which must be redressed with offerings so that the sin is removed from the offenders and they may be forgiven. Thus, it seems that clearing the altar during the dedication prepares it to effect clearing for the people from their sins.

The following chapters (6–10) add to the already complex portrait. After complementary details about offerings and a description of the dedication and inauguration of the cult, the Nadab and Abihu incident serves as a clear warning of the (super)natural consequences of sin. Although supramundane,[2] the dedication seems relatively straightforward, suggesting that all is well. Lest the people become too comfortable in their newfound relationship, God demonstrates the fatal consequences of approaching him inappropriately.

---

[1] Rather than providing full definitions before examining the terms meant to be defined by those definitions, a preliminary explanation of key Priestly terms was offered in chapter 3 and at the beginning of chapter 6. Having analyzed the context in which the terms are embedded, we are now prepared to offer a fuller analysis.

[2] Using mundane means to enact something that transcends the mundane, namely the purification and consecration of YHWH's sanctuary.

Leviticus 11–15 then adds to the danger by addressing it from another direction, indicating that certain impurities as well as sins are an affront to YHWH. Like sins, (often) unavoidable impurities also must be removed from the offerer, this time so that he or she may become clean, rather than forgiven. Leviticus 15 finishes with a warning that spells out the fatal consequences of impurity, adding to the legislation for sin by indicating why impurities are lethal; impurities make the tabernacle unclean (טמא), presumably by coming into direct contact with impurity-bearing individuals. At this point, the danger and unnaturalness of YHWH's presence are readily apparent. If the people's sins and impurities are not appropriately cleared from the individuals, they will incite divine wrath to prevent them from infecting the sanctuary.

As if this is not enough, Leviticus 16 goes well beyond the bounds previously set for damage control. More than simply requiring clearing to restore a suitable ground state, the tabernacle complex requires an annual Clearing Day to remove the people's evils. Thus, Leviticus 16 suggests that the tabernacle and its altar absorb the people's pollution, even from afar, and even if previously cleared from the people through the prescribed offerings.[3] In turn, although it may limit the damage, divine wrath does not prevent the tabernacle from being polluted.[4]

By returning to the unresolved Nadab and Abihu incident at the beginning of the chapter, Leviticus 16 indicates that it offers the solution. It simultaneously prescribes the appropriate means of approach and deals with the consequences of Nadab and Abihu's inappropriate approach. The text highlights that even correct approach is fraught with peril, and the frequency and intimacy of contact with the deity are severely limited. Although limited, such an approach with the blood of the חטאת offerings is nonetheless sufficient to remove the people's pollution from the sanctuary, at once introducing and nullifying a new danger. In addition to its fatal effect on the carriers, pollution pollutes YHWH's sanctuary, thereby threat-

---

[3] Although it is by no means ironclad, Milgrom's miasmic theory seems to make the most sense of the data. Although possible, Gane's theory (2005; cf. Propp 2006:698–700; Scurlock 2006a:20–28) that the offerings themselves pollute the sanctuary is slightly less likely (see, e.g., Eberhart 2006; Nihan 2007:190–192; Sklar 2007). It is even possible to combine the two systems. If the tabernacle absorbs pollution from afar, the transfer of pollution to the sanctuary during individual pollution removal rites may have little additional effect on the sanctuary, since it already absorbed the pollution when it was generated. The rite then could simply serve to drain the pollution from individuals into the safest possible environment, where it would remain until Clearing Day with minimal effect. Whatever the solution may be, it does not significantly affect our conclusions.

[4] While killing the offender punishes him for polluting the sanctuary and prevents further pollution, it cannot undo the damage already done.

ening to incite YHWH to return to his natural home in heaven.[5] In the face of this new danger, the removal of pollution invites him to stay. At the same time, the goat for Azazel suggests that simple removal from the people and the sanctuary is not enough. Sins and the culpability for those sins must be fully removed from the community so that they have no further bearing on its welfare and no longer affect the dangerous intrusion that is YHWH's home on earth.[6]

7.2. The Implications of Priestly Damage Control

By progressively unveiling the complexity of the divine dwelling and the damage control necessary to maintain it, the Priestly writers cleverly introduce the final solution just as they introduce the full extent of the problem. The Priestly texts are well aware of the "jerry-rigged" nature of the tabernacle as the receptacle of divine presence.[7] Instead of unraveling in the face of this insurmountable obstacle, their system succeeds when it seems most in danger of foundering.[8] The divinely mandated and divinely empowered Clearing Day is their ultimate solution.

Clearing Day suggests that YHWH will never leave his sanctuary as long as the Clearing Day rituals are performed correctly.[9] In Genesis 17 the Priests introduce the concept of individual punishment without collective sanction. Although every male must be circumcised so that he is not cut off (כרת) from his people, the fact that the covenant is eternal (ברית עולם) indicates that "individual transgression, though punished, does not put an end to it."[10] The Holiness Legislation goes even further, indicating that,

---

[5] The people must clear the pollutants from the tabernacle that dwells in the midst of their impurities (16:16). By mentioning the dwelling of the tabernacle instead of YHWH himself, the text is careful to shroud the nature of YHWH's presence in mystery so that it is not misunderstood as simply anthropomorphic.

[6] The purpose statements also contribute to this progressive revelation of danger. Lev 4–5 and 11–15 are ultimately concerned with forgiveness and cleansing; clearing pollutants from the offerers is merely a means of achieving these ends. However, clearing is the ultimate purpose of Lev 16. The pollutants also must be removed from the sanctuary and the community for forgiveness and cleansing to have any meaning, i.e., in addition to simply being prescribed, the system must also prove effective. Clearing on Clearing Day establishes the system's credibility (see further sections 7.2. and 7.4.3.).

[7] Sommer 2001:61; cf. Blum 1990:332.

[8] Contra Sommer 2001.

[9] Nihan 2007:195, 372; *pace* Milgrom 1991:258–259, 980; Schwartz 1995:5, 21; Gane 2005:231.

[10] Nihan 2007:195; see further Gross 1998:45–70; see similarly the non-Priestly Numbers 14:17–20, where punishment of the offending generation does not nullify the promise for future generations (Gane 2005:334–337).

even after collective sanction, God will not break his covenant by abandoning his people (Lev 26:44–45). In other words, Israelite sin will not stop YHWH from being their God; they may always renew their relationship through repentance (26:40–41).[11]

Clearing Day employs similar logic, but, as usual, expands on its parallels so that its solution matches its comprehensive parameters. Clearing Day goes well beyond simply keeping the relationship alive; it also vindicates the system that makes the relationship possible and applies the benefits of the system to the people. For the people, Clearing Day functions as a judgment day[12] wherein God's cult fully accounts for the imperfections of the faithful and fully condemns the rebellious. On a corporate level, all evils, even the defiant sins for which there is no sacrificial remedy, have been expelled,[13] so that the people as a whole no longer must bear their load. The people receive this benefit simply by performing the prescribed Clearing Day rituals correctly.[14]

While corporately the people stand secure before God, individuals fall into one of two groups: the loyal who stand fully right with God and the rebels who are condemned.[15] God's system allows for and remedies ritual impurities and simple moral faults, provided that the offender performs the appropriate cultic response. Those who stay within these bounds may receive the benefits of Clearing Day. If, however, an individual commits an irremediable sin, fails to correctly remedy (known) remediable sins, or fails to humble himself on Clearing Day, he will prove himself disloyal and thus become irrevocably condemned.[16]

For the faithful, forgiveness and cleansing find full meaning in the final clearing on Clearing Day. If the effects of sin and impurity linger in the community, forgiveness and cleansing would lose much of their force, as the forgiven or cleansed pollution would continue to affect the community. Worse yet, if the pollution continues to loiter, it would naturally lead to divine abandonment of the community. In turn, forgiveness and cleansing

---

[11] H here seems to be making a concession to the Deuteronomistic and Prophetic traditions that breaking covenant is possible, while maintaining God's commitment to keeping it intact (Nihan 2007:542).

[12] Gane 2005:305–309.

[13] Schwartz 1995:21.

[14] Lev 16 thus agrees with Gen 17 that there is no corporate sanction, as long as the people remain loyal by yearly performing the Clearing Day rituals. This ritual performance alone prevents the collective punishment envisioned in H.

[15] For this distinction, see Gane 2005:305–323.

[16] The latter sin is a particularly offensive פשע sin because, by not humbling himself, he rebels against God on the very day that the sanctuary is being purged of his forgiven offenses (Lev 23:26–32).

7.2. The Implications of Priestly Damage Control

would lose all significance, since their meaning is found only in relation to the (resident) deity.

By expelling the pollutants from the community, the forgiven and cleansed people realize the full benefits of their newfound condition, as these pollutants have now become "irrevocably irrelevant" to them.[17] In other words, pollution and its responsibility no longer have any bearing on the community at large or the individuals who exercise loyalty because they have been fully and finally cleared.[18] The loyal are forgiven, and their guilt has been removed.[19] The record of their crimes is thoroughly expunged.

Clearing Day also proves that YHWH's system works. On Clearing Day, YHWH's continued relationship with his people is at once assured and justified, since all of the people's imperfections, including their defiant sins, have been removed from the sanctuary and the community. YHWH's forgiveness and cleansing are also fully justified because the situation that necessitated them in the first place has been completely resolved.

Similarly, Clearing Day preserves YHWH's reputation and his holiness. Removing pollution from the people at YHWH's expense would impugn him, especially if accruing pollution in his home forces him to abandon it. As a result, he would seem incapable of leading and protecting his people or of overcoming the rival (evil) forces that threaten to drive him from his dwelling.[20] More simply, pollution is incompatible with the perfection of the divine sphere and its divine ruler. For him and his heaven to truly remain on earth, perfection must be maintained, or at least approximated. By banishing all pollutants from the community, clearing on Clearing Day restores the relative perfection of the sanctuary and the community, if only for a day. Such a restoration vindicates the perfection of both the system and its designer, thereby demanding from the Israelites continued adherence to it and to him.[21]

---

[17] Gane 2005:318.

[18] Cf. Ps 103:12: "As far as the east is from the west, so far has he removed our transgressions (פשעינו) from us."

[19] Cf. Geller 1992:108.

[20] Thus, in Ezekiel he seeks to return and restore his people for the sake of his name, which permanent exile will tarnish.

[21] God's people must daily demonstrate their loyalty to him to remain in good standing. Consistent submission alone preserves God's people (Gane 2005, e.g., 305–323, drawing heavily on the parallel between God and human kings, wherein loyalty to the king is paramount); cf. Marx's interpretation of offerings as feudal tribute (2005:50, 77–80, 86–87, 202–204).

7.2.1. Excursus: The Possibility of System Failure in H and Ezekiel

Although a brilliant stroke, the Priests' final solution does not extend far enough to satisfy the two traditions closest to them, the Holiness Legislation and Ezekiel. First, the Holiness Legislation at once upholds the efficacy of the Priestly system and allows for a (temporary) dissolution of that system. To do so, H introduces a new category, serious sins that generate impurity and pollute (טמא) from afar.[22] Such sins pose no threat to the cultic system. Since they likely fall under the פשע category, Clearing Day, mentioned in Leviticus 23:27–32, presumably removes their pollution from the sanctuary and the community, but not from the individual offender.[23] However, H also indicates that these sins pollute (טמא) the land, for which the Priestly texts offer no sacrificial remedy.[24] In other words, although Clearing Day annually replaces the tabernacle's pollution-filter, thereby ensuring that the divine abode does not reach its saturation point, it has no stated effect on the land. Thus, the land will spew out the Israelites if they saturate its filter with their abominations just as it spewed out the Canaanites before them (18:24–30; 20:22). The resultant exile will remove the people from the land and its cultic system while the land regenerates, enjoying its neglected sabbaths (26:34–35). As indicated in the previous section, H also goes beyond the Priestly texts into corporate sanction and beyond corporate sanction into (the potential for) individual and corporate renewal. Even in exile, the Israelites may again receive the benefits of a renewed relationship with YHWH by humbly repenting (26:40–41), just as they receive the benefits of Clearing Day by humbling themselves (23:27–32).

Second, Ezekiel diverges from the Priestly texts by mandating a decisive break with the Priestly system because of the people's irremediable corruption.[25] Although it does not mention Clearing Day, the text implicitly suggests that such a remedy will not avail.[26] The people's abominations are so great in the sanctuary that nothing may be salvaged (Ez 8). Clearing Day would only perpetuate the people's profligacy.[27] Thus, YHWH in the

---

[22] Cf. Schwartz 1987:103–108; Klawans labels the result 'moral impurity' (2000:26).

[23] Although only the pollution mentioned in Lev 20:3, Num 19:13, and 20 explicitly pollutes the tabernacle, we may presume that all such sins function similarly. The latter two texts, like most in Numbers, are hard to assign. They may belong to P as traditionally assigned, H according to Knohl 1995, or a later theocratic revision according to Achenbach 2003 and Nihan 2007.

[24] Cf. Klawans 2000:26–30.

[25] Albertz 2003:360.

[26] Here, we presume that Clearing Day was in place, at least in some form, before Ezekiel was composed.

[27] See Albertz 2003:360–361 for a fuller list of the sins that prompt the exile.

form of his glory abandons his sanctuary (8–11; cf. 5:11).[28] In depicting the divine withdrawal, Ezekiel draws from and expands on Priestly ideas. For Ezekiel, the precarious and ambulatory nature of YHWH's presence both allows for and ensures a divine exodus in the face of flagrant human imperfection.

Nonetheless, for Ezekiel, as for H, this communal sanction is not permanent. YHWH promises to return to a perfected temple surrounded by a perfected people for the sake of his name (11:17–20; 36:17–38; 40–48), thereby keeping the parameters in place for a renewed master-servant relationship even after exile. Once this relationship is restored, the people may profitably perform rites akin to Clearing Day (45:20).

7.3. Key Priestly Concepts

7.3.1 Sins and Impurities

After examining the data, we are now ready to clarify key items of Priestly vocabulary. Impurity is different from the physical conditions that generate it. Contacting impure persons or objects,[29] contracting skin disease, giving birth, and having certain genital discharges produce but are not in themselves impurity.[30] Impurity is the name given to the stain produced by certain, often unavoidable, biological factors.[31] Although it sounds merely like a point of etiquette, this stain is perceived to be real. As in the ANE, it is a malevolent force that harms whatever it comes into contact with and thus must be removed.[32] More specifically, this stain affixes itself to the afflicted individual, to persons and objects that come into contact with that individual, and to the sanctuary.

Like other physical conditions (e.g., illnesses), the condition that generates impurity may heal over time.[33] While the source of impurity may be impermanent, impurity itself remains active until it has been appropriately remedied. After the condition heals, washing and waiting remove enough pollution to enter the sanctuary. Because impurity's force seems to dissipate when cut off from its source, it fades with time and may be removed by water, with the result that it is no longer contagious. However, if the

---

[28] To ensure that there is no return to the present sanctuary, he even defiles his own house (בית) with corpses (9:7).

[29] Impure animals seem to carry within themselves pollution akin to the portentous dog mentioned above (section 5.3.1. p. 125 and n. 30) that bore evil in Mesopotamia.

[30] Schwartz 1995:5.

[31] Cf. Klawans 2000:23–24.

[32] Cf. Levine 1974:77.

[33] Cf. Klawans 2000:25–26.

stain is severe enough, entering the tabernacle complex requires offerings to remove the last vestiges of pollution. Although innocuous in the human sphere, such pollution remains an affront to the divine and must be removed. As in the ANE, final removal leads to the afflicted individual becoming clean in the sense of being free from all polluting influences.

Although analogous, the stain generated by a sinful act is not the same as impurity resulting from certain bodily conditions.[34] Lacking a suitable term, the sinful stain is also called 'sin' to differentiate it from impurity. Thus, as in the ANE, sin is both an evil action and the evil stain that results from it. This stain affixes itself to the sinner and the sanctuary and also seems to plague the community and must be removed from all three spheres (Lev 4–5, 16). However, unlike impurity, it is not contagious to individual persons or objects.

The removal process for sin differs from that for impurity. First, the individual himself, rather than a condition in his body, generates the sinful stain. Second, unlike unclean bodily conditions, the individual's sinful act does not continue to produce contamination. Since the passage of time will not eradicate an individual's proclivity to sin and the sacrificial system cannot root it out, the Priestly cult may only deal with the one-off pollution generated by a sinful act. Thus, a single offering may effectively remove the pollutant from him so that he is forgiven.

In addition to being an act and a stain, sin is also connected to guilt. However, although sin leads inexorably to guilt, the Priestly texts are careful to distinguish between the two. The consequence of sin is expressed with אשם and נשא עון, referring to objective guilt and the suffering that results from it, and legal and cultic culpability respectively.[35]

Impurity generated by certain sins represents a third category, favored by the Holiness Legislation. Certain sins, including bloodshed (Num 35:33–34), sexual misconduct (Lev 18:24–30), idolatry (Lev 19:31; 20:1–3),[36] and failure to properly handle corpse contamination (Num 19:13, 20) are said to pollute (טמא) the individual, the community, the sanctuary, and

---

[34] Schwartz 1995; Contra Levine 1974:76; Wright 1987:18; Gorman 1990:78–89; Milgrom 1991:258–261.

[35] While H and Numbers employ נשא חטא as a synonym of נשא עון (Lev 20:20; 22:9; 24:15; Num 9:13; 18:22, 32), Leviticus 1–16 is careful to use only the latter to distinguish between חטא and עון, between sin and its consequences; cf. *DCH* 198–200, which lists Gen 18:20, Num 16:26, 32:23, Jer 17:1, and Ez 3:20, 18:24 as instances where חטאה expresses guilt resulting from sin.

[36] Frymer-Kensky 1983:404; Klawans 2000:26, 30. Idolatry is not simply worshiping idols; it refers more expansively to any interaction with other gods that does not involve destroying their images and sanctuaries.

the land.³⁷ Like both sin and impurity, they generate a real stain that must be removed.³⁸

Faced with the same dilemma as the Priestly texts – i.e., how to express the polluting effects of sins – H borrows from the language of bodily impurities.³⁹ H indicates that certain sins, like P's bodily conditions, generate impurity, thereby establishing that the pollutions are analogous and that 'moral' impurity is a real force.⁴⁰ Nonetheless, although analogous, H is careful to distinguish his new category from bodily impurities by both language and effect. H employs the complementary terms תועבה and חנף, which do not appear with bodily impurities. The text also indicates that, unlike bodily impurities, these abominable sins are not contagious to persons or objects and that they alone pollute the land.⁴¹

Lest we assume that the sins described by H are the same as those in the Priestly texts, thereby assuming that impurity is H's way of describing the pollution generated by all sins, H indicates the greater severity of its sins. Unlike the sins mentioned in Leviticus 1–16, these sins are labeled תועבה and חנף and defile (טמא) the land. Thus, it would seem that these abominable sins are the worst kind of inexpiable פשעים.

The Priestly texts (here including H) commendably and carefully preserve the similarities and differences between categories. To express their similarities and differences to each other and to impurity, the authors describe the two categories of sin with carefully chosen language. As a result, various conclusions emerge. Each of the three contaminants (sin and impurity in P and abominable sins in H) pollutes in a real, albeit different, way. Each continues to pollute until it is properly remedied, and each requires a different remedy. Those with bodily conditions must be healed and cleansed, while sinners must be forgiven. Unfortunately for those who commit abominable sins, there is no individual remedy; the only remedy for the land and people is exile.

---

³⁷ By analogy with the פשעים, these sins must be removed from both the sanctuary and community, yet cannot be removed from the land or the sinner (see further section 7.2.1.).

³⁸ Klawans (2000:32–36) rightly argues that the defilement is real and, in doing so, rejects the various metaphorical interpretations (e.g., Wright 1991:163). However, although certain metaphorical interpretations should be dismissed, namely those that the view the pollution itself as merely figurative, we need not reject metaphor altogether (see further pp. 12-14).

³⁹ As Klawans emphasizes (2000:34–35), the secondary nature of the impurity resulting from sins has not been established. However, it seems best to understand it as secondary in these texts, especially if P is prior to H.

⁴⁰ Cf. ibid. 38.
⁴¹ Ibid. 26.

7.3.1.1. How Do Contaminants Pollute the Sanctuary?

It seems that pollution in P functions analogously to holiness in H. Just as the Israelite people absorb YHWH's contagious holiness, so too does YHWH's tabernacle absorb the people's pollution, their sins and impurities. In other words, just as YHWH's presence and perfection have a significant effect on the community, so too do the people's presence and imperfection significantly affect YHWH's sanctuary.[42] The people's impurities and sins emit an imperceptible stain that the tabernacle, as the source of perfection, absorbs. Although noncontagious to individuals and objects, sins affix themselves to the tabernacle. Even after they have been rendered innocuous to individuals and objects, severe impurities also cling to the tabernacle.[43] Thus, in the Priestly system, the tabernacle as the source of perfection and blessing is especially susceptible to the people's sins and impurities, the source of imperfection and danger. Because of its extreme holiness, YHWH's abode can tolerate no imperfection. Paradoxically, because of its susceptibility to imperfection, it must tolerate imperfection (at least temporarily) to dwell among an imperfect people. To resolve this tension, Clearing Day is a Priestly masterstroke, as the tabernacle and its resident deity must tolerate pollution only temporarily, only until the polluted filter is annually replaced.

7.3.2. חטא and אשם

Just as the Priestly writers carefully choose language that differentiates sin from impurity, so too do they carefully choose language that connects the remedies. Sin and impurity are clearly different in nature. Nevertheless, in rightly differentiating between the two, commentators have often downplayed their similar effect upon the sanctuary. Whatever their causes and natures may be, both sin and (severe) impurity offend the deity and pollute his sanctuary. This similar effect requires an offering and remedial process with the same names (חטאת and כפר), both of which are (largely) limited to

---

[42] The source of any extreme power is especially susceptible to any breach of protocol. An anomaly that would be harmless anywhere else could cause a power plant to meltdown (Chernobyl). Similarly, an anomaly in the tabernacle could have devastating results: the people could be destroyed (e.g., Nadab and Abihu) or the source of the power could leave (e.g., YHWH in Ez 8–11); cf. Quirke 1992:70; Hutton 1994:147; Propp 2006: 490.

[43] When offerings are unnecessary, it seems that time and washing sufficiently remove the pollutants so that approaching the sanctuary will inflict no further damage. However, it is unclear if the minor impurity remedied outside of the tabernacle still pollutes the tabernacle and, thus, must be removed from it on Clearing Day.

the tabernacle complex.⁴⁴ By making this connection, the authors stress that, even after preliminary cleansings, severe impurities, like sins, are an affront to the deity. In other words, regardless of their cause, severe impurities function like sin (חטאת) that must be cleared with a חטאה offering.

Leviticus 4–5 serves as an introduction to the damage control legislation, functioning as a lens through which the rest is meant to be interpreted.⁴⁵ In these chapters, the authors intentionally and unabashedly juxtapose the roots חטא and אשם, both of which refer to the consequences of the offense and its remedy.⁴⁶ More than simply referring to the act and its effect, the root חטא, like עון elsewhere, also refers to the punishment, in this case the חטאת offering.⁴⁷ In fact, the Priests use the same form, חטאת, to express both sin and the offering for it.⁴⁸ אשם as well refers to the result, suffering guilt's consequences, and the compensation for it as a general category (e.g., 5:6–7) and as an offering (e.g., 5:15–16; 14:12–14). As noted above in chapter 6, חטא(ת) and אשם, as action, result, and remedy, also appear side-by-side throughout the chapters, with the balance swinging from the former to the latter as the text progresses from the act to its consequences.

---

⁴⁴ The clearing of the 'diseased' house (14:53) is the lone exception of the latter in Lev 1–16, while the חטאת goat for Azazel, presented in the tabernacle complex yet ultimately led away from it, is also somewhat anomalous.

⁴⁵ This holds whether we read the text synchronically or diachronically. Diachronically, it may be an addition to the חטאת legislation in 12–15 and 16. As such, it fills out the system and offers a final interpretation of it (Nihan 2007:186–195). By placing it first, the authors offer it as an interpretive lens, regardless of its chronological priority.

⁴⁶ Most scholars eschew sin and guilt language with the the odd result "that the translations of contemporary commentators completely obscure the fact that the Hebrew uses the same words, or at least what look and sound like the same words, for two offerings and for the common nouns 'sin' and 'guilt'" (Watts 2007:82; see, e.g., ironically, Milgrom 1991:226 for his translation of 4:3 and p. 254 for his explanation; cf. p. 319 for his translation of 5:19).

⁴⁷ In Akkadian as well, the roots *arnu* and *ḫīṭu* refer to both sin and punishment (*CAD* A.2 294–299; H 210–212; AHw I: 53, 70, 350).

⁴⁸ Cf. Watts 2007:87. The doubled middle radical in both instances suggests a possible derivation from the *piel*. If this is the case, 'sin' seems to be mispointed. It should be related to the *qal*, meaning sin, instead of the *piel*, meaning de-sin = purify, and thus pointed without the dagesh (Levine 1974:101–102; see, however, חַטָּא, sinner, which he associates not with the *piel* form, but as a *nomen opificium* in the *qattal* form [see, e.g., Joüon-Muraoka I:252] so that the *piel* form is never translated 'to commit an offense'; cf. Propp [2006:460] who calls deriving the meaning of חטאת from חַטָּא "methodologically backwards"). Even if this were the case, the two would look and sound so similar that the reader would be compelled to make a connection between the two, especially when the verb and noun expressing the action appear in the same verse as the offering (see also 6:19 where the author uses the *piel* verb to indicate sin removal, or, perhaps, it simply refers to offering a חטאת). The new meanings would also be evocative, placing sin alongside removing sin.

Behind this Priestly word choice lies a powerful rhetorical strategy. By selecting emotionally evocative words and engaging in emotionally evocative wordplay,[49] they highlight the seriousness of the crimes and the necessity of the appropriate remedy.[50]

With Leviticus 4–5 in mind, 11–15 takes on new meaning. By calling the removal of impurity חטאת and by describing the removal process as כפר, the authors clearly connect impurity with sin. They thus stress the need for the proper remedy and the danger of an improper remedy (Lev. 5:2–3; 7:20–21; 15:31; cf. 22:3–7; Num 19:13, 20). The danger and necessity are especially pronounced when referring to tabernacle offerings, as both serious impurities and neglected minor impurities require sacrificial solutions. Even after a severely impure person has been properly healed and cleansed, he still must offer a חטאת sacrifice in the tabernacle to effect clearing for him and render him fully clean. Likewise, failing to purify himself appropriately requires a reparation without which the consequences are fatal (15:31). In both cases, the Priests limit their use of חטאת and clearing language to tabernacle offerings in order to indicate the shared consequences of sin and impurity, regardless of their origins. In other words, when individuals reenter the divine sphere, they must deal with the effect their pollution has on YHWH and his abode. Read in this light, the use of the *piel* of חטא, which is potentially innocuous, takes on new meaning. Although it generally refers to purification, here it seems to evoke thoughts of the more etymologically related sin removal.[51]

A point of clarification is necessary at this juncture. The use of sin-like language to describe the remedy for impurities does not mean that we should conclude that the Priests are (primarily) concerned with making impurity a moral issue. Instead, their primary aim is to elicit compliance from the people by stressing the seriousness of the offense and assigning it a straightforward remedy. To ensure maximum rhetorical effect, the Priests nonetheless use morally evocative language.

The Priests, then, differentiate between the natures of the cause and effect and its remedy. Although impurity's cause may be acceptable and its result differs from that of sin in many ways, it nonetheless has a sin-like effect on the sanctuary that must be redressed in a similar fashion. For example, even if procreation is beneficial, it nonetheless has negative consequences for the sanctuary that are functionally equivalent to minor sins.

---

[49] Watts 2007:79–89; cf. Paran 1989:vii.

[50] Cf. Watts 2007:91; Bergen (2005:40) notes that the persuasive power of the text invites the reader, whether ancient or modern, to be "deeply concerned about sin and its effects."

[51] Cf. Propp 2006:469, who translates it as 'un-sin'; Levine (1974:101) associates חטא with the removal of חֵטְא (which he erroneously connects with impurity).

The name of impurity's remedy serves to ensure that the reader will make this connection.⁵² Leviticus 16 then drives home the seriousness and necessity of the removal rites by stressing that sins and impurities do more than threaten the relationship between man and his God; they also pollute God's sanctuary and must be removed from it.

Thus, the Priestly writers simultaneously posit well-defined offerings for well-defined offenses and opt to give these offerings shocking names for rhetorical effect. The חטאת then is in some way related to sin just as the אשם is in some way related to guilt, as both address the negative consequences that Israelite imperfection has on YHWH and his tabernacle. This intentional connection then serves to compel the audience to respond appropriately.

In addition, the offering names חטאת and אשם both seem to have roots in the legal realm, giving their cultic usage (potential) legal overtones.⁵³ Thus, it would not be too far a leap to refer to these offerings as a legal payment that annuls legal debt, a כֹּפֶר of sorts.⁵⁴ Mixing instrumental and legal metaphors,⁵⁵ this payment may then enable the divinely ordained removal of pollution. In other words, as in Mesopotamia, the sacrificial ritual may be conceived of as a contract, whereby the offerer provides the offering as payment for the pollution removal service of YHWH and his priests. This implied meaning reinforces the efficacy and necessity of the system, especially since YHWH is the initiator of the contract. Damage control offerings would then be the only surefire way to avert the consequences of the damage, death (since proximity + pollution = death [Lev 10; 15:31]). In turn, more than simply being eager to comply, the people would also be grateful to YHWH and the priests for making this necessary service available. Thus, juxtaposing pollution and penal language doubles the rhetorical effect, thereby providing further incentive to support the system. In the end, Priestly offerings are at once precise and rhetorically potent.⁵⁶

---

⁵² Cf. Propp 2006:460.

⁵³ For the former, see Levine 1974:102; cf. Utzschneider 1988:100, 106, 118–119; for the latter, see Milgrom 1976:13–16.

⁵⁴ In Akkadian, *arnu* and *ḫīṭu* also may refer to both a legal offense and its obligation clearing punishment.

⁵⁵ In speaking of metaphors, I do not mean to suggest that the people doubted that the pollutants were real or that a debt was owed. Rather, I speak of different conceptions of sin (and impurity), whose terminology is borrowed from other analogous spheres (for this conceptualization of metaphor, see Soskice 1985:15 and passim).

⁵⁶ Since I am more interested in the interpretation than the translation and no problem-free translation emerges, I will leave the terms חטאת and אשם untranslated. Regarding the question of interpretation versus translation, see Lemardelé 2002:284 and Watts 2007:89.

7.3.3. כפר

To this point, we have demurred, translating כפר as clearing to communicate the term's multivalence. At last, with the data in hand, we are prepared to examine the enigmatic and controversial כפר more fully. כפר is the most prominent and prolific of the few interpretive statements in the Priestly texts.[57] However, interpreting this interpretive statement strewn throughout the Priestly corpus is problematic, since כפר is never fully defined in the Priestly texts and it carries with it different connotations.[58] Its usage falls into roughly three categories[59] (instrumental, legal/penal, and social, respectively): to wipe and by extension to purge or remove pollution,[60] to substitute or ransom,[61] and, more generally, to atone, all of which feature in Priestly literature.

Given the variability, it would seem "imperative to determine which sense is being used in each separate passage."[62] However, this is not an easy task, as the first and second categories naturally overlap with the third.[63] In other words, removing pollution and the payment of a redemptive fine have social consequences, such that YHWH and the offender are functionally at one again.[64]

---

[57] Watts 2007:130.

[58] In H (Lev 17:11), we find a definition of sorts that implicitly connects כִּפֶּר to כֹּפֶר, ransom. However, in addition to falling outside (and after) the Priestly corpus, this definition, ransom, seems unable to account for certain uses of כִּפֶּר (e.g., that the sanctuary must somehow be ransomed from sin and impurity [16:16]) and ill-equipped to explain purgation (which also inheres in the cognate Akkadian root *kuppuru*); cf. Gilders 2004: 158–180 on 17:11.

[59] Milgrom 1991:1079–1084; cf. Schwartz 1991:52–53, who argues that the third category is better understood as referring to a metaphorical cleansing or actions that obtain or grant forgiveness or purification, an expiation or eradication of pollution. It is also unclear whether כפר represents two distinct homographs or a single root with two distinct meanings (compare Schwartz 1991:62, 64 with Levine 1974:61–62). The latter seems most likely, or at least most convenient, since the two meanings share the basic sense 'to wipe away' (Gilders 2004:29, who translates כפר as 'to effect removal'). Ultimately, whether connected originally or not, the two usages both find their way into Priestly parlance and were likely mutually influential.

[60] See Milgrom 1991:1079–1084; this use is related to or derived from the Akkadian *kuppuru* (see *CAD* K 178–180).

[61] The expression כפר על נפש is especially characteristic of this usage (Levine 1974:67, 73 and Milgrom 1991:1082–1083); for a fuller definition of כֹּפֶר, see Sklar 2005:44–79, 183–184; cf. Brichto 1976.

[62] Schwartz 1991:55.

[63] See Lang 1995:292–293, whose interpretation focuses on the social dimension.

[64] Milgrom denies the social dimension of the חטאת, likely as a response to overly symbolic interpretations in which חטאת has little or no purgative effect (e.g., Gese 1977; Janowski 1982; Schenker 1991), and in which Israelite sacrifices are often considered inferior to Jesus' sacrifice. However, although he is right to stress the purgative effect and

7.3. Key Priestly Concepts

Moreover, while the context often suggests that either purgation or payment is primary, these options are not mutually exclusive. Leviticus 17:11 is especially germane in this respect. H explicitly connects כפר with the animal's lifeblood,[65] thereby suggesting that the blood is a mitigated כֹּפֶר-payment in place of the offerer's life.[66] As the only clear instance of a sacrifice serving as כֹּפֶר-payment, the passage seems to be offering a novel interpretation, an example of inner-biblical exegesis akin to spinning a midrash.[67] Rather than purging sancta or persons, clearing redeems the offerer's life with a mitigated payment.[68] However, since it is the only interpretation offered, it is unclear if it is meant to compete with, complement, or complete the Priestly portrayal of purgation.[69]

Although we cannot discover P's intention, enough evidence exists to conclude that the seeds of a dual interpretation are present in the Priestly corpus.[70] First, the presentation of the purgative חטאת and אשם as legal language paves the way for a bivalent כפר.[71] If the offerings serve both as legal payment and the means of removing pollution, it is only natural that the כפר process would both remove pollution and ransom the previously pol-

---

to be wary of symbolic, and at times anti-Jewish, interpretations, he goes too far in doing so, in essence throwing out the baby with the bathwater (cf. Watts 2007:81–82).

[65] Contra Milgrom (2000:1472–1479), 17:11 seems to explain the clearing power of all sacrifices (Schenker 1983:209; Gorman 1990:184–187; Schwartz 1991:58–60; Hartley 1992:275; Rendtorff 1992:169).

[66] Schwartz 1991:55. By demanding the life of the animal, this payment operates on the talionic principle life for life. Paradoxically, it undermines, or at least alleviates, this principle since the life offered is not the offerer's own, "but that of a substitute, an exchange that God is willing to receive in place of the real thing" (ibid. 56–57). YHWH thus differentiates himself from his human community. While he decrees that the people may not accept a כֹּפֶר in exchange for human life (Num 35:31–34), YHWH is not subject to his own decree and thus may accept a כֹּפֶר (ibid. 57–58).

[67] Ibid. 55, 59–60.

[68] Schwartz (1991:59) argues that the interpretation of כפר as ransom may either stem from a doctrinal dispute between P and H or merely serve a rhetorical function, namely, "to explain the rationale for the prohibition of eating blood in a manner suited to the internal logic of the chapter."

[69] See the diachronic progression from כפר as a purgative to כפר as a debt payment (Anderson 2005; cf. Schwartz 1994). However, the fact that the latter interpretation gains prominence over time does not mean that it was not present during the Priestly composition. All we can say with certainty is that the latter interpretation gained popularity at the expense of the former.

[70] Sklar (2005) goes too far in arguing that כפר always refers to both a כֹּפֶר-payment and purgation. The fact that a כֹּפֶר-payment is largely consonant with Priestly כפר (which is likely why H made the connection in the first place) does not mean that P ever interpreted כפר as a כֹּפֶר-payment, much less that P always interpreted כפר in this way (furthermore, evidence from non-Priestly texts cannot be used to conclusively interpret Priestly terms).

[71] See also נשא עון (Wells 2004:60–62, 73–82).

luted. Second, the application of כִּפֶּר to sacrificial contexts would be a logical extension of non-sacrificial כִּפֶּר-payments in the Priestly corpus (e.g., Ex 30:12–16) and elsewhere (e.g., Ex 21:30). Leviticus 17:11 may even be intended to explain the mechanism through which כפר-purgation is effected. The offerings may serve as the price of purgation. More specifically, YHWH's portion burned on the altar and the priests' portion consumed in the tabernacle precincts would be the price of their participation.[72] Since removal rites are not efficacious without divine and priestly participation,[73] such a price is necessary to ensure that the removal rite produces the desired effect.[74] Third, a dual meaning is consonant with ritual, as ritual authorities are often loath to offer binding interpretive statements and liable to approve of multiple interpretations. Binding interpretations may prevent rituals from adapting to new situations,[75] while multiple interpretations highlight the necessity, importance, and effectiveness of the ritual.

To make matters more complicated, כפר is occasionally associated with consecration (קדש) (e.g., Lev 16:19).[76] As argued above,[77] this use of כפר seems to be an inexact extension of purgation. Removing pollution is the people's part in the consecration process of shared space, which is ultimately achieved by YHWH.[78] Thus, כפר may be loosely associated with consecration.[79]

Why translate כפר as clearing?[80] In its multiple uses, כפר has cultic, legal, and social connotations. כפר refers to the pollution removal and consecration processes, the payment of a mitigated penalty, and the reconciliation of human and divine. These processes result in the human being

---

[72] As elsewhere in the ANE, the deity's aid is not free; cf. Ex 23:15 and Dt 16:16, which state that none shall appear before YHWH empty-handed.

[73] The non-Priestly presentation of YHWH as the subject of כפר and the Priestly presentation of the priests as the subject affirms this interpretation.

[74] In addition, wiping away language is inexact as the blood is left on the sancta and not rubbed off as in Mesopotamia and ancient Greece (Propp 2006:466). It would be more appropriate to call it a disinfectant that eradicates pollution (Gilders 2004) or somehow simply removes it.

[75] See, e.g., North 1988:983–984 on Roman sacrifice and ritual; more expansively, Kreinath, Hartung and Deschner 2004; cf. Bell 1992:184.

[76] Gilders (2004:135–137) associates כפר with removing "both impurity and the state of being common." קדש then, like חטא and טהר, adds specificity to כפר; cf. Kiuchi 1987: 94–99; Hartley 1992:64; Sklar 2005:121–127; Nihan 2007:177.

[77] Sections 3.3.3.1.b.1. and 3.4.

[78] Although removing common imperfection does not make an object holy, it is prerequisite to divine consecration.

[79] Similarly, although כפר often results in forgiveness or cleansing, כפר itself does not mean that an individual is forgiven or cleansed. It is merely a prerequisite to divine forgiveness or cleansing.

[80] After Propp 2006:466–467.

free from pollution and death, the divine abode and community being free from human pollution and the responsibility for it, and the deity being free from any temptation to leave. Each instance shares the basic meaning 'to remove (= to clear away) an unwanted barrier.'[81] Although by no means perfect, 'clearing' is a particularly resonant term that captures the common meaning, accommodates each individual emphasis and communicates כפר's inexact consecratory function.[82] Pollution must be cleared away to enable divine forgiveness, cleansing, and consecration.[83] A debt must be cleared so that the deity is suitably compensated and the offender no longer bears the burden of his misdeed or is subject to punishment. After effecting כפר, the offender is ultimately cleared, reconciled with YHWH and free from any further obligation. Finally, when all is cleared, there is no more left to do, since all is as it should be.

7.3.3.1. Why Would the Priests Choose a Multivalent Term That They Fail to Define Properly?

Rituals in general, and damage control rituals in particular, aim to bring divine power to bear on the mundane world. To adequately describe this process, ritual language is often characterized by condensation of meaning, multivocality, and ambiguity.[84] The Priests achieve all three objectives in one term, כפר. First, כפר is flexible enough to encapsulate multiple meanings and interpretations in a single term. As such, it is used to interpret most meaningful ritual actions in the tabernacle complex, often carrying with it at least two meanings at once.[85] It is also broad enough to cover multiple implied meanings and to incorporate various potential innovations.[86] Second, כפר is dynamic enough to signify different concepts to different people and to be interpreted in different ways in different contexts.[87]

---

[81] In speaking of a shared meaning, I am not speaking of etymology, but of use in context.

[82] Gilders' proposal "to effect removal," by which he means "the 'removal' of anything that disrupts the proper workings of the divine human relationship" is also acceptable (2004:28–29, 135–139). 'Atone' and 'purge,' however, emphasize the social and instrumental dimensions respectively at the expense of other possible uses.

[83] Clearing is akin to wiping away, which lies at the heart of the Akkadian *kuppuru*.

[84] See chapter 1.

[85] E.g., cultic and social, or legal and social.

[86] See similarly the unspecified scope of the חטאת and אשם offerings; cf. the Mesopotamian *Šurpu* rituals; North (1988:981–986) on the adaptability of Roman rituals; Detienne (1989:1–20) on Greek rituals. Such flexibility allows the ritual to remain eternally relevant.

[87] The clearing function of the חטאת ritual, in particular, has been variously understood (compare, e.g., Milgrom [1991:253–292], who interprets it strictly as a purgative and Janowski [1982] who connects it with symbolic atonement with little or no purgative

Third, כפר is undefined enough to avoid any binding interpretation. In other words, it has no fixed meaning since its meaning depends on its context.[88] Rather, its undefined meaning leaves open multiple possibilities without committing itself to one.[89]

Since the Priests' primary aim is to persuade, not to explain, the multifaceted כפר is especially effective. כפר adds to the persuasive power of the Priestly legislation without detracting from its precise and effective performance. It does so because the interpretation of כפר itself "is not an issue of ritual but of rhetoric," as כפר interprets ritual action instead of describing it.[90] Its pliability enhances its persuasive power, as it may be adapted to fit the complex Priestly agenda. Priestly damage control rituals simultaneously seek to concretize the abstract, making the divine accessible through otherwise mundane actions, and to preserve the transcendent mystery and majesty of the divine and the divinely ordained ritual. Thus, a precise ritual procedure with an assured result and an imprecise explanation maximizes a ritual's rhetorical effect. To this end, ritual does not state how the system works; it simply states that the intended effect is the logical outcome of the prescribed ritual actions.

Priestly damage control rituals offer imprecise explanations for two reasons: precision is elusive and a precise explanation may undermine ritual authority. The Priests lack suitable language to adequately encapsulate the transcendent realities enacted in ritual. כפר is thus a productive way of describing phenomena that defy mundane explanation. כפר as purgation, redemption, atonement, and even consecration serves to approximate transcendent reality. However, even if suitable language existed, the Priests would not offer it. Precise interpretations leave the system open to critique and competition. If people understand the system too well, they may become convinced that they no longer need it, thereby questioning its authority. In extreme cases, they may reject it altogether. More likely, many would seek alternate means of recreating the ritual's effects without priests and potentially even without the deity. In short, too much information is bad for business.[91] In addition, a fixed system has a fixed reach; once fully

---

function). Likewise, the word clearing may refer to such concepts as purgation, consecration, ransoming, and reconciliation in different contexts.

[88] Since it is related to such diverse concepts as payment and purgation, the lexeme כפר has no single fixed meaning. Its meaning derives both from the context and the interpreter's gap-filling abilities.

[89] "The complexity and uncertainty of the meaning of symbols are sources of their strength" (Kertzer 1988:11; cf. Sperber 1975; Lewis 1980:9).

[90] Watts 2007:138; cf. Bergen 2005:40.

[91] In fact, since they cannot make people bring offerings, priestly livelihood depends on their persuasive power (cf. Bibb 2009:87).

defined, a system cannot easily expand to fit new circumstances.[92] Fixed rites with a flexible explanation, however, possess both the authority of antiquity and the freedom to change. Finally, transcendent mystery is necessary to keep the people enraptured and, thus, compliant. Just as a magician's trick loses its allure once the audience knows its secret, so too does ritual lose its 'magic' when it is becomes too concrete and too common.[93]

Priestly כפר remains ever-potent and ever-necessary precisely because it remains a mystery, a mystery inextricably linked to the all-important forgiveness, cleansing, and consecration. By leaving כפר undefined, limiting it to the sanctuary and making it absolutely necessary for the removal of sins and serious impurities, the Priests convince people that they need כפר even if they do not know precisely what it is. Having established it as a constituent part of the ultimate goals of forgiveness and cleansing, clearing can become the ultimate goal itself in reference to the tabernacle. The mere presence of כפר convinces people that Clearing Day is necessary so that their sins and impurities can be cleared from the tabernacle. In fact, the people believe that they cannot survive without it, for without it they can never become right with God or safe from the negative repercussions of their actions. They become equally convinced that the only way that they can procure clearing is by following Priestly procedure and that, if they offer the prescribed offerings, all will be well. Thus, YHWH and his system are obeyed and venerated.

The switch in subject from YHWH to the priests adds rhetorical freight, as does the placement of כפר in a ritual context with legal language and an assured result. Whereas elsewhere, YHWH is often the subject of כפר (Dt 21:8; 32:43; Ez 16:63; 2 Ch 30:18; Ps 65:4; 78:38; 79:9; Jer 18:23), in the Priestly texts the priests are the subjects. This (not so) subtle shift builds on the principle that the deity is the ultimate source of clearing and adds to it the necessity of a priestly mediator.[94] By placing clearing almost exclusively in the tabernacle complex, the Priests add more evidence to their case. Together the pieces seek to ensure that people assent to the central-

---

[92] The explanation in Lev 17:11 is an aside to Moses, meant for his ears yet deemed unnecessary to ensure compliance from the people. However, because it has reached our ears, it has often limited our understanding of כפר (e.g., to symbolic substitutionary conceptions that are seen to prefigure and pale in comparison to Christ's sacrifice, such that the ritual's purgative power is ignored).

[93] The lively scholarly debate about the nature and function of כפר testifies to the fact that it has not lost its magic, even across the millennia.

[94] In addition, priestly authority is reinforced by divine decree and by the failure of Korah to occupy a priestly role. The transfer of ritual authority from Moses to Aaron, from the ultimate leader to the office of the priest, reinforces the necessity and authority of the priests (cf. Bibb 2009:83). In the Priestly system, with Moses gone, the priests are the sole mediators between human and divine.

ized Priestly system, using that system and its priests as the only means of accessing divine clearing. Before concluding their case, the Priests have one more element to add to their arsenal. Outside of the Priestly texts, clearing often occurs in the context of pleas to YHWH (Dt 21:8; 2 Ch 30:18; Ps 79:9; Jer 18:23).[95] In the Priestly texts, clearing occurs in a ritual context in quasi-legal terms. Instead of making a petition to YHWH, the aggrieved individual has access to a divinely ordained system wherein clearing is ensured, as long as he offers the appropriate sacrifice.

7.3.3.2. The Consequences of Priestly Language

Whether or not the Priestly writers intend the multiple interpretations offered above, they would likely welcome them since they enhance the system's prestige, necessity, and efficacy. However, the Priests' care not to limit meaning opens the door for other (unwelcome) interpretations, especially when the Priests are no longer around to police their system, such that clearing "has developed far beyond" the Priestly rhetoric "that made it the only interpretive comment in the ritual texts of Leviticus."[96] Even with such unwanted consequences, the continued interest in the nature and function of כפר testifies to the powerful legacy left by the Priestly term.

7.4. A Comparison of Priestly and ANE Damage Control Systems

The Priestly system is constructed to both resemble and distinguish itself from the systems of the surrounding ANE cultures. From the outset, the Priestly writers posit a fundamental difference regarding the nature of the deity and his relationship to the world and its people. The ANE gods and their people are functionally interdependent. As the masters, the gods are neither obligated to help their servants nor to disclose their wills. They do both only as it serves their purposes. YHWH too is the master; in fact, unlike in the ANE, he is the exclusive master. Nonetheless, he binds himself to respond to certain of their afflictions by prescribing a damage control system. In addition, while the ANE gods are part of this world and, thus, subject to its fate, YHWH exists outside of the world he created and has no rival in it. In other words, the people's behavior affects his relationship to

---

[95] See also Ez 16:63, which speaks of divine clearing because the sacrificial cult will not avail, so that Israel may start again after punishment and institute a sacrificial cult that will prove efficacious.

[96] Watts 2007:140; 139–140 for examples.

them, his reputation, and his spatial proximity to the world, yet does not ultimately threaten him.

These fundamental differences have profound implications on their respective damage control systems. In each system, various evils afflict sanctuaries and people alike, yet their sources and effects on the gods differ in significant ways. In each culture, evils are conceived of as stains that arise from certain actions and conditions, which weigh upon individuals and sanctuaries until properly remedied. However, while ANE afflictions have various sources, in the Priestly system, sin and (in many cases) impurity only result from human imperfection; since, in this monolatrous system, YHWH and the people are the only actors that matter.[97] Even where disputed, the Priestly system is constructed in such a way that pollution's source is irrelevant, as the afflicted must come to the supreme deity YHWH and his system to become whole (clean) again.

The nature of the gods also determines how this pollution affects them. In the ANE, both sanctuaries and deities are vulnerable to evil forces. In the Priestly system, only the sanctuary is vulnerable. Although imperfection is incompatible with his presence, it poses no real danger to YHWH, only to his precarious and unnatural place in the created world. Without endangering himself, he may eradicate imperfection either 1) through destruction, 2) through removal rites, or 3) by removing himself from it, returning to his heavenly abode. However, two of the three options would separate God from humanity, ending his unnatural sojourn among them. If YHWH chooses to destroy imperfection, he alone would remain in creation. Similarly, if he returned home, he would by necessity be absenting himself from humanity. Cultic removal then is the only tenable option left to him. Thus, in the Priestly texts, YHWH's only battle is to preserve his place in the world by preserving his system designed to eradicate imperfection.[98]

Given pollution's nature, each culture places a heavy emphasis on removing it from sanctuaries and people to achieve relative wholeness, i.e., freedom from negative influences. Each recognizes the necessity of divine participation to divinely empower ritual transactions requiring more than what can be accomplished by mundane means alone. In spite of this com-

---

[97] Menstruation, seminal emissions and the aftereffects of childbirth are all natural processes that nonetheless produce unwanted results, polluting both individuals and the sanctuary. The source of skin-disease and irregular genital discharges remains unstated (potentially deriving from YHWH himself, other supernatural forces, or simple human frailty).

[98] Other books in the Hebrew Bible offer different solutions. Nonetheless, many are concerned with the same central issue: how the perfect God may cohabit peacefully with his imperfect people.

mon ground, the ANE and Priestly systems differ with regard to the application of this power.

While the ANE cultures for the most part separate individual and communal removal from sanctuary removal, the Priestly texts incorporate both into one all-encompassing system. Because human imperfection is incompatible with and dangerous to the divine sphere and because the gods are not bound to help their servants, ANE communal removal rites are often divorced from the sanctuary. In the Priestly system, however, YHWH binds individual and communal rites to his sanctuary, thereby binding himself to participate in them.

7.4.1. Sanctuary Rites

Before addressing these communal rites, we turn to the sanctuary rites, which are analogous in P and the ANE but have been cleverly adapted in the Priestly texts to serve Priestly ends. In each context, since sanctuary removal rites benefit the sanctuary, divine participation is assumed. In the Priestly texts, it is all but promised in the prescriptive legislation (Lev 16). Thus, such rites often are relatively straightforward, albeit elaborate enough to express the importance and thoroughness of the removal process, and operate according to a fixed schedule.

In each context, human imperfection is unwelcome in the divine sphere, especially in the Priestly sanctuary since the divide between perfect YHWH and imperfect creation is greater than in the rest of the ANE.[99] In an attempt to maintain a safe distance, human imperfection in the ANE must dealt with before contact with the deity or simply denied. In P, as well, human imperfection must be redressed as much as possible beforehand.[100] This is often achieved by performing offerings in the divine sphere to remove that pollution, and, in the case of impurities, through waiting and washing prior to contact with the sanctuary. Even on Clearing Day, the priests must be pure and perfectly attired and must wash themselves before beginning ritual service.

However, recognizing that it is impossible to fully eradicate imperfection outside of the sanctuary or in individual sanctuary rites, the Priestly

---

[99] E.g., his presence on earth is unnatural, he can only be approached in a limited way both spatially and temporally, he eschews anthropomorphic description, and his glory at once reveals and conceals his presence.

[100] Often by performing offerings in the divine sphere to remove that pollution; and in the case of impurities, through waiting and washing prior to contact with the sanctuary. On Clearing Day, the priests must be pure and perfectly attired and must wash themselves before beginning ritual service.

texts require corporate confession[101] so that imperfection may be conclusively removed on Clearing Day. Indeed, whereas ANE temple removals are often part of a larger rite, the purpose of Clearing Day is simply to remove human pollution. In the Priestly system, human pollution is the only threat; without it, there would be no need for purification.[102] Paradoxically then, for the Priestly authors, imperfection is both more incongruous with and more permissible in the sanctuary. The Priests account for this tension because their system has the power to ultimately resolve it. Evils must be fully acknowledged so that their effects can be fully negated.

To do so, the Priests combine three otherwise discrete ANE elements into one ritual complex,[103] each with significant alterations. First, whereas in the ANE, temple personnel are given regular intimate access to the divine presence, in P, the high priest is only granted limited yearly access. Beginning the legislation with the proper entry protocol highlights the precariousness of the following rites, indicating that although assured, YHWH's presence is less accessible than the other ANE gods and that any interaction with him is fraught with danger.

Second, instead of entering for regular anthropomorphic service, Aaron is granted access for the express purpose of clearing the tabernacle complex of human pollution, once again stressing the anomalousness and importance of this day. Although similar, temple purification rites in the ANE remove all sorts of evils, including demonic influence. Instead of being a yearly occurrence,[104] such rites are common, usually as part of a larger ritual complex. In fact, temple purification rites even accompany the regular care and feeding of the gods.[105] By contrast, Clearing Day is set apart and exists for the sole purpose of removing human pollution. More fundamentally, whereas ANE sanctuary purifications seek to ensure that the rituals and festivals in which they are embedded are successful, Clearing Day exists to ensure that Israel has a future. That such a rite is necessary indicates that it is not a foregone conclusion, that human imperfection is a real threat to YHWH's terrestrial habitation and the people's continued existence in his presence. Only after fully dealing with this threat through a reinauguration of the system can the Israelites look to the future fruitful interchange between YHWH and his people (e.g., in service, offerings, and

---

[101] Jacobsen identifies Clearing Day as the only instance of national confession in the ANE (1976:174).

[102] There is no cosmic battle to be reenacted or cosmic foe to guard against (compare *Enūma eliš* with Gen 1).

[103] Nihan 2007:350–351.

[104] Assuming Lev 16:29–34 is a later addition, in its original form Clearing Day may have been an emergency rite to be practiced as the high priest saw fit.

[105] E.g., in Egypt, service is accompanied by various purifications in the divine cella. Such rites are often a prelude to the ritual main event, as in the *akītu* festival.

festivals). By isolating Clearing Day and limiting its scope to the removal of human imperfection, the Priestly writers thereby suggest that human imperfection is a greater threat to YHWH's precarious presence than that of his ANE counterparts. They imply that the threat is greater because YHWH is greater, wholly without rival and wholly incompatible with imperfection. By juxtaposing the full revelation of the threat with the final solution to it, the Priests then brilliantly highlight the comprehensive genius of their system.

Third, the goat for Azazel bears the stamp of an ANE communal removal rite, with the surprising innovation that it has been grafted onto the most sacred (sanctuary) rite in the Priestly system. Among the Hittites, people and/or animals serve both as gifts to a plague-causing deity and as bearers of plague themselves.[106] Such an odd combination seems to reflect the idea that the Hittites are making peace with the deity by acknowledging his wrath and offering him a gift that is more pleasant, and thus more pleasant to afflict with pollution than themselves.[107] In these rites, the transfer of pollution is not automatic; instead it is expressed as a plea pending divine approval.[108] The gift then sweetens the deal and provides a convenient transfer vessel.

The Priestly writers take what may have originally been a similar rite and adapt it to fit their system. Unlike the Hittite texts, P removes any suggestion that the goat for Azazel is a gift. First, Azazel is in no way responsible for the afflictions sent to him.[109] The people are responsible for their sins, while the impurities of uncertain origin are not delivered to him, lest he be understood as their source. Second, the goat for Azazel is presented to YHWH in the sanctuary, i.e., it has been translated into a sanctuary rite. Because YHWH himself approves of the transfer,[110] Azazel is simply forced to accept a severely polluted carcass.[111] The people do not need Azazel's permission to transfer their sins to the goat and ultimately to

---

[106] See Wright 1987:45–60 for various Hittite removal rites; cf. ibid. 60–72 for Assyrian rites; Janowski and Wilhelm 1993:134–158 for South Anatolian (Hurrian) sources; Zatelli 1998:254–258 for interesting Eblaite examples; Dietrich and Loretz 1990:19–38 for a possible Ugaritic parallel.

[107] In the Ashella ritual (Wright 1987:50–51), the angry god is offered a more pleasant object to feast upon than human flesh (ibid. 53).

[108] Scurlock 2002b argues for a similar transfer principle in Mesopotamia.

[109] Contra Levine 1989:252; Gorman 1990:99; Gane 2005:61–265, who argue that Azazel is the source of the community's evils.

[110] Cf. Lev 17:7, where sacrificing to goat demons (שעירים) is strictly prohibited. Lev 16 divests the goat of this (role) and transforms it into an acceptable vehicle of removal.

[111] Cf. Gane 2005:242–266.

him.¹¹² Thus, the Priestly system transforms an offering to a foreign deity into the capstone of its removal system. After the pollution has been banished on its bovid vessel, YHWH's system is fully vindicated, as Clearing Day renders human evils and their consequences irrevocably innocuous to the community and its sanctuary.

7.4.2. Individual and Communal Rites

Although significant overlap remains, the differences between individual and communal removal rites in the various ANE and the Priestly texts are particularly striking. In each context, individual and communal removal rites are autonomous and occur sporadically in response to a perceived crisis, with the sole purpose of removing human affliction.¹¹³ However, the afflictions removed are much more limited in the Priestly corpus, addressing only sins and impurities instead of all suffering, including various illnesses and their resulting pollution. Within Priestly legislation, the priests then take no part in physical healing;¹¹⁴ the system is concerned solely with the stains generated by Israelites' conditions and conduct.¹¹⁵

Thus, the Priestly texts pragmatically refrain from attempting to legislate primary health care.¹¹⁶ Instead they devote their energies to ensuring that, for all sins and certain physical conditions, ultimate healing – the return to relative wholeness after the full removal of all evil effects – comes from YHWH and only through his prescribed offerings.¹¹⁷ By implication, consulting any other supernatural forces in the purification process is strictly prohibited. Worse yet, it threatens to undermine the final healing that comes from YHWH alone.

While the monolatrous Israelite system demands sole allegiance to YHWH and contends that this devotion is absolutely necessary, ANE systems operate according to different principles.¹¹⁸ Complex and variable means are available to the afflicted ANE individual. Since there is no as-

---

¹¹² In addition, in the Hittite rites, the gift turned pollution bearer is not sent to the deity, but elsewhere, e.g., to afflict the enemy realm.

¹¹³ Other purposes may be implied in Lev 4–5 and 12–15 yet are by no means explicit.

¹¹⁴ They do, however, diagnose skin-disease and quarantine the patient accordingly.

¹¹⁵ In the Priestly system, the health of the individual is secondary to the 'health' of the sanctuary. Since the individual cannot access the sanctuary until he has been healed, he cannot directly pollute the sanctuary. Any pollution absorbed from afar by the tabernacle, regardless of whether the individual is healed, is remedied on Clearing Day.

¹¹⁶ Cf. H's ban on various alternatives (Lev 19:26; 19:31; 20:6; 20:27).

¹¹⁷ It simply would not be feasible for the Priestly writers to prescribe various remedies for all afflictions. Moreover, since the Priests cannot guarantee the successful healing of ailments, providing ritual remedies would ultimately threaten to undermine their authority.

¹¹⁸ Cf. Avalos 1995:397.

surance of divine cooperation, individuals often choose to make use of various options, adopting a maximalist approach to maximize the efficacy of their remedy. In the ANE, legitimacy is measured by effectiveness; regardless of its nature, a remedy is judged to be worthwhile if it helps.[119] Individual removal rites stand alone – that is, they exist for the sole purpose of removing human affliction – instead of being part of a larger ritual that benefits the deity. These rites neither directly concern the deity nor is he obligated to participate in them. Moreover, human pollution is dangerous to the divine and does not seem to pollute their temples from afar. Thus, because of divine self-interest, individual removal rites are often barred from the temples. To secure divine cooperation, individuals must give the deities compelling reasons to leave the safe confines of their temples and come to the rescue. Recognizing that success is not guaranteed, individuals hedge their bets, hoping that multiple imperfect means will somehow be sufficient to ensure a favorable divine response.

In the Priestly texts, legitimacy is determined by divine dictate and defended on the grounds that it alone is effective. YHWH himself prescribes the rites, which bear the divine stamp and are thus guaranteed to be effective. He also demands that individuals come to his sanctuary to participate in those rites. Because they are divinely sanctioned, pose no threat to YHWH, occur in the divine precincts, and operate according to a fixed protocol, the people may rest assured in the security of the system. Without the need to coerce the divine or combine partial solutions, these rites are far simpler and more straightforward than their ANE counterparts. Instead of putting their energy into constructing coercive rites to secure divine favor, the Priests devote their time to convincing the people to follow the system.

This difference finds clear expression in the use of both contractual and cultic language to describe offerings. In both the ANE and the Priestly corpus, offerings may be cast as a legally binding payment that ensures divine cooperation. In both, purgation may be cast as the logical outcome of offering rituals. Nevertheless, the ANE texts offer such explanations as a way of making an otherwise unstable effort more secure. By contrast, since the efficacy of their system is guaranteed, the Priestly texts offer such explanations in order to persuade the people to comply with its ordinances.

The Priests even successfully incorporate anomalous removal rites into their system. Having already discussed the goat for Azazel, we turn to the bird rite in Leviticus 14. With clear parallels in the ANE,[120] the bird rite is

---

[119] However, certain ritual series pick up a quasi-canonical status over time as they are deemed the officially accepted, and thus most effective and appropriate remedies (e.g., the Mesopotamian *Šurpu* series).

[120] See Wright 1987.

obviously an elimination rite. The Priestly writers, however, adapt it to fit their system. As with the goat for Azazel, the Priests are especially careful to distinguish the bird rite from both normal procedure and its ANE antecedents. The Azazel goat rite may safely keep its anomalous form, since although it begins in the sanctuary, it is an anomalous rite that uniquely carries pollution into the wilderness. Once put in its Priestly context, it forms an integral part of the Priestly system, and serves as implicit critique of other ANE removal rites. Seen as ineffectual in their 'primitive' forms, these removal rites must be combined with other more central Priestly clearing rites and with priestly and divine supervision to avail.

Incapable of fully effecting purification, the bird rite and an accompanying ablution serve simply to remove enough pollution for the individual to reenter society. Since the individual has no access to the sanctuary and its normal procedures, a makeshift ritual is required outside of divine space.[121] Lest it is misunderstood, the rite is placed under priestly, and thus divine, purview. Finally, the ritual's subordinate role is confirmed, as after time and other ritual actions, the offender may enter the sanctuary to receive clearing and ultimate cleansing through normal channels.

7.4.3. Why Does the Priestly System Allow Pollution in the Divine Sphere?

The sanctuary admits pollution because and so that it can be conclusively eliminated. Individual and communal damage control rites form an essential component of the construction and preservation of the Priests' perfect society, which is a primary goal of their theology.[122] To construct such a society, all human imperfection must be conclusively eradicated; unlike in the ANE, eradicating imperfection from humanity is thus in the divine self-interest. To ensure that imperfection is fully and finally removed from Israel, the afflicted must come to the tabernacle. In a way, individual removal rites unleash ordered chaos in the heart of the ordered world so that the chaos may be conclusively expelled.[123] These rites are situated in the best

---

[121] Cf. Num 16:46–47, where incense must be employed to effect clearing outside of the sanctuary.

[122] Although an idealist, P is also in some ways a realist, since his 'perfect' society makes room for and redresses non-rebellious imperfections. While it is implicit in the Priestly texts, perfection is more explicitly expressed in H in the command to pursue holiness (e.g., Lev 19:2).

[123] Again, it is unclear if the tabernacle complex absorbs pollution in the removal process or simply removes it. If the former, pollution would then be stored in the only place that could suitably handle it, the tabernacle, pending its expulsion on Clearing Day (Propp 2006:698–700). It is also possible that the absorption of the people's pollution would be relatively innocuous. If the tabernacle absorbs pollution from afar, the transfer of pollution to the sanctuary during individual pollution removal rites may not have much effect, since the tabernacle has already absorbed the transferred pollutants. The rite then

and most controlled environment to ensure thorough removal in the divine sphere, with the deity present and cooperative, the priests to officiate, and the legislation to back it up.

Complemented and completed by the annual Clearing Day, all pollutants are removed so thoroughly from the loyal community, loyal individuals within it, and the divine abode that they are rendered irrevocably irrelevant to all three. Because they have no more bearing on Israel, the people and the sanctuary are perfectly pure, i.e., free from imperfection, as YHWH is perfectly pure. Disloyal individuals, however, stand condemned, as isolated pockets of imperfection awaiting judgment amid the relatively perfect community.

Comprehensive clearing is the primary means of achieving this unlikely reality, enabled by a single system that juxtaposes communal and sanctuary clearing. The Priests recognize that the sanctuary and its community are inextricably linked, that the state and fate of the one affects the state and fate of the other. In putting the two systems together in the tabernacle under divine and priestly aegis, the Priests construct a perfect system that fully accounts for imperfection in both spheres.

With the system functioning as intended, YHWH, his divine intrusion into creation, and the system designed to enable it are all vindicated. The instrumental removal of pollution and the payment of a mitigated penalty indicate that the system works. In both expressions, individuals receive clearing to escape death that is the consequence of contact between human imperfection and divine perfection (Lev 10; 15:31).[124] In both, people become reconciled with their god. As a result, human and divine may continue to live in relative harmony, preserving the precarious equilibrium for another year. YHWH, in turn, receives honor for his perfect system, while his relatively perfect people reflect the greatness of their divine overlord.[125] To make this picture a reality, the Priests direct their rhetoric at expounding the system in such a way that the people are compelled to obey its stipulations, so that YHWH remains content, Israel receives blessing, and the priests keep their place as overseers of the all-important cult.

---

could simply serve to drain the pollution from individuals into an environment where it would have little additional effect.

[124] Even when perfectly pure, Aaron must take great precautions in approaching the divine presence lest he be destroyed by YHWH's absolute holiness (Lev 16).

[125] In H, certain rebellious actions reflect poorly and YHWH, thereby desecrating (חלל) his name. Other positive actions reflect well on YHWH and thus do not desecrate his name. In other words, they honor him (Lev 18:21; 19:12; 20:3; 22:2, 32 cf. 21:6, where being holy is likened to not profaning the divine name).

Conclusion

Rather than analyzing an aspect of the Priestly cultic system (e.g., blood manipulation, the חטאת offering) or looking at the system through a narrow lens (e.g., graded holiness, cosmology), my study began with a broader, empirically-based focus. It asked a fundamental and largely unexamined question,[1] as applicable to the ANE cultures as it is to the Priestly writers: how does one secure and safeguard the divine presence in the midst of human community? My primary aim has been to elucidate the Priestly system designed to safeguard the divine presence in the tabernacle. Nonetheless, to do so adequately, I situated the Priestly system alongside the analogous ANE systems, examining its fundamental components that are universally applicable in the ANE world: the nature of the divine presence (chapter 2); the dedication and inauguration of the divine abode and its cult (chapter 3); regular service (chapter 4); and damage control (chapters 5-7). This analytical approach had an empirical foundation, as it allowed the material itself to dictate the conclusions as much as possible.[2]

In order to accommodate my broad focus and empirically-based approach, my study required a wide interpretive lens. Since the best ritual theories only address aspects of the ritual systems, my interpretive framework combined the various elements into one comprehensive system (chapter 1).

Ritual itself is a meaningful way of bridging the divide between human and divine on multiple levels. Ritual transforms a series of mundane actions so that the results of those actions transcend normal cause-effect relations. By bringing the divine presence and power to bear on the mundane world, ritual transforms that world in a way that no mundane action can hope to accomplish. For example, in the חטאת for sins in Leviticus 4–5 and 16, a bloody mess successfully removes the intangible stain caused by sin from individuals and the tabernacle to the end that the individual is forgiven, the sanctuary is suitably pure, human and divine are at one, and world

---

[1] Previous studies have been either cursory or selective in their analyses.

[2] Of course, placing the Priestly system alongside the Egyptian, Mesopotamian, Hittite and Syro-Palestinian systems ensures that I make connections whether or not they exist. Nonetheless, the strong implicit thread that connects the Israelite system to its ANE forbears is difficult to deny.

order is restored. In the process, ritual roles and the power relations they embody are reinforced. YHWH is the author, recipient, and ultimate power behind ritual action. The people are the servants, who through ritual action may interact with the deity to remove the effects of their imperfections from themselves and the sanctuary. The priests act as the mediators, who alone are qualified to perform the ritual actions to enable this cosmic interchange. The ritual elements themselves are also illustrative, often carrying with them symbolic and ideological undertones.

To accommodate this multivocality, I developed a three-pronged ritual analysis. First, structure analyzed the relationships between people, places, and objects that can be derived verifiably from the rituals themselves.[3] Second, use examined what participants expect ritual action to accomplish, often instrumentally, by analyzing the *causa* that prompts ritual and the various purpose statements assigned to ritual actions.[4] Third, ideology explored the text's underlying rationale and the non-obvious, often symbolic connections it makes.[5] Finally, since the Priestly texts are not rituals themselves, but texts describing rituals, my analysis also took into account the text's persuasive purposes.[6] This broad interpretive lens and the wide landscape that it examined thus provided a more comprehensive portrait than has been attempted before, yielding various large- and small-scale insights in each of the major sections.[7] Instead of systematically differentiating myself from other interpreters, my conclusion will focus on the unique portrait of the Priestly system that emerges from my investigation.

Identifying the rhetorical purpose(s) of P, especially in relation to the the ANE, is a primary innovation of my approach, which expands on Watts' work. From an analysis of P itself, a clear purpose emerges. In comparing P with the ANE, this purpose emerges in a broader, more ambitious light. The Priestly texts aim to persuade their audience that the system they describe is necessary and important. When placed alongside the ANE texts

---

[3] Gilders' indexical approach is especially helpful in this regard as it explains ritual roles and the power dynamics that undergird them.

[4] See Modeus 2005 and Gane 2005.

[5] See, e.g., Klawans 2006. Making connections with ANE material falls into this category, since they are non-verifiable and address the text's theoretical underpinnings.

[6] More than simply explaining ritual, the Priestly corpus also serves rhetorical purposes (see esp. Watts 2007; cf. id. 1999).

[7] On a large scale, my study offers new interpretations of the nature of the divine presence (esp. in comparing it with non-P and ANE conceptions), the dedication of the tabernacle, regular service (especially since no comprehensive study exists for either the tabernacle dedication or regular service), and damage control (especially in comparing P with ANE systems and their underlying rationales). On a smaller scale, I offer new interpretations of the divine glory, consecration, divine meals, and clearing. Selected insights will be mentioned throughout the conclusion.

and the systems they describe, it becomes clear that the Priestly texts pursue their goal largely by differentiating themselves from their ANE counterparts.[8]

In designing a worthy system, the Priestly writers naturally first examine whatever source data are available to them. The various ANE peoples surrounding them whose systems have similar elements, even if those elements are expressed in different ways, provide the most logical fodder.[9] Although the Priestly writers may not have access to the intricacies of ANE ritual practice, they, like most ANE people, know its fundamental principles.[10] In turn, they construct their system according to this shared blueprint, but with significant alterations to distinguish themselves from it.

More than simply aiming to establish the importance of their system, the Priestly writers hope to establish its exclusive necessity, so that the audience obeys YHWH, his system, and the priests who oversee it.[11] To do so, they must establish the supremacy and ultimate efficacy of YHWH and his system, and that following any other course is perilous.[12] In constructing the supreme system and convincing the Israelites of its necessity, the Priestly writers minimize the perceived weaknesses of the model they align themselves with so as to maximize the persuasive power of their exclusive appeal.

Such intentionality is difficult to prove, especially since the polemic is not explicit as in Second Isaiah, for example.[13] However, although implicit, the polemic against ANE systems is no less powerful,[14] proving its worth again and again over the course of my examination. On the face of it, the Priestly texts simply explain the system and, in the process, convince their audience of its necessity. At the same time, a closer look indicates that they

---

[8] The Priests undoubtedly built on present and previous Israelite ritual systems. Their system responds to and hopes to supersede internal claimants as much as external. However, given the paucity of non-Priestly biblical materials on the matter, it is difficult to trace this internal development. Thus, my analysis focused on the more expansive, and perhaps no less intentional, interconnections with the ANE.

[9] Of course in addition to their own (rival) traditions.

[10] Modern interpreters have access to these principles largely through an examination of specialist texts, whose ideology, if effective, would pervade popular culture, shaping its religious worldview, and influence those like the Israelites who come into contact with it.

[11] For the Priestly writers his system is their system. Thus, they differentiate themselves from both external and internal rivals.

[12] This is especially important given the monolatrous Israelite/Priestly tendencies and the relative inability (perhaps even absence) of the Israelite state to counteract the allure of and exposure to more powerful cultures.

[13] In fact the Priestly texts do not even acknowledge the existence of other ANE systems (cf. H on the Canaanite abominations).

[14] As also, e.g., Ps 29 and 93.

are constructed to implicitly supersede their closest analogues, so as to convince those familiar with (or soon-to-be familiar with) ANE practice that the Priestly system is superior, and thus the best option.

We now turn our attention to a synthesis of the fundamental components of the Priestly and ANE systems with a view to placing the Priestly system in sharper and more comprehensive focus. This optical enhancement functions on two levels. First, since the Priestly system shares common ground with its ANE counterparts, examining the ANE systems better illumines the place of the Priestly system in its wider context, especially where the Priestly worldview is otherwise largely inaccessible to the modern mind.[15] Second, comparing ANE elements with Priestly elements allows the Priestly innovations to emerge with greater clarity, as they adapt the ANE systems to construct a supreme system underwritten by the supreme deity. Our synthesis will likewise proceed on two levels – through a general comparative lens and, more specifically, through the use of language – both with a view toward situating each element in the larger Priestly system and its rhetorical trajectory.

Priestly innovation is immediately apparent in the conceptualization of the divine presence. In the Priestly system, as in the ANE, divine presence is both necessary and difficult to conceptualize. Ritual tradents thus make the gods accessible by providing them with a home and an image, yet not so accessible that they are misunderstood. In the ANE, gods inhabit statues, which they are connected to but not encapsulated by. However, in practice, the gods are often equated with their statues. In response to this potential problem, the Priestly texts distance YHWH from any human-made object,[16] instead positing the divine glory as a new and improved version of a divine statue. Unlike the ANE statue, YHWH's glory emanates from his person; it is part of him, at once locating him and concealing his true form behind its luminous veil. Unlike the ANE statue, YHWH's glory and, by extension, YHWH himself are not bound to space or form, nor can they be deported, transported, or destroyed. Although not bound to space, YHWH displays his glory in and around the centralized tabernacle structure, thereby eliminating the possibility of multiple and potentially rival YHWHs in various locales. Thus, the Priestly conceptualization of divine presence is more elusive and independent, with fewer limitations and an-

---

[15] In other words, since the Priestly texts contain the same basic elements and a similar worldview as the ANE texts, a comparison of texts is mutually beneficial. For example, modern scholars find it difficult to explain how multiple ritual actions accomplish a single end, often resorting to diachronic solutions or acrobatic harmonizations that smooth over embarrassing ritual repetition. When understood in context, it becomes clear that the cumulative approach, where multiple means accomplish a single end, is the preferred method in the ANE.

[16] YHWH appears near the ark but is in no way ontologically connected to it.

thropomorphic entanglements. Although more mysterious, YHWH's majestically veiled presence is likewise more reassuring. Even though little understood, the participation of such a transcendent deity promises to be more effective than that of its anthropomorphic equivalent.

Priestly language ably serves the Priestly agenda, providing enough detail to suggest practical presence – i.e., divine aid and supervision of the cult – while shrouding the nature of that presence in mystery. The Priestly texts add precision when precision is possible and profitable, e.g., in systematizing the elements of a theophany into three tiers of presence. However, as precision becomes increasingly elusive the closer one gets to YHWH himself, so too does Priestly language. The Priests intimate that God will dwell with Israel, yet when the time comes for him to take up residence, they are circumspect about what divine dwelling entails, careful to differentiate YHWH's indwelling presence from all known analogues. In addition, by concealing YHWH's true form behind the glory, YHWH himself is ultimately unapproachable both spatially and conceptually.

In the dedication and inauguration of the tabernacle and the cult, the Priestly writers steer closer to their ANE counterparts, but with one significant distinction. In P as in the ANE, the entrance of the deity stands at the heart of the dedication rite, the rest of which is orchestrated to ensure initial, continued, and contented divine presence. Although redundant by modern sensibilities, the Priestly system shares with its ANE heritage the proclivity for positing multiple means to achieve a single end. In both P and the ANE, ritual is also a joint effort of human and divine. Humans follow (divinely inspired) instruction, providing the deity with a conducive environment to ensure that mundane ritual action achieves its supramundane goals. In the Priestly texts, multiple human actions and mysterious divine supervision effect a suitable ground state, rendering the tabernacle suitable for divine presence and effective ritual commerce between humanity and the divine. However, the treatment of the divine presence provides a strong point of contrast. In the ANE, the divine statue undergoes an elaborate ritual transformation from statue to fully-functioning locus of divine presence, after which the deity, in the form of his statue, enters the temple with great fanfare. In the Priestly texts, the ark, as the closest human-made approximation of the ANE statue, is simply placed in the sanctuary before its dedication and anointed like all other sancta. The highlight of the dedication is instead the arrival of YHWH's glory. Finally, lest YHWH's arrival be misconstrued as his animation of the ark, YHWH in the form of his glory later emerges from the tabernacle without the ark (Lev 9:23–24).

Priestly language used to describe the dedication follows the previously established pattern. The Priests add precision to the non-Priestly and ANE texts by more clearly differentiating between holiness and purity. Nonetheless, there is still some conceptual overlap in the Priestly texts, since the two concepts are so closely allied. Furthermore, while human action is carefully enumerated and regulated, Priestly language renders divine participation both assumed and enigmatic.

Regular service once again highlights the Priestly debt to and departure from the other ANE cultures. In P as in the ANE, regular divine service consists of the care and feeding of the god(s). However, although the elements are similar (food, drink, light, and incense), the Priestly writers blur the definitional edges. While service remains essential and retains anthropomorphic elements, the Priestly texts obscure the nature and meaning of the service (e.g., how YHWH partakes of food). Thus, the audience cannot conclusively identify why YHWH wants and what he does with the gifts so carefully proffered. However, enough detail exists to indicate that whatever his purposes may be, YHWH's service and his appropriation of it are different from his ANE divine and royal analogues. Similarly, the Priestly account adds distance to the already mysterious divine service. Whereas ANE priests have regular, intimate, and often anthropomorphic contact with their gods, in P none may behold YHWH's true form, much less cater to his bodily needs.

The language used to describe divine service is precise enough to distinguish YHWH's service from that of his ANE counterparts, yet elusive enough to preserve divine privacy and primacy. Priestly language becomes increasingly elusive the closer one gets to YHWH himself.[17] The Priestly texts imply selective ambiguity by omitting expected elements of divine service (e.g., meat to accompany the bread on the table) and inserting simple and simply impenetrable purpose statements (e.g., the purpose of the bread is to set it before YHWH). Thus, while YHWH demands anthropomorphic service, it remains unclear what YHWH does with his gifts, rendering him more mysterious and less anthropomorphic than his ANE rivals.

Finally, Priestly damage control conforms closely to the established precedent. In both P and the ANE, sins and impurities produce a danger that threatens peoples, places, and objects and thus must be redressed through ritual action involving human and divine cooperation. However, whereas the ANE peoples separate individual/communal and sanctuary removal rites, the Priestly writers combine both into one all-encompassing system. Whereas ANE individual and communal removal rites are often isolated from the sanctuary and require the suppliant to convince the deity to participate, YHWH himself details the ritual procedure and demands

---

[17] For example, while offerings at the bronze altar may safely be referred to as food (e.g., Lev 3:11), the nature of the bread of presence on the table in the outer sanctuary remains undefined.

that it occur in his sanctuary complex, thus ensuring its success. Whereas ANE sanctuary removal rites expel unwanted (often demonic) influences from the sanctuary as part of a larger ritual (e.g., a divine procession), the Priestly Clearing Day is solely devoted to removing human pollution from the divine sphere and the human community that surrounds it. This Priestly combination brilliantly underscores the ultimate efficacy of their system. The juxtaposition of individual and sanctuary removal rites conclusively removes all human pollution[18] from the loyal community and the divine sanctuary so that it becomes "irrevocably irrelevant" to both,[19] thereby safeguarding the divine presence and keeping heaven on earth for another year.

Whereas Priestly language is especially precise in enumerating ritual practice and its instrumental results, its interpretative statements are more elusive. The nature of the all-important כפר, 'clearing,' is particularly hard to define. As a result the Israelites cannot be sure what כפר is, yet know that it is necessary to enable forgiveness and cleansing (Lev 4–5 and 12–15, respectively) and for the ultimate removal of pollution (16). Likewise, the Priests give evocative names to the carefully legislated חטאת and אשם offerings in order to convince the Israelites of their necessity. In short, precise ritual practice with undefined ritual interpretation serves the Priestly ritual agenda, keeping the 'magic' intact and thus keeping the priests in business.

The Priestly writers use whatever means they have at their disposal to establish the importance of their system, in the process exalting YHWH, his system, and its priestly overseers. Because they cannot compete with the more powerful ANE cultures materially, the Priestly writers do battle conceptually and rhetorically. Knowing that they can never make their temple, statue, service, and installation and damage control rituals as lavish as their neighbors, the Priests instead make their deity and his regular service more elusive and less materially-reliant. As a result, they render him more transcendent and thus superior to his ANE rivals. At the same time, by providing precise, divinely inspired ritual legislation, performed in the sanctuary complex with divine and priestly supervision, the Priests render YHWH's system more efficacious. In turn, a more transcendent deity in charge of a more effective system logically compels human participation and makes a compelling case for their continued relevance. In the end, the enduring legacy of the Priestly system in both scholarly and popular circles testifies to its clever construction and rhetorical power.

---

[18] In the monolatrous Priestly system, all human pollution equals all meaningful pollution.

[19] Gane 2005:318. The disloyal, however, must face the fatal consequences of their pollution.

Works Cited

Abusch, I. Tzvi
1987–90   "Maqlû." *RlA* 7: 346–351. Berlin: de Gruyter.
1991   "The Ritual Tablet and Rubrics of *Maqlû*: Towards the History of the Series." Pages 233–253 in *Ah Assyria...: Studies in Assyrian History and Ancient Near Eastern Historigraphy Presented to Hayim Tadmor*. Edited by M. Cogan and I. Eph'al. ScrHier 33. Jerusalem: Magnes Press.
1992   "Ritual and Incantation: Interpretation and Textual History of Maqlû VII: 58–105 and IX: 152–159." Pages 367–380 in *"Sha'arei Talmon": Studies in the Bible, Qumran, and the Ancient Near East Presented to Shemaryahu Talmon*. Edited by M. A. Fishbane and E. Tov. Winona Lake, IN: Eisenbrauns.
1999   "Witchcraft and the Anger of the Personal God." Pages 81–121 in *Mesopotamian Magic: Textual, Historical, and Interpretive Perspectives*. Edited by T. Abusch and K. van der Toorn. Ancient Magic and Divination 1. Groningen: Styx.
2002   *Mesopotamian Witchcraft: Toward a History and Understanding of Babylonian Witchcraft Beliefs and Literature*. Ancient Magic and Divination 5. Groningen: Styx.
2004a   "Prayers, Hymns, Incantations, and Curses: Mesopotamia." Pages 353–355 in *Religions of the Ancient World: A Guide*. Edited by S. Johnston. Cambridge, MA: Belknap Press of Harvard University Press.
2004b   "Illnesses and Other Crises: Mesopotamia." Pages 456–459 in *Religions of the Ancient World: A Guide*. Edited by S. Johnston. Cambridge, MA: Belknap Press of Harvard University Press.

Achenbach, Reinhard
2003   *Die Vollendung der Tora: redaktionsgeschichtliche Studien zum Numeribuch im Kontext von Hexateuch und Pentateuch*. BZAR 3. Wiesbaden: Harrassowitz Verlag.

Albertz, Rainer
1978   *Persönliche Frömmigkeit und offizielle Religion: religionsinterner Pluralismus in Israel und Babylon*. Calwer theologische Monographien A, Bibelwissenschaft 9. Stuttgart: Calwer.
1994   *A History of Israelite Religion in the Old Testament Period*. Translated by J. Bowden. 2 vols. London: SCM Press.
2003   *Israel in Exile: The History and Literature of the Sixth Century B.C.E.* Translated by D. Green. SBL Studies in Biblical Literature 3. Atlanta: SBL.

Anderson, Gary A.
1992   "Sacrifice and Sacrificial Offerings: Old Testament." *ABD* 5: 870–886. New York: Doubleday.
2005   "From Israel's Burden to Israel's Debt: Toward a Theology of Sin in Biblical and Early Second Temple Sources." Pages 1–30 in *Reworking the Bible:*

Apocryphal and Related Texts at Qumran. Proceedings of a Joint Symposium by the Orion Center for the Study of the Dead Sea Scrolls and Associated Literature and the Hebrew University Institute for Advanced Studies Research Group on Qumran, 15–17 January, 2002. Edited by E. G. Chazon, D. Dimant and R. A. Clements. STDJ 58. Leiden: Brill.

Assmann, Jan
    2001   *The Search for God in Ancient Egypt*. Translated by D. Lorton. Ithaca, NY: Cornell University Press.
    2004   "Prayers, Hymns, Incantations, and Curses: Egypt." Pages 350–353 in *Religions of the Ancient World: A Guide*. Edited by S. Johnston. Cambridge, MA: Belknap Press of Harvard University Press.

Austin, John L.
    1962   *How to Do Things with Words*. New York: Oxford University Press.

Avalos, Hector
    1995   *Illness and Health Care in the Ancient Near East: The Role of the Temple in Greece, Mesopotamia, and Israel*. HSM 54. Atlanta: Scholars Press.

Baentsch, Bruno
    1903   *Exodus–Leviticus–Numeri*. HK 1, 2. Göttingen: Vandenhoeck und Ruprecht.

Bahrani, Zainab
    2003   *The Graven Image: Representation in Babylonia and Assyria*. Philadelphia: University of Pennsylvania Press.

Beckman, Gary M.
    1989   "The Religion of the Hittites." *BA* 52: 98–108.
    2000   "Royal Ideology and State Administration in Hittite Anatolia." Pages 529–544 in *Civilizations of the Ancient Near East*. Edited by J. M. Sasson. Peabody, MA: Hendrickson.
    2004   "Sacrifices, Offerings, and Votives: Anatolia." Pages 336–339 in *Religions of the Ancient World: A Guide*. Edited by S. Johnston. Cambridge, MA: Belknap Press of Harvard University Press.

Bell, Catherine
    1992   *Ritual Theory, Ritual Practice*. Oxford: Oxford University Press.
    1997   *Ritual: Perspectives and Dimensions*. Oxford: Oxford University Press.

Bell, Lanny
    1985   "Luxor Temple and the Cult of the Royal *Ka*." *JNES* 44: 251–294.
    1998   "The New Kingdom 'Divine' Temple: The Example of Luxor." Pages 127–184 in *Temples of Ancient Egypt*. Edited by B. Shafer. London: I. B. Tauris.

Bergen, Wesley J.
    2005   *Reading Ritual: Leviticus in Postmodern Culture*. JSOTSup 417. London: T&T Clark.

Berlejung, Angelika
    1997   "Washing the Mouth: The Consecration of Divine Images in Mesopotamia." Pages 45–72 in *The Image and the Book: Iconic Cults, Aniconism, and the Rise of Book Religion in Israel and the Ancient Near East*. Edited by K. van der Toorn. Leuven: Peeters.
    1998   *Die Theologie der Bilder: Herstellung und Einweihung von Kultbildern in Mesopotamien und die alttestamentliche Bilderpolemik*. OBO 162. Fribourg: Universitatsverlag.

Berquist, Bergitta
    1993   "Bronze Age Sacrificial Koine in the Eastern Mediterranean? A Study of Animal Sacrifice in the Ancient Near East." Pages 11–43 in *Ritual and Sac-*

rifice in the Ancient Near East: Proceedings of the International Conference Organized by the Katholieke Universiteit Leuven from the 17th to the 20th of April 1991. Edited by J. Quaegebeur. OLA 55. Louvain: Peeters.

Bertholet, Alfred
1901 *Leviticus*. KHC 3. Tübingen: J.C.B. Mohr.

Bibb, Bryan
2009 *Ritual Words and Narrative Worlds in the Book of Leviticus*. LHBOTS 480. London: T&T Clark.

Bidmead, Julye
2004 *The Akītu Festival: Religious Continuity and Royal Legitimation in Mesopotamia*. Gorgias Dissertations 2. Near Eastern Studes 2. Piscataway, NJ: Gorgias Press.

Blackman, Aylward M., and Herbert W. Fairman
1946 "The Consecration of an Egyptian Temple according to the Use of Edfu." *JEA* 32: 75–91.

Bloch, Maurice
1992 *Prey into Hunter: The Politics of Religious Experience*. Cambridge: Cambridge University Press.

Blum, Erhard
1984 *Die Komposition der Vätergeschichte*. WMANT 57. Neukirchen-Vluyn: Neukirchener.
1990 *Studien zur Komposition des Pentateuch*. BZAW 189. Berlin: de Gruyter.

Borger, Riekele
1956 *Die Inschriften Asarhaddons, Königs von Assyrien*. AfO Beiheft 9. Graz: E.Weidner.
1973 "Die Weihe eines Enlil-Priesters." *BiOr* 30: 163–176.

Borghouts, Joris F.
1978 *Ancient Egyptian Magical Texts*. Nisaba: Religious Texts Translation Series 9. Leiden: Brill.
2000 "Witchcraft, Magic, and Divination in Ancient Egypt." Pages 1775–1785 in *Civilizations of the Ancient Near East*. Edited by J. M. Sasson. Peabody, MA: Hendrickson.

Bottéro, Jean
2001 *Religion in Ancient Mesopotamia*. Translated by T. L. Fagan. Chicago: The University of Chicago Press.

Brichto, Herbert C.
1976 "On Slaughter and Sacrifice, Blood and Atonement." *HUCA* 47: 19–55.

Buchler, Justus
1955 *The Philosophical Writings of Peirce*. NY: Dover.

Caplice, Richard I.
1974 *The Akkadian Namburbi Texts: An Introduction*. Sources from the Ancient Near East 1, 1. Los Angeles: Undena Publications.

Carpenter, Eugene, and Michael A. Grisanti
1999 "פשׁע." *NIDOTTE* 3: 706–710. Grand Rapids, MI: Zondervan.

Cassin, Elena
1968 *La splendeur divine: introduction à l'étude de la mentalité mésopotamienne*. Civilisations et Sociétés 8. Paris: Mouton.

Cassuto, Umberto
1967 *A Commentary on the Book of Exodus*. Translated by I. Abrahams. Jerusalem: Magnes Press.

Černý, Jaroslav
  1952   *Ancient Egyptian Religion.* London: Hutchinson's University Library.
Cholewiński, Alfred
  1976   *Heiligkeitsgesetz und Deuteronomium: eine vergleichende Studie.* Rome: Biblical Institute Press, 1976.
Cohen, Mark E.
  1981   *Sumerian Hymnology: The Eršemma.* HUCASup 2. Cincinnati: Hebrew Union College Press.
  1993   *The Cultic Calendars of the Ancient Near East.* Bethesda, MD: CDL Press.
Collins, Billie Jean
  2004a   "Deities and Demons: Anatolia." Pages 404–407 in *Religions of the Ancient World: A Guide.* Edited by S. Johnston. Cambridge, MA: Belknap Press of Harvard University Press.
  2004b   "Illnesses and Other Crises: Anatolia." Pages 461–463 in *Religions of the Ancient World: A Guide.* Edited by S. Johnston. Cambridge, MA: Belknap Press of Harvard University Press.
  2004c   "Sin, Pollution, and Purity: Anatolia." Pages 504–505 in *Religions of the Ancient World: A Guide.* Edited by S. Johnston. Cambridge, MA: Belknap Press of Harvard University Press.
  2005   "A Statue for the Deity: Cult Images in Hittite Anatolia." Pages 13–42 in *Cult Image and Divine Representation in the Ancient Near East.* Edited by N.H. Walls. Boston, MA: ASOR.
  2007   *The Hittites and their World.* Archaeology and Biblical Studies 2. Atlanta: SBL.
Collins, C. John
  1999   "כבד." *NIDOTTE* 2:577–587. Grand Rapids, MI: Zondervan.
Converse, Philip E.
  1964   "The Nature of Belief Systems in Mass Publics." Pages 206–261 in *Ideology and Discontent.* Edited by D. Apter. New York: Free Press.
Cross, Frank Moore
  1973   *Canaanite Myth and Hebrew Epic: Essays in the History of the Religion of Israel.* Cambridge, MA: Harvard University Press.
Crüsemann, Frank
  1992   *Die Tora: Theologie und Sozialgeschichte des alttestamentlichen Gesetzes.* München: Kaiser.
Dahm, Ulrike
  2003   *Opferkult und Priestertum in Alt-Israel: ein kultur- und religionswissenschaftlicher Beitrag.* BZAW 327. Berlin: de Gruyter.
David, A. Rosalie
  1981   *A Guide to Religious Ritual at Abydos.* Warminster: Aris & Philips.
Davies, Douglas
  1977   "Interpretation of Sacrifice in Leviticus." *ZAW* 89: 387–399.
Detienne, Marcel
  1989   "Culinary Practices and the Spirit of Sacrifice." Pages 1–20 in *The Cuisine of Sacrifice among the Greeks.* Edited by M. Detienne and J.-P. Vernant. Translated by P. Wissing. Chicago: University of Chicago.
Dietrich, Manfred, and Oswald Loretz
  1990   *Mantik in Ugarit: keilalphabetische Texte der Opferschau, Omensammlungen, Nekromantie.* ALASPM 3. Münster: Ugarit-Verlag.

Dozeman, Thomas B., and Konrad Schmid, eds.
2006   *A Farewell to the Yahwist? The Composition of the Pentateuch in Recent European Interpretation.* SBL Symposium Series 34. Atlanta: SBL.

Douglas, Mary
1966   *Purity and Danger: An Analysis of the Concepts of Pollution and Taboo.* London: Routledge.
1995   "Poetic Structure in Leviticus." Pages 239–256 in *Pomegranates and Golden Bells: Studies in Biblical, Jewish, and Near Eastern Ritual, Law, and Literature in Honor of Jacob Milgrom.* Edited by D. P. Wright, D. N. Freedman, and A. Hurvitz. Winona Lake, IN: Eisenbrauns.

Driver, Godfrey R.
1969   "Ugaritic and Hebrew Words." *Ug* 6: 181–184.

Driver, Samuel R.
1911   *The Book of Exodus.* Cambridge Bible for Schools and Colleges. Cambridge: Cambridge University Press.

Driver, Tom F.
1996   "Transformation: The Magic of Ritual." Pages 170–187 in *Readings in Ritual Studies.* Edited by R. Grimes. Upper Saddle River, NJ: Prentice Hall.

Dumont, Louis
1967   *Homo hierarchicus: essai sur le système des castes.* Bibliothèque des Sciences Humaines. Paris: Gallimard.

Durham, John I.
1987   *Exodus.* WBC 3. Waco, TX: Word.

Eberhart, Christian
2002   *Studien zur Bedeutung der Opfer im Alten Testament: die Signifikanz von Blut- und Verbrennungsriten im kultischen Rahmen.* WMANT 94. Neukirchen-Vluyn: Neukirchener.
2006   Review of R. Gane, *Cult and Character: Purification, Day of Atonement, and Theodicy. RBL* 2006. Online: http://www.bookreviews.org/pdf/5068_5341.pdf.

Ehrlich, Arnold B.
1899–1901 *Hamiqra Kifshuto.* Berlin: M. Poppelauer (Hebrew).
1909   *Randglossen zur Hebräischen Bibel 2: textkritisches, sprachliches und sachliches.* Leipzig: Hinrichs.

Eilberg-Schwartz, Howard
1990   *The Savage in Judaism: An Anthropology of Israelite Religion and Ancient Judaism.* Bloomington, IN: Indiana University Press.

Elliger, Karl
1952   "Sinn und Ursprung der priesterlichen Geschichtserzählung." *ZTK* 49: 121–142.
1959   "Heiligkeitsgesetz." *RGG* 3: 175–176. Tübingen: Mohr.
1966   *Leviticus.* HAT 1, 4. Tübingen: Mohr.

Englund, Gertie
1987   "Gifts to the Gods – a Necessity for the Preservation of Cosmos and Life: Theory and Praxis." Pages 57–66 in *Gifts to the Gods: Proceedings of the Uppsala Symposium 1985.* Edited by T. Linders and G. Nordquist. BOREAS 15. Stockholm: Almqvist & Wiksell International.
2002   "Offerings." Pages 276–286 in *The Ancient Gods Speak: A Guide to Egyptian Religion.* Edited by D. Redford. Oxford: Oxford University Press.

Evans-Pritchard, Edward E.
  1956   *Nuer Religion*. Oxford: Clarendon.
Fabry, Heinz-Josef, and Hans-Winfried Jüngling, eds.
  1999   *Levitikus als Buch*. BBB 119. Berlin: Philo.
Fernandez, James
  1965   "Symbolic Consensus in a Fang Reformative Cult." *AA* 67: 902–929.
Fleming, Daniel E.
  1992   *The Installation of Baal's High Priestess at Emar: A Window on Ancient Syrian Religion*. HSS 42. Atlanta: Scholars.
  1998   "The Biblical Tradition of Anointing Priests." *JBL* 117: 401–414.
Fohrer, Georg
  1970   *Introduction to the Old Testament*. Translated by D. Green. London: SPCK.
Foster, Benjamin R.
  1995   *From Distant Days: Myths, Tales, and Poetry of Ancient Mesopotamia*. Bethesda, MD: CDL Press.
  2005   *Before the Muses: An Anthology of Akkadian Literature*. 3rd ed. Bethesda, MD: CDL Press.
Fox, Kate
  2005   *Watching the English: The Hidden Rules of English Behaviour*. London: Hodder & Stoughton.
Frandsen, Paul John
  2000   "On the Origin of the Notion of Evil in Ancient Egypt." *Göttinger Miszellen* 179: 9–34.
  2004   "Sin, Pollution, and Purity: Egypt." Pages 497–499 in *Religions of the Ancient World: A Guide*. Edited by S. Johnston. Cambridge, MA: Belknap Press of Harvard University Press.
Frankfort, Henri
  1948   *Kingship and the Gods: A Study of Ancient Near Eastern Religion as the Integration of Society and Nature*. Chicago: The University of Chicago Press.
Frantz-Szabó, Gabriella
  2000   "Hittite Witchcraft, Magic, and Divination." Pages 2007–2019 in *Civilizations of the Ancient Near East*. Edited by J. M. Sasson. Peabody, MA: Hendrickson.
Friedman, Richard E.
  1981   *The Exile and Biblical Narrative*. HSM 22. Chico, CA: Scholar's Press.
  1992   "Tabernacle." *ABD* 6: 292–300. New York: Doubleday.
Frymer-Kensky, Tikva
  1983   "Pollution, Purification and Purgation in Ancient Israel." Pages 399–415 in *The Word of the Lord Shall Go Forth: Essays in Honor of David Noel Freedman in Celebration of His Sixtieth Birthday*. Edited by C. L. Meyers and M. O'Connor. Winona Lake, IN: Eisenbrauns.
Gane, Roy E.
  1992   "'Bread of Presence' and Creator in Residence." *VT* 42: 179–203.
  2004   *Ritual Dynamic Structure*. Gorgias Dissertations 14. Piscataway, NJ: Gorgias Press.
  2005   *Cult and Character: Purification Offerings, Day of Atonement and Theodicy*. Winona Lake, IN: Eisenbrauns.
  2008   "Privative Preposition מן in Purification Offering Pericopes and the Changing Face of 'Dorian Gray.'" *JBL* 127: 209–222.

Garr, W. Randall
    2003   *In His Own Image and Likeness: Humanity, Divinity and Monotheism*. Culture and History of the Ancient Near East 15. Leiden: Brill.

Gee, John L.
    1998   "The Requirements of Ritual Purity in Ancient Egypt." Ph.D. Diss., Yale University.

Geller, Markham J.
    1980   "The Šurpu Incantations and Lev. V.1–5." *JSS* 25: 181–192.

Geller, Stephen A.
    1992   "Blood Cult: Toward a Literary Theology of the Priestly Work of the Pentateuch." *Proof* 12: 97–124.

Gerstenberger, Erhard S.
    1996   *Leviticus: A Commentary*. Translated by D.W. Stott. OTL. Louisville, KY: Westminster John Knox.

Gertz, Jan Christian
    2000   *Tradition und Redaktion in der Exoduserzählung: Untersuchungen zur Endredaktion des Pentateuch*. FRLANT 186. Göttingen: Vandenhoeck & Ruprecht.

Gertz, Jan Christian, Konrad Schmid and Marcus Witte, eds.
    2002   *Abschied vom Jahwisten: die Komposition des Hexateuch in der jüngsten Diskussion*. BZAW 315. Berlin: de Gruyter.

Gese, Hartmut
    1977   "Die Sühne." Pages 85–106 in *Zur biblischen Theologie: Alttestamentliche Vorträge*. BEvT 78. München: Kaiser.

Gilders, William K.
    2004   *Blood Ritual in the Hebrew Bible: Meaning and Power*. Baltimore, MD: The Johns Hopkins University Press.

Gluckman, Max
    1962   *Essays on Ritual and Social Relations*. Manchester: Manchester University Press.

Goetze, Albrecht
    1957   *Kleinasien*. 2nd ed. Handbuch der Altertumswissenschaft 3, 2. Kulturgeschichte des Alten Orients 3, 1. München: Beck.

Gorman, Frank H.
    1990   *The Ideology of Ritual: Space, Time and Status in the Priestly Theology*. JSOTSup 91; Sheffield: JSOT Press.
    1999   Review of Gerald Klingbeil, *A Comparative Study of the Ritual of Ordination as Found in Leviticus 8 and Emar 369*. *JBL* 118: 534–536.

Grabbe, Lester L.
    1993   *Leviticus*. OTG. Sheffield: JSOT Press.

Graham, M. Patrick
    1990   *The Utilization of 1 and 2 Chronicles in the Reconstruction of Israelite History in the Nineteenth Century*. SBLDS 116. Atlanta: John Knox.

Green, Alberto R. W.
    2003   *The Storm-God in the Ancient Near East*. Biblical and Judaic Studies 8. Winona Lake, IN: Eisenbrauns.

Grimes, Ronald L.
    1990   *Ritual Criticism: Case Studies in its Practice, Essays on its Theory*. Columbia: University of South Carolina Publishing.
    1995   *Beginnings in Ritual Studies*. Columbia: University of South Carolina Press.

1996 "Ritual Criticism and Infelicitous Performance." Pages 279–293 in *Readings in Ritual* Studies. Edited by R. Grimes. Upper Saddle River, NJ: Prentice Hall.

Gröndahl, Frauke
1967 *Die Personennamen der Texte aus Ugarit.* Studia Pohl 1. Rome: Päpstliches Bibelinstitut.

Gross, Walter
1998 *Zukunft für Israel: alttestamentliche Bundeskonzepte und die aktuelle Debatte um den Neuen Bund.* SBS 176. Stuttgart: Verlag Katholisches Bibelwerk.

Gruenwald, Ithamar
2002 *Rituals and Ritual Theory in Ancient Israel.* Brill Reference Library of Judaism 10. Leiden: Brill.

Gurney, Oliver R.
1977 *Some Aspects of Hittite Religion.* Oxford: Oxford University Press.

Güterbock, Hans G.
1974 "Appendix: Hittite Parallels," *JNES* 33: 323–327.

Haas, Volkert
1970 *Der Kult von Nerik: ein Beitrag zur hethitischen Religionsgeschichte.* Studia Pohl 4. Rome: Päpstliches Bibelinstitut.

Hallo, William W.
1990 "Compare and Contrast: The Contextual Approach to Biblical Literature." Pages 1–30 in *The Bible in Light of Cuneiform Literature.* Edited by W. Hallo, B. Jones, and G. Mattingly. Scripture in Context III. Ancient Near Eastern Texts and Studies 8. Lewiston, NY: Mellen.
1997 "Ancient Near Eastern Texts and Their Relevance for Biblical Exegesis." Pages xxiii–xxviii in *The Context of Scripture.* Edited by W. Hallo and L. Younger. Vol. 1. Leiden: Brill.

Haran, Menahem
1960 "Uses of Incense in the Ancient Israelite Ritual." *VT* 10: 113–129.
1978 *Temples and Temple-Service in Ancient Israel.* Oxford: Clarendon.

Hardin, Richard S.
1996 "'Ritual' in Recent Literary Criticism: The Elusive Sense of Community." Pages 308–324 in *Readings in Ritual Studies.* Edited by R. Grimes. Upper Saddle River, NJ: Prentice Hall.

Haroutunian, Hripsime
2004 "Religious Practices of the Individual and Family: Anatolia." Pages 430–431 in *Religions of the Ancient World: A Guide.* Edited by S. Johnston. Cambridge, MA: Belknap Press of Harvard University Press.

Hartley, John E.
1992 *Leviticus.* WBC 4. Dallas: Word.

Heger, Paul
1997 *The Development of Incense Cult in Israel.* BZAW 245. Berlin: Walter de Gruyter.

Heinisch, Paul
1935 *Das Buch Leviticus.* HSAT. Bonn: Hanstein.

Hendel, Ronald S.
1997 "Aniconism and Anthropomorphism in Ancient Israel." Pages 205–228 in *The Image and the Book: Iconic Cults, Aniconism, and the Rise of Book Re-*

ligion in Israel and the Ancient Near East. CBET 21. Edited by K. van der Toorn. Leuven: Peeters.

Hoffmeier, James K.
1985 "Sacred" in the Vocabulary of Ancient Egypt: The Term DṢR, with Special Reference to Dynasties I–XX. OBO 59. Fribourg: Universitätsverlag.

Hoftijzer, Jacob
1967 "Das sogenannte Feueropfer." Pages 114–134 in Hebräische Wortforschung: FS zum 80. Geburtstag von Walter Baumgartner. VTSup 16. Edited by B. Hartmann et al. Leiden: Brill.

Hornung, Erik
1983 Conceptions of God in Ancient Egypt: The One and The Many. Translated by J. Baines. London: Routledge & Kegan Paul.

Houston, Walter
1993 Purity and Monotheism: Clean and Unclean Animals in Biblical Law. JSOTSup 140. Sheffield: JSOT Press.
2003 "Towards an Integrated Reading of the Dietary Laws of Leviticus." Pages 142–161 in The Book of Leviticus: Composition and Reception. Edited by R. Rendtorff and R.A. Kugler. VTSup 93. Formation and Interpretation of Old Testament Literature 3. Leiden: Brill.

Houtman, Cornelis
1992 "On the Function of the Holy Incense (Exodus XXX 34–8) and the Sacred Anointing Oil (Exodus XXX 22–33)." VT 42: 458–465.
2000 Exodus. Vol. 3. HCOT. Leuven: Peeters.

Hubert, Henri, and Marcel Mauss
1964 Sacrifice: Its Nature and Function. Translated by W. D. Halls. Chicago: University of Chicago Press.

Hundley, Michael
2009 "To Be or Not to Be: A Reexamination of Name Language in Deuteronomy and the Deuteronomistic History." VT 59: 533–555.

Hurowitz, Victor A.
1985 "The Priestly Account of Building the Tabernacle." JAOS 105: 21–30.
1989 "Isaiah's Impure Lips and Their Purification in Light of Mouth Purification and Mouth Purity in Akkadian Sources." HUCA 60: 39–89.
1992 I Will Build You an Exalted House: Temple Building in the Bible in the Light of Mesopotamian and Northwest Semitic Writings. JSOTSup 115. JSOT/ASOR Monograph Series 5. Sheffield: JSOT Press.
1994 "Ancient Israelite Cult in History, Tradition and Interpretation." Association of Jewish Studies Review 19: 213–236.
2002 Review of G. Klingbeil, A Comparative Study of the Ritual of Ordination as Found in Leviticus 8 and Emar 369. JQR 92: 604–608.
2003 "The Mesopotamian God Image, from Womb to Tomb." JAOS 123: 147–157.

Hurvitz, Avi
1982 A Linguistic Study of the Relationship between the Priestly Source and the Book of Ezekiel: A New Approach to an Old Problem. Cahiers de la RB 20. Paris: J. Gabalda.

Hüsken, Ute, ed.
2007 When Rituals go Wrong: Mistakes, Failure, and the Dynamics of Ritual. SHR 115. Leiden: Brill.

Hutton, Rodney R.
 1994 *Charisma and Authority in Israelite Society.* Minneapolis, MN: Fortress Press.
Imparati, Fiorella
 2000 "Private Life Among the Hittites." Pages 571–586 in *Civilizations of the Ancient Near East.* Edited by J. M. Sasson. Peabody, MA: Hendrickson.
Jacobsen, Thorkild
 1970 *Toward the Image of Tammuz and Other Essays on Mesopotamian History and Culture.* HSS 21. Cambridge, MA: Harvard University Press.
 1976 *The Treasures of Darkness: A History of Mesopotamian Religion.* New Haven, CT: Yale University Press.
 1987 *The Harps that Once...: Sumerian Poetry in Translation.* New Haven, CT: Yale University Press.
Janowski, Bernd
 1982 *Sühne als Heilsgeschehen: Studien zur Sühnetheologie der Priesterschrift und zur Wurzel KPR im Alten Orient und im Alten Testament.* WMANT 55; Neukirchen-Vluyn: Neukirchener.
 1999 "Azazel." Pages 128–131 in *Dictionary of Deities and Demons in the Bible.* 2nd Edition. Edited by K. van Der Toorn, B. Becking, and P.W. Van Der Horst. Leiden: Brill.
Janowski, Bernd, Klaus Koch, and Gernot Wilhelm, eds.
 1993 *Religionsgeschichtliche Beziehungen zwischen Kleinasien, Nordsyrien und dem Alten Testament.* OBO 129. Fribourg: Universitätsverlag.
Janowski, Bernd, and Gernot Wilhelm
 1993 "Der Bock, der die Sünden hinausträgt: Zur Religionsgeschichte des Azazel-Ritus Lev 16,10.21f." Pages 106–169 in *Religionsgeschichtliche Beziehungen zwischen Kleinasien, Nordsyrien und dem Alten Testament.* Edited by B. Janowski, K. Koch, and G. Wilhelm. OBO 129. Fribourg: Universitätsverlag.
Janzen, David
 2004 *The Social Meanings of Sacrifice in the Hebrew Bible: A Study of Four Writings.* BZAW 344. Berlin: Walter de Gruyter.
Janzen, J. Gerald
 1997 *Exodus.* Westminster Bible Companion. Louisville, KY: Westminster John Knox.
Jay, Nancy B.
 1992 *Throughout Your Generations Forever: Sacrifice, Religion and Paternity.* Chicago: Chicago University Press.
Jennings, Theodore W.
 1996 "On Ritual Knowledge." Pages 324–334 in *Readings in Ritual Studies.* Edited by R. Grimes. Upper Saddle River, NJ: Prentice Hall.
Jenson, Philip P.
 1992 *Graded Holiness: A Key to the Priestly Conception of the World.* JSOTSup 106. Sheffield: JSOT Press.
Jeremias, Jörg
 1977 *Theophanie: die Geschichte einer alttestamentlichen Gattung.* WMANT 10. 2nd edition. Neukirchen: Neukirchener.
Johnston, Sarah Iles, ed.
 2004 *Religions of the Ancient World: A Guide.* Cambridge, MA: Belknap Press of Harvard University Press.

Joosten, Jan
 1996 *People and Land in the Holiness Code: An Exegetical Study of the Ideational Framework of the Law in Leviticus 17–26*. VTSup 67. Leiden: Brill.
Joüon, Paul, and Takamitsu Muraoka
 2005 *A Grammar of Biblical Hebrew*. 2 vols. SubBi 14. Rome: Editrice Pontificio Istituto Biblico.
Jürgens, Benedikt
 2001 *Heiligkeit und Versöhnung: Levitikus 16 in seinem literarischen Kontext*. HBSt 28. Freiburg: Herder.
Kawashima, Robert S.
 2006 "The Priestly Tent of Meeting and the Problem of Divine Transcendence: An 'Archaeology' of the Sacred." *JR* 86: 226–257.
Keel, Othmar
 1977 *Jahwe-Visionen und Siegelkunst: eine Neue Deutung der Majestätsschilderungen in Jes 6, Ez 1 und 10 und Sach 4*. SBS 84/85. Stuttgart: Verlag Katholisches Bibelwerk.
Kertzer, David I.
 1988 *Ritual, Politics, and Power*. New Haven: Yale University Press.
 1996 "Ritual, Politics and Power." Pages 335–352 in *Readings in Ritual Studies*. Edited by R. Grimes. Upper Saddle River, NJ: Prentice Hall.
King, Leonard W.
 1912 *Babylonian Boundary Stones and Memorial-Tablets in the British Museum*. London: British Museum.
Kiuchi, Nobuyoshi
 1987 *The Purification Offering in the Priestly Literature: Its Meaning and Function*. JSOTSup 56. Sheffield: JSOT Press./
 2003 *A Study of Ḥāṭāʾ and Ḥaṭṭāʾt in Leviticus 4–5*. FAT 2, 2. Tübingen: Mohr Siebeck.
Klawans, Jonathan.
 2000 *Impurity and Sin in Ancient Judaism*. Oxford: Oxford University Press.
 2006 *Purity, Sacrifice, and the Temple: Symbolism and Supersessionism in the Study of Ancient Judaism*. Oxford: Oxford University Press.
Klingbeil, Gerald
 1998 *A Comparative Study of the Ritual of Ordination as Found in Leviticus 8 and Emar 369*. Lewiston, NY: Edwin Mellen.
Knierim, Rolf P.
 1965 *Die Hauptbegriffe für Sünde im Alten Testament*. Gütersloh: Gütersloher Verlagshaus, 1965.
 1992 *Text and Concept in Leviticus 1:1–9: A Case in Exegetical Method*. FAT 2. Tübingen: Mohr.
 1997a "עָוֺן *ʿāwōn* perversity." *TLOT* 2:862–866. Peabody, MA: Hendrickson, 1997.
 1997b "פֶּשַׁע *pešaʿ* crime." *TLOT* 2:1033–1037. Peabody, MA: Hendrickson, 1997.
Knohl, Israel
 1987 "The Priestly Torah Versus the Holiness School: Sabbath and the Festivals." *HUCA* 58: 65–117.
 1995 *The Sanctuary of Silence: The Priestly Torah and Holiness School*. Minneapolis: Fortress Press.
Koch, Klaus
 1999 "עָוֺן." *TDOT* 10: 546–552. Grand Rapids, MI: Eerdmans.

Köckert, Matthias
1989 "Leben in Gottes Gegenwart: Zum Verständnis des Gesetzes in der priesterschriftlichen Literatur." *JBTh* 4: 29–61.
Kornfeld, Walter
1983 *Levitikus*. NEB 6. Würzburg: Echter.
Kornfeld, Walter, and Helmer Ringgren
2003 "קדש." *TDOT* 12: 521–545. Grand Rapids, MI: Eerdmans.
Korpel, Marjo C.A.
1990 *A Rift in the Clouds: Ugaritic and Hebrew Descriptions of the Divine*. UBL 8. Münster: Ugarit-Verlag.
Kratz, Reinhard G.
2000 *Die Komposition der erzählenden Bücher des Alten Testaments: Grundwissen der Bibelkritik*. Göttingen: Vandenhoeck & Ruprecht.
Kratz, Reinhard, and Hermann Spieckermann, eds.
2006 *Götterbilder, Gottesbilder, Weltbilder. I: Polytheismus und Monotheismus in der Welt der Antike. Band I: Ägypten, Mesopotamien, Kleinasien, Syrien, Palästina*. FAT 2,17. Tübingen, Mohr Siebeck.
Kreinath, Jens, Constance Hartung, and Annette Deschner, eds.
2004 *The Dynamics of Changing Rituals: The Transformation of Religious Rituals within their Social and Cultural Context*. Toronto Studies in Religion 29. New York: Peter Lang.
Læssøe, Jørgen
1955 *Studies on the Assyrian Ritual and Series Bît Rimki*. København: Munksgaard.
Lambert, Wilfred G.
1962 "A Catalogue of Texts and Authors." *JCS* 16: 59–77.
1968 "Myth and Ritual as Conceived by the Babylonians." *JSS* 13: 104–112.
1974 "Dingir.šà.dib.ba Incantations." *JNES* 33: 267–322.
1990 "Ancient Mesopotamian Gods: Superstition, Philosophy, Theology." *RHR* 207: 115–130.
1993 "Donations of Food and Drink to the Gods in Ancient Mesopotamia." Pages 191–201 in *Ritual and Sacrifice in the Ancient Near East: Proceedings of the International Conference Organized by the Katholieke Universiteit Leuven from the 17th to the 20th of April 1991*. Edited by J. Quaegebeur. OLA 55. Louvain: Peeters.
Lang, Bernhard
1995 "כפר." *TDOT* 7: 288–303. Grand Rapids, MI: Eerdmans.
Laroche, Emmanuel.
1971 *Catalogue des textes hittites*. Paris: Éditions Klincksieck.
Lawrence, Jonathan D.
2006 *Washing in Water: Trajectories of Ritual Bathing in the Hebrew Bible and Second Temple Literature*. Academia Biblica 23. Atlanta: SBL.
Leach, Edmund R.
1976 *Culture and Communication: The Logic by which Symbols are Connected: An Introduction to the Use of Structuralist Analysis in Social Anthropology*. Cambridge: Cambridge University Press.
1985 "The Logic of Sacrifice." Pages 136–150 in *Anthropological Approaches to the Old Testament*. IRT 8. Edited by Bernhard Lang. Philadelphia: Fortress Press.

Lebrun, René
1976 *Samuha, foyer religieux de l'empire hittite.* Publications de l'Institut orientaliste de Louvain 11. Louvain-la-Neuve: Institut orientaliste, Université catholique de Louvain.
2004 "Prayers, Hymns, Incantations, and Curses: Anatolia." Pages 359–360 in *Religions of the Ancient World: A Guide.* Edited by S. Johnston. Cambridge, MA: Belknap Press of Harvard University Press.

Lemardelé, Christophe
2002 "Le sacrifice de purification: un sacrifice ambigu?" *VT* 52: 284–289.

Lévi-Strauss, Claude
1978 *Myth and Meaning.* London : Routledge and Kegan Paul.

Levine, Baruch A.
1963 "Ugaritic Descriptive Rituals." *JCS* 17: 105–111.
1965 "The Descriptive Tabernacle Texts of the Pentateuch." *JAOS* 17: 307–318.
1974 *In the Presence of the Lord: A Study of Cult and Some Cultic Terms in Ancient Israel.* SJLA 5. Leiden: Brill.
1983 "The Descriptive Ritual Texts from Ugarit: Some Formal and Functional Features of the Genre." Pages 467–475 in *The Word of the Lord Shall Go Forth: Essays in Honor of David Noel Freedman in Celebration of His Sixtieth Birthday.* Edited by C.L. Meyers and M. O'Connor. Winona Lake, IN: Eisenbrauns.
1989 *Leviticus.* JPSTC. Philadelphia: JPS.
2000 *Numbers 21–36.* AB 4A. New York: Doubleday.

Levinson, Bernard M.
1997 *Deuteronomy and the Hermeneutics of Legal Innovation.* Oxford: Oxford University Press.

Lewis, Gilbert
1980 *Day of Shining Red: An Essay on Understanding Ritual.* Cambridge: Cambridge University Press.

Lichtheim, Miriam
1976 *Ancient Egyptian Literature: A Book of Readings. Volume 2: The New Kingdom.* Berkeley: University of California Press.

Lie, Arthur G.
1929 *The Inscriptions of Sargon II King of Assyria. I. The Annals: Transliterated and Translated with Notes.* Paris: Paul Geuthner.

Linssen, Marc J. H.
2004 *The Cults of Uruk and Babylon: The Temple Ritual Texts as Evidence for Hellenistic Cult Practice.* Cuneiform Monographs 25. Leiden: Brill.

Lohfink, Norbert
1978 "Die Priesterschrift und die Geschichte." Pages 189–225 in *Congress Volume, Göttingen 1977.* Edited by J. A. Emerton. VTSup 29. Leiden: Brill.
1994 "The Priestly Narrative and History." Pages 136–172 in *Theology of the Pentateuch.* Minneapolis, MN: Fortress.

Löhr, Max
1925 *Das Ritual von Lev. 16.* Untersuchungen zum Hexateuchproblem III. Schriften der Königsberger Gelehrten Gesellschaft 2, 1. Berlin: Deutsche Verlagsgesellschaft für Politik und Geschichte.

Lorton, David
    1999   "The Theology of Cult Statues in Ancient Egypt." Pages 123–210 in *Born in Heaven, Made on Earth: The Making of the Cult Image in the Ancient Near East.* Edited by M. B. Dick. Winona Lake, IN: Eisenbrauns.
Luciani, Didier
    2005   *Sainteté et Pardon. Vol. 1: Structure littéraire du Lévitique. Vol. 2: Guide Technique.* BETL 185. Leuven: Peeters.
Maul, Stefan M.
    1999   "How the Babylonians Protected Themselves Against Calamities Announced by Omens." Pages 123–129 in *Mesopotamian Magic: Textual, Historical, and Interpretive Perspectives.* Ancient Magic and Divination 1. Edited by T. Abusch and K. van der Toorn. Groningen: Styx.
Malul, Meir
    2002   *Knowledge, Control and Sex: Studies in Biblical Thought, Culture and Worldview.* Tel Aviv-Jaffa: Archaeological Center Publication.
Marx, Alfred
    2003   "The Theology of Sacrifice According to Leviticus 1–7." Pages 103–120 in *The Book of Leviticus: Composition and Reception.* Edited by R. Rendtorff and R.A. Kugler. VTSup 93. Formation and Interpretation of Old Testament Literature 3. Leiden: Brill.
    2005   *Les Systèmes Sacrificiels de l'Ancien Testament: Formes et Fonctions du Culte Sacrificiel à Yhwh.* VTSup 105. Leiden: Brill.
Mauss, Marcel
    1990   *The Gift: The Form and Reason for Exchange in Archaic Societies.* Translated by W. D. Halls. London: Routledge.
McCarthy, Dennis J.
    1969   "The Symbolism of Blood and Sacrifice." *JBL* 88: 166–176.
McMahon, Gregory
    2000   "Theology, Priests, and Worship in Hittite Anatolia." Pages 1981–95 in *Civilizations of the Ancient Near East.* Edited by J. M. Sasson. Peabody, MA: Hendrickson.
Meeks, Dimitri.
    1975   "Pureté et purification en Égypte." *SDB* 9: 430–452.
    1999   *The Daily Life of the Egyptian Gods.* Translated by G. M. Goshgarian. London: Pimlico.
Meier, Gerhard
    1937   *Die Assyrische Beschwörungssammlung Maqlû.* AfO Beiheft 2. Berlin: Im Selbstverlage des Herausgebers.
Mendenhall, George E.
    1973   *The Tenth Generation: The Origins of the Biblical Tradition.* Baltimore: Johns Hopkins University Press.
Mettinger, Tryggve N. D.
    1982   *The Dethronement of Sabaoth: Studies in the Shem and Kabod Theologies.* ConBOT 18. Lund: CWK Gleerup.
    1998   "The Name and the Glory: The Zion-Sabbath Theology and Its Exilic Successors." *JNSL* 24: 1–24.
Milgrom, Jacob
    1963   "The Biblical Diet Laws as an Ethical System." *Int* 17: 288–301.
    1970   *Studies in Levitical Terminology. I. The Encroacher and the Levite: The Term 'Aboda.* Berkeley, CA: University of California.

1976   *Cult and Conscience: the Asham and the Priestly Doctrine of Repentance.* SJLA 18. Leiden: Brill.
1983   *Studies in Cultic Theology and Terminology.* SJLA 36. Leiden: Brill.
1986   "The Priestly Impurity System." Pages 121–127 in *Proceedings of the Ninth World Congress of Jewish Studies.* Vol. 1. Jerusalem: Magnes Press.
1989a   "Ethics and Ritual: The Foundation of the Biblical Dietary Laws." Pages 159–191 in *Religion and Law: Biblical-Judaic and Islamic Perspectives.* Edited by E.B. Firmage, B.G. Weiss and J.W. Welch. Winona Lake, IN: Eisenbrauns.
1989b   "Rationale for Cultic Law: The Case of Impurity." *Semeia* 45: 103–109.
1990   *Numbers.* JPSTC. Philadelphia: JPS.
1991   *Leviticus 1–16.* AB 3. New York: Doubleday.
2000   *Leviticus 17–22.* AB 3A. New York: Doubleday.
2001   *Leviticus 23–27.* AB 3B. New York: Doubleday.
2003   HR in Leviticus and Elsewhere in the Torah." Pages 24–40 in *The Book of Leviticus: Its Composition and Reception.* Edited by R. Rendtorff and R.A. Kugler. VTSup 93. Leiden: Brill.
2007   "The Preposition מן in the חטאת Pericopes." *JBL* 126: 161–191.

Miller, Patrick D., and J.J.M. Roberts
1977   *The Hand of the Lord: A Reassessment of the "Ark Narrative" of 1 Samuel.* Baltimore: Johns Hopkins University Press.

Modéus, Martin
2005   *Sacrifice and Symbol: Biblical Šĕlāmîm in a Ritual Perspective.* ConBOT 52. Stockholm: Almqvist & Wiksell.

Munn, Nancy D.
1973   "Symbolism in Ritual Context: Aspects of Symbolic Action." Pages 579–612 in Handbook of Social and Cultural Anthropology. Edited by J. Honigmann. Chicago: Rand McNally.

Nelson, Harold H.
1949   "Certain Reliefs from Karnak and Medinet Habu," JNES 8: 201–232.

Nicholson, Ernest W.
1998   The Pentateuch in the Twentieth Century: The Legacy of Julius Wellhausen. Oxford: Clarendon.

Nielsen, Kjeld
1986   Incense in Ancient Israel. VTSup 38. Leiden: Brill.
1992   "Incense." *ABD* 3: 404–409. New York: Doubleday.

Nihan, Christophe
2007   *From Priestly Torah to Pentateuch: A Study in the Composition of the Book of Leviticus.* FAT 2, 25. Tübingen: Mohr Siebeck.

North, John A.
1988   "Sacrifice and Ritual: Rome." Pages 981–986 in *Civilizations of the Ancient Mediterranean: Greece and Rome.* Edited by M. Grant and R. Kitzinger. New York: Scribner's.

Noth, Martin
1948   *Überlieferungsgeschichte des Pentateuch.* Stuttgart: Kohlhammer.
1962   *Das dritte Buch Mose: Leviticus.* ATD 6. Göttingen: Vandenhoeck und Ruprecht.
1965   *Leviticus: A Commentary.* OTL. Translated by J. E. Anderson. London: SCM Press.

1981 *A History of Pentateuchal Traditions*. Translated by B. W. Anderson. Atlanta: Scholars Press.
1987 *The Chronicler's History*. Translated by H.G.M. Williamson. JSOTSup 50. Sheffield: JSOT Press.

Oppenheim, A. Leo
1943 "Akkadian *pul(u)ḫ(t)u* and *melammû*." *JAOS* 63: 31–34.
1977 *Ancient Mesopotamia: Portrait of a Dead Civilization*. Chicago: University of Chicago Press.

Otto, Eckart
1994 "Das Heiligkeitsgestetz Leviticus 17–26 in der Pentateuchredaktion." Pages 65–80 in *Altes Testament, Forschung und Wirkung: FS für Henning Graf Reventlow*. Edited by P. Mommer and W. Thiel. Frankfurt am Main: Peter Lang.
1997 "Forschungen zur Priesterschrift." *TRu* 62: 1–50.
1999 "Innerbiblische Exegese im Heiligkeitsgesetz Levitikus 17–26." Pages 125–196 in *Levitikus als Buch*. BBB 119. Edited by H.-J. Fabry and H.-W. Jüngling. Berlin: Philo.
2002 "Forschungen zum nachpriesterschriftlichen Pentateuch." *TRu* 67: 125–155.

Otto, Rudolf
1923 *The Idea of the Holy: An Inquiry into the Non-rational Factor in the Idea of the Divine, and its Relation to the Rational*. Translated by J. W. Harvey. London: H. Milford.

Paran, Meir
1989 *Forms of the Priestly Style in the Pentateuch*. Jerusalem: Magnes Press (Hebrew).

Pardee, Dennis
2002 *Ritual and Cult at Ugarit*. SBLWAW 10. Atlanta: SBL.

Parpola, Simo
1970–83 *Letters from Assyrian scholars to the Kings Esarhaddon and Assurbanipal*. AOAT 5. Neukirchen-Vluyn: Neukirchener.

Péter-Contesse, René
1993 *Lévitique 1–16*. CAT 3a. Genève: Labor et Fides.

Pongratz-Leisten, Beate
1994 *Ina šulmi īrub: die kulttopographische und ideologische Programmatik der akītu-Prozession in Babylonien und Assyrien im 1. Jahrtausend v. Chr.* Baghdader Forschungen 16. Mainz: von Zabern.

Popko, Maciej
1995 *Religions of Asia Minor*. Translated by I. Zich. Warsaw: Academic Publications Dialog.

Preuss, Horst Dietrich
1985 "Heiligkeitsgesetz." *TRE* 14: 713–719.

Propp, William H. C.
2006 *Exodus 19–40*. AB 2A. New York: Doubleday.

Quaegebeur, Jan
1993 "L'autel-à-feu et l'abattoir en Égypte tardive." Pages 329–353 in *Ritual and Sacrifice in the Ancient Near East: Proceedings of the International Conference Organized by the Katholieke Universiteit Leuven from the 17th to the 20th of April 1991*. Edited by J. Quaegebeur. *OLA* 55. Louvain: Peeters.

Quirke, Stephen
1992 *Ancient Egyptian Religion*. New York: Dover.

Ramsey, Ian T.
 1957   *Religious Language: An Empirical Placing of Theological Phrases.* London: SCM Press.
Rappaport, Roy A.
 1999   *Ritual and Religion in the Making of Humanity.* Cambridge Studies in Social and Cultural Anthropology 110. Cambridge: Cambridge University Press.
Reiner, Erica
 1956   "Lipšur Litanies." *JNES* 15: 129–149.
 1958   *Šurpu: A Collection of Sumerian and Akkadian Incantations.* AfO Beiheft 11. Graz: Ernst Weidner.
 1985   *Your Thwarts in Pieces, Your Mooring Rope Cut: Poetry from Babylonia and Assyria.* Michigan Studies in the Humanities 5. Ann Arbor: Horace H. Rackham School of Graduate Studies at the University of Michigan.
Rendtorff, Rolf
 1985   *Leviticus.* BKAT 3. Neukirchen-Vluyn: Neukirchener.
 1995   "Another Prolegomenon to Leviticus 17:11." Pages 23–28 in *Pomegranates and Golden Bells: Studies in Biblical, Jewish, and Near Eastern Ritual, Law, and Literature in Honor of Jacob Milgrom.* Edited by D. P. Wright, D. N. Freedman, and A. Hurvitz. Winona Lake, IN: Eisenbrauns.
Rendtorff, Rolf, and Robert A. Kugler, eds.
 2003   *The Book of Leviticus: Composition and Reception.* VTSup 93. Formation and Interpretation of Old Testament Literature 3. Leiden: Brill.
Ritner, Robert K.
 1993   *The Mechanics of Ancient Egyptian Magical Practice.* Studies in Ancient Oriental Civilization. Chicago: Oriental Institute of the University of Chicago.
 2002a "Magic." Pages 191–198 in *The Ancient Gods Speak: A Guide to Egyptian Religion.* Edited by D. Redford. Oxford: Oxford University Press.
 2002b "Magic in Medicine." Pages 198–204 in *The Ancient Gods Speak: A Guide to Egyptian Religion.* Edited by D. Redford. Oxford: Oxford University Press.
 2002c "Magic in Daily Life." Pages 204–209 in *The Ancient Gods Speak: A Guide to Egyptian Religion.* Edited by D. Redford. Oxford: Oxford University Press.
Robbins, Gay
 2005   "Cult Statues in Ancient Egypt." Pages 1–12 in *Cult Image and Divine Representation in the Ancient Near East.* Edited by N.H. Walls. Boston, MA: ASOR.
Rogerson, John W.
 1985   *Old Testament Criticism in the Nineteenth Century: England and Germany.* Philadelphia: Fortress.
Römer, Thomas
 2008   *The Books of Leviticus and Numbers.* BETL 215. Leuven: Peeters.
Römer, Thomas, and Konrad Schmid, eds.
 2007   *Les dernières rédactions du Pentateuque, de l'Hexateuque et de l'Ennéateuque.* BETL 203. Leuven: Peeters.
Römer, Willem H. P.
 1975   "Beiträge zum Lexikon des Sumerischen." *BiOr* 32: 145–162, 296–308.

Roth, Ann Macy
    2006   "The Representation of the Divine in Ancient Egypt." Pages 24–37 in *Text, Artifact, and Image: Revealing Ancient Israelite Religion*. Edited by G. M. Beckman and T. J. Lewis. BJS 346. Providence, RI: Brown Judaic Studies.

Ruwe, Andreas
    1999   *"Heiligkeitsgesetz" und "Priesterschrift": literaturgeschichtliche und rechtssystematische Untersuchungen zu Leviticus 17,1–26,2*. FAT 26. Tübingen: Mohr Siebeck.
    2003   "The Structure of the Book of Leviticus in the Narrative Outline of the Priestly Sinai Story (Exod. 19:1–Num 10:10*). Pages 55–78 in *The Book of Leviticus: Composition and Reception*. Edited by R. Rendtorff and R. A. Kugler. VTSup 93. Formation and Interpretation of Old Testament Literature 3. Leiden: Brill.

Sauneron, Serge
    1966   "Le monde du magicien égyptien." Pages 27–65 in *Le monde du sorcier: Égypte, Babylone, Hittites, Israël, Islam, Asie centrale, Inde, Nepal, Cambodge, Vietnam, Japon*. Edited by S. Sauneron. Sources Orientales 7. Paris: Éditions du Seuil.
    2000   *The Priests of Ancient Egypt*. Ithaca: Cornell University.

Sasson, Jack M., ed.
    2000   *Civilizations of the Ancient Near East*. 2 vols. Peabody, MA: Hendrickson.

Schenker, Adrian
    1983/91   "Das Zeichen des Blutes und die Gewissheit der Vergebung im Alten Testament: Die sühnende Funktion des Blutes auf dem Altar nach Lev 17,10–12." Pages 167–185 in *Text und Sinn im Alten Testament: Textgeschichtliche und bibeltheologische Studien*. OBO 103. Freiburg: Universitätsverlag, 1991. Reprinted from *MTZ* 34:195–213.
    1999   "Welche Verfehlungen und welche Opfer in Lev 5,1–6?" Pages 249–261 in *Levitikus als Buch*. BBB 119. Edited by H.-J. Fabry and H.-W. Jüngling. Berlin: Philo.
    2000   *Recht und Kult im Alten Testament: achtzehn Studien*. OBO 172. Fribourg: Academic Press Fribourg.

Schiffman, Lawrence H. Edited by Florentino García Martínez
    2008   *The Courtyards of the House of the Lord: Studies on the Temple Scroll*. STDJ 75. Leiden: Brill.

Schlögl, Hermann A.
    1983   Echnaton-Tutanchamun: Fakten und Texte. Weisbaden: Harrasowitz.

Schmidt, Ludwig
    1993   *Studien zur Priesterschrift*. BZAW 214. Berlin: de Gruyter.

Schmitt, Rainer
    1972   *Zelt und Lade als Thema alttestamentlicher Wissenschaft: eine kritische forschungsgeschichtliche Darstellung*. Gütersloh: Gütersloher Verlagshaus G. Mohn.

Schwartz, Baruch J.
    1987   *Selected Chapters of the Holiness Code – A Literary Study of Leviticus 17–19*. Ph.D. diss., Hebrew University (Hebrew).
    1991   "The Prohibition Concerning the 'Eating' of Blood in Leviticus 17." Pages 34–66 in *Priesthood and Cult in Ancient Israel*. JSOTSup 125. Edited by G. A. Anderson and S. M. Olyan. Sheffield: JSOT Press.

1994	"'Term' or Metaphor: Biblical nāśā' 'ăwōn/peša'/ḥēṭ'." *Tarbiz* 63: 149–171 (Hebrew).
1999	*The Holiness Legislation: Studies in the Priestly Code.* Jerusalem: Magnes Press (Hebrew).
2000	"Israel's Holiness: The Torah Traditions." Pages 47–59 in *Purity and Holiness: The Heritage of Leviticus.* Edited by M.J.H.M. Poorthuis and J. Schwartz. Jewish and Christian Perspectives Series 2; Leiden: Brill.

Scurlock, JoAnn
1999	"Physician, Exorcist, Conjurer, Magician: A Tale of Two Healing Professions." Pages 69–79 in *Mesopotamian Magic: Textual, Historical, and Interpretive Perspectives.* Ancient Magic and Divination 1. Edited by T. Abusch and K. van der Toorn. Groningen: Styx.
2002a	"Animal Sacrifice in Ancient Mesopotamian Religion." Pages 389–403 in *A History of the Animal World in the Ancient Near East.* Edited by B. Collins. Leiden: Brill.
2002b	"Translating Transfers in Ancient Mesopotamia." Pages 209–223 in *Magic and Ritual in the Ancient World.* Edited by P. Mirecki and M. Meyer. Leiden: Brill.
2006a	"The Techniques of the Sacrifice of Animals in Ancient Israel and Ancient Mesopotamia: New Insights Through Comparison, Part 1." *AUSS* 44: 13–49.
2006b	"The Techniques of the Sacrifice of Animals in Ancient Israel and Ancient Mesopotamia: New Insights Through Comparison, Part 2." *AUSS* 44: 241–264.

Seidl, Theodor
1982	*Tora für den "Aussatz"-Fall: literarische Schichten und syntaktische Strukturen in Levitikus 13 und 14.* ATSAT 18. St. Ottilien: Eos. Seux, Marie-Joseph
1976	*Hymnes et prières aux dieux de Babylonie et d'Assyrie.* LAPO 8. Paris: Éditions du Cerf.

Shafer, Byron E.
1998	"Temples, Priests, and Rituals: An Overview." Pages 1–30 in *Temples of Ancient Egypt.* Edited by B. Shafer. London: I. B. Tauris.

Sigrist, Marcel
2004	"Sacrifices, Offerings, and Votives: Mesopotamia." Pages 330–332 in *Religions of the Ancient World: A Guide.* Edited by S. Johnston. Cambridge, MA: Belknap Press of Harvard University Press.

Sklar, Jay
2005	*Sin, Impurity, Sacrifice, Atonement: The Priestly Conceptions.* Hebrew Bible Monographs 2. Sheffield: Sheffield Phoenix Press.
2007	Review of R. Gane, *Cult and Character: Purification, Day of Atonement, and Theodicy. RBL* 2007. Online: http://www.bookreviews.org/pdf/5068_6109.pdf.

Smith, Christopher R.
1996	"The Literary Structure of Leviticus." *JSOT* 70: 17–32.

Smith, Jonathan Z.
1982	*Imagining Religion: From Babylon to Jonestown.* Chicago: University of Chicago Press.

Smith, Mark S.
1987   *The Early History of God: Yahweh and the Other Deities in Ancient Israel*. San Francisco: Harper & Row.
2005   "Like Deities, Like Temples (Like People)." Pages 3–27 in *Temple and Worship in Biblical Israel: Proceedings of the Oxford Old Testament Seminar*. LHBOTS 422. London: T&T Clark.
2006   "The Structure of Divinity at Ugarit and Israel: The Case of Anthropomorphic Deities versus Monstrous Divinities." Pages 38–63 in *ext, Artifact, and Image: Revealing Ancient Israelite Religion*. Edited by G. M. Beckman and T. J. Lewis. BJS 346. Providence, RI: Brown Judaic Studies.

Smith, William Robertson
1894   *Lectures on the Religion of the Semites*. London: Black.

Snaith, Norman H.
1967   *Leviticus and Numbers*. NCB. London: Nelson.

Sommer, Benjamin D.
2000   "The Babylonian Akitu Festival: Rectifying the King or Renewing the Cosmos?" *JANES* 27: 81–95.
2001   "Conflicting Constructions of Divine Presence in the Priestly Tabernacle." *BibInt* 9: 41–63.

Soskice, Janet M.
1985   *Metaphor and Religious Language*. Oxford: Clarendon.

Spalinger, Anthony
1998   "The Limitations of Formal Ancient Egyptian Religion." *JNES* 57: 241–260.

Sperber, Daniel
1975   *Rethinking Symbolism*. Translated by A. L. Morton. Cambridge: Cambridge University Press.

Staal, Frits
1979   "The Meaninglessness of Ritual." *Numen* 26: 2–22.
1989   *Rules Without Meaning: Ritual, Mantras and the Human Sciences*. New York: Peter Lang.

Stackert, Jeffrey
2007   *Rewriting the Torah: Literary Revision in Deuteronomy and the Holiness Legislation*. FAT 52. Tübingen: Mohr Siebeck.

Stade, Bernhard
1887–88 *Geschichte des Volkes Israel*. 2 vols. Berlin: Grote.

Stager, Lawrence E., and Samuel R. Wolff.
1981   "Production and Commerce in Temple Courtyards: An Olive Press in the Sacred Precinct at Tel Dan." *BASOR* 243: 95–102.

Sternberg, Heike
2004   "Illnesses and Other Crises: Egypt." Pages 453–456 in *Religions of the Ancient World: A Guide*. Edited by S. Johnston. Cambridge, MA: Belknap Press of Harvard University Press.

Streck, Maximilian
1916   *Assurbanipal und die letzten assyrischen Könige bis zum Untergang Niniveh's, I, II, III*. VAB 7. Leipzig: Hinrichs.

Stromberg, Peter
1981   "Consensus and Variation in the Interpretation of Religious Symbolism: A Swedish Example." *American Ethnologist* 8: 544–559.

Tambiah, Stanley J.
    1968   "The Magical Power of Words." *Man* 3: 175–208.
Tawil, Hayim
    1980   "'Azazel The Prince of the Steepe [sic]: A Comparative Study." *ZAW* 92: 43–59.
Terrien, Samuel L.
    1978   *The Elusive Presence: Toward a New Biblical Theology.* NY: Harper and Row.
Thompson, Robert J.
    1963   *Penitence and Sacrifice in Early Israel Outside the Levitical Law: An Examination of the Fellowship Theory of Early Israelite Sacrifice.* Leiden: Brill.
Thompson, Stephen E.
    2002   "Cults." Pages 61–71 in *The Ancient Gods Speak: A Guide to Egyptian Religion.* Edited by D. Redford. Oxford: Oxford University Press.
Thureau-Dangin, François
    1921   *Rituels Accadiens.* Paris: E. Leroux.
Tobin, Vincent A.
    2002a   "Amun and Amun-Re." Pages 18–20 in *The Ancient Gods Speak: A Guide to Egyptian Religion.* Edited by D. Redford. Oxford: Oxford University Press.
    2002b   "Myths." Pages 239–246 in *The Ancient Gods Speak: A Guide to Egyptian Religion.* Edited by D. Redford. Oxford: Oxford University Press.
    2002c   "Creation Myths." Pages 246–251 in *The Ancient Gods Speak: A Guide to Egyptian Religion.* Edited by D. Redford. Oxford: Oxford University Press.
Toorn, Karel van der
    1985   *Sin and Sanction in Israel and Mesopotamia: A Comparative Study.* SSN 22. Assen: Van Gorcum.
    1991   "The Babylonian New Year Festival: New Insights from the Cuneiform Texts and their Bearing on Old Testament Study." Pages 331–344 in *Congress Volume Leuven 1989.* Edited by J. A. Emerton. VTSup 43. Leiden: Brill.
    1996   *Family Religion in Babylonia, Syria, and Israel: Continuity and Changes in the Forms of Religious Life.* Studies in the History and Culture of the Ancient Near East 7. Leiden: Brill.
    2004a   "Religious Practices of the Individual and Family: Mesopotamia." Pages 424–427 in *Religions of the Ancient World: A Guide.* Edited by S. Johnston. Cambridge, MA: Belknap Press of Harvard University Press.
    2004b   "Sin, Pollution, and Purity: Mesopotamia." Pages 499–501 in *Religions of the Ancient World: A Guide.* Edited by S. Johnston. Cambridge, MA: Belknap Press of Harvard University Press.
Turner, Victor
    1967   *The Forest of Symbols.* Ithaca, NY: Cornell University Press.
Tylor, Edward B.
    1871   *Primitive Culture: Researches into the Development of Mythology, Philosophy, Religion, Art, and Custom.* London: John Murray.
Ünal, Ahmet
    1988   "The Role of Magic in the Ancient Anatolian Religions according to the Cuneiform Texts from Boğazköy-Ḫattuša." Pages 52–85 in *Essays on Anatolian Studies in the Second Millennium B.C.* Edited by P. T. Mikasa.

Bulletin of the Middle Eastern Culture Center in Japan 3. Wiesbaden: Harrassowitz.

Utzschneider, Helmut
    1988   *Das Heiligtum und das Gesetz: Studien zur Bedeutung der sinaitischen Heiligtumstexte (Ex 25–40; Lev 8–9)*. OBO 77. Göttingen: Vandenhoeck und Ruprecht.

Vaux, Roland de
    1961   *Ancient Israel: Its Life and Institutions*. Translated by J. McHugh. London: Darton, Longman, & Todd.
    1964   *Studies in Old Testament Sacrifice*. Cardiff: University of Wales Press.

Vorländer, Hermann
    1975   *Mein Gott: die Vorstellungen vom persönlichen Gott im Alten Orient und im Alten Testament*. AOAT 23. Neukirchen-Vluyn: Neukirchener.

Wagner, Volker
    1974   "Zur Existenz des sogenannten 'Heiligkeitsgesetzes.'" *ZAW*: 307–316.

Waldman, Nahum
    1984   "A Note on Ezekiel 1:18." *JBL* 103: 614–618.

Walker, Christopher B. F., and Michael B. Dick
    1999   "The Induction of the Cult Image in Ancient Mesopotamia: The Mesopotamian *mīs pî* Ritual." Pages 55–121 in *Born in Heaven, Made on Earth: The Making of the Cult Image in the Ancient Near East*. Edited by M. B. Dick. Winona Lake, IN: Eisenbrauns.
    2001   *The Induction of the Cult Image in Ancient Mesopotamia: The Mesopotamian Mīs Pî Ritual*. SAALT 1. Helsinki: The Neo-Assyrian Text Corpus Project.

Warning, Wilfried
    1999   *Literary Artistry in Leviticus*. BIS 35. Leiden: Brill.

Watts, James W.
    1999   *Reading Law: The Rhetorical Shaping of the Pentateuch*. BS 59. Sheffield: Sheffield Academic Press.
    2006   "'Ōlāh: The Rhetoric of Burnt Offerings." *VT* 56: 125–137.
    2007   *Ritual and Rhetoric in Leviticus: From Sacrifice to Scripture*. Cambridge: Cambridge University Press.

Weimar, Peter
    1984   "Struktur und Komposition der priesterschriftlichen Geschichtsdarstellung." *BN* 32: 81–134; 33: 138–162.

Weinfeld, Moshe
    1972   *Deuteronomy and Deuteronomic School*. Oxford: Clarendon.
    1983   "Social and Cultic Institutions in the Priestly Source Against Their Ancient Near Eastern Background". Pages 95–129 in *Proceedings of the Eighth World Congress of Jewish Studies*. Vol. 5. Jerusalem: Magnes Press.
    1993   "Traces of Hittite Cult in Shiloh, Bethel, and in Jerusalem." Pages 455–472 in *Religionsgeschichtliche Beziehungen zwischen Kleinasien, Nordsyrien und dem Alten Testament*. Edited by B. Janowski, K. Koch, and G. Wilhelm. OBO 129. Fribourg, Universitätsverlag.
    1995   "כָּבוֹד." *TDOT* 7: 22–38. Grand Rapids, MI: Eerdmans
    2004   *The Place of the Law in the Religion of Ancient Israel*. VTSup 100. Leiden: Brill.

Wellhausen, Julius
    1963   *Die Composition des Hexateuchs und der historischen Bücher des Alten Testaments* (1899). 4th edition. Berlin: de Gruyter.

Wells, Bruce
    2004   *The Law of Testimony in the Pentateuchal Codes.* BZAR 4. Wiesbaden: Harrassowitz.

Westbrook, Raymond
    1994   "The Deposit Law of Exodus 22,6–12." *ZAW* 106: 390–403.

Westenholz, Joan
    2004   "Religious Personnel: Mesopotamia." Pages 292–295 in *Religions of the Ancient World: A Guide.* Edited by S. Johnston. Cambridge, MA: Belknap Press of Harvard University Press.

Whitekettle, Richard
    1991   "Leviticus 15.18 Reconsidered: Chiasm, Spatial Structure and the Body." *JSOT* 49: 31–45.
    1995   "Leviticus 12 and the Israelite Woman: Ritual Process, Liminality and the Womb." *ZAW* 107: 393–408.
    1996   "Levitical Thought and the Female Reproductive Cycle: Wombs, Wellsprings, and the Primeval World." *VT* 46: 376–391.
    2001a   "Rats Are Like Snakes, and Hares are Like Goats: A Study in Israelite Land Taxonomy." *Bib* 82: 345–362.
    2001b   "Where the Wild Things Are: Primary Level Taxa in Israelite Zoological Thought." *JSOT* 93: 17–37.
    2002   "All Creatures Great and Small: Intermediate Level Taxa in Israelite Zoological Thought." *SJOT* 16: 162–183.

Wiggermann, Frans A. M.
    1996   "Scenes from the Shadow Side." Pages 207–220 in Mesopotamian Poetic Language: Sumerian and Akkadian. Edited by M. E. Vogelzang and H. L. J. Vanstiphout. Cuneiform Monographs 6. Groningen: Styx
    2000   "Theologies, Priests and Worship in Ancient Mesopotamia." Pages 1857–70 in *Civilizations of the Ancient Near East.* Edited by J. M. Sasson. Peabody, MA: Hendrickson.

Wilkinson, Richard H.
    2005   *The Complete Temples of Ancient Egypt.* Cairo: The American University in Cairo Press.

Willems, Harco
    2004   "Sacrifices, Offerings, and Votives: Egypt." Pages 326–330 in *Religions of the Ancient World: A Guide.* Edited by S. Johnston. Cambridge, MA: Belknap Press of Harvard University Press.

Wilson, Brian
    1984   *Systems: Concepts, Methodologies, and Applications.* Chichester: Wiley.

Wilson, E. Jan
    1994   *"Holiness" and "Purity" in Mesopotamia.* AOAT 237. Neukirchen-Vluyn: Neukirchener.

Wright, David P.
    1987   *The Disposal of Impurity: Elimination Rites in the Bible and in Hittite and Mesopotamian Literature.* SBLDS 101. Atlanta: Scholar's Press.
    1991   "The Spectrum of Priestly Impurity". Pages 150–181 in *Priesthood and Cult in Ancient Israel.* JSOTSup 125. Edited by G. A. Anderson and S. M. Olyan. Sheffield: JSOT Press.

	1992	"Unclean and Clean." *ABD* 6: 729–741. New York: Doubleday.
	2004	"Histories: Syria and Canaan." Pages 173–180 in *Religions of the Ancient World: A Guide*. Edited by S. Johnston. Cambridge, MA: Belknap Press of Harvard University Press.

Zatelli, Ida
    1998   "The Origin of the Biblical Scapegoat Ritual: The Evidence of Two Eblaite Texts." *VT* 48: 254–263.

Zenger, Erich
    1983   *Gottes Bogen in den Wolken: Untersuchungen zu Komposition und Theologie der priesterschriftlichen Urgeschichte*. SBS 112. Stuttgart: Verlag Katholisches Bibelwerk.
    1999   "Das Buch Levitikus als Teiltext der Tora/des Pentateuch: Eine synchrone Lektüre mit kanonischer Perspektive." Pages 47–83 in *Levitikus als Buch*. BBB 119. Edited by H.-J. Fabry and H.-W. Jüngling. Berlin: Philo.

Zimmerli, Walter
    1980   "'Heiligkeit' nach dem sogenannten Heiligkeitsgesetz." *VT* 30: 493–512.

Source Index

Genesis
1	115, 136, 195
1:3	104
8:21	87
17	175, 176
18	114
18:20	180
18:22	181
37:3	74
41:40ff	74

Exodus
13:21	48
14:19–20	48
16:10	47
16:16	101
16:36	101
19	2
19:9	48
19:10	71, 77
19:14-15	71
19:16–18	48
19:16–17	48
19:18	48
19:21	48
19:22	77
21:30	188
23:15	188
24	2, 157
24:4–8	88
24:15–18	47
24:16–17	45, 47
24:16	40
24:17	13, 43
25–Lev 16	1
25–31	2, 7
25	97
25:8	39
25:11	99
25:22	39, 40, 57
25:29	100
25:30	100
25:31	104
25:37	104
25:38–39	104
27:20–21	103, 104
27:20	104
28–30	53
28–29	82, 91
28	60, 61, 93
28:1	81
28:2	41, 43, 63, 74
28:3	63, 74
28:4–39	61
28:4	63, 74
28:10–14	63
28:25	71
28:35	71
28:40–43	61
28:40	41, 43, 63, 74
28:41	63, 82
28:42–43	71
28:43	111
29	2, 59, 60, 63, 65, 73, 79, 80, 82, 91, 93, 109, 163, 168
29:1–37	97
29:1	75, 81
29:4–10	60
29:6	74
29:7	79
29:12	61
29:16	61
29:18	63
29:19–28	87
29:19–21	60
29:21	29, 61, 74, 78, 79
29:23–25	64
29:25	64, 86
29:29–30	80

29:29	63, 74	39:30	74
29:32–33	88	39:37	104
29:32	64	39:41	74
29:33	64, 75, 82, 83, 85, 86,	40	2, 53, 56, 57, 58, 59,
29:35	64		60, 91, 92, 93, 96, 97
29:36	61, 63, 64, 81, 82	40:9–11	57
29:36–37	64, 79	40:13	74
29:37	57, 72, 78	40:23	97
29:38–46	109	40:25	97
29:38–42	64, 97	40:27	97
29:38–41	110	40:29	97
29:41	60, 110	40:32	111
29:42–43	39, 109	40:34–Lv 1:1	40
29:43–46	63, 95, 96	40:34–38	57
29:43–44	44, 64, 79, 87, 92	40:34–35	43, 47
29:45–46	39, 72, 109	40:35	43
30	60	40:38	45
30:1	105		
30:6–8	39, 105	Leviticus	
30:7–8	105	1–16	2, 3, 7, 135, 160, 166,
30:7	105		167, 170, 173, 181,
30:9	101, 105		183
30:10	105	1–15	165
30:12–16	188	1–7	4, 135
30:17–21	70	1–3	135, 138, 144, 173
30:20	111	1:1–2	138
30:21	63	1:4	86, 87
30:23–33	75	1:9	110
30:25–32	57	1:13	110
30:25	61, 63	1:17	110
30:26–30	63	2	110
30:26–28	61	2:2	86, 110
30:31–33	63	2:3	110
30:34–38	105	2:9	86, 110
30:34–36	105	2:10	110
30:35–37	105	2:16	110
30:36	39, 105	3	62
30:37–38	105	3:3–5	23
31:8	104	3:9–11	23
31:10	74	3:11	64, 99, 111, 206
32–34	1	3:14–16	23
33:11	102	3:16	64, 99, 111
33:14–15	102	4–5	119, 135, 136, 137,
33:18ff	64		138, 139, 140, 141,
33:18–23	51		142, 144, 145, 147,
33:20	102		148, 149, 150, 155,
34	13		158, 159, 160, 162,
35–40	2, 7		163, 166, 171, 173,
37:16	100		175, 180, 183, 184,
37:29	105		197, 201, 207

Source Index

4-5:13	141, 143	5:6–7	138, 158, 183
4–5:6	139	5:6	137, 138, 139, 142, 146, 147
4	20, 80, 140, 144, 146, 147, 159	5:7–13	139
4:1–12	146	5:7	138, 141, 142
4:1–2	138	5:8–10	139
4:3–12	73	5:9	138, 139
4:3	138, 139, 158, 183	5:10	137, 138, 141, 142, 147
4:5–12	139		
4:5–7	138, 139	5:11	138, 139, 146
4:6–10	139	5:12–13	139
4:7	105, 139	5:13	138, 142, 147
4:8–10	23	5:14–26	140, 142, 143, 145, 147, 148
4:12	139		
4:13–20	18	5:14–19	139, 140, 144
4:14	139	5:14–16	142, 144, 148
4:15	138	5:14	138, 139
4:16–21	139	5:15–16	183
4:16–18	138, 139	5:15	138, 139, 148, 158
4:18	139	5:16	138, 140, 147
4:19	23	5:17–19	140, 143, 145, 149, 156
4:20	18, 138, 146		
4:21	139	5:18	138, 139, 143, 147
4:22–26	32	5:19	183
4:23–24	138	5:20–26	139, 140, 143, 145, 149
4:23	139		
4:25–26	139	5:20	138
4:25	138, 139	5:21	140, 148
4:26	23, 137, 138, 142, 146	5:22	149
4:28–29	138	5:24	149
4:28	139	5:25	138, 139, 158
4:30–35	139	5:26	143, 147
4:30	138, 139, 160	6–10	171
4:31	23, 138, 142, 146, 148	6–7	135
4:32–33	138	6:8	107
4:32	139	6:16	110
4:33–35	139	6:17–7:7	138
4:34	138, 139	6:18–7:7	137
4:35	138, 142, 147	6:19	139
4:35	23	7:2	139, 140, 141
5	3, 7, 140, 144, 147, 150, 156, 183	7:3–5	138, 158
		7:5	143, 149
5:1–6	139, 140, 144, 147, 148	7:6	139
		7:19–21	137
5:1–4	144	7:20–21	184
5:1	139, 148	8–9	43, 91, 135
5:2–4	139	8	53, 57, 58, 59, 60, 62, 63, 65, 73, 79, 80, 82, 91, 92, 137, 139, 141, 163, 168
5:2–3	137, 148, 153, 184		
5:4	148		
5:6–13	23		

8:2–14	60	12–15	119, 135, 136, 137, 140, 143, 150, 155, 157, 158, 159, 160, 162, 166, 183, 197, 207
8:3–4	74		
8:5	66		
8:7–13	61		
8:7–9	61		
8:10–15	157	12	159
8:10–12	61, 63	12:1–8	143
8:10–11	57, 60, 65, 75	12:4	152
8:10	61, 63	12:6	141
8:12	61, 79	12:7–8	140
8:13	61	12:7	144, 155
8:14–17	63	12:8	141
8:15	61, 63, 75, 78, 81, 82, 93, 170	13–14	3
		13:6	154
8:19	61	13:13	151, 154
8:21	63	13:17	151, 154
8:22–29	87	13:37	154
8:23–24	60	13:47–59	141
8:28	64, 86	14	70, 88, 156, 157, 188
8:30	60, 61, 64, 78, 79	14:1–32	143
8:33–35	64, 71	14:1–20	141
8:33	62	14:3	151
8:34	81, 82, 83, 85, 88	14:4–7	156
8:35	62, 71	14:7	81, 154
9	57, 60, 62, 64, 79, 85, 90, 92, 93, 97, 139	14:8	90
		14:9	90
9:2–4	62, 64	14:11	154
9:4	40, 51, 62, 90	14:12–17	156, 157
9:6	40, 51, 66	14:12–14	183
9:7	64, 83, 84, 85, 86, 87, 88, 147	14:12	141
		14:14–18	141
9:9	62	14:17	141
9:12	62	14:19	141, 143, 144, 155
9:18	62	14:20	86, 87, 90, 110
9:23–24	57, 89	14:22	141
9:23	40, 43, 44, 45, 46, 51, 62	14:31	140, 141
		14:33–57	141
9:24	46, 57, 62	14:34–53	164
10	24, 25, 71, 107, 165, 185, 190	14:49	81
		14:52	81
10:1–2	119	14:53	140, 155, 183
10:2	46	15	153, 155, 174
10:7	71	15:2–12	141
11–15	137, 149, 150, 155, 158, 163, 174, 175, 184	15:5–11	154
		15:13–15	143
		15:13	144, 155
11	4, 135, 153, 157, 158	15:15	140, 141, 143
11:27	143	15:16	143
11:46	165	15:19–24	141
		15:19	143

15:21–23	154	16:33–34	170
15:25–30	143	16:33	162
15:27	154, 155	16:34	162, 163, 166
15:28	144	17–26	1, 2
15:30	140	17:7	196
15:30	137, 140, 143	17:11	186, 187, 188, 191
15:31–33	155	18:21	200
15:32–33	155	18:24–30	178, 180
15:31	150, 184, 185, 190	19	72
16	1, 2, 3, 19, 60, 85, 119, 135, 137, 139, 159, 160, 163, 165, 174, 175, 176, 180, 183, 185, 194, 196, 200, 201, 207	19:2	199
		19:12	200
		19:19	61
		19:26	197
		19:31	180, 197
		20:1–3	180
16:2–28	160	20:3	178, 200
16:2	39, 44, 45, 162	20:6	197
16:4–24	171	20:7–8	72
16:4	161, 168	20:20	180
16:6	23, 162, 169	20:22	178
16:10	162, 164	20:27	197
16:11	162, 169	21:6	99, 111, 200
16:13	39, 44, 45, 105, 108, 109, 162	21:8	99, 111
		21:17	99, 111
16:14–16	23	21:21	99, 111
16:14	20	21:22	99, 111
16:15	169	22:2	200
16:16–19	162	22:3–7	184
16:16–18	162	22:9	180
16:16	116, 160, 161, 162, 163, 164, 167, 175, 186	22:25	99, 111
		22:31–33	72
		22:32	200
16:18–19	163, 171	23:26–32	176
16:18	105, 160	23:27–32	178
16:19	23, 75, 78, 160, 161, 167, 188	23:27	119
		24:2–4	103–104
16:20	161, 162, 168	24:2–3	104
16:21–22	160, 163, 164	24:2	104
16:21	164, 166, 167	24:4	104
16:22	162, 166	24:5	101
16:23–24	161, 168	24:6-7	99
16:24	23, 86, 87	24:7	99, 100, 107
16:25–28	171	24:8	100
16:26	160	24:9	99, 100
16:27–28	160	24:15	181
16:29–34	1, 160, 162, 163, 196	26	97
16:29–31	162	26:18	165
16:29	162	26:21	165
16:30	81, 162, 163, 166, 170, 171, 172	26:24	165
		26:28	165

26:34–35	178	5:4	48
26:40–41	176, 178	5:22	48
26:44–45	176	5:24	48
27	1	5:26	48
		16:16	188
Numbers		21:8	146, 191, 192
1–10	2	23:15	77
1:51	72	32:43	146, 191
3:10	72	33:2	48
3:38	72	33:10	109
4:7	100		
4:20	93	*Joshua*	
5:3	39	3:5	77
7	57	7:3	77
8:21	81		
9:13	180	*Judges*	
9:15	45	5:4–5	48
10:34	48	13:9–23	112
11:18	77	13:19–20	111
14:10	44		
15	165	*1 Samuel*	
15:30	72	16:5	77
16:19	44		
16:26	180	*2 Samuel*	
16:38	73	6	56
16:46–47	199	6:3–7	73
17	108	6:14	55
17:7	44	11:4	78
17:11–15	105	13:18	74
17:11–13	109		
18:22	180	*1 Kings*	
18:32	180	8	53, 54, 57, 58
19	108, 137, 150, 157	8:1–11	54
19:13	178, 180, 184	8:10–11	56
19:19	81	8:5	54, 56
19:20	178, 180, 184	8:30	56
20:6	44	8:39	56
20:26	74	8:43	56
20:28	74	8:49	56
28:1	109	8:62–66	54
28:2	99, 109, 110, 111	8:62–63	54
28:7	100	8:64	58
28:24	99, 111	8:65	54
32:23	180	8:66	55
35:9–34	2	19:19	74
Deuteronomy		*2 Kings*	
1:33	48	2:13–14	74
4:11	48		
4:33	48		

Source Index

Isaiah
1:10–17	115
19:1	49
22:21ff.	74
29:6	48
30:27	48
31:4	48
30:30	48
61:1–3	28
61:10	74

Jeremiah
6:20	115
17:1	180
18:23	146, 191, 192
33:8	81

Ezekiel
1	45
1:4	49
1:26–27	41
1:26	41
1:27	41
1:28	41
3:20	180
5:11	179
8–11	179, 182
8	178
9:7	179
11:17–20	179
16:63	146, 191, 192
18:24	180
36:17–38	179
36:33	81
37:23	81
40–48	179
43:18–26	91
43:20	81
43:26	81
44:7	99, 111
45:18	81
45:20	81, 179

Amos
5:21–27	115

Micah
1:3	48

Habakkuk
3:3	48
3:4	48
3:11	48

Zechariah
3:3	74
3:5	74

Psalms
18:9	48
18:10–11	49
18:13	48
18:14	48
18:15	48
29	204
32:5	167
45:14	74
50:2	48
50:12–13	114, 115
51:4	81
51:9	81
65:4	146, 191
77:19	48
78:14	48
78:38	146, 191
79:9	146, 191, 192
80:2	48
93	203
94:1	48
97	48
97:2–3	48
97:3	48
103:12	177
104:1–2	41
104:1	74
104:3	49
105:39	48

Proverbs
15:8	115

Job
37:22	48

Lamentations
3:22	48

Esther
8:15	74

Daniel
5:16 74
8:11–13 97
8:11 111
11:31 97
12:11 97

Nehemiah
9:12 48
9:19 48

1 Chronicles
15:12 77
15:14 77
29:10–22 114

2 Chronicles
5:11 77
5:14 56
7 56
29:5–8 97
29:24 81
29:34 77
30:3 77
30:15 77
30:17 77
30:18 146, 191, 192
30:34 77
35:6 77

Dead Sea Scrolls
Temple Scroll
22:04 149

Rabbinic Literature
Num. R.
21:19 112

Mid. Aggadah 108

Greek Texts
Iliad 8:550–52 112

Egyptian Texts
Book of the Dead
125 123

Deir el Medina 131

Thutmose III at
Medinet Habu 58

Opening of
the Mouth 55, 58, 66–67,
83, 123, 127

Re 42

Rest. Stele of Tutankhamun
(Urk. IV 2027) 113

Utt.
29 109
267 107
412 106
508 106

Mesopotamian Texts
Akītu 58, 80, 106, 109,
123, 124, 129, 195
33–35 124
350 129
353–354, 355 129
357–360 129
374 80
382 80

Assurbanipal 55

Assurnasirpal II 55

Atrahasis
III.iii.31 106, 113
iv.21–22 106, 113

Bît rimki 120

Daily Temple Ritual (AO 6460)
10 127

Enki's Journey
93–114 55

Enūma eliš 13, 55, 195
I.73–75 55
I.94–5 13

Erra and Ishum 122

Esarhaddon 54–55

Gilgamesh
XI.159–161 106, 113
XI.161 110

Gudea cylinder	54, 56, 58	Temple Rest.	126
A iii.10–12	56		

Ugaritic Texts
Baal epic

Hymn to Enlil with a Prayer to Ur-Nammu	54

VI 38–43	54
VI 38–59	55
KTU 1.39	96

Kettledrum Ritual	126–127
Maqlû series	7, 120

Emar Texts

Installation of Baal's High Priestess	59, 69–70

Mouth-Washing and Mouth-Opening
(*mīs pî* and *pīt pî*) 55, 58, 68, 83–84, 87, 128, 129

Hittite Texts

Ashella	196
IT 3.6–25, 33–37	83
CTH 264	121
IT 3.70–71	83
IT 4.A.23–33	68
Inst. for Temple Personnel	96, 121
STT 199.1–5	68
STT 200.42–44	83
Temple of Night	54–55, 69, 83, 87, 123

Nabonidus' Rebuilding of Ehulhul	56

KUB

17.27 ii 28–41	127
30.31 4, 36–40	127
31.113	96
32.114 rev 4'–8'	127

Namburbû texts	120, 123, 124, 133
Nebuchadnezzar I	55
Ordination of the Priest of Enlil	59, 68

Plague Prayers of Murshili II	121, 131
Samuha 36–41	132

Sargon	54
Šurpu series	120, 124, 131–133, 198
V–VII	124
V–VI.52/53, 60, 70	132
IX	133
V–VII	124

Telipinu	128–129
Tunnawi	132

Temple Awakening (*dīk bīti*)	127, 129

Author Index

Abusch, I.T., 7, 120, 125, 130, 131, 132, 133
Achenbach, R., 2, 178
Albertz, R., 2, 130, 178
Anderson, G.A., 20, 187
Assmann, J., 10, 121, 123, 126, 130, 131
Austin, J.L., 25
Avalos, H., 124, 126, 130, 141, 197

Baentsch, B., 3, 48
Bahrani, Z., 51
Beckman, G.M., 101, 121, 122, 125, 128, 130, 132
Bell, C., 5, 17, 22, 24, 25, 26, 27, 35, 66, 188
Bell, L., 106, 115, 121
Bergen, W.J., 4, 5, 18, 29, 66, 184, 190
Berlejung, A., 68, 83, 128
Berquist, B., 87
Bertholet, A., 3, 149
Bibb, B., 4, 5, 190, 191
Bidmead, J., 129
Blackman, A.M., 58, 67
Bloch, M., 18
Blum, E., 2, 6, 81, 175
Borger, R., 54, 55, 59
Borghouts, J.F., 120, 123, 124, 125, 132
Bottéro, J., 96, 101, 113, 120, 127
Brichto, H.C., 186
Buchler, J., 29

Caplice, R.I., 120
Carpenter, E., 165
Cassin, E., 42
Cassuto, U., 100, 104
Černý, J., 67
Cholewiński, A., 2
Cohen, M.E., 127, 129

Collins, B.J., 54, 69, 96, 121, 122, 125, 127, 128, 130, 132, 133
Collins, C.J., 41
Converse, P.E., 22
Cross, F.M., 6
Crüsemann, F., 2

Dahm, U., 4
David, A.R., 55, 58, 59, 67, 127
Davies, D., 27
Deschner, A., 188
Detienne, M., 189
Dick, M.B., 68
Dietrich, M., 196
Douglas, M., 3, 4, 26, 27
Dozeman, T.B., 4
Driver, G.R., 63
Driver, S.R., 84
Driver, T.F., 20
Dumont, L., 157
Durham, J.I., 104

Eberhart, C., 4, 5, 137, 145, 174
Ehrlich, A.B., 63, 64
Eilberg-Schwartz, H., 4
Elliger, K., 2, 3, 166
Englund, G., 101, 122
Evans-Pritchard, E.E., 18

Fabry, H.-J., 3
Fairman, H.W., 58, 67
Fernandez, J., 27
Fleming, D.E., 59, 69, 75
Fohrer, G., 6
Foster, B.R., 122, 132
Fox, K., 158
Frandsen, P.J., 125, 126, 130
Frankfort, H., 42
Frantz-Szabó, G., 130
Friedman, R.E., 5

Frymer-Kensky, T., 180

Gane, R.E., 4, 7, 8, 18, 20, 23, 24, 27, 31, 33, 34, 36, 63, 66, 80, 84, 99, 100, 101, 102, 114, 129, 137, 146, 147, 162, 164, 165, 166, 167, 168, 169, 170, 172, 174, 175, 176, 177, 196, 202, 207
Garr, W.R., 43
Gee, J.L., 62, 68, 71, 74, 76, 115
Geller, M.J., 7
Geller, S.A., 177
Gerstenberger, E.S., 104
Gertz, J.C., 4, 6
Gese, H., 145, 186
Gilders, W.K., 4, 5, 18, 19, 23, 28, 29, 30, 32, 34, 35, 62, 66, 79, 87, 88, 186, 188, 189, 202
Gluckman, M., 26
Goetze, A., 96
Gorman, F.H., 4, 18, 21, 28, 60, 61, 62, 160, 165, 168, 169, 180, 187, 196
Grabbe, L.L., 20
Graham, M.P., 1
Green, A.R.W., 49
Grimes, R.L., 17, 18, 25, 27, 32
Grisanti, M.A., 165
Gröndahl, F., 121
Gross, W., 175
Gruenwald, I., 22
Gurney, O.R., 121
Güterbock, H.G., 131

Haas, V., 96
Hallo, W.W., 9
Haran, M., 4, 6, 61, 97, 99, 100, 105, 110, 111
Hardin, R.S., 17
Haroutunian, H., 115
Hartley, J.E., 84, 149, 164, 187, 188
Hartung, C., 188
Heger, P., 105
Heinisch, P., 164
Hendel, R.S., 13
Hoffmeier, J.K., 76
Hoftijzer, J., 63
Hornung, E., 42, 121, 122
Houston, W., 4, 158
Houtman, C., 61, 62, 74, 80, 97, 105, 106, 107, 108

Hubert, H., 18
Hundley, M., 52, 56
Hurowitz, V.A., 54, 55, 56, 57, 58, 68, 69, 83, 128, 145
Hurvitz, A., 6
Hüsken, U., 25
Hutton, R.R., 182
source index
Imparati, F., 132

Jacobsen, T., 68, 130, 195
Janowski, B., 7, 60, 145, 159, 186, 189, 196
Janzen, D., 4
Janzen, J.G., 114
Jay, N.B., 29, 30
Jennings, T.W., 18, 20
Jenson, P.P., 4, 31, 72, 84, 164
Jeremias, J., 48
Johnston, S.I., 7, 130
Joosten, J., 2, 72, 73, 96
Joüon, P., 183
Jüngling, H.-W., 3
Jürgens, B., 4

Kawashima, R.S., 53, 121, 136
Keel, O., 41
Kertzer, D.I., 22, 23, 27, 190
King, L.W., 55
Kiuchi, N., 4, 63, 81, 84, 146, 148, 165, 188
Klawans, J., 4, 17, 26, 27, 28, 37, 178, 179, 180, 181, 202
Klingbeil, G., 59, 91
Knierim, R.P., 20, 165, 166
Knohl, I., 1, 2, 12, 53, 162, 170, 178
Koch, K., 7, 167
Köckert, M., 3
Kornfeld, W., 2, 76
Korpel, M.C.A., 121
Kratz, R.G., 2, 7
Kreinath, J., 188
Kugler, R.A., 3

Læssøe, J., 120
Lambert, W.G., 10, 87, 100, 115, 124, 131, 132
Lang, B., 186
Laroche, E., 120
Lawrence, J.D., 70, 71

Leach, E.R., 21, 27
Lebrun, R., 124, 132
Lemardelé, C., 185
Levine, B.A., 4, 19, 40, 60, 71, 100, 111, 112, 145, 146, 149, 168, 179, 180, 183, 184, 185, 186, 196
Levinson, B.M., 6
Lévi-Strauss, C., 27
Lewis, G., 190
Lichtheim, M., 131
Lie, A.G., 54
Linssen, M.J.H., 68, 80, 124, 126, 127, 129
Lohfink, N., 2, 3
Löhr, M., 166
Loretz, O., 196
Lorton, D., 67, 80, 95
Luciani, D., 4

Malul, M., 4
Marx, A., 4, 11, 20, 96, 97, 114, 149, 171, 177
Maul, S.M., 123, 124, 125
Mauss, M., 18, 131
McCarthy, D.J., 95
McMahon, G., 121, 122
Meeks, D., 121, 130
Meier, G., 120
Mendenhall, G.E., 41, 42
Mettinger, T.N.D., 39, 40, 41, 46, 48, 49, 50
Milgrom, J., 1, 2, 4, 5, 7, 8, 10, 12, 23, 27, 39, 47, 50, 57, 60, 63, 64, 65, 66, 70, 71, 74, 75, 77, 78, 79, 82, 84, 86, 87, 88, 89, 97, 99, 100, 101, 102, 104, 108, 110, 112, 119, 124, 137, 139, 140, 141, 142, 144, 145, 147, 148, 149, 151, 152, 153, 156, 162, 163, 164, 165, 166, 170, 172, 174, 175, 180, 183, 185, 186, 187, 189
Miller, P.D., 55
Modéus, M., 4, 18, 27, 29, 32, 33, 35, 36
Munn, N.D., 23
Muraoka, T., 183

Nelson, H.H., 106
Nicholson, E.W., 1
Nielsen, K., 105, 106, 107, 109

Nihan, C., 1, 2, 3, 4, 27, 60, 65, 92, 137, 139, 140, 146, 148, 149, 150, 157, 159, 160, 165, 166, 168, 171, 174, 175, 176, 178, 183, 188, 195
North, J.A., 188, 189
Noth, M., 1, 2, 3, 62

Oppenheim, A.L., 41, 42, 95, 101
Otto, E., 2, 4, 6
Otto, R., 72

Paran, M., 184
Pardee, D., 96
Parpola, S., 133
Péter-Contesse, R., 60
Pongratz-Leisten, B., 129
Popko, M., 121, 123, 125, 129, 130
Preuss, H.D., 2
Propp, W.H.C., 63, 64, 65, 71, 74, 75, 78, 80, 83, 88, 89, 99, 100, 102, 104, 106, 107, 111, 112, 114, 146, 174, 182, 183, 184, 185, 188, 199

Quaegebeur, J., 87
Quirke, S., 122, 182

Ramsey, I.T., 13
Rappaport, R.A., 19, 20, 21, 24, 29
Reiner, E., 59, 120, 124
Rendtorff, R., 3, 4, 5, 60, 146, 149, 187
Ringgren, H., 76
Ritner, R.K., 120, 124, 130, 132, 133
Robbins, G., 122
Roberts, J.J.M., 55
Rogerson, J.W., 1
Römer, T., 3, 4
Römer, W.H.P., 42
Roth, A.M., 42
Ruwe, A., 2, 4

Sasson, J.M., 7
Sauneron, S., 68, 120
Schenker, A., 4, 145, 148, 149, 186, 187
Schiffmann, L.H., 6
Schlögl, H.A., 113
Schmid, K., 4
Schmidt, L., 6
Schmitt, R., 46

Schwartz, B.J., 1, 72, 77, 96, 136, 164, 166, 167, 168, 169, 175, 176, 178, 179, 180, 186, 187
Scurlock, J., 124, 131, 139, 174, 196
Seidl, T., 3
Shafer, B.E., 54, 58, 59, 67
Sigrist, M., 101
Sklar, J., 138, 140, 147, 166, 174, 186, 187, 188
Smith, C.R., 4
Smith, J.Z., 19
Smith, M.S., 21, 49, 122
Smith, W.R., 18
Snaith, N.H., 119
Sommer, B.D., 53, 129, 175
Soskice, J.M., 12, 185
Spalinger, A., 121
Sperber, D., 190
Spieckermann, H., 7
Staal, F., 23
Stackert, J., 2
Stade, B., 149
Stager, L.E., 104
Sternberg, H., 125, 133
Streck, M., 55
Stromberg, P., 27

Tambiah, S.J., 20
Tawil, H., 7
Terrien, S.L., 12
Thompson, R.J., 86, 87
Thompson, S.E., 128
Thureau-Dangin, F., 129
Tobin, V.A., 121, 122
Toorn, K. van der, 107, 125, 126, 127, 129, 130, 131
Turner, V., 23
Tylor, E.B., 18

Ünal, A., 120
Utzschneider, H., 185

Vaux, R. de, 4, 102
Vorländer, H., 130

Wagner, V., 2
Waldman, N., 42
Walker, C.B.F., 68, 83
Warning, W., 4
Watts, J.W., 5, 7, 18, 28, 37, 86, 110, 138, 140, 144, 183, 184, 185, 186, 187, 190, 192, 202
Weimar, P., 2, 3
Weinfeld, M., 7, 8, 40, 41, 42, 43, 48, 96, 110
Wellhausen, J., 1, 60
Wells, B., 148, 149, 166, 187
Westbrook, R., 149
Westenholz, J., 115
Whitekettle, R., 4
Wiggermann, F.A.M., 120, 122
Wilhelm, G., 7, 196
Wilkinson, R.H., 54, 58, 67
Willems, H., 101
Wilson, B., 33
Wilson, E.J., 72, 76
Witte, M., 4
Wolff, S.R., 104
Wright, D.P., 4, 7, 8, 9, 10, 120, 121, 125, 127, 129, 130, 132, 133, 165, 166, 168, 180, 181, 196, 198

Zatelli, I., 196
Zenger, E., 3, 4
Zimmerli, W., 72

Subject Index

Aaron, Aaron's sons, *see* Priests
Access 115–116
Altar
– Bronze 30–31, 57, 61–62, 63–64, 81, 83–85, 87–93, 99, 100, 105, 108, 110–112, 115–117, 138–140, 158, 160, 163, 169, 171, 174
– Incense 100, 105, 107, 138, 158, 159
Ancient Near East
– Conceptions of Presence 41–42
– Daily Temple Services 95–96, 127–128
– Divine Meals 100–101, 113
– Divine Relationships to Creation 120–122
– Festivals 128–129
– Incense 105–106
– Individual Removal Rituals 130–133
– Nature and Source of Evils 124–125
– Priests 69–70, 128–130
– Purity 125–126
– Temple Removal Rituals 126–130
Animals
– Bird 141, 150–152, 155–156, 198–199
– Bull 67, 139, 161–162, 168–171
– Goat
  – for Azazel 160–162, 164, 166, 168–170, 175, 196
  – Sacrificial 139, 161–162, 168–171
– Lamb 110, 141, 156
– Ram 63–64, 78, 86–88, 129, 139
– *see also* Offerings
Anointing
– in the ANE 69, 75, 95
– Oil 74–75, 79, 171
– Priestly Ordinands 60–61, 63–64, 73–75, 78–79, 82, 88–90
– the Tabernacle and its Furniture 57, 61, 63–64, 73, 78, 89, 92, 171

Anthropomorphisms
– and Divine Presence 41, 45, 205
– and Divine Service 11, 95–98, 100–103, 108–109, 112–113, 117, 206
– Language of 13–14, 49, 98
– Transcendent Anthropomorphisms 13, 83, 97–98
Ark 14, 40, 43, 50–51, 55–57, 92, 205
– *see also* כפרת
Atonement, *see* Clearing
Azazel 159, 161–162, 164, 168–170, 196, 198–199

Basin 61, 68, 128
"Before YHWH" 39, 46, 50, 92, 99–100, 102–103, 105, 109, 116, 138, 142, 145, 161–162, 164, 206
Blood
– in the ANE 128
– Blood-Oil Mixture 61-62, 64, 73–74, 78, 88–89, 141, 156
– Effect of 75, 78–79, 81–82, 88–89, 128, 162–163, 169, 171, 174
– Lifeblood 187
– Manipulation of 30–31, 60–62, 64, 74, 78–79, 81–82, 87–89, 105, 128, 138–141, 145, 154, 156–157, 159–163, 171, 174
– Menstrual 144
Bread of Presence 99–103
– *see also* Regular Divine Service

Cherubim 44, 50
Circumcision 175
Clean/Unclean 24, 71, 76–77, 115, 126, 129, 148, 150, 152–155, 174, 178, 184, 193
Cleansing (טהר) 24, 71, 81, 140–141, 143–144, 148, 150–159, 162–163,

170–171, 176–177, 181, 183–184,
191, 199
– from Sin 170
– *see also* Impurity
Clearing (כפר) 18, 20, 23, 63–64, 75,
81–86, 88–90, 105, 108, 116, 137–
138, 140, 142–148, 150–152, 154–
155, 158–159, 161–164, 167–172,
173–174, 176–177, 186–192, 195,
199–200, 202, 207
– of the Altar 84–85
– of the People 85, 136–159, 162, 169–
170
– of the Tabernacle and its Furniture
159–172
– Secondary Clearing of People 85,
169–170
– Secondary Clearing of the Tabernacle
and its Furniture 137
– Translation of 188–189
Clearing Day 20, 23, 80, 90, 159–172,
174–176, 178, 182, 191, 195–197,
207
Clothing, *see* Garments
Cloud
– Divine 40, 44–49, 51, 57
– Incense 43–44, 106, 108, 115
Comparative Method 7–12
Confession
– in the ANE 123, 131
– in P 139, 148, 160, 162, 164, 195
Consecration 44, 57–58, 63–64, 68–70,
71–81, 82–85, 87–93, 97, 105, 115,
117, 128–129, 157, 162–163, 171–
172, 182, 188–189, 190–191
Contagion 64, 72, 93, 141, 153–154,
179–182
Corporate Renewal 178–179
Corporate Sanction 175–176, 178–179
Creation 115, 120–122, 136, 200
Covenant 88, 100, 102, 157, 175–176
Culpability (עון) 160–164, 166–167,
170, 175
Cult Statue, *see* Divine Statue

D 6, 52
Damage Control
– Comparison of Systems in P and ANE
192–199, 206–207
– Individual Removal Rites 197–199

– Nature and Source of Evils 193
– Sanctuary Removal Rites 194–197
– Vulnerability to Evil 193
Day of Atonement, *see* Clearing Day
Death
– Consequences of Ritual Failure 25,
72, 93, 150, 162, 165, 173–174, 184–
185
– Ritual Action to Prevent 63-64, 70–
71, 89, 105, 107–109, 162, 184–185,
200
– and Skin Disease 154
– Through Contact with YHWH 44–45
Divinity in P
– Divine Form in P 44–55
– Divine Meal 101–103
– Divine Mystery 14, 39, 50–51, 56, 80,
93, 96, 101, 111, 112, 114, 117, 121,
190–191, 205
– Divine Relationship to People and
World 136
Divine Statue 11, 14, 42, 50–51, 56, 59,
67–69, 83, 95–96, 113, 127–128, 204,
205
Dtr 54–56, 176

Egypt
– Opening of the Mouth 67, 83, 128
– Priestly Installation 67
– Purity and Holiness 76
– Temple Dedication 67
Emar
– Installation of the High Priestess 69–
70, 79
Entrance of the Tent of Meeting 30, 35,
62, 89
Evil, *see* Pollution, Sin.
Exile 179–180, 182
Ezekiel
– Clearing in 81, 180
– Divine Food in 99, 111
– Glory in 41, 45, 51
– Possibility of System Failure in 179–
180

Fat 139, 142–143, 148–149, 161, 171
Festivals 96, 128–129, 196–197
Fire
– Divine 40–41, 43–46, 48, 51, 60, 62,
90, 93

– Regular 23, 33–34, 48, 129
Food
– Divine Food 8, 83, 97, 99-103, 110–115, 117, 206
– in Ezekiel 99, 111
– (Food) Gift (אשה) 63–64, 86, 100, 102, 107, 110, 143, 149
– Human 101, 114
– Priestly Food 82
– *see also* Divine Meal
Forgiveness (סלח) 24, 138, 142–143, 145–148, 158–159, 162, 170, 173–174, 176–177, 180–181, 191, 207

Garments
– Divine Clothing 41–3, 48
– Priestly Garments 60–61, 63–64, 73–74
– 'Skin'-Diseased Garments 141, 153
Genital Discharges 141, 143, 151–153, 155, 179
Glory 40–41, 43–48, 50–53, 56–57, 60, 64, 74, 80, 87, 90, 92–93, 97–98, 179, 204–205
Goal Statements
– ANE Removal Rites 125
– on Clearing Day 162–163, 191
– Divine Service 97–100, 104–105, 110,
– Impurity Removal 143–144, 150–152, 154, 158–159, 191
– Sin Removal 142–143, 144–147, 158–159, 191
– Tabernacle Dedication and Priestly Installation 62-66, 82, 87, 91
– Theory of 33–34
Gold
– in the ANE 68, 80, 129
– Priestly Apparel 61, 71
– Tabernacle Furniture 99–100
Guilt/Guilt's Consequences (אשם) 123, 138, 140, 142–143, 145, 147–148, 166, 177, 180
– אשם: Root 182–183, 185
– Guilt Offering, *see* Offerings: אשם

Hand-laying 30, 60, 87, 138, 158, 160
Healing
– Physical Healing 24, 150–152, 154-155, 179, 181, 184, 197
– Rituals, Health Care 24, 197

Hierarchy
– Graded Holiness 72–73
– Polytheistic 121–122, 131
– Priestly 61–62
– of Ritual Actors 99, 103, 105, 109, 138–139, 141
– of Systems 31
Hittites
– Blood Manipulation 128
– Communal Removal Rites 196
– Enlivening the Divine Statue 69, 83, 128
– Temple Dedication 69
Holy, Holiness, *see* Consecration
Holy-of-Holies, *see* Inner Sanctuary

Idol, Image, *see* Divine Statue
Imperfection
– in the ANE 119, 123–124, 126–128, 131, 133, 198
– as an all-inclusive Category 119, 124, 126–128, 156, 182, 193–195, 200
– Human 119, 123, 131, 133, 136, 171, 176–177, 182, 185, 193–196, 199–200
– Language 12–14
– Mundane 75, 194
– Physical 126, 158
– Ritual 198
– *see also* Impurity, Sin, Pollution
Impurity (טמא) 70–71, 79, 106, 125, 135–137, 140–141, 143–144, 149–158, 159, 161–164, 167–169, 174, 176, 178, 185, 196–197, 206
– From Sin 180–181
– Rationale for 157–158
– Removal from Individuals 137, 140–141, 143–144
– Removal from Sancta 161–163, 166–169
Incense, *see* Regular Divine Service
– *see also* Altar, Cloud
Inner Sanctuary 43–45, 57, 73, 78, 115–116, 159–164, 169

כפרת 40, 105–106, 160
כרת 175
Korah 73, 107, 108, 191

Lampstand 60, 97, 100, 103–104
Land 111, 178, 181

Language in P
- of Divine Presence 39, 48
- Imprecision of 75–78, 81, 82, 91–92, 151–152, 163, 164, 170–171, 185
- Interpreting Religious Language 12–14, 21, 119
- Precision of 12–14, 47–49, 76–77, 181, 185, 190, 205, 206, 207
- (Purposely) Elusive 12–14, 39, 45, 49–51, 56, 98–99, 101–103, 107–109, 112, 114, 116–117, 144, 189– 192, 204–207
Leprosy, see Skin Disease
Light 103–104
- see also Regular Divine Service
Loyalty to YHWH 168, 176–177, 200, 207

Mesopotamia
- Akītu Festival 58, 80, 106, 109, 123, 124, 129–130, 195
- Mouth-Washing and Mouth-Opening 68, 83, 128
- Priestly Installation 68
- Purity and Holiness 76
Moses 5, 43–44, 46–47, 60, 64, 66, 74–75, 81, 87, 92, 136

Nadab and Abihu, see Priests

Odor, see Scent
Offerings
- אשם 8, 137, 138–145, 147, 149–150, 153, 155–157, 180, 182–183, 185, 187, 207
- Burnt (עלה) 8, 11, 23, 36, 62–64, 83, 86–87, 89–90, 111, 141, 153, 155, 161–162
- Grain (מנחה) 11, 23, 60, 82, 86, 87–89, 97, 109–111, 113, 141
- חטאת 8, 18, 20–24, 30–34, 36, 62–64, 75, 81–85, 88–90, 135–148, 155, 159, 161, 168, 170–171, 182–185, 201, 207
  - see also Clearing
- Ordination Offering 63–64, 78–79, 82, 86–89, 156–157
- Well-being Offering (זבח שלמים) 23, 62, 90, 157

Outer Sanctuary 43–44, 78, 99–112, 114–116, 138–139, 161–163, 169

P
- as a Ritual Text 5, 18–19, 59
- Setting of 5–6
Parturient 141, 143, 152, 155
Perfection
- in the ANE 68, 83, 122, 126–128, 131
- Divine 119, 128, 131, 177, 182, 200
- in Ezekiel 179
- Perfect Purity 68, 75, 83–4, 89, 126–8, 163, 169, 171, 200
- Priestly System 177, 199–200
- Relative 177, 200
Pleasing Gift 70, 86–87, 88–89, 103, 105, 111, 114, 116, 131–132, 148, 171, 196, 206
Pollution 11, 44, 73, 76–77, 83–85, 124–125, 133, 135, 137, 152–153, 156, 159–164, 167–170, 174–182 185–189, 193–200
- Pollution of Tabernacle 174, 182
- see also Imperfection, Impurity, Sin
Priestly system
- Success of 175–176
- Summary of 203–207
Priests 5–7, 14, 23, 30, 32, 35, 44, 58–64, 67–71, 73–75, 78–83, 85, 87–92, 98–100, 102–105, 108–109, 114–117, 128–130, 138–139, 142, 144, 146, 154, 157, 159–160, 162–164, 169–170, 185, 188, 191, 197, 199–200, 202, 207
- Aaron 5, 43–44, 60–64, 74, 78–79, 82, 90, 92, 107–109, 138, 159–160, 162, 195
- Aaron's Sons 60–62, 78–79, 82
- High priest(ess) 61, 69–70, 73–74, 79–80, 89–90, 115–116, 195
- Nadab and Abihu 24, 46, 119, 162, 165, 173, 174
Purity
- in the ANE 68, 76, 115–116, 125–126, 128
- in P 71, 75, 79, 83–85, 88–90, 99, 104, 105, 115–116, 163, 169, 171, 180, 194, 200
- Purity and Holiness 75–78, 205
- see also Clean, Cleansing, Perfection

Purification
- in the ANE 58, 67–70, 76, 95, 105–6, 123, 127–130, 195
- in P 58, 70, 77–79, 84–85, 88–90, 108, 168, 184, 195, 197, 199
- *see also* Cleansing, Clearing, Purity

Ransom (כֹּפֶר) 185–188
Rebellion against YHWH 176, 200
Regular Divine Service in P
- Bread of Presence 98–103, 111, 113, 114, 116–117, 206
- Burnt, Grain, and Drink Offerings 109–112
- Drink Offering 99–100, 103
- Incense 105–109
- Light 103–104
Removal Rites in P
- Individual and Communal 136–159
- Sanctuary 159–172
Reparation (אשם) 140, 148–149, 157, 184
Repentance 176, 178
Ritual
- Cumulative Effect of 64, 65–70, 83, 89–90, 128, 130–131, 152, 155, 156, 162, 167, 189, 197–198, 205
- Effects of 24–26
- Importance of Ritual Performance 18, 66, 71, 117
- Nature of Ritual 20–22, 201
- Necessary Divine Role in 67, 68, 69, 80, 92, 123, 126, 128, 129–133, 146, 154, 171, 189, 194, 197, 205
- Ritual Failure 24–25, 66, 71
- System Failure 178–179
- Ritual Unity 66–67
Ritual Theory
- Approaches to 26–34
- Cumulative Approach 34–37, 201
- Ritual Signs 22–24, 190

Sacrifice, *see* Offerings
Sacrilege (מעל) 142, 144–145, 148–149

Scapegoat, *see* Azazel, Animals: Goat for Azazel
Scent
- Importance of 83, 106–109, 115
- Soothing Scent (ריח ניחוח) 63–64, 86–87, 89, 107, 110–112, 142–143, 148
Self-Abasement 160, 162, 172, 176, 178
Sinai 2, 5–6, 137
Sin 18, 22, 81, 125, 136, 159, 160, 163, 165–166, 167–170, 173–176, 180–183, 193, 196–197, 206
- Affixed to the Sanctuary 167
- Expiable 145, 165–166, 176
- from Impurity 137, 148
- Inadvertent Sins (שגג) 139–140, 142, 144–145
- Inexpiable Sins 145, 165–167, 176–178, 181
- Intentional Sins 140, 142–144, 148
- Rebellious Sin (פשע) 164–165, 167, 178, 181
- Removal from Individuals: 137, 138–140, 142–143, 144–149
- Removal from Sancta 162–163, 165–169
- Root: חטא 182–185
- Sin-Bearing (נשא עון) 166–167, 180
- Sins and Impurities: Nature and Relationship of 179–181, 182–183
Skin Disease 141, 143, 150–156

Tabernacle, Tent of Meeting, *see* Clearing, Entrance of the Tent of Meeting, Inner Sanctuary, Offerings, Outer Sanctuary, Removal Rites, Ritual
Theophany 41, 47–49, 70–71, 205
Transcendence 7, 13–14, 21, 34, 39–40, 50, 53, 97–98, 100–101, 103, 109, 114, 116, 119, 136, 190–191, 205, 207

Washing 60, 63, 70–71, 127, 143, 151, 152, 153, 154, 161, 179
Wilderness 2–3, 48, 159–164, 169, 199

Forschungen zum Alten Testament

Edited by Bernd Janowski, Mark S. Smith
and Hermann Spieckermann

Alphabetical Index

Adam, Klaus-Peter: Saul und David in der judäischen Geschichtsschreibung. 2006. *Vol. 51.*
Baden, Joel S.: J, E, and the Redaction of the Pentateuch. 2009. *Vol. 68.*
Bäckersten, Olof: Isaiah's Political Message. 2008. *Vol. II/29.*
Barthel, Jörg: Prophetenwort und Geschichte. 1997. *Vol. 19.*
–: see *Hermisson, Hans-Jürgen.*
Barstad, Hans M.: History and the Hebrew Bible. 2008. *Vol. 61.*
Basson, Alec: Divine Metaphors in Selected Hebrew Psalms of Lamentation. 2006. *Vol. II/15.*
Bauks, Michaela: Jephtas Tochter. 2010. *Vol. 71.*
Baumann, Gerlinde: Die Weisheitsgestalt in Proverbien 1–9. 1996. *Vol. 16.*
Berlejung, Angelika / Janowski, Bernd (Ed.): Tod und Jenseits im Alten Israel und in seiner Umwelt. 2009. *Vol. 64.*
Berner, Christoph: Die Exoduserzählung. 2010. *Vol. 73.*
Bester, Dörte: Körperbilder in den Psalmen. 2007. *Vol. II/24.*
Blair, Judit M.: De-Demonising the Old Testament. 2009. *Vol. II/37.*
Blischke, Mareike V.: Die Eschatologie in der Sapientia Salomonis. 2007. *Vol. II/26.*
Blum, Erhard: Textgestalt und Komposition. 2010. *Vol. 69.*
Bodendorfer, Gerhard und *Matthias Millard* (Ed.): Bibel und Midrasch. Unter Mitarbeit von B. Kagerer. 1998. *Vol. 22.*
Chapman, Stephen B.: The Law and the Prophets. 2000; student ed. 2009. *Vol. 27.*
Diehl, Johannes F.: see *Witte, Markus.*
Dimant, Devorah / Kratz, Reinhard G. (Ed.): The Dynamics of Language and Exegesis at Qumran. 2009. *Vol. II/35.*
Diße, Andreas: see *Groß, Walter.*
Driver, Daniel R.: Brevard Childs, Biblical Theologian. 2010. *Vol. II/46.*
Dyma, Oliver: Die Wallfahrt zum Zweiten Tempel. 2009. *Vol. II/40.*
Eberhardt, Gönke: JHWH und die Unterwelt. 2007. *Vol. II/23.*
Ego, Beate: see *Janowski, Bernd.*
Ehrlich, Carl S. / White, Marsha C. (Ed.): Saul in Story and Tradition. 2006. *Vol. 47.*
Emmendörffer, Michael: Der ferne Gott. 1997. *Vol. 21.*
Finlay, Timothy D.: The Birth Report Genre in the Hebrew Bible. 2005. *Vol. II/12.*
Finsterbusch, Karin: Weisung für Israel. 2005. *Vol. 44.*
Fischer, Stefan: Das Hohelied Salomos zwischen Poesie und Erzählung. 2010. *Vol. 72.*
Frevel, Christian (Ed.): Medien im antiken Palästina. 2005. *Vol. II/10.*
Green, Douglas J.: "I Undertook Great Works". 2010. *Vol. II/41.*
Grohmann, Marianne: Fruchtbarkeit und Geburt in den Psalmen. 2007. *Vol. 53.*
Groß, Walter: Die Satzteilfolge im Verbalsatz alttestamentlicher Prosa. Unter Mitarbeit von A. Diße und A. Michel. 1996. *Vol. 17.*

Gulde, Stefanie Ulrike: Der Tod als Herrscher in Ugarit und Israel. 2007. *Vol. II/22.*
Hägglund, Fredrik: Isaiah 53 in the Light of Homecoming after Exile. 2008.
Vol. II/31.
Halpern, Baruch: From Gods to God. 2009. *Vol. 63.*
Hanhart, Robert: Studien zur Septuaginta und zum hellenistischen Judentum. 1999.
Vol. 24.
Hardmeier, Christof: Erzähldiskurs und Redepragmatik im Alten Testament. 2005.
Vol. 46.
Hartenstein, Friedhelm: Das Angesicht JHWHs. 2008. *Vol. 55.*
Hausmann, Jutta: Studien zum Menschenbild der älteren Weisheit (Spr 10ff). 1995.
Vol. 7.
Heckl, Raik: Hiob – vom Gottesfürchtigen zum Repräsentanten Israels. 2010. *Vol. 70.*
Hermisson, Hans-Jürgen: Studien zu Prophetie und Weisheit. Hrsg. von J. Barthel,
H. Jauss und K. Koenen 1998. *Vol. 23.*
Hibbard, J. Todd: Intertextuality in Isaiah 24–27. 2006. *Vol. II/16.*
Hjelde, Sigurd: Sigmund Mowinckel und seine Zeit. 2006. *Vol. 50.*
Hulster, Izaak J. de: Iconographic Exegesis and Third Isaiah. 2009. *Vol. II/36.*
Hundley, Michael: Keeping Heaven on Earth. 2011. *Vol. II/50.*
Huwyler, Beat: Jeremia und die Völker. 1997. *Vol. 20.*
Janowski, Bernd / Ego, Beate (Ed.): Das biblische Weltbild und seine altorientalischen
Kontexte. 2001. *Vol. 32.*
– / *Stuhlmacher, Peter* (Ed.): Der Leidende Gottesknecht. 1996. *Vol. 14.*
–: see *Berlejung, Angelika.*
Jauss, Hannelore: see *Hermisson, Hans-Jürgen.*
Jeremias, Jörg: Hosea und Amos. 1996. *Vol. 13.*
Kagerer, Bernhard: see *Bodendorfer, Gerhard.*
Kakkanattu, Joy Philip: God's Enduring Love in the Book of Hosea. 2006. *Vol. II/14.*
Kerr, Robert M.: Latino-Punic Epigraphy. 2010. *Vol. II/42.*
Kiuchi, Nobuyoshi: A Study of Hata' and Hatta't in Leviticus 4–5. 2003. *Vol. II/2.*
Knierim, Rolf P.: Text and Concept in Leviticus 1:1–9. 1992. *Vol. 2.*
Köckert, Matthias: Leben in Gottes Gegenwart. 2004. *Vol. 43.*
Köhlmoos, Melanie: Das Auge Gottes. 1999. *Vol. 25.*
–: Bet-El – Erinnerungen an eine Stadt. 2006. *Vol. 49.*
Koenen, Klaus: see *Hermisson, Hans-Jürgen.*
Körting, Corinna: Zion in den Psalmen. 2006. *Vol. 48.*
Konkel, Michael: Sünde und Vergebung. 2008. *Vol. 58.*
Kratz, Reinhard Gregor: Das Judentum im Zeitalter des Zweiten Tempels. 2004.
Vol. 42.
–: Kyros im Deuterojesaja-Buch. 1991. *Vol. 1.*
– und *Spieckermann, Hermann* (Ed.): Divine Wrath and Divine Mercy in the World
of Antiquity. 2008. *Vol. II/33.*
– Götterbilder – Gottesbilder – Weltbilder.
Vol. I: Ägypten, Mesopotamien, Kleinasien, Syrien, Palästina. 2006. *Vol. II/17.*
Vol. II: Griechenland und Rom, Judentum, Christentum und Islam. 2006.
Vol. II/18.
– see *Dimant, Devorah.*
Lange, Armin: Vom prophetischen Wort zur prophetischen Tradition. 2002. *Vol. 34.*

Levinson, Bernard M.: "The Right Chorale": Studies in Biblical Law and Interpretation. 2008. *Vol. 54.*
Liess, Kathrin: Der Weg des Lebens. 2004. *Vol. II/5.*
Løland, Hanne: Silent or Salient Gender? 2008. *Vol. II/32.*
Lund, Øystein: Way Metaphors and Way Topics in Isaiah 40–55. 2007. *Vol. II/28.*
Lux, Rüdiger: Prophetie und Zweiter Tempel. 2009. *Vol. 65.*
MacDonald, Nathan: Deuteronomy and the Meaning of 'Monotheism'. 2003. *Vol. II/1.*
Maier, Bernhard: William Robertson Smith. 2009. *Vol. 67.*
Marttila, Marko: Collective Reinterpretation in the Psalms. 2006. *Vol. II/13.*
Mayfield, Tyler D.: Literary Structure and Setting in Ezekiel. 2010. *Vol. II/43.*
Michel, Andreas: Gott und Gewalt gegen Kinder im Alten Testament. 2003. *Vol. 37.*
–: see *Groß, Walter.*
Millard, Matthias: Die Komposition des Psalters. 1994. *Vol. 9.*
–: see *Bodendorfer, Gerhard.*
Miller, Patrick D.: The Way of the Lord. 2004. *Vol. 39.*
Müller, Reinhard: Königtum und Gottesherrschaft. 2004. *Vol. II/3.*
Niemann, Hermann Michael: Herrschaft, Königtum und Staat. 1993. *Vol. 6.*
Nihan, Christophe: From Priestly Torah to Pentateuch. 2007. *Vol. II/25.*
Otto, Eckart: Das Deuteronomium im Pentateuch und Hexateuch. 2001. *Vol. 30.*
Perlitt, Lothar: Deuteronomium-Studien. 1994. *Vol. 8.*
Petry, Sven: Die Entgrenzung JHWHs. 2007. *Vol. II/27.*
Pilger, Tanja: Erziehung im Leiden. 2010. *Vol. II/49.*
Podella, Thomas: Das Lichtkleid JHWHs. 1996. *Vol. 15.*
Pola, Thomas: Das Priestertum bei Sacharja. 2003. *Vol. 35.*
Radebach-Huonker, Christiane: Opferterminologie im Psalter. 2010. *Vol. 44.*
Radine, Jason: The Book of Amos in Emergent Judah. 2010. *Vol. II/45.*
Riedweg, Christoph: see *Schmid, Konrad.*
Rösel, Martin: Adonaj – Warum Gott „Herr" genannt wird. 2000. *Vol. 29.*
Ruwe, Andreas: „Heiligkeitsgesetz" und „Priesterschrift". 1999. *Vol. 26.*
Sager, Dirk: Polyphonie des Elends. 2006. *Vol. II/21.*
Sals, Ulrike: Die Biographie der „Hure Babylon". 2004. *Vol. II/6.*
Saxegaard, Kristin M.: Character Complexity in the Book of Ruth. 2010. *Vol. II/47.*
Schaper, Joachim: Priester und Leviten im achämenidischen Juda. 2000. *Vol. 31.*
– (Ed.): Die Textualisierung der Religion. 2009. *Vol. 62.*
Schenker, Adrian (Ed.): Studien zu Opfer und Kult im Alten Testament. 1992. *Vol. 3.*
Schmid, Konrad / Riedweg, Christoph (Ed.): Beyond Eden. 2008. *Vol. II/34.*
Schmidt, Brian B.: Israel's Beneficent Dead. 1994. *Vol. 11.*
Schmitz, Barbara: Prophetie und Königtum. 2008. *Vol. 60.*
Schöpflin, Karin: Theologie als Biographie im Ezechielbuch. 2002. *Vol. 36.*
Seeligmann, Isac Leo: The Septuagint Version of Isaiah and Cognate Studies. Edited by Robert Hanhart and Hermann Spieckermann. 2004. *Vol. 40.*
–: Gesammelte Studien zur Hebräischen Bibel. Herausgegeben von Erhard Blum mit einem Beitrag von Rudolf Smend. 2004. *Vol. 41.*
Ska, Jean-Louis: The Exegesis of the Pentateuch. 2009. *Vol. 66.*
Smith, Mark S.: God in Translation. 2008. *Vol. 57.*
Spieckermann, Hermann: Gottes Liebe zu Israel. *Vol. 33.*
–: see *Kratz, Reinhard Gregor.*
Stackert, Jeffrey: Rewriting the Torah. 2007. *Vol. 52.*

Forschungen zum Alten Testament

Steck, Odil Hannes: Gottesknecht und Zion. 1992. *Vol. 4.*
Stuhlmacher, Peter: see *Janowski, Bernd.*
Süssenbach, Claudia: Der elohistische Psalter. 2005. *Vol. II/7.*
Suriano, Matthew J.: The Politics of Dead Kings. 2010. *Vol. II/48.*
Sweeney, Marvin A.: Form and Intertextuality in Prophetic and Apocalyptic Literature. 2005. *Vol. 45.*
Taschner, Johannes: Die Mosereden im Deuteronomium. 2008. *Vol. 59.*
Tiemeyer, Lena-Sofia: Priestly Rites and Prophetic Rage. 2006. *Vol. II/19.*
Turkanik, Andrzej S.: Of Kings and Reigns. 2008. *Vol. II/30.*
Uhlig, Torsten: The Theme of Hardening in the Book of Isaiah. 2009. *Vol. II/39.*
Vos, Christiane de: Klage als Gotteslob aus der Tiefe. 2005. *Vol. II/11.*
Weber, Cornelia: Altes Testament und völkische Frage. 2000. *Vol. 28.*
Weimar, Peter: Studien zur Priesterschrift. 2008. *Vol. 56.*
Weippert, Manfred: Jahwe und die anderen Götter. 1997. *Vol. 18.*
Weyde, Karl William: The Appointed Festivals of YHWH. 2004. Vol. II/4.
White, Marsha C.: see *Ehrlich, Carl S.*
Widmer, Michael: Moses, God, and the Dynamics of Intercessory Prayer. 2004. *Vol. II/8.*
Wilke, Alexa F.: Kronerben der Weisheit. 2006. *Vol. II/20.*
Willi, Thomas: Juda – Jehud – Israel. 1995. *Vol. 12.*
Williamson, Hugh: Studies in Persian Period History and Historiography. 2004. *Vol. 38.*
Wilson, Kevin A.: The Campaign of Pharaoh Shoshenq I into Palestine. 2005. *Vol. II/9.*
Witte, Markus and *Johannes F. Diehl* (Ed.): Orakel und Gebete. 2009. *Vol. II/38.*
Young, Ian: Diversity in Pre-Exilic Hebrew. 1993. *Vol. 5.*
Zwickel, Wolfgang: Der Tempelkult in Kanaan und Israel. 1994. *Vol. 10.*

For a complete catalogue please write to the publisher
Mohr Siebeck • P.O. Box 2030 • D-72010 Tübingen/Germany
Up-to-date information on the internet at www.mohr.de